BERLIN ALEXANDERPLATZ

The Story of Franz Biberkopf

Alfred Döblin

Translated by Eugene Jolas

Foreword by Alexander Stephan

continuum
LONDON • NEW YORK

Continuum

The Tower Building
11 York Road
London SE1 7NX

15 East 26th Street
Suite 1703
New York
NY 10010

www.continuumbooks.com

This edition 2004

British Library Cataloguing-in-Publication Data
A catalogue record for this book is available from the British Library

ISBN 0–8264–7789–5

Typeset by RefineCatch Limited, Bungay, Suffolk
Printed and bound in Great Britain by
Antony Rowe, Chippenham, Wiltshire

Foreword

Berlin Alexanderplatz (1929) by Alfred Döblin (1878–1957) ranks among the masterpieces of modern literature. Like John Dos Passos's *Manhattan Transfer*, it explores the speed, anonymity, and chaos of the contemporary metropolis. From Upton Sinclair and *The Jungle*, it borrows the concern over social injustice in modern mass society. James Joyce's *Ulysses* has been mentioned as a source for Döblin's writing style, with its rapid shifts between interior monologue, collage of quotations, and montage of fragmented details. Filmmakers from Phil Jutzi (1931) to Rainer Werner Fassbinder (1980) have been attracted by its technique.

In the words of one of its first reviewers, *Berlin Alexanderplatz* is a book that "gets under the skin." German Expressionism reached its zenith with Döblin's masterpiece. The "Americanization" of the Weimar Republic and its culture is reflected in the hectic life at Alexanderplatz in the heart of Berlin, in the emergence of a new, socially and sexually independent woman, and in the at-once fascinating and threatening aspects of technology.

Döblin was a physician who lived and practiced in a working-class district of Berlin. He had firsthand experience with antiheros like Franz Biberkopf, who wheels and deals in an underworld of thieves and pimps, makes friends with bums, and is twice done in by a small-time gangster. Like his contemporary Bertolt Brecht, Döblin uses running synopses of the plot to focus the reader's attention on the process rather than the outcome of Franz Biberkopf's story. But unlike the Marxist Brecht, Döblin does not aim to change, by political means, the social injustice he sees around Alexanderplatz. Instead, the beginning and conclusion of the book deal with "fate." "Hell-fire" blazes from people's eyes in the periods of dreams and delusions experienced by "Franzeken." The surface of reality is ruptured by symbolic, metaphysical, and religious references to fundamental human situations. Animals and people are sacrificed to Death and the Whore of Babylon. The prison from which Biberkopf is released at the start of the story, the madhouse in which he vanishes suffering from "psychic trauma" near the ending, and the crazy world of Berlin between Alexanderplatz and Rosenthalerplatz, all blur into one.

When Hitler came to power in Germany, Döblin fled first to France and then to the United States. *Berlin Alexanderplatz*, which very soon after publication had been translated into many languages, was banned by the Nazis. Virtually ignored following his return to Europe in 1945, Döblin's books fortunately since have been rediscovered.

Alexander Stephan

Contents

This book reports the story of Franz Biberkopf, an erstwhile cement- and transport-worker in Berlin. He has just been discharged from prison where he has been doing time because of former incidents, and is now back in Berlin, determined to lead a decent life.

And, at first, he succeeds. But then, though economically things go rather well with him, he gets involved in a regular combat with something that comes from the outside, with something unaccountable, that looks like fate.

Three times this thing crashes against our man, disturbing his scheme of life. It rushes at him with cheating and fraud. The man is able to scramble up again; he is still firm on his feet.

It drives and beats him with foul play. He finds it a bit hard to get up, they almost count him out.

Finally it torpedoes him with huge and monstrous savagery.

Thus our good man, who has held his own till the end, is laid low. He gives the game up for lost; he does not know how to go on and appears to be done for.

But, before he puts a definite end to himself, his eyes are forcibly opened in a way which I do not describe here. He is most distinctly given to understand how it all came about. To wit, through himself, that's obvious, through his scheme of life, which looked like nothing on earth, but now suddenly looks entirely different, not simple and almost self-evident, but prideful and impudent, cowardly withal, and full of weakness.

This awful thing which was his life acquires a meaning. Franz Biberkopf has been given a radical cure. At last we see our man back on Alexander-platz, greatly changed and battered, but, nevertheless, bent straight again.

To listen to this, and to meditate on it, will be of benefit to many who, like Franz Biberkopf, live in a human skin, and, like this Franz Biberkopf, ask more of life than a piece of bread and butter.

FIRST BOOK

Here in the beginning, Franz Biberkopf leaves Tegel Prison into which a former foolish life had led him. It is difficult to gain a foothold in Berlin again, but he finally does. This makes him happy, and now he vows to lead a decent life.

On Car 41 into Town

He stood in front of the Tegel Prison gate and was free now. Yesterday in convict's garb he had been raking potatoes with the others in the fields back of the building, now he was walking in a tan summer topcoat; they were still raking back there, he was free. He let one street-car after another go by, pressed his back against the red wall, and did not move. The gateman walked past him several times, showed him his car-line; he did not move. The terrible moment had come (terrible, Franze, why terrible?), the four years were over. The black iron gates, which he had been watching with growing disgust for a year (disgust, why disgust?), were shut behind him. They had let him out again. Inside, the others sat at their carpentry, varnishing, sorting, gluing, had still two years, five years to do. He was standing at the car-stop.

The punishment begins.

He shook himself and gulped. He stepped on his own foot. Then, with a run, took a seat in the car. Right among people. Go ahead. At first it was like being at the dentist's, when he has grabbed a root with a pair of forceps, and pulls; the pain grows, your head threatens to burst. He turned his head back towards the red wall, but the car raced on with him along the tracks, and only his head was left in the direction of the prison. The car took a bend; trees and houses intervened. Busy streets emerged, Seestrasse, people got on and off. Something inside him screamed in terror: Look out, look out, it's going to start now. The tip of his nose turned to ice; something was whirring over his cheek. *Zwölf*

Uhr Mittagszeitung, B. Z., Berliner Illustrierte, Die Funkstunde. "Anybody else got on?" The coppers have blue uniforms now. He got off the car, without being noticed, and was back among people again. What happened? Nothing. Chest out, you starved sucker, you, pull yourself together, or I'll give you a crack in the jaw! Crowds, what a swarm of people! How they hustle and bustle! My brain needs oiling, it's probably dried up. What was all this? Shoe stores, hat stores, incandescent lamps, saloons. People got to have shoes to run around so much; didn't we have a cobbler's shop out there, let's bear that in mind! Hundreds of polished window-panes, let 'em blaze away, are they going to make you afraid or something, why, you can smash 'em up, can't you, what's the matter with 'em, they're polished clean, that's all. The pavement on Rosenthaler Platz was being torn up; he walked on the wooden planks along with the others. Just go ahead and mix in with people, then everything's going to clear up, and you won't notice anything, you fool. Wax figures stood in the show-windows, in suits, overcoats, with skirts, with shoes and stockings. Outside everything was moving, but—back of it—there was nothing! It—did not—live! It had happy faces, it laughed, waited in twos and threes on the traffic islands opposite Aschinger's, smoked cigarettes, turned the pages of newspapers. Thus it stood there like the street-lamps—and—became more and more rigid. They belonged with the houses, everything white, everything wooden.

Terror struck him as he walked down Rosenthaler Strasse and saw a man and a woman sitting in a little beer-shop right at the window: they poured beer down their gullets out of mugs, yes, what about it, they were drinking, they had forks and stuck pieces of meat into their mouths, then they pulled the forks out again and were not bleeding. Oh, how cramped his body felt, I can't get rid of it, where shall I go? The answer came: Punishment.

He could not turn back, he had come this far on the car, he had been discharged from prison and had to go into this thing, deeper and deeper into it.

I know, he sighed to himself, that I have to go into this thing and that I was discharged from prison. They had to discharge me, the punishment was over, that's as it should be, the bureaucrat does his duty. I'll go into it, too, but I'd rather not, my God, I can't do it.

He wandered down Rosenthaler Strasse past Wertheim's department store, at the right he turned into the narrow Sophienstrasse. He thought, this street is darker, it's probably better where it's darker. The prisoners are put in isolation cells, solitary confinement and general confinement. In isolation cells the prisoner is kept apart from the others night and day. In solitary confinement the prisoner is placed in a cell, but during his walks in the open air, during instruction or religious service, he is put in company with the others. The cars roared and jangled on, house-fronts were rolling along one after the other without stopping. And there were roofs on the houses, they soared atop the houses, his eyes wandered straight upward: if only the roofs don't slide off, but the houses stood upright. Where shall I go, poor devil that I am, he shuffled alongside the walls of the houses, there was no end to it. I'm really a big duffer, a fellow ought to be able to traipse his way through hereabouts, five minutes, ten minutes, then drink a cognac and sit down. When the given signal rings, work must being immediately. It can only be interrupted at the time set aside for eating, walking, and instruction. During the walk the prisoners must hold their arms stiff and swing them back and forth.

A house appeared, he took his glance away from the pavement, he pushed open the door of a house, and a sad growling oh, oh, came from his chest. He thrashed his arms about, well, old boy, you won't freeze here. The door of the courtyard opened, someone shuffled past him, stood behind him. Now he groaned, it did him good to groan. In the first days of his solitary confinement he had always groaned like this, and had been happy to hear his own voice, there you have at least something, everything is not lost yet. Many did that in the cells, some in the beginning, others later on, when they felt lonely. Then they started it, it was something human, it consoled them. Thus our man stood in the hallway, did not hear the terrible noise from the street, those mad houses were not there. With pursed lips he grunted to give himself courage, his hands clenched in his pockets. His shoulders in the tan summer topcoat were hunched for defense.

A stranger had stopped beside the discharged prisoner and was watching him. He asked: "What's the matter, anything wrong, are you in pain?" until the man noticed him and stopped his grunting at once. "Are you sick, do you live here in this house?" It was a Jew with a full red beard, a little man in an overcoat, with a black plush felt hat, a cane in his hand. "No, I don't live here." He had to get out of the hallway, the hallway had been all right. And now the street started once more, the house-fronts, the show-windows, the hurrying figures with trousers or light socks, all so quick, so smart, each moment another. And making up his mind, he stepped again into an entrance-way, but just here the gates opened to let a wagon pass. Then quickly into the next-door house, into a narrow hall-way next to the staircase. No wagon could get in here. He clung to the banister-post. And while he held on to it, he knew he wanted to escape punishment (oh, Franz, what do you want to do? You'll not be able to do it), he would certainly do it, he knew now where there was an escape. And softly he started his music again, the grunting and grumbling, and I won't go back to the street either. The red Jew stepped back into the house, did not at first notice the man by the banister. He heard him humming. "Say, tell me, what are you doing here? Are you sick?" He moved away from the post, walked towards the courtyard. As he grasped the gate, he saw it was the Jew from the other house. "Leave me alone, what do you want anyway?" "Well, well, nothing. You moan and groan so, can't a body ask how you are?" And through the crack in the door across the way he saw the blamed old houses again, the swarming people, the sliding roofs. The discharged prisoner opened the courtyard gate, the Jew behind him: "What could happen? Now, now, it's not going to be as bad as all that. You're not going to go under. Berlin is big. Where a thousand live, one more can also live."

He was in a deep dark courtyard. He stood beside the dustbin. And suddenly he started singing in a resonant voice, singing towards the walls. He took his hat off, like an organ-grinder. The echo resounded from the walls. That was fine. His voice filled his ears. He sang in such a very loud voice, he would never have been allowed to sing like that in prison. And what did he sing, that it should echo from the walls? "There comes a call like thunder's peal." Martially hard and pithy. And then: "Tra-la-la-la-la-la-la," a bit from a song. Nobody paid any attention to him. The Jew received him at the gate: "You sang beautifully. You really sang beauti-fully. You could earn gold with a voice like you've got." The Jew followed him to the street, took him by the arm, pushed him farther along, talking endlessly all the way, until they turned into Gormannstrasse, the Jew and the raw-boned, big fellow in the summer topcoat with his lips pressed tight together, as if he wanted to spit gall.

Still not There

He led him into a room, where an iron stove was burning, and sat him down on the sofa: "Well, here you are. Make yourself at home. Can leave your hat on or take it off, just as you please. I just want to get somebody you'll like. As a matter of fact, I don't live here. Am just a guest like yourself. Well, that's the way it is, one guest brings another, if only the room is warm."

The discharged convict was sitting alone. There comes a call like thunder's peal, like billows' roar and clash of steel. He was riding in the car, looking out the window, the red walls were visible between the trees, many-colored leaves were raining down. The walls stood before his eyes, he looked at them from the sofa, kept on looking at them. A fellow's very lucky to live within these walls, he knows at least how the day starts and how it goes on. (Franz, you wouldn't hide, I hope, four years you've been hidden, courage, look around, this hiding will have to stop some time.) All singing, whistling, and noise is prohibited. The prisoners must immediately rise in the morning at the signal to get up, they must put their bunks in order, wash, comb their hair, clean their clothes, and dress. Soap should be issued in adequate quantities. Boom, a bell, get up, boom five-thirty, boom six-thirty, doors unlocked, boom boom, we go outside, distribution of breakfast, working hours, recreation hour, boom boom boom, noon, don't make such a wry face, old boy, you're not going to be fattened up here, singers should step forward, they are to appear at five-forty, I'll report myself hoarse, at six the doors are locked, good evening, that's that. A fellow's lucky to live within these walls, they dragged me down in the dirt, I almost committed murder, but it was only manslaughter, bodily injury with fatal consequences, wasn't as bad as all that, I had become a great reprobate, a hooligan—almost a real bum.

A big, long-haired old Jew, a little black skull-cap on the back of his head, had been sitting opposite him for a long time. Now in Shushan there was a certain Jew, whose name was Mordecai and he brought up Esther, his uncle's daughter, and the maid was fair and beautiful. The old man looked away from him and turned his head back to the redbeard: "Where did you pick this one up?" "He was running around from house to house. He stood in a courtyard and he sang." "Sang?" "War songs." "He must be freezing." "Maybe." The old man looked at him. Jews must not handle a corpse on the first feastday, nor shall Israelites do this on the second feastday; and this applies to both New Years' days, as well. And who is the author of the following rabbinic teaching: If a man eats from the carcass of a clean bird, he is not unclean; if, however, he eats of the intestines or of the craw, he is unclean? With his long yellow hand the old man groped for the hand of the discharged prisoner lying on the topcoat. "Heh, don't you want to take your coat off? It's warm here. We're old people, we freeze all the year round, maybe it will be too much for you."

He sat on the sofa, he squinted down at his hand, he had walked from courtyard to courtyard through the streets, gotta look and see where something can be found in this world. And he wanted to get up, walk out of the door, his eyes looked for the door in the dark room. And the old fellow pushed him back to the sofa: "Why don't you stay, what do you want?" He wanted to get outside. The old man, however, held his wrist and squeezed and squeezed: "Just want to see who is stronger, you or I. Now are you going to remain seated, or not? You are going to listen to what I am saying, young fellow. Pull yourself together, rascal." And turning to the red-haired chap who grasped the man by the shoulders: "Get out of here, you. Did I call you? I'll fix him up."

What did these people want with him? He wanted to get out, he tried to rise, but the old man pushed him down again. Then he shouted: "What are you doing with me?" "Go ahead and curse, you'll be cursing more than that." "You better lemme go. I've got to be off." "Into the street again, I suppose, or the courtyard, maybe?"

Then the old man got up from his chair, went rustling up and down the room: "Let him scream as much as he wants to. Let him do as he pleases. But not in my house. Open the door for him." "What's the matter, haven't you got noise here anyway?" "Don't bring people here who make a noise. The daughter's children are sick, they're back there in bed, I got enough noise already." "Eh, eh, what a shame, I didn't know, you must excuse me." The redbeard grasped the man by the hands: "Come along. The Rebbe's got his house full. The grandchildren are sick. We'll go somewhere else." But the other chap did not want to get up. "Come along." He had to get up. Then he whispered: "Don't pull. Why don't you leave me here?" "His house is full up, I tell you, didn't you hear?" "Just lemme stay here."

With sparkling eyes the old man looked at the strange man who was now pleading. Thus spake Jeremiah, we would have healed Babylon, but she is not healed; forsake her, and let us go everyone into his own country. A sword is upon the Chaldeans and upon the inhabitants of Babylon.

"If he doesn't keep still, send him away." "All right, all right, we won't make any noise. I'll sit with him, you can depend on me." Without a word the old man rustled towards the door.

Instruction through the Example of Zannovich

And so the discharged prisoner in the tan summer topcoat was sitting on the sofa again. Sighing and shaking his head, the redbeard walked through the room: "Now don't be angry because the old man was so excited. Are you from out of town?" "Yes, I am—I was—" The red walls, the beautiful walls, cells, he couldn't help looking at them with longing, his back seemed glued to the red wall, it was a clever man had built it, he did not leave. And the man, like a doll, rolled from the sofa down to the carpet. In falling, he knocked the table to one side. "What's that?" cried the red chap. The discharged convict stooped over the carpet, his hat rolled down beside his hands, he thrust his head downward, moaned: "Down into the ground, into the earth, where it's dark!" The red-haired man tugged at him: "For God's sake. You're among strangers. Suppose the old man should come in. Get up." But the other one did not let himself be pulled up, he held fast to the carpet, continued moaning. "Just keep quiet, for God's sake, suppose the old man should hear you. We'll get along all right." "Nobody'll get me away from here." Like a mole.

And as he could not get him up, the redbeard rubbed the curls on his temples, locked the door, and resolutely sat down on the floor beside him. He drew up his knees and looked at the table-legs in front of him: "It's O. K. with me. Just stay where you are. I'll sit down, too. Of course, it's not comfortable, but what of it? You won't tell me what's wrong with you, so I'm going to tell you a story." The discharged prisoner groaned, his head on the carpet. (Why's he groaning and moaning? He's gotta make a decision, that's why, he's gotta walk down some road—and, Franze, you don't know of any road? You're through with that bunk from the old days, and in the cell, too, all you did was groan and hide away, and you didn't think about anything, Franze.) The red-haired fellow said fiercely: "You shouldn't bother so much about your own person. You should listen to others. Who told you there's such a lot the matter with you? God won't let any man drop out of his hands, but then there are also other people, don't forget. Didn't you read what Noah put into his ark, into his ship, when the great flood came? A pair of each. God didn't forget any of them. Not even the lice on our heads did he forget. All of them were near and dear to him." The other man was whimpering on the floor. (Whimpering doesn't cost anything, a sick mouse can whimper, too.)

The red chap let him go on whimpering and scratched his cheeks:

"There's a lot on earth—a man could tell a lot of stories about it, when he's young and when he's old. You see, I'm going to tell you the story of Zannovich, Stefan Zannovich. You never heard it. When you feel better, just sit up a bit. The blood goes to your head, it's not good for you. My late father—God bless him—told us a good deal, he traveled a lot like the people of our race do, he lived to be over seventy, died after our dear mother, knew a lot, a clever man. We were seven hungry mouths, and whenever there was nothing to eat, he told us stories. It don't fill your stomach, but you forget things." The muffled groaning below continued. (A sick jackass can groan, too.) "Well, well, we know that in this world there ain't only gold, beauty, and happiness. Now, who was Zannovich, who was his father, who were his parents? Beggars like most of us, hawkers, peddlers, tradespeople. Old Zannovich came from Albania, and went to Venice. He knew why he went to Venice. Some fellows go from the city to the country, others from the country to the city. In the country it's quieter, people turn everything around and around, you can talk for hours, and if you're lucky, you've earned a couple of pfennigs. Now, in town, too, it's hard, but the people live closer together, and they have no time. If it's not one thing, it's the other. Got no oxen, but fast horses with cabs. You lose and you win. Old Zannovich knew that. First sold what he had with him and then he took to cards and played with the folks. He wasn't straight. He made a bizniz out of it, he did, knowing that folks in the city have got no time and want to be amused. He entertained 'em all right! It cost 'em hard cash. A swindler, a cardsharp—that was old Zannovich, but he had a head on him. The peasants made things hard for him, here he made a softer living. Things went well with him. Till one of them suddenly imagined he had been done a wrong. Noo, old Zannovich hadn't exactly counted on that. It came to blows, the police mixed in, and finally old Zannovich had to scoot with his children. The law of Venice was after him, the old man thought he'd rather have no dealings with the law, they don't understand me, they couldn't catch him either. He had horses and money with him and settled again in Albania and bought himself an estate, a whole village, he did, and his children he sent to college. And when he became very old, he died peacefully and respected. That was old Zannovich's life. The peasants wept over him, but he never could bear them, because he always thought of the time when he had stood before them with his trinkets, rings, bracelets, and coral chains, while they turned them around and around, fiddling with them, and finally went away and left him standing there.

"Y'know, when the father's a li'l plant, he wants his son to be a tree. When the father's a stone, he wants his son to be a mountain. Old Zannovich said to his sons: 'I was nothing here in Albania, as long as I went peddling for twenty years, and why not? Because I didn't take my head where it belonged. I send you to the big school, to Padua, get horses and wagons, and when you're through studying, think of me, who had many cares together with your mother and you and who slept at night with you in the forest, like a boar: it was my own fault. The peasants had drained me dry like a bad year, and I would have gone to pieces. But I went among people and I didn't go under.'"

The red-haired chap laughed to himself, wagged his head, rocked his body. They were sitting on the carpet. "If anybody should come in now, he might think we're both *meschugge*, we've got a sofa and we sit on the floor. Noo, if we want to, why not? If we only get some fun out of it. Young Zannovich Stefan was already a great orator as a young man of twenty. He could scrape and bow, make himself popular, he could make goo-goo eyes at the women and act noble with the men. In Padua the nobles learn from the professors, Stefan learnt from the nobles. They were all nice to him. And when he came home to Albania, his father was still living, how happy he was about him and he liked him, too, and said: 'Look at him, there's a man of the world for you, he won't trade with the peasants for twenty years as I did, he's twenty years ahead of his father.' And the youngster stroked his silk sleeve, brushed his beautiful curls from his brow and kissed his happy old father: 'But you, father, you spared me those bad twenty years.' 'May they be the best of your life,' said the old man, and patted and petted his youngster.

"And then things went like a miracle with young Zannovich, and yet it was no miracle. Everywhere people rushed to him. He had the key to all hearts. He went to Montenegro on an excursion as a cavalier with coaches and horses and servants, his father was overjoyed at seeing his son a big man—the father a little plant, the son a tree—and in Montenegro they called him count and prince. They wouldn't have believed him, if he had said: My father's name is Zannovich, we live in Pastrovich in a village and my father's proud of it! They wouldn't have believed him, he appeared on the scene so like a nobleman from Padua, and he looked like one, too, and knew them all. Then Stefan laughed and said: 'You shall have your way.' And pretended to the people he was a wealthy Pole, which they really believed, a Baron Warta, and then they were happy about it, and he was happy about it, too."

The discharged prisoner had sat up with a sudden lurch. He was crouching on his knees and slyly watching the other from above. Now he said with an icy look: "Monkey!" The redhead replied contemptuously: "Well, then, I am a monkey. But monkeys know really more than many a man." The other was forced down to the floor again. (Repent thou shalt; know what has happened; know what is needed.)

"So we can go on talking. A lot can still be learned from other people. Young Zannovich was on this road, and so it went. I didn't experience it, nor did my father experience it, but you can imagine it, can't you? If I ask you, you, who call me a monkey—you should not despise any animal on God's earth, they give us meat, and they show us many a kindness, think of a horse, a dog, singing birds; monkeys I only know from the county fair, they have to do tricks, on a chain, a hard lot, sure, no man has such a hard lot—now I'm going to ask you, I can't call you by your name, because you won't tell me your name: how did Zannovich get that far, both the young and the old man? You think because they had brains, they were clever. Other people were clever, too, and hadn't got as far at eighty as Stefan was at twenty. But the main things about a man are his eyes and his feet. He should be able to see the world and go after it.

"Now listen to what Stefan Zannovich did, he who had seen men and who knew how little we should be afraid of them. Just look how they smooth your way, how they almost show the blind man his road. They wanted this from him: You're Baron Warta. That's nize, says he, then I'm Baron Warta. Later on that wasn't enough for him, or not for them. If he was a Baron, why not be more? There's a celebrity in Albania, who had been dead a long time, but they honor him like people honor heroes, his name was Skanderbeg. If Zannovich could have done it, he would have said: he himself is Skanderbeg. After Skanderbeg was dead, he said, so he did, I'm a descendant of Skanderbeg's, and threw out his chest, he was called Prince Castriota of Albania, and he's going to make Albania great again; his followers are waiting for him. They gave him money, so that he could live like a descendant of Skanderbeg's should live. He did the people a lot of good. They go to the theater and hear a lot of cooked-up things that are agreeable to them, and they pay for it. They could pay for it, too, couldn't they, if the agreeable things happened to them in the afternoon, or in the morning, and they themselves could play a part in them."

And again the man in the tan summer topcoat sat up, his face wrinkled and gloomy; he looked down at the red-haired man, coughed, his voice was changed: "Say, listen, young feller, you're cuckoo, heh? You're off your noodle, ain't you?" "Cuckoo, maybe. First I'm a monkey, then I'm *meschugge*." "Say, listen here, you, what do you mean sitting here and giving me a lot of your bunk?" "Who's sitting on the floor and don't want to get up? Me? When there's a sofa standing right behind me? Well, if it bothers you, I'll stop talking."

Then the other man, who had been looking around the room at the same time, drew his legs from under him and sat down with his back to the sofa, resting his hands on the carpet. "That's right, you can sit more comfortably this way." "Well, you might stop your blathering now." "If you like. I've often told the story before, I don't care, if you don't care." But after a moment of silence the other turned to him again: "Just go on with your story." "Noo, you see, a man tells stories and talks with another man, time passes better that way. I only wanted to open your eyes. Stefan Zannovich, who you heard about, got money, a lot of it, and he traveled to Germany with it. They didn't unmask him in Montenegro. What's to be learnt from Stefan Zannovich is that he knew about himself and about people. He was innocent like a little bird that twitters. Look here, he was so little afraid of the world, the greatest and most powerful men of his time, men to be properly afraid of, were his friends: the Elector of Saxony, the Crown Prince of Prussia, who later became a great war hero, and before whom the Austrian Empress Theresa trembled on her throne. Zannovich didn't tremble before them. And once when Stefan came to Vienna and got in with people who were prying around him, the Empress herself raised her hand and said: Leave the youngster alone."

Completion of the Story in an unexpected Manner and the tonic Effect it has on the discharged Prisoner

The other chap sitting on the sofa began to laugh, he fairly neighed: "You're a card. You should join the circus as a clown." The redhead sniggered, too: "So you see how it was. But keep quiet, the old man's grandchildren. Maybe we'd better sit down on the sofa, after all. What do you say?" The other laughed, crept up and raised himself slowly, sat down in one corner of the sofa, while the red-haired man sat in the other corner: "You sit softer that way, you don't rumple your coat, either." The man in the summer topcoat stared at the redhead from his corner: "You certainly are a funny bird—I haven't seen the likes of you in ages." The redhead, quietly: "Maybe you didn't take a good look, there are some. You got your coat dirty, they don't clean their shoes here." The discharged prisoner, a man of about thirty, had merry eyes, his face was fresher: "Say, tell me, what are you selling anyway? You must be living on the moon." "Well, that's fine, let's talk about the moon, now."

A man with a curly, brown beard had been standing at the door for about five minutes. He went to the table, sat down in a chair. He was young, wore a black plush hat like the other. He described a circle in the air with his hand, then began in his shrill voice: "Who's that? What are you doing with him?" "And what are you doing here, Eliser? I don't know him, he won't tell his name." "You've been telling him stories." "Well, what's it to you?" The brownbeard to the convict: "Did he tell you stories, that one?" "He don't talk. He just walks around and sings in the courtyards." "Then let him go." "It's none of your business what I'm doing." "But I overheard what happened at the door. You told him about Zannovich. What else would you do but tell stories and stories?" Then the stranger, who had been staring at the brownbeard, grumbled: "Who are you and how'd you get in here, anyway? What do you want to mix in his affair for?" "Did he tell you about Zannovich, or not? He's been tellin' you stories. Nachum, my brother-in-law, goes around everywhere telling stories and stories and can't do anything for himself." "Did I ever ask you to help me? Don't you see he's feeling bad, you low-life?" "What of it, if he's not feeling well? You didn't get an order from God, just look at him, God waited till he came along. Alone God wasn't able to help." "Low-life." "Keep away from that man, I tell you. He probably told you how Zannovich or some other feller got up in the world." "You better get out o' here soon!" "Just listen to the swindler, the charity hound. Wants to talk to me. Is it his house? Noo, what did you tell him again about your Zannovich, and how a man can learn from him? You should o' become one of our Rebbes. We would o' fattened you up, sure enough." "I don't need your charity." The brownbeard shouted again: "And we don't need any sponges around here always hanging on to a man's coat-tails. Did he also tell you what happened to his Zannovich finally, in the end?" "You rascal, you low-life." "Did he tell you that?" The prisoner blinked wearily at the red-haired chap who shook his fist and walked towards the door, he growled after the red-haired man: "Hey, there, don't run away; don't get excited, let him shoot his bull."

The brown-bearded fellow was already talking violently to him, fidgeting with his hands, shifting back and forth, clucking, and jerking his head, with a different expression every moment, turning now to the stranger, now to the redhead: "He makes people *meschugge*. Let him tell you what kind of an end his Stefan Zannovich came to. He don't tell it, why don't he tell it, why, I ask you?" "Because you are a low-life, Eliser." "A better man than you are. They" (the brownbeard lifted both hands disgustedly, making terrible goggle-eyes) "chased his Zannovich out of Florence like a thief. Why? Because they found him out." The red-haired fellow placed himself menacingly before him, the brownbeard brushed him aside: "It's my turn to talk now. He wrote letters to princes, a prince gets lots of letters, you can't tell from the handwriting what a man is. Then he stuck out his chest and went to Brussels as a Prince of Albania and mixed up in high politics. It was his bad angel told him to do that. He goes to the government, just imagine Stefan Zannovich, the youngster, and promises to give them a hundred thousand men or two hundred, it don't matter, for a war, with somebody or other. The government writes a little letter, thank you very much, they're not interested in uncertain enterprises. Then his bad angel told Stefan Zannovich, take the letter and get a loan on it. Didn't you have the letter from the minister with the address, To His Royal Highness the Prince of Albania on it? They loaned him money, and that was the end of the swindler. How old did he get to be? Thirty years, he didn't get to be any older than that as a punishment for his evil-doing. He couldn't pay the money back, they reported him to the authorities in Brussels and that's how everything came out. Your hero, Nachum! Did you tell about his black end in prison where he opened his veins? And after he was dead—a fine life, a fine end, go on and tell it—the executioner came, then the knacker with a wagon for dead dogs and horses and cats, and loaded him on the wagon, Stefan Zannovich himself, yes, sir, and chucked him out by the gallows and dumped garbage from the town all over him."

The man in the summer topcoat was standing with his mouth open: "That's true?" (A sick mouse can groan, too.) The red-haired fellow had counted every word his brother-in-law had been shouting. He waited with his index finger lifted in the face of the brownbeard as though for a cue, then touched him lightly on the chest and spat before him on the ground, peh, peh: "That's for you. So you are one of those fellows. My brother-in-law." The brownbeard sprawled towards the window: "Now you go ahead and talk, and say it isn't true."

The walls no longer existed. A small room with a hanging lamp, two Jews running around, one with brown hair and one with red hair, both wearing black plush hats, quarreling with each other. He pursued his red-haired friend: "Say, listen to me, is that true, what he told about the man, how he went to pieces and how they killed him?" The brownbeard yelled: "Killed, did I say killed? He killed himself." The redbeard: "Well, then, he killed himself." The ex-convict: "And what did they do, the others?" The redbeard: "Who, who?" "Well, there probably were others like him, like Stefan. Most likely they weren't all ministers and knackers and bankers." The red and the brown fellow exchanged glances. The redhead: "Well, what could they do? They looked on."

The discharged prisoner in the tan summer topcoat, the big fellow, stepped from behind the sofa, took up his hat, brushed it, and put it on the table; then he threw his coat back, and without saying a word, unbuttoned his waistcoat. "Here, take a look at my pants. I was that stout and now they stand out, two thick fists, one on top of the other, that's from short victuals. All gone. The whole caboodle gone to the devil. That's how you go to pieces, because you weren't always the way you should have been. I don't know as the others are much better. Nope. Don't believe it. They just try to drive a man crazy."

The brownbeard whispered to the redbeard: "There you got it." "What have I got?" "Well, a convict." "What of it?" The discharged prisoner: "Then they say: you are discharged and back you go, right back into the dirt, and it's the same dirt as before. It's no laughing matter." He buttoned his waistcoat again: "You can see from that, the way they do. They take the dead man out of his hole, the lousy fool with the dog wagon comes and dumps a dead man, who killed himself, on the wagon, the damned stinking swine—why didn't they knock his brains out? Sinning against a human being like that, and it don't matter who it is." The red-haired man sadly: "What can you do about it?" "Yes, sir, are we nothing, just because we did something once? Everybody who has been in jail can get back on his feet again and it don't matter what he did." (To repent! A fellow's got to have air! Hit out! Then everything will lie behind us, then everything'll be over, fear and everything.) "I just wanted to show you: Don't you listen to everything my brother-in-law tells you. You can't always do everything you want to, sometimes it works just as well another way." "That's no justice to throw a fellow on the dungheap like a cur and then dump garbage on top of him, and that's the justice they give a dead man. Ough, hell. But now I've got to leave you. Give me your paw. You mean well and you, too, (he pressed the red-haired fellow's hand). My name's Biberkopf, Franz. Was nice of you to take me in. My dicky-bird has already sung its bit in the courtyard. Well, here's how, merry business, it'll soon be over." The two Jews shook hands with him and smiled. The redhead held his hand for a long time, beamed: "Now you're all right. And I'll be glad if you have time and can come around one day." "Thanks, we'll fix that up, we'll find time all right, only no money. And give the old gentleman who was there my regards. That boy's got strength in that hand of his, say, he musta been a butcher once. Ow, we'll have to put the rug straight, it's all crumpled up. No, let's do it all ourselves, and the table, like this." He worked on the floor, laughed over his shoulder to the redhead: "Well, here we sat and told each other a lot. A good place to sit down, askin' your pardon."

They accompanied him to the door, the red-haired fellow was still worried: "Will you be able to walk alone?" The brownbeard nudged him: "Don't call him back." The ex-convict, walking erect, shook his head, pushed the air from him with both arms (we must get air, air, air, and that's all). "Don't bother about it. You can let me run along. Didn't you talk about feet and eyes? I've still got them all right. Nobody's chopped 'em off for me yet. Bye-bye, gents."

And across the narrow, obstructed courtyard he went; the two men looked down the stairs after him. He had his stiff hat down over his face, mumbled, as he stepped over a puddle of gasoline: "Lotta poison. Now for a cognac. The first man who comes along gets one in the jaw. Let's see, where can I get a cognac?"

Market dull, later Bears very active, Hamburg depressed, London weaker

It was raining. To the left in Münzstrasse signs sparkled in front of the movies. At the corner he was unable to pass, the people were standing in front of a fence, then it got very steep, the street-car tracks ran on planks laid across the space, a car was just riding slowly over them. Look here, they are building a subway station, must be work to be had in Berlin. Another movie. Children under seventeen not allowed. On the huge poster a beet-red gentleman was standing on a staircase, while a peach of a young girl embraced his legs, she lay on the stairs, and he stood up above with a leering expression on his face. Underneath was written: No

Parents, Fate of an Orphaned Child, in Six Reels. Yes, sir, I'll take a look at that. The orchestrion was banging away. Price sixty pfennigs.

A man to the woman cashier: "Say, Fräulein, is it any cheaper for an old territorial without a belly?" "Nope, only for children under five months with a sucking nipple." "Sure. That's our age. New-born babies on the instutterment plan." "All right, make it fifty then, get along in." Behind him there meandered a young chap, slim of build, with a muffler on: "Hey, lady, I'd like to git in free." "How do you get that way? Tell your Mommer to put you on the pottie." "Well, kin I get in?" "In where?" "The movie." "There ain't no movie here." "You really mean it, there ain't no movie here?" She called through the window of the ticket-office to the watchman at the door: "Say, Max, come here a minute. Here's a fellow wants to know if there's a movie here. He's got no money. Go ahead show him what we got here." "What we got here, young fellow? You ain't noticed it yet? This is the poor-box, Münzstrasse division." He pushed the slim fellow out of the ticket-office, showed him his fist: "If ye want me to, I'll give ye what's comin' to you right off the bat."

Franz pushed on in. It just happened to be an intermission. The long room was packed full, 90 per cent men with work-caps on, they don't take them off. The three lamps on the ceiling are covered with red. In front, a yellow piano with packages on top of it. The orchestrion makes a continuous racket. Then it gets dark and the film starts. A goose-girl is to be given culture, just why, is not made so clear, at least not right in the middle. She wiped her nose with her hand, she scratched her behind on the staircase, everybody in the movie laughed. Franz thought it was quite wonderful, when the tittering started up around him. Just folks, free folks, amusing themselves, nobody has a right to say anything to them, simply lovely, and I right here among 'em! It went on. The high-toned Baron had a sweetheart who lay in a hammock and stretched her legs vertically in the air. The girl had drawers on. That's something. Wonder why people get so excited about that dirty goose-girl and her licking the platters clean? Again the girl with the slim legs flashed by. The Baron had left her alone, now she toppled out of the hammock, and flopped onto the grass, lay there a long time. Franz stared at the screen, there was already another picture, he still saw her toppling out and lying there for a long while. He gnawed his tongue, hell's bells, what was that? But when finally the one who had been the goose-girl's lover embraced this fine lady, the skin of his chest felt hot as if he had been embracing her himself. It went all over him and made him weak.

A jane. (There's something else besides anger and fear. What about all this bunk? Air, m'boy, and a jane!) Queer he shouldn't have thought of that. You stand at the window of the cell and look into the courtyard through the bars. Sometimes women pass by, visitors or children or house-cleaning up at the old man's. How they all stand at the windows, the convicts, and look, every window occupied, devouring every woman. A guard once had a two weeks' visit from his wife from Eberswalde, formerly he used to drive over to see her once every two weeks, now she made good use of the time, every moment of it, at work his head hangs with fatigue, he can hardly walk any longer.

Franz was now outside on the street in the rain. What'll we do? I'm a free man. I've got to have a woman! A woman I've got to have! Gee, how great, life is nice outside. But I must hold on to myself so I can walk. He was walking on springs, not on solid earth. Then, at the corner of Kaiser-Wilhelm Strasse, behind the market-wagons, he came upon a woman; he posted himself beside her, any old gal will do. The devil, how did I suddenly git such cold feet. He went off with her, bit his under-lip, he was so excited, if you live far, I won't come along. It was just across the Bülowplatz, past the fences, through a hallway, to the courtyard, down six steps. She turned back, laughed: "Don't be so dithery, sweetie, why, you'll knock me down." She had hardly shut the door behind him, when he grabbed her. "Boy, just give me time to put my umbrella down first." He pressed her, hugged her, pinched her, rubbed his hands across her coat, he still had his hat on, angrily she let the umbrella drop. "Let me go, won't you." He groaned, and smiled an awkward, dizzy smile: "Whazze matter?" "You're going to ruin all my get-up. Are you going to shell out for it afterwards? All right then, we never get anything for nothing either." He did not let her go. "Say, you fool, I can't breathe. You must be loony." She was stout and slow, small, he first had to give her the three marks, which she put carefully into the chest of drawers. The key she put in her pocket. He couldn't keep his eyes off her. "It's because I've been behind the bars a coupla years, fat gal. Out there in Tegel, you can imagine it." "Where?" "Tegel, you know."

The flabby wench guffawed. She unbuttoned her blouse at the top. There were once two royal children, who held each other so dear. And the cow jumped over the moon. She grabbed him, pressed him to her. Putt, putt, putt, my little chick, putt, putt, putt, my rooster.

19

He soon had beads of sweat on his face, he groaned. "Well, whatcha groaning for?" "Who's that bird running around next door?" "It's not a bird, it's my landlady." "What's she doing there?" "What do you think she's doing? She's got her kitchen there." "Well, she ought to stop running around like that. What does she want to run around for now? I can't stand it." "Oh Lordylordy, I'll go and tell her." What a sweaty fellow he is, I'll be glad to get rid of him, the old bum! I'll soon put him out. She knocked next door: "Frau Priese, won't you be quiet for just a few minutes? I've got to talk to a gentleman here, something important." Well, that's done, dear fatherland, be comfort thine, come to my heart, but you're going to be ditched soon.

She thought to herself, her head on the pillow: those tan oxfords need soling, Kitty's new boy-friend does that for two marks, if she don't mind, I ain't goin' to swipe him away from her, he can also dye 'em brown to go with my brown blouse, it's an old rag anyway, just good enough to be made into a coffee-cozy: them ribbons'll have to be pressed, I'll ask Frau Priese right away, she's probably still got a fire going, what's she cooking today anyway? She sniffed. Green herring.

Incomprehensible verses keep running through his head in a circle. When you cook soup, Fräulein Stein, I'll get a spoon, Fräulein Stein. If you cook noodles, Fräulein Stein, give me some noodles, Fräulein Stein. Tumbling down, tumbling up. He groaned aloud: "Maybe you don't like me?" "Why not, come on, I'm a lovin' gal, I am." He fell back into bed, grunted and moaned. She rubbed her neck. "I have to laugh myself sick. Just keep quiet there. You don't bother me." She laughed, raised her fat arms, stuck her stockinged feet out from under the cover. "I can't help it."

Lets get out of this. Air. Still raining. What's the matter? I'll have to get myself another gal. First let's get some sleep, Franz, what'se matter with you, anyway?

Sexual potency depends upon the concentered action of 1. the internal secretory system, 2. the nervous system, and 3. the sexual apparatus. The glands participating in this potency are: the pituitary gland, the thyroid gland, the suprarenal gland, the prostate gland, the seminal vesicle, and the epididymis. In this system the spermatic gland preponderates. Through the matter prepared by it, the entire sexual apparatus is charged from the cerebral cortex to the genitals. The erotic impression releases the erotic tension of the cerebral cortex, the current flows as an erotic stimulus from the cerebral cortex to the switch center in the interbrain. The stimulus then rolls down the spine. Not unimpeded, however, for, before leaving the brain, it has to pass the brakes of the inhibitions, those predominantly psychic inhibitions which play a large rôle in the form of moral scruples, lack of self-confidence, fear of humiliation, fear of infection and impregnation, and things of this order.

In the evening there he is, shambling down Elsasser Strasse. Don't be afraid, m'boy, don't pretend you're tired. "How much for the pleasure, kid?" The black gal is fine, got hips, a toothsome piece. When a gal's got a man, that she loves, ain't it gran'? "My you're a gay one, sweetie. Did you just come into a fortune?" "And how! You'll get some change out of it." "Why not." But, nevertheless, he is afraid.

And afterwards in the room, flowers behind the curtain, a clean little room, a nice little room, why, the girl even has a phonograph, she sings for him, artificial silk stockings, rayon, no blouse, pitch-black eyes: "I'm a cabaret singer, I am. You know where? Anywhere I like. Just now I got no engagement, you know. I go into nice-looking joints and I ask. Then I do my stunt. It's a wow. Hey, quit tickling." "Aw, come on." "Nope, hands off, that knocks hell out of my business. My act—be nice now, sweetie—you see, I hold an auction in the place, no plate collection either; whoever gives me something, can kiss me. Crazy, ain't it! In a public place, too. Nobody under fifty pfennigs. Say, I get everything. Here on my shoulder. There, go ahead, it's all right." She puts on a man's top hat, croaks into his face, shakes her hips, her arms akimbo: "Theodore, what did you mean last night, when you smiled at me so gay and bright? Theodore, what was it you hoped to gain, when you stood me to pig's knuckles and fine champagne?"

While sitting on his lap, she pulls a cigarette out of his waistcoat and sticks it into her mouth; she looks yearningly into his eyes, tenderly rubs her ear on his and chirps: "Do you know what homesickness is? When your heart is torn by homesickness? Everything seems so cold and dreary." She hums a tune, stretches herself on the sofa. She puffs, strokes his hair, trills, laughs.

Sweat on his brow. Again that fear. And suddenly his head slithers off. Boom, the bell rings, get up, five-thirty, six o'clock, cells opened, boom, boom, brush your coat quickly, suppose the old man makes inspection, no, not today. I'll get discharged soon. Psst, say, one of the boys got out last night, pard, the rope's still dangling out there over the wall, they got the police after him. He groans, he lifts his head, he sees the girl, her chin, her neck. If I only knew how to get out of prison. They ain't going to discharge me. I'm not out yet. She puffs blue rings from the side at him, sniggers: "You're sweet, come on, I'll pour you a glass of Mampe brandy, thirty pfennigs." He lies there, stretched out at full length. "What do I care for Mampe? They knocked hell out of me. I did time at Tegel, I did, what for, I'd really like to know. First with the Prussians in the trenches, and then in Tegel. I ain't a human being any more." "Well, but you're not going to cry here. Come on, open your li'l beakie, big mans gotta drink. We're a jolly lot, we are, we're as happy as can be, we laugh and sing with delight from morning until night." And the dump heap for that. Why, they might have chopped off the fellow's head at once, and be done with it, the lousy dogs. Could have dumped me on the garbage heap, why not. "Come on, big man, take another glass. I'd walk a mile for Mampe's brandy, it makes you feel so hale and dandy."

"To think the girls ran after me like a bunch of sheep and I didn't even spit at 'em, and there I was, flat on my nose." She picks up another one of his cigarettes which have fallen to the floor. "Yes, you ought to go to the policeman sometime and tell him." "I'm going." He is looking for his suspenders. And says nothing more and doesn't look at the girl with her slobbery mouth, she smokes and smiles and looks at him, shoves a few cigarettes quickly under the sofa with her foot. And he grabs his hat and hurries down the stairs, takes the 68 car to Alexanderplatz, and sits brooding in a café over a glass of light beer.

Testifortan, authorized patent No. 365695, sexual therapeutic agent approved by Sanitary Councillor Dr. Magnus Hirschfeld and Dr. Bernard Schapiro, Institute of Sexual Science, Berlin. The main causes of impotence are: A. insufficient charging through functional disorder of the internal secretory glands, B. too strong resistance through extreme psychic inhibitions, exhaustion of the erective center. At what moment the impotent patient will be able to resume his functions can be determined only through the progress of each individual case. A period of abstention is often effective.

And gluttonously he eats and sleeps his fill, and the next day on the street he thinks: I'd like to have this gal, and that gal I'd like to have, but doesn't go near any of them. And the one in the show-window, what a plump little morsel. She could suit me, but I won't go near any of 'em. And he hangs around the café again and doesn't look at any of the girls and guzzles and boozes. Now I won't do anything the whole livelong day but eat my fill and booze and sleep and life is over for me. Over. Over.

Victory all along the Line! Franz Biberkopf buys a Veal Cutlet

As Wednesday rolls around, the third day, he puts on his coat.

Whose fault is it all? Ida's of course. Who else's? I knocked that tart's ribs to pieces, that's why I had to go to the jug. Now she's got what she wanted, the wench is dead, and here I am. And he snivels to himself and races along the streets in the cold. Where to? Where she had lived with him, at her sister's. Through the Invalidenstrasse, into Ackerstrasse, right into the house like a whirlwind, second courtyard. Prison had never existed, nor the conversation with the Jews in the Dragonerstrasse. Where is the wench, it's her fault. Seen nothing in the street but found my way. A little twitching of the face, a little twitching in the fingers, then we'll go there, bumbledy, bumbledy, bumbledy, bee, tumbledy, rumbledy, tumbledy, bee, rumbledy, bumbledy.

Ring-a-ling. "Who is it?" "Me." "Who?" "Open that door, old girl." "Lordy, you, Franz." "Open that door." Rumbledy, bumbledy, bumbledy, bee. Rumbledy. A piece of twine on my tongue; got to spit it out. He is standing in the hallway, she shuts the door behind him. "Whatche want here? Suppose somebody seen you on the stairs." "Too bad, eh. Let 'em see me. Howdy." He walks along to the left, swings into the room. Rumbledy, bumbledy. That piece of twine on my tongue won't come off. He scrapes it with his fingers. But it's nothing, just a lousy feeling on the tip of my tongue. So that's the room, the stiff-backed sofa, the Kaiser hanging on the wall, a Frenchman in red trousers giving him his sword. I have surrendered. "What do you want here, Franz? Are you crazy, or what?" "I'll sit down." I have surrendered, the Kaiser presents his sword, the Kaiser must return the sword to him, that's the way the world runs. "If you don't go, I'll call for help, I'll yell murder." "What for?" Rumbledy, bumbledy, I have run this far, I'm here, I'll stay. "Have they let you out already?" "Yes, it's all over."

He stares at her and gets up: "Because they let me out, that's why I'm here. They let me out all right, but how?" How, he wants to tell it, but chews on his twine, the trumpet is broken, it's all over, and he trembles, and can't cry, and looks at her hand. "What do you want now? Is anything wrong?"

There are mountains that have been standing for centuries, that have always been standing, and armies with guns have gone over them, there are islands, people on them, chock-full, all strong, solid business houses, banks, industry, dancing, dives, import, export, social questions, and one day there starts a rrrrrrrr, rrrr, not from the warship, the rumpus starts all by itself—from down below. The earth gives a jump, nightingale, nightingale, how beautifully you sang, the ships fly to the skies, the birds fall to the earth. "Franz, I'll yell, let me go. Karl will soon be here. Karl will be here any minute. You started the same way with Ida."

What is a woman worth among friends? The London divorce courts, in the suit of Captain Bacon, pronounced a dissolution of his marriage on the ground of his wife's adultery with Captain Furber, a fellow-officer, and granted him £750 damages. The captain does not seem to have put too high a value on his faithless wife, who is soon going to get married to her lover.

Oh, there are mountains that have been lying quiet for myriads of years, and armies with guns and elephants have gone over them, what is one to do, when they suddenly start to caper, because down below there's a noise that goes: rrrr, rumm. Don't let's say anything about that, let's leave it alone. Minna cannot get her hand away from him, and his eyes look into hers. The face of a man like that is laid with rails, a train passes over it, see the smoke, it passes along, Berlin-Hamburg-Altona express, 6.05 till 9.35, three hours and thirty-five minutes, can't do anything about it, the arms of a man like that are made of iron, iron. I'll call for help. She screamed. She was lying on the carpet now. His stubby cheek against hers, his mouth greedily fumbles up towards hers, she turns away. "Franz, Oh God, have pity, Franz." And—she saw it all right.

Now she knows, she is Ida's sister, that's the way he looked at Ida sometimes. He has Ida in his arms, it's she, that's why he has his eyes closed and looks happy now. And there is no longer the terrible fighting and this moping about, it's no longer prison! It's Treptow, Paradiesgarten, with a display of fireworks, where he met her and brought her home, the little seamstress, she had won a vase at dice shooting; in the hallway, with her key in her hand, he had kissed her for the first time, she stood on tiptoe, she had canvas shoes on, he dropped the key, after that he could not tear himself away from her. That's good old Franz Biberkopf.

And now he smells her again, at the throat, it's the same skin, the same odor, it makes him dizzy, what will it lead to? And she, the sister, what strange thing is happening to her? She feels from his face, from his lying still on her, that she has to give in, she defends herself, but a sort of transformation comes over her, her face loses its tension, her arms can no longer push him off, her mouth grows helpless. The man says nothing, she lets lets lets him have her mouth, she grows soft as in a bath, do with me whatever you please, she dissolves like water, it's all right, just come, I know it all, I love you, too.

Magic, quivering. The goldfish gleams in the bowl. The room sparkles, it is not Ackerstrasse, no house, no gravitation, no centrifugal force. It has disappeared, it has sunk away, extinguished is the red deflection of radiations in the sun's dynamic field, the kinetic theory of gases, transformation of heat into energy, electric vibrations, induction phenomena, the density of metals, of liquids, of non-metallic solids.

She was lying on the floor, tossing herself about. He laughed and stretched himself: "Well, go ahead and choke me. I'll keep still, if you can do it." "You deserve it, all right." He clambered up, laughed, and spun around with joy, delight, beatitude. The trumpets are blowing, hussars ride forth, hallelujah. Franz Biberkopf is back again! Franz is discharged! Franz Biberkopf is free! He had pulled up his trousers, hobbling from one leg to the other. She sat on a chair, was on the point of bursting into tears: "I'll tell my husband about it, I'll tell Karl, they oughta've kept you there another four years." "Tell him right away, Minna!" "So I will, I'll get a copper right away, too." "Minna, my li'l Minnakin, pull yourself together, I'm so happy, I'm a human being again, li'l Minna." "You're crazy, you are, they must have turned your head around in Tegel." "You haven't got anything to drink, a pot of coffee or something?" "And who's going to pay for my apron, just look at it, all in shreds." "Leave it to Franz, leave it to Franz! Franz is alive again, Franz is back again!" "Take your hat and beat it. If he meets you, and me with a black eye! And don't let me see you again." "Bye-bye, Minna."

But next morning he came back again with a little package. She did not want to open the door, he wedged his foot in between. She whispered through the crack: "You oughta go about your business. I've told you that before." "Minna, it's only the aprons." "What aprons?" "You can pick out a couple." "You can keep that stuff you pinched for yourself." "Didn't pinch it. Go ahead, open that door, Minna." "The neighbors'll see you. Go away." "Open that door, Minna."

And so she opened the door, he threw the package in, and as she did not want to come in with the broomstick in her hand, he hopped around the room alone. "I'm so happy, Minna. I'm so happy all day long. Dreamt about you last night."

Then he opened the package on the table; she came nearer, touched the material, chose three aprons, but wouldn't yield when he grabbed her hand. He wrapped up his package again, she still stood there with the broom, insisted: "Now quick, get out of here." He waved to her from the door. "So long Minnakin." She pushed the door shut with the broomstick.

A week later he came to her door again: "Just want to ask about your eye." "Everything's fine, you got no business here." He appeared stronger, had on a blue winter overcoat and a brown derby: "I just wanted to show you how I'm making out, how I look." "Makes no difference to me." "But just let me drink a cup of coffee." At that moment steps were heard coming down the stairs, a child's ball rolled along the steps; scared, the woman opened the door, pulled him in. "Stay there, that's the Lumkes, now you can go again." "Just want to drink a cup of coffee. Surely you got a little pot of coffee for me?" "You don't need me for that. You probably got another girl already, from the way you look." "Just a cup of coffee." "You do make a body miserable."

And as she stood by the coat-rack in the hall, and he looked beseechingly at her from the kitchen door, she picked up the nice new apron, shook her head and wept: "You make me miserable, you sure do." "But what's the matter?" "Karl didn't believe me about that black eye. How could I have bumped into the press like that? I had to show him how. But a person really can get a black eye on that press, if the door's open. Let him try it. Say, I don't know why he don't believe me." "I don't understand it either, Minna." "Because I've got some marks here too, on my neck. I hadn't noticed them at all. What can I say, when he shows 'em to me, and I look in the mirror and don't know where they came from?" "Humph, can't a person scratch himself, suppose something is itching you. Don't let Karl razz you like that. I certainly would knock that into his head." "And you keep on coming up here. And the Lumkes probably saw you." "Well, they don't have to get all ruffled up about that." "But if you'd only go away, Franz, and don't come back again. You make me miserable." "Did he ask about the aprons, too?" "I've been wanting to get some aprons for a long time." "All right, then, I'll go, Minna."

He grabbed her around the neck, she let him do it. After a while, when he didn't let go, without pressing her to him, she noticed that he was stroking her, and looked up, astonished: "But you must go now, Franz." He drew her gently towards the room, she resisted, but followed step by step. "Franz, is it going to start all over again?" "Why, no, I just want to sit by you, in the room."

They sat quietly talking next to each other on the sofa for a while. Then he left of his own accord. She accompanied him to the door. "Don't come again, Franz." She wept and laid her head on his shoulder. "It's certainly queer, Minna, what you can do to a fellow. Why shouldn't I come back again? Well, then, I won't come again." She clung to his hand: "No, Franz, don't come back." Then he opened the door, she still held his hand tight and pressed it hard. She still held his hand while he stood outside. Then she dropped it and gently, quickly, shut the door. From the street he sent her up two big slices of veal cutlet.

And now Franz swears to all the World and to himself to stay Respectable in Berlin with Money or Without

He was already quite well on his feet in Berlin—he had turned his old furniture into cash, he had a few pennies from Tegel, his landlady and his friend Meck gave him a small loan—then he got another terrible blow. But it turned out later on to be only a slap. One morning, which otherwise wasn't so bad, he found on his table an official yellow paper with printing and typewriting on it.

Police commissioner, division 5, reference number, you are requested in case of possible claims in the above affair to mention the above reference number. According to documents in my possession, you have been convicted of assault and battery with fatal consequences, as a result of which you are to be regarded as dangerous to public safety and morality. Accordingly I have decided on the authority granted me in paragraph 2 of the Law of Dec. 31, 1842, and paragraph 3 of the Prisoner Restriction Act of Nov. 1, 1867, as well as the Laws of June 12, 1889 and June 13, 1900, to expel you through the constabulary from Berlin, Charlottenburg, Neukölln, Berlin-Schöneberg, Wilmersdorf, Lichtenberg, Stralau, as well as from the districts of Berlin-Friedenau, Schmargendorf, Tempelhof, Britz, Treptow, Reinickendorf, Weissensee, Pankow, and Berlin-Tegel, and therefore instruct you to leave the districts specified above within a period of 14 days, with the warning that, should you be found after that period within the said area, or should you return therein, you will be fined, under Paragraph 132, Clause 2, of the General Administration Act of July 30, Q 11 E 1883, the sum of 100 marks, or, in default of payment, be sentenced to 10 days' imprisonment. I also direct your attention to the fact that, in the event of your being found in any of the following places adjacent to Berlin: Potsdam, Spandau, Friedrichsfelde, Karlshorst, Friedrichshagen, Oberschöneweide and

Wuhlheide, Fichtenau, Rahnsdorf, Carow, Buch, Frohnau, Cöpenick, Lankwitz, Steglitz, Zehlendorf, Teltow, Dahlem, Wannsee, Klein-Glienicke, Nowawes, Neuendorf, Eiche, Bornim, and Bornstedt, you are liable to expulsion from these places. I. Ve. Copy No. 986a.

A staggering blow, that. There was a fine house alongside the city car-line, Grunerstrasse 1, on the Alex, Prisoners' Aid. There they take a look at Franz, ask him this and that, sign: Herr Franz Biberkopf has sought our protective supervision, we will make inquiries whether you are working, and you will have to report here every month. O. K., full stop, everything, everything going slick.

Forgotten all fear, forgotten Tegel and the red walls, and the groaning and all that sort of thing—to hell with it. A new life's about to begin, the old life's all in, Franz Biberkopf is back to stay and the Prussians are happy and shout hurray.

Then for four weeks he filled his belly with meat, potatoes, and beer, and went once more to see the Jews in Dragonerstrasse to express his thanks. Nachum and Eliser were going after each other again. They did not recognize him when he entered, all dolled up, stout and smelling of brandy as he was, and asked in a whisper, his hat respectfully before his mouth, whether the old gentleman's grandchildren were still sick. In the saloon at the corner where he stood up the drinks, they asked him, what kind of business he was in. "Me and business. I ain't got any business. With me things just go along any old way." "And where do you get your money from?" "From the old days, savings, I guess a man can save something, can't he?" He nudged Nachum in the ribs, puffed up his nose, looked at him with canny, mysterious eyes: "You still know that story about Zannovich? A crazy hound. Was a fine chap. Afterwards they killed him. Funny how you know everything. I'd like to be a prince, too, and study. No, I ain't goin' to study. Maybe I'll get married, instead." "Good luck." "You must come around and see me then, we'll put on the feed-bag and soak it up."

Nachum, red-haired Nachum, looked at him, rubbed his chin: "You'll listen to another story, mebbe. A man once had a ball, you know, the kind children have, but not made out of rubber, of celluloid, transparent, and inside there are little lead shots. Children can rattle it and throw it. Then the man took the ball and threw it and he thought: there are lead shots in it, so I can throw it, and the ball won't run any farther, it'll stand still right on the spot I intend it to. But when he threw the ball, it didn't go the way he had intended, it made one more jump, and then it rolled a bit, about two hands sideways." "Leave him alone with your stories, Nachum. The man don't need you, does he?" The stout chap: "What about that ball, and why are you scrapping again? Say, boss, look at them two here, they been scrapping ever since I know 'em." "You gotta let people be the way they are. Scrapping is good for the liver." The red-haired man: "I'll tell you, I saw you in the street, in the courtyard, and heard you sing. You sing very nice. You're a good man. But don't get so excited. Just hold your horses. Be patient in this world. What do I know about how it looks inside you and what God intends to do with you? You see, the ball don't go the way you throw it and the way you want it to, it goes about this way, you see, but it goes a li'l bit sideways, too."

The stout fellow threw his head back and laughed, stretched out his arms, fell around the red-haired man's neck: "You sure can tell stories, that man can tell stories. Franz has had his own experiences. Franz knows life. Franz knows who he is." "I just wanted to tell you, you sang very sadly there for a while." "For a while, for a while. Well, let bygones be bygones. Now my vest's filled out again. Folks, everything's goin' fine! Ain't nobody can come near me. Bye-bye, and when I get married, you'll be there."

Thus Franz Biberkopf, the concrete-worker, and later furniture-mover, that rough, uncouth man of repulsive aspect, returned to Berlin and to the street, the man at whose head a pretty girl from a locksmith's family had thrown herself, a girl whom he then made into a whore, and at last mortally injured in a scuffle. He has sworn to all the world and to himself to remain respectable. And as long as he had money, he remained respectable. Later, however, his money gave out: and that was the moment he had been waiting for, to show everybody, once and for all, what a real fellow is like.

Second Book

And thus we have brought our man safely to Berlin. He has made his vow, and the question is: Hadn't we better simply stop here? The end seems amiable and without artifice, almost a fitting end, and the whole has the great advantage of brevity.

But this is no ordinary man, this Franz Biberkopf. I did not call him here for sport, but to share his hard, true, and enlightening existence.

Franz Biberkopf is badly burnt. He now stands safe and sound contentedly on Berlin ground, and if he says he wants to be good, we can believe him, he will be good.

You're going to see how he stayed decent for many a week, but it's only a respite, so to speak.

Once upon a time there lived in Paradise two human beings, Adam and Eve. They had been put there by the Lord, who had also created the beasts and plants and heaven and earth. And Paradise was the wonderful garden of Eden. Flowers and trees were growing there, animals were playing about, and none oppressed the other. The sun rose and set, the moon did the same, there was abiding joy the whole day long in Paradise.

Thus let us start off merrily. We want to sing and move about: with our little hands going clap, clap, clap, our little feet going tap, tap, tap, moving to, moving fro, roundabout, and away we go.

Franz Biberkopf Enters
BERLIN

 Trade and Commerce

 Street Cleaning and Transport

Health Department

 Underground Construction

 Art and Culture

 Traffic

 Municipal Savings Bank

 Gas Works

 Fire Department

 Finance and Tax Office

Notice of a scheme regarding the building lot situate An der Spandauer Brücke No. 10.

The scheme for the permanent restriction of the building lot situate in the Communal District of Berlin Center due to the addition of an ornamental rosette to the street wall of No. 10 An der Spandauer Brücke is hereby published, together with a sketch plan, for public inspection. During this time all parties concerned may file any objections to the scheme, within the extent of their interests. The municipal authorities of the communal district are also authorized to state their objections, if any. Such objections should be made in writing to the District Office Center,

Berlin C 2, Klosterstrasse 68, Room 76, or be made orally before the Registrar.

—I have granted to Herr Bottich, hunting lessee, with the consent of the Police President, authority, liable to cancellation at any time, for the shooting of wild rabbits and other vermin in the area of the Faule Seepark on the following days in the year 1928: Shooting must cease in summer, from April 1st to September 30th, by 7 p. m., in winter, from October 1st to March 31st, by 8 p. m. The public are hereby notified of this permit, and are warned against entering the said area during the shooting time fixed hereby. The Chief Burgomaster, Controller of Hunting Licenses.

—Albert Pangel, master furrier, who may look back upon an activity of almost three years as honorary official, has resigned his honorary office because of age and removal from the district in question. During this long period he was uninterruptedly active as president of the charity commission, or rather as charity guardian. The district office has expressed recognition of his merits in a note of thanks to Mr. Pangel.

The Rosenthaler Platz is busily active.

Weather changing, more agreeable, a degree below freezing. For Germany, a low-pressure region is extending, which in its entire range has ended the weather prevailing up to now. The few pressure changes now going on indicate a slow extension of the low-pressure area towards the south, so that the weather will remain under its influence. During the day the temperature will probably be lower. Weather forecast for Berlin and surrounding country.

Car No. 68 runs across Rosenthaler Platz, Wittenau, Nordbahnhof, Heilanstalt, Weddingplatz, Stettiner Station, Rosenthaler Platz, Alexanderplatz, Straussberger Platz, Frankfurter Allee Station, Lichtenberg, Herzberge Insane Asylum. The three Berlin transport companies—streetcar, elevated and underground, omnibus—form a tariff-union. Fares for adults are 20 pfennigs, for schoolchildren 10 pfennigs, reduced fares allowed for children up to the age of 14, apprentices and pupils, poor students, war cripples, persons physically unfit for walking as certified by the district charity offices. Get to know about the lines. During the winter months the front entrance shall not be opened for passengers entering or leaving, 39 seating capacity, 5918, to alight from the car, warn the motorman in time, the motorman is forbidden to converse with passengers, getting off or on while the car is in motion may lead to fatal accidents.

In the middle of the Rosenthaler Platz a man with two yellow packages jumps off from the 41, an empty taxi glides just past him, the copper looks at him, a street-car inspector appears, cop and inspector shake hands: damned lucky, that fellow with his packages.

Various fruit brandies at wholesale prices, Dr. Bergell, notary and attorney-at-law, Lukutate, the Indian rejuvenation treatment for elephants, Fromms Akt, the best rubber sponge, what's the use of so many rubber sponges, anyway?

The wide Brunnenstrasse runs north from this square, the A. E. G. runs along its left side in front of the Humboldthain. The A. E. G. is an immense enterprise, which embraces, according to the 1928 telephone directory: Electric Light and Power Works, Central Administration, NW 40, Friedrich-Karl-Ufer 2–4, Local Call and Long Distance Call Office, North 4488, General Management, Janitor, Electric Securities Bank Inc., Division for Lighting Fixtures, Division for Russia, Oberspree Metal Division, Treptow Apparatus Plant, Brunnenstrasse Plant, Henningsdorf Plant, Plant for Insulators, Rheinstrasse Plant, Oberspree Cable Works, Wilhelminenhofstrasse Plant, Rummelsburger Chaussee, Turbine Plant NW 87, Huttenstrasse 12–16.

The Invalidenstrasse trails off to the left. It goes towards the Stettin Station where the trains from the Baltic Sea arrive: Why, you're all covered with soot—yes, there is a lot of dust here.—How do you do? So long.—Has the gentleman anything to carry, 50 pfennigs.—Your vacation certainly did you a lot of good.—Oh, that tan will come off soon.—Wonder where people get all the money from to travel around like that.—In a little hotel over there in that dark street two lovers shot themselves early yesterday morning, a waiter from Dresden and a married woman, both of whom, however, had registered under false names.

From the south the Rosenthaler Strasse runs into the square. Across the way Aschinger provides food as well as beer to drink, music, and wholesale bakery. Fish are nutritious, some are happy when they have fish, and others are unable to eat it, eat more fish, the healthy slenderizing dish. Ladies' stockings, genuine artificial silk, here you have a fountain pen with a 14-carat gold point.

On the Elsasser Strasse they have fenced in the whole street leaving only a narrow gangway. A power engine puffs behind the billboards. Becker-Fiebig, Building Contractor Inc., Berlin W 38. There is a constant din, dump carts are lined up as far as the corner, on which stands the Commercial and Savings Bank, Deposit Branch L, Custody of Securities,

Payment of Savings Bank Deposits. Five men, workmen, kneel in front of the bank driving small stones into the ground.

Four persons have just gotten on No. 4 at Lothringer Strasse, two elderly women, a plain man with a worried look, and a boy with a cap and ear-muffs. The two women are together, they are Frau Plück and Frau Hoppe. They want to get an abdominal bandage for Frau Hoppe, the older woman, because she has a tendency to navel hernia. They have been to the truss-maker's in the Brunnenstrasse, and now they both want to call by to fetch their husbands for lunch. The man is a coachman named Hasebrück, who is having a lot of trouble with an electric iron which he bought for his boss second-hand and cheap. They had given him a defective one, the boss tried it for a few days, then it failed to work properly, so he is supposed to exchange it, the people refuse to do so, this is the third time he has gone there, today he has been told he has to pay something on it. The boy, Max Rüst, will later on become a tinker, father of seven more Rüsts, he will go to work for the firm of Hallis & Co., Plumbing and Roofing, in Grünau. At the age of 52 he will win a quarter of a prize in the Prussian Class Lottery, then he will retire from business and die during an adjustment suit which he has started against the firm of Hallis & Co., at the age of 55. His obituary will read as follows: On September 2, suddenly, from heart-disease, my beloved husband, our dear father, son, brother, brother-in-law, and uncle, Paul Rüst, in his 55th year. This announcement is made with deep grief on behalf of his sorrowing family by Marie Rüst. The notice of thanks after the funeral will read as follows: Acknowledgment. Being unable to acknowledge individually all tokens of sympathy in our bereavement, we hereby express our profound gratitude to all relatives, friends, as well as to the tenants of No. 4 Kleiststrasse and to all our acquaintances. Especially do we thank Herr Deinen for his kind words of sympathy. At present this Max Rüst is 14 years old, has just finished public school, is supposed to call by on his way there at the clinic for the defective in speech, the hard of hearing, the weak-visioned, the weak-minded, the incorrigible, he has been there at frequent intervals, because he stutters, but he is getting better now.

Small café on Rosenthaler Platz.

In front they are playing billiards, in the back, in a corner, two men sit puffing and smoking and drinking tea. One of them has a flabby face and gray hair, he is sitting with his raglan on: "Well, shoot. But keep still, don't fidget around like that."

"You won't get me to play billiards today. My hand's shaky."

He chews a dry Vienna roll, does not touch the tea.

"But you needn't. We're all right here."

"It's always the same old story. Now it's come to a head."

"Who's come to a head?"

The other man, young, very blond, firm face, firm figure: "Me, too, of course; you thought maybe it was only them? Now everything's cleared up."

"In other words, you've been let out."

"I talked some real German with the boss, then he started to jump on me. That evening I had my notice for the first."

"It's best never to talk German in certain situations. If you had talked French with the man, he wouldn't have understood you, and you'd still be there."

"I'm still there, what do you mean? Very much there! Maybe they think I'm going to make their lives easy! Every day, at two o'clock sharp, I'll be on the spot, and I'll make life a hell for 'em, you can bet your boots on it."

"Why, sonny, I thought you were married."

The other holds his head. "That's the mean thing about it, I haven't told her yet, I can't tell her."

"Maybe it'll all blow over."

"She is expecting."

"The second?"

"Yes."

The man in the raglan pulls his overcoat tighter round him, smiles mockingly at the other, then nods: "That's all right, children give a fellow courage. You'll need it now."

The other jerks forward: "I won't need it. What for? I'm in debt up to here. Those eternal installments. I can't tell her. And then to ditch a fellow like that. I'm used to order, and that damned business is rotten from top to bottom. The boss has his furniture factory, and whether I get orders for the shoe department or not, is something he doesn't worry about. That's the way it is. You're the fifth wheel on the wagon. You stand around the office and ask and ask: Did those estimates go out? Which estimates? Six times I told them, what's the use then of calling on the customers? You make yourself ridiculous. Either he lets the department go to hell, or he don't."

"Well, take a swallow of tea. Right now he's letting you go to hell."

A man in shirt-sleeves comes up from the billiard table, taps the younger man on the shoulders: "A game?"

The elder answers for him: "He's just been socked pretty bad."

"Billiards is good for bad socks." Then he walks away. The man in the raglan swallows some hot tea, it's good to drink hot tea with sugar and rum, and listen to somebody else yapping. It's cozy here in this place. "You're not going home today, Georg?"

"Haven't got the nerve, haven't got the nerve. What'll I tell her? I can't look her in the face."

"Onward, brother, keep the pace, look them calmly in the face."

"What do you know about it?"

The other sprawls over the table, the lapels of his raglan between his fingers: "Drink, Georg, or eat, and don't talk. I know something about it. I know the whole shooting-match, yes, sir. When you were that high, I had already been through the mill."

"Just put yourself in my place. A good position, and then they go and mess things up for a fellow."

"I was a high school teacher. Before the war. When the war broke out, I was already the way I am now. The café was like it is today. They didn't take me. They got no use for people like me, people who take dope. Or rather, they did take me. I thought I'd get a stroke. The needle, of course, they took that away, and the morphine, too. And into the mess I went. I stood it two days, as long as I still had some reserves, drops, and then goodbye, Prussians, and me for the insane asylum. Then they let me go. Well, what was I saying, then I was fired by the school, morphine, of course, a fellow is sometimes fuddled when he starts taking the stuff; now that don't happen to me anymore; worse luck. Well, and the wife? And the child? Good-bye, my dear old fatherland. Georg, old bird, I could tell you some romantic stories." The gray-haired man drinks, both hands around his glass, drinks slowly, earnestly, peering into the tea. "A wife, a child, it looks as if that were the whole world. I have no regrets. I don't feel any guilt about it, we have to take facts, like ourselves, the way they come. We shouldn't brag about our fate. I'm an enemy of Destiny, I'm not a Greek, I'm a Berliner. Why do you let that nice tea get cold? Put some rum in it." The young man holds his hand over his glass, but the other shoves it aside, pours something into it from a small tin flask which he pulls out of his pocket. "I have to go. Thanks. I'll have to walk off my bad temper." "Just stay here and keep quiet. Georg, drink a bit, then play some billiards. At any rate, don't get yourself all muddled up. That's the beginning of the end. When I didn't find my wife and child at home and there was only a letter, gone to mother in West Prussia and so on, life a failure, a man like me, and the scandal and so on and so forth, I slit myself here, here on the left arm, looks like attempted suicide, eh? We should never neglect the opportunity to learn something, Georg, I knew Provençal all right but anatomy—I mistook the tendon for the pulse. I don't know much more about it today, but that doesn't matter now, that's all over. In a word: pain and regrets were nonsense, I went on living, the woman also went on living, the child, too. In fact, more kids came on the scene in West Prussia, a brace I think, seems I operated at a distance; we're all alive and healthy. I enjoy the Rosenthaler Platz, I enjoy the cop at the Elsasser corner, I like my game of billiards, I'd like anyone to come and tell me that his life is better than mine and that I don't understand women."

The blond fellow eyes him with disgust: "Why, you're a wreck, Krause, and you know it, too. A fine sort of example you are. You make no bones about your bad luck, Krause. Didn't you tell me yourself how you often go hungry with your private lessons? I wouldn't be caught dead like that." The gray-haired man has emptied his glass, he leans back in his iron chair in his raglan, blinks at the youngster for a moment in a hostile way; then snorts and laughs convulsively: "Nope, I'm no example, you're right, I never claimed to be. Not for you, anyway. The fly, let's see, it's all in the point of view. A fly stands under the microscope and thinks it's a horse. Just let the fly get in front of my telescope some time! Who are you anyway, sir, Herr Georg? Go ahead and introduce yourself: The Honorable City Sales Representative of the firm of XY, shoe department. Nope, stop that nonsense. Always telling me about your troubles; your troubles— spelled t for tripe, r for rotter, a damned rotter, eh?—and o for oaf. And you got the wrong number, the wrong number, my dear sir, absolutely the wrong number."

A young girl gets out of the 99, Mariendorf, Lichtenrader Chaussee, Tempelhof, Hallesches Tor, Hedwigskirche, Rosenthaler Platz, Badstrasse, Seestrasse corner Togostrasse, during the night of Saturday to Sunday continuous service between the Uferstrasse and Tempelhof, Friedrich-Karl Strasse, at intervals of 15 minutes. It is 8 p.m., she has a music-case under her arm, she has pulled her lambskin collar high about her face, she paces to and fro at the corner of Brunnenstrasse and Weinbergsweg. A man in a fur coat speaks to her, she starts back, crosses quickly to the other side. She stands underneath the high street-lamp, watches the opposite corner. A small elderly man with horn-rimmed spectacles appears on the other side, and she goes up to him at once. She walks beside him, giggling. They turn up the Brunnenstrasse.

"I mustn't come home too late, really I mustn't. As a matter of fact I shouldn't have come at all. But I can't call you up, can I?" "No, only exceptionally, if it's urgent. They listen in at the office. It's for your sake, child." "Yes, I am afraid, suppose it should be known, you won't tell anybody, honest?" "Honest." "If Papa should hear anything about it, and Mama, Oh, my Lord." The elderly gentleman holds her delightedly by the arm. "Nothing's going to leak out. I won't tell anybody about it. Did you have a nice lesson?" "Chopin. I'm playing the Nocturnes. Are you musical?" "Yes, when it's necessary." "I'd like to play something for you some time, when I can. But I am afraid of you." "Well, well." "Yes, I am always afraid of you, a little, not very much. No, not very much. But I needn't be afraid of you, need I?" "Not at all. What a way to talk! Why, you've known me three months now." "Really it's Papa I'm afraid of. If he should find it out." "Girlie, surely you can go out a few steps alone at night. You're not a baby any more." "That's what I always tell Mama. And I do go out, too." "We'll go where we please, sweetie." "Don't call me sweetie. I only told you that so—well, just in passing. Where shall we go today? I have to be home by nine." "Right up here. We're there already. Friend of mine lives here. We can go up without being bothered." "I'm afraid. Is anybody going to see us? You go ahead. I'll come up after you."

Upstairs they smile at each other. She stands in the corner. He has taken off his coat and hat, she lets him take her hat and music-case. Then she runs to the door, switches off the light: "But not long today, I have so little time, I must get home, I won't undress, you are not going to hurt me?"

Franz Biberkopf goes on the Quest, a Man must earn Money, Man cannot live without Money. Concerning the Frankfort Crockery Fair

Franz Biberkopf sat down with his friend Meck at a table where several loud-voiced men were sitting, and waited for the meeting to start. Meck declared: "You don't want to take the dole, Franz, and you don't want to go into a factory, and it's too cold for ditch-work. Business is the best thing. In Berlin or in the country. You can take your choice. But it keeps a fellow going." The waiter called out: "Mind your heads!" They drank their beer. At that moment steps were heard overhead, Herr Wünschel, the manager, up on the next floor, was running for help, his wife had fainted. Then Meck explained once more: "As sure as my name's Gottlieb, take a look at these people here! Aren't they well off! And tell me, do they look starved? Are they respectable people, or aren't they?" "You know, Gottlieb, I won't stand any joking about respectability. Honest now, is it a respectable profession or not?" "Well, look at these people! I'm not saying anything at all. Tip-top, I'm tellin' you, look at 'em!" "A steady kind of a life, that's what we need, yes, sir." "It's the steadiest you can find anywhere. Suspenders, socks, stockings, aprons. Maybe head-shawls, too. The profit's in the buying."

On the stage a hunchback was talking about the Frankfort fair. People can't be warned enough against sending merchandise to the fair from other towns. The fair is badly situated. Especially the crockery fair. "Ladies and gentlemen, my esteemed colleagues, all who were present at the Frankfort crockery fair last Sunday can bear me out, it's asking too much of the public." Gottlieb nudged Franz: "He's talking about the Frankfort crockery fair. You're not goin' there anyway." "What's the odds, he's a good man, that one, he knows what he wants." "Anybody who's been to the Magazinplatz in Frankfort will never go there again. That's as sure as you're alive. It was nothing but a filthy morass. Also I should like to state further that the municipal authorities of Frankfort took no steps till three days before the opening of the fair. Then they said: Magazinplatz for us, not Marktplatz, as it always was before. Why? I'd like my colleagues here to take a sniff at that: because the weekly market is held on the market-place, and if we go there, it would cause traffic congestion. It's an unheard-of thing for the Frankfort authorities to do, it's a smack in the face. Imagine giving an excuse like that. They now have market four half-days a week, and yet we are supposed to go? Why us, especially? Why not the vegetable-man and the butter-woman? Why doesn't Frankfort build a covered market? The fruit, vegetable, and food dealers are treated just as badly by the municipal authorities as we are. We all suffer from the blunders of the authorities. But it has got to stop. The receipts on the Magazinplatz were small, practically nothing, nothing at all, it didn't pay. Nobody came in all that filth and rain. Most of our colleagues who were there didn't even make enough dough to get away from the place with their wagons. Railroad fares, booth rent, parking charges, getting there, getting back. And then I would most distinctly submit and state to the entire public that the toilet conditions in Frankfort are indescribable. All those who were there can tell a tale or two about that. Such unhygienic conditions are unworthy of a big city, and the public should brand them, wherever it can. Such conditions will never attract visitors to Frankfort, and they do a lot of harm to the tradespeople. And then those narrow booths, like sardines in a can!"

After the discussion, in which the board of directors was also attacked for its inactivity up till now, the following resolution was unanimously adopted:

"The fair-merchants feel that the removal of the fair to the Magazinplatz is a slap in the face. The business results for the merchants fell considerably short of those of former fairs. The Magazinplatz as a fair-site is absolutely unsuitable, because it cannot possibly hold all the fair-visitors, and because in regard to sanitation it is a perfect disgrace to the city of Frankfort-on-the-Oder, without taking into consideration that, if a fire had broken out, the merchants themselves, as well as their wares, would have perished. The members assembled here demand that the municipal authorities remove the fair back to the Marktplatz, because only in this event can a guarantee be given for the holding of the fair. At the same time the members assembled strongly urge a reduction of the booth rent, since they are not in a position to fulfill even approximately their obligations under the given conditions, and may well become a charge upon the city's charitable institutions."

But Biberkopf was irresistibly attracted by the speaker. "Meck, that's some orator, a man just made for the world." "Go ahead and step on his toes, maybe something will fall your way, too." "You can't tell about that, Gottlieb. But you know, them Jews did give me a lift. I went from one courtyard to another singing the Watch on the Rhine, that's how dizzy I was in my head. Then the two Jews fished me out and told me stories. Words are a good thing, too, Gottlieb, and what a man says." "That story about Stefan the Polak. Franz, you're still a little cracked." The latter shrugged his shoulders: "Gottlieb, cracked or not cracked, put yourself in my place and then talk. That man up there, the little hunchbacked fellow, he's all right. I tell you, he's first-class, first-class." "Well, have your way. You better begin to worry about business, Franz." "We'll get around to that; one thing at a time. Why, I don't talk against business, do I?"

And he wended his way towards the hunchback. Respectfully he asked him for a piece of information. "What do you want?" "I should like to ask for some information." "The debate is over now. Finished, this is the end. We get sick of it, too, sometimes, up to here." The hunchback was venomous. "But what do you really want?" "Me?—They've been talking a lot about the Frankfort fair here, and you did your job wonderfully, first-class, sir. I wanted to tell you that, as coming from me. I'm entirely of your opinion." "Glad of that, comrade, if I may ask, what's your name?" "Franz Biberkopf. I saw with pleasure how you did your job and how you gave it to the Frankforters." "The municipal authorities." "First-class. That was a smooth ironing out. They won't say boo after that. They'll have to take a back seat now." The little fellow collected his papers, stepped from the stage into the smoke-filled hall. "Fine, comrade, that's great." And Franz beamed, bowing and scraping behind him. "But didn't you want some information? Are you a member of the association?" "No, sorry." "You can get it from me right away. Come along and sit down at the table." Thus Franz sat at the chairman's table below, among the flushed faces, drank, saluted, got a ticket in his hand. The fees he promised to pay the first of next month. Handshake.

From a distance he started signaling to Meck with the sheet of paper: "I'm a member now, yes, sir! I'm a member of the Berlin Local Group. There, read that, there it is: Berlin Local Group, National Association, and what does it say here: of the Itinerant Tradesmen of Germany. Great, heh!" "And what are you, a dealer in textiles? Here it says textiles. But since when is that your line, Franz? What kind of textiles have you got?" "But I didn't say textiles, I said stockings and aprons. He just would have it that way, textiles. But it doesn't matter, I don't have to pay till the first of the month." "Well, old boy, first of all, suppose you should go in for china plates now, or kitchen pails, or let's say you trade in animals, like these gentlemen here: gentlemen, isn't it nonsense for a man to get himself a membership card for textiles when he might be going to deal in cattle?" "I advise you not to do anything in cattle. Cattle are low. You'd better go in for small live-stock." "But he isn't going in for anything at all, yet. That's a fact. Gentlemen, this fellow's only sitting around here and would like to do something. You might just as well tell him, yes, sir, Franz, go in for mouse-traps or plaster heads." "If it's necessary, Gottlieb, if you can make a living at it, why not? Not particularly mouse-traps, there's already a strong competition on the part of the drug-stores with their patent poisons, but plaster heads, why shouldn't a man take plaster heads into the small towns?" "You see, there you are: he gets himself a ticket for aprons and is going in for plaster heads."

"Gottlieb, that's not it; gentlemen, you're right, but you mustn't turn the thing around like that. You ought to explain a thing properly and show it in its proper light, like the hunchbacked chap did about that

Frankfort business, when you weren't listening." "Because I got nothing to do with Frankfort. And these gentlemen ain't either." "All right, Gottlieb, that's fine, gentlemen, don't wanta reproach you, only I, for my part, in my humble way, I was listening, and it was great, the way he illustrated everything, so calmly, but forcefully too, although he had a weak voice, and the man has a weak chest, too, and the way everything was arranged in order and the way he led up to the resolution, every point clean-cut, a fine thing, he's got a good head on him, and accurate even to mentioning the toilets they didn't like. Of course, I had that business with the Jews, you know, don't you? Once, gentlemen, when I felt very low, two Jews helped me by telling me stories. They spoke to me, decent people, who didn't know me, and then they told me about a Pole or somebody or other, and it was nothing but a story and still it was very good, a good lesson for me in the situation I was in. I thought: Cognac would have done the work, too. But who knows? Afterwards I was going good, and on my feet again." One of the live-stock dealers puffed and grinned: "Before that you must have got a pretty big wallop in the neck?" "No joking, gentlemen. Besides, you are right. It was some wallop! Might happen to you, too, in life, that things come plopping down on your head and make your knees wobble. Might happen to anybody, a dirty break like that. What are you going to do with your wobbly knees afterwards? You run around the streets, Brunnenstrasse, Rosenthaler Tor, Alex. You run around sometimes and can't even read the street signs. Clever people helped me then, they talked to me and told me a lotta things, people with heads on 'em, and from that you learn this: You shouldn't swear by money or cognac or the lousy pennies you pay in dues. The main thing is, head high, and see that you use it and that you know what's goin' on around you, so you don't get knocked out before you know it. Then everything's not half bad. That's it, gentlemen. That's how it strikes me."

"And so, sir, I mean fellow-member, let's drink something. To our organization!" "To our organization, here's how, gentlemen. Here's how, Gottlieb!" The latter laughed and laughed: "Boy, the only question that's left now is how you're goin' to pay your dues the first of the month." "And then see to it, young colleague, now that you got a membership card and you are a member of our organization, that the organization helps you to make some real money." The live-stock dealers tried to outlaugh Gottlieb. One of the dealers: "You'd better go with that paper to Meiningen, next week is market week there. I'll take my stand on the right-hand side. You can go on the other side, to the left, and I'll watch how business goes with you. Let's imagine it; Albert, he has his card and is a member of the organization and is standing in his booth. Here on my side they're yelling: Hot dogs with real Meiningen crackers, and he yells opposite me: Right this way! First time here, member of the organization, the great sensation of the Zwick market of Meiningen. The people will come in droves. Say, Isaac, you make my eyes ache!" They beat on the table, Biberkopf along with them. Cautiously he shoved the paper into his breast-pocket: "If a man wants to walk, he simply buys himself a pair of shoes. I haven't said anything yet about doing a fat lot of business. But I ain't looney, either." They got up.

Out in the street Meck got into a violent discussion with the two live-stock dealers. Both expressed their views about a lawsuit one of them was engaged in. He had been trading cattle in the Province of the Mark, but had a trade permit for Berlin only. A competitor had then met him in a village and reported him to the police. Whereupon the two dealers, who were traveling together, played a deep game: the defendant testifies in court that he was only the other's companion, and had acted according to his orders.

The cattle dealers were explaining: "We won't foot the bill. We'll take the oath. That is, we gotta take an oath in court. He'll swear he was only my companion and that he's done it often before, and we'll swear to that and that's all there is to it."

Then Meck got quite excited, holding the two cattle dealers by their overcoats: "There you are, you're crazy, why, you belong in Loonyville. Imagine taking an oath for a lousy thing like that, just to do that scoundrel a service, so that he can get you in trouble for good. It ought to be put in the papers that the law is giving its support to things like that, why, that's not straight, those gents with their monocles. But now we're talking justice."

The second live-stock dealer insists: "I'll swear, well, why not? Me—cough up, three appeals, and that crook getting a lot of fun out of it? No, sir. That guy's green with envy. As far as I'm concerned, nothin' doin', I won't shell out."

Meck tapped his forehead with his fist: "You fat-head, you deserve to lie in the gutter where you are."

They took leave of the cattle dealers, Franz took Meck by the arm and they bowled along through the Brunnenstrasse. Meck hurled a threat after the cattle dealers: "Funny birds. Got something on their conscience. The whole country's got something on its conscience." "What did you say, Gottlieb?" "They're a lot o' jellyfish, instead of showing their fists to the court, nothin' but jellyfish, the whole country, business men, working men, the whole bunch of 'em."

Suddenly Meck stopped in his tracks and planted himself in front of Franz: "Franz, we gotta have a talk together. Otherwise I can't let you come with me, nohow." "Well, go ahead then." "Franz, I gotta know who you are. Look me in the face. Tell me honestly and on your word of honor, you got a taste of it out there in Tegel, you know what's right and just. And right is always right." "That's true, Gottlieb." "Well then, Franz, honest and true, what did they do to you out there?" "Don't you worry. You can believe me: if you got a fight to pick, just leave it outside. Out there they read books and learned shorthand and then they played chess, me, too." "You know how to play chess, too?" "Well, don't you worry, we'll go on shuffling our little game of skat, Gottlieb. So you sit around, you haven't got much gray matter to think with, with us transport workers it's more the muscles and bones that count, so you say one day: Damn it all, don't get yourself mixed up with people, go your own way. Hands off people! Gottlieb, what's a man like us got to do with the law and police and politics? Out there we had a communist, he was bigger than me, he did his share in the '19 show in Berlin. They didn't get him then, but afterwards he got reasonable, got to know a widow and went right into her business. A clever boy, you see!" "Well, how did he get out there?" "Probably tried some shady deal. Out there we always stuck together, and if one of us squealed, he got what was coming to him. But it's better if you ain't got nothin' to do with the others. That's suicide. Just let 'em go their own way. Stay respectable and keep to yourself! That's my idea."

"Is that so?" said Meck and looked at him severely. "Why then we might as well all shut up shop, that's pretty wishy-washy of you, we'd all go to pieces that way." "Let 'em shut it, if they want to shut up shop, we're not worrying about it." "Franz, you're a sap, no doubt about that. You'll regret it some day, Franz."

Franz Biberkopf is walking down the Invalidenstrasse, his new girl-friend, Polish Lina, is walking along with him. At the corner of the Chausseestrasse there is a newsstand in the hallway, a few people are standing there, gabbling and chattering.

"Hey, don't stand around here." "Can't a man look at the pictures?" "Why don't you buy 'em? Don't block the passage-way." "Dumbbell."

Tourists' Supplement. When in our cold North there comes that disagreeable season which lies between snow-glittering winter days and the first green of May, something draws us—an urge thousands of years old—to the sunny South beyond the Alps, to Italy. He who is so fortunate as to be able to follow this urge to roam. "Don't get so excited about people. Just look here, how barbarous they're getting; here's a fellow who attacks a girl in the street-car, and beats her half dead for fifty marks." "I'd do it too for that much." "What?" "Why, do you know what fifty marks is? You don't know anything about fifty marks. That's a pile o' money for a man in our position, a big pile, say. All right then, some day when you know what fifty marks is, I'll talk to you again."

Fatalistic speech made by Chancellor Marx: Whatever is to happen lies, in my opinion, in the hands of a Divine Providence, which has its special intentions for each people. Human accomplishment, on the other hand, will remain only fragmentary. All we can do is to continue to give our utmost effort, according to our convictions, and thus I shall have fulfilled, faithfully and honestly, the office I now hold. I conclude, gentlemen, with best wishes for a successful conclusion of your laborious and devoted activities in behalf of beautiful Bavaria. God speed your further efforts. So live, that when you die, hope you had a pleasant evening.

"Well, sir, are you through reading?" "Why?" "Shall I take the paper off the hook for you? There was a guy once, asked me for a chair so he could read in comfort." "Guess you only display your pictures so they—" "What I do with my pictures, that's my affair. You're not paying for my stand. But fellows that simply sponge, I don't want 'em around my stand, they only drive customers away."

There he goes, he'd better have his shoes polished, probably camps out in that "Palme" flop-house on Fröbelstrasse, there he is taking the street-car, I bet he's riding on a fake ticket or has picked up an old one, and is trying it out. When they catch him, then it just happens he lost the right one. Those sponges, here come two more now. I'll have to put up a railing here, the next thing. Got to get some lunch now.

Franz Biberkopf comes marching along in a derby hat, plump Polish Lina on his arm. "Lina, eyes right, let's get into the hallway. The weather's not made for the unemployed. Let's look at the pictures. Nice pictures, but there's a draft here. Say, comrade, how's business? Why, a fellow could freeze to death here." "Well, it's not meant for a Turkish bath." "Lina, would you like to stay in a place like that?" "Come on, let's go, that fellow's got such a dirty grin." "Say, Fräulein, I bet it gives the boys a thrill, when you stand in the hallway and sell papers. Service from dainty hands."

Gusts of wind, the papers blow loose from the clamps. "Say, bo, you ought to put up an umbrella outside here." "So nobody could see anything?" "You could put a glass pane in front of it." "Come along, Franz." "Well, wait a minute. Jest a second. That man stands here for hours on end and isn't blown over. Don't be so fussy, Lina." "But what makes him keep on grinning like that?" "That's the expression of my face, Fräulein, my features, I can't help that." "He's always grinning, I tell you, Lina, the poor guy."

Franz pushed his hat back, looked the newsvender in the face and burst out laughing, holding Lina's hand in his. "Why, he can't help it, Lina. He got it from his mother's breast. Do you know, bo, what kind of a face you make, when you grin? Nope, not like that, I mean, when you grin like you did before? You know, Lina. As if he was lying at his mother's breast and the milk had got sour." "That's where you're on the wrong track. They raised me on the bottle." "A lot of boloney." "Listen, bo, what does a man earn in this business?" "*Rote Fahne*, thanks. Let this man get by, please. Watch out, a box coming." "But you're sure in a nice mob here, all right."

Lina pulled him away, they floated down the Chausseestrasse as far as the Oranienburger Tor. "That'd be something for me, all right. I don't catch a cold so very easy. If it wasn't for all that hanging around in the hallway."

Two days later it is warmer. Franz, who has sold his overcoat, and is wearing thick underwear, which Lina got him somewhere, stands on the Rosenthaler Platz in front of Fabisch & Co., high-class men's tailoring to measure, excellent work and low prices are the characteristics of our products. Franz is hawking necktie-holders. He shouts his spiel:

"Why does the smart man in the West End wear a bow tie when the proletarian doesn't? Ladies and gents, right up here, you too, Fräulein, with your husband, minors allowed, it costs no more for minors. Why doesn't the proletarian wear bow ties? Because he can't tie 'em. Then he has to buy a tie-holder, and after he's bought it, it's no good and he can't tie the tie with it. That's swindling, it makes the people bitter; it pushes Germany still deeper into poverty than she is already. Why, for instance, don't they wear those big tie-holders? Because nobody wants to put a dustpan around his neck. No man or woman wants that, not even the baby, if he could speak for himself. Please don't laugh at that, ladies and gents, don't laugh, we don't know what's going on in that dear little child brain. Oh, Lord, the dear little head, the little head and the little curls, it's pretty, ain't it, but when you got to pay alimony, it's not to be laughed at, that gets a man into trouble. Go buy yourself a tie like this at Tietz's or Wertheim's or, if you don't want to buy it from Jews, get it somewhere else. I'm a Nordic, I am." He raises his hat, blond hair, red ears standing out, merry bull's eyes. "The big department stores don't have to get me to advertise them, they can exist without me. Buy a tie like the one I have here, and then decide how you're going to tie it tomorrow.

"Ladies and gents, who has time nowadays to tie his tie in the morning, when he would rather take one more minute of sleep? We all need a lot of sleep, because we have to work so much to earn so little. A tie-holder like this helps you go to sleep. It competes with the drug stores, for whoever buys a tie-holder like the one I have here don't need any sleeping powder and no night-cap or nothing. He sleeps without rocking, like a child at his mother's breast, because he knows there'll be no hurrying around in the morning; all he needs lies, ready for use, on his chest of drawers, and has only to be shoved into the collar. You spend your money for a lot of junk. Last year, for instance, you saw the crooks at the Krokodil bar, in the front they sold hot dogs, in the back Jolly was fasting in a glass case with sauerkraut growing around his mouth. Every one of you saw that—just come up a little closer, I wanta save my voice, I ain't insured my voice, I never had the money for the first premium—you saw Jolly lying in the glass box, didn't you? But how they smuggled chocolate to him, that you didn't see. Here you are buying honest goods, it's not celluloid, it's vulcanized rubber, twenty pfennigs a piece, fifty for three.

"Get away from the curb, young man, or you'll be run over by an auto, and who is going to sweep up the rubbish afterwards? Now I'll explain to you, how the tie is tied, or do I have to knock you on the head with a wooden hammer? You'll understand it at once. Here you take about twelve to thirteen inches from one side, then you fold the ends together, but not like this. That looks as if a flattened out bedbug was sticking to the wall, a wallpaper splotch, a man of the better class don't wear that. That's when you take my contraption. We gotta save time. Time is money. The romantic days are over and won't come back again, we all have to take that into consideration nowadays. You can't pull a rubber hose slowly around your neck every day, you need a ready and efficient article like this here. Just look, that's your Christmas present, that suits your taste, ladies and gents, it's for your own good. If the Dawes Plan has left you anything at all, it's your head under your lid, and it ought to tell you that this is just what you want; buy it and take it home, it'll be a consolation to you.

"Ladies and gents, we need consolation, all of us together, and when we are foolish, we try to find it in the saloon. But if you're reasonable, don't do anything of the kind, for the pocketbook's sake anyway, because the kind of rotten liquor the bartender hands out nowadays cries to heaven, and the good kind is expensive. Therefore, take this contraption, put a small loop through here, you can also make a large loop, like the ones the fairies wear in their shoes, when they step out. You pull it through here and then take hold of one end. A German citizen buys only genuine goods, that's what you get here."

Lina gives it to the Pansies

But that isn't enough for Franz Biberkopf. He rolls his eyeballs. In the company of sloppy Lina he observes the street life between the Alex and Rosenthaler Platz and decides to sell newspapers. Why? They had told him all about it. Lina could lend a hand, and it's just the thing for him. Moving to, moving fro, roundabout and away we go.

"Lina, I can't make speeches, I'm not a popular orator. When I'm selling something, they understand me, but it's not just right, either. Do you know what 'mind' is?" "Nope." Lina ogles him expectantly. "Look at the boys on the Alex and here, too, none of them has any mind. The fellows with the stalls and wagons, too, that ain't nothin' either. They're smart, clever boys, a lot of sap in 'em, needn't tell me anything about that. But just imagine a speaker in the Reichstag, Bismarck or Bebel, why, the ones we got now ain't nothing, take it from me, they got mind all right, mind, that means head, not just any old noodle. None of them can get anything out of me with their soft soap. A speaker that is a speaker." "Ain't you a speaker, Franz?" "You make me laugh—me a speaker! Know who's a speaker, well, you'll never believe it, your landlady." "That Schwenk woman?" "Nope, the other one, where I got the things, in the Karlstrasse." "The one near the circus? Don't talk to me about her."

Franz bends mysteriously forward: "She sure was a speaker, Lina, a real one, I tell you." "Not on your life. Comes into my room, and me lying in bed and wants to get my valise on account of one month." "All right Lina, now listen, it wasn't nice of her. But when I went upstairs and asked about the valise, she started off." "I know that bunk of hers. I didn't listen to her. Franz, you mustn't let a woman like that put the skids under you." "I tell you, Lina, she started off about criminal law, the civil code, and how she squeezed out a pension for her dead old man, when the old fool had an apoplectic fit, which didn't have anything to do with the war. Since when has apoplexy got anything to do with the war? She said so herself, but she didn't give in, and she won her case. She's got mind, Fatty, no two ways about it. Whatever she wants she gets, that's more than earning a coupla pfennigs. That's where you show what you are. That's how you get air, baby. I'm still knocked flat." "You go up to see her once in a while?" Franz protests with both hands: "Suppose you go up there, Lina, you want to get a valise; you're there at eleven sharp, you got something to do at twelve, and about a quarter to one you're still standing there. She talks and talks to you, and you haven't got your valise yet, and maybe you trot off without it. She can talk, that one, take it from me."

He meditates across the table-top, and draws a design in a beer puddle with his finger: "I'm going to get a license somewhere and sell newspapers. That's a good thing."

She remains speechless, slightly insulted. Franz does what he pleases. One noon, he's on Rosenthaler Platz, she brings him sandwiches, then he lights out at twelve, plunks the box with the tripod and all the cardboard-boxes under her arms and goes out looking for information about newspapers.

To start with, an elderly man on the Hackesche Market in front of Oranienburger Strasse advises him to take an interest in sexual education. It's now being practiced on a big scale and doing quite well. "What's sexual education?" Franz asks, and hesitates. The white-haired man points to his exhibit. "Better first take a look at this, then you won't ask questions about it." "Those are naked girls painted there." "That's the only kind I got." They puff silently side by side. Franz stands and gapes at the pictures from top to bottom, puffing into the air, the man looks past him. Franz looks him in the eye: "Listen here, comrade, do you get any fun out of this, these here girls and pictures like that? The *Gay Life*. Here they go and paint a nude girl with a little kitten. Wonder what she's after, on the stairs, with a li'l kitty. Suspicious bird. Am I disturbing you, pardner?" The latter, seated on his camp-chair, takes a deep breath and sinks into himself: there are jackasses in this world as big as mountains, the real thing in blockheads, who run around the Hackesche Market in broad daylight and stop in front of a fellow, if he's in bad luck, to talk a lot of tommyrot. As the white-haired man becomes silent, Franz takes a few magazines from the hook: "You mind, pardner? What's this? *Figaro.* And this one, *Marriage.* And this, *Ideal Marriage.* Now I s'pose that's different from marriage. *Woman's Love.* Everything to be had separately. Why a fellow can get all kinds of information here, if he's got any money, but it's mighty expensive. Beside there's a catch in it somewhere." "Well, I'd like to know what kind of a catch is in it. Everything goes. Nothing's forbidden. What I sell, I got authorization for, and there ain't no catch in it. Things like that I leave alone." "I can tell you one thing, I just want to tell you, looking at pictures is no good. I could tell you a thing or two about that. It does a man harm, yes, sir, that botches you up. You start by looking at pictures and afterwards, when you want to, there you are, and it won't go naturally any more." "Don't know what you're talking about. And don't spit on my papers, they cost a lot o' money, and don't paw the covers like that. Here read this: *The Unmarried.* There's everything, even a special magazine for people like that." "Unmarried, well, well, why shouldn't there be people like that, why, I'm not married with Polish Lina either." "Well, here; look what's here, if that isn't true, it's only an example: To attempt to regulate the sexual life of the two parties by contract, or to decree conjugal duties in this respect, is the most loathsome and humiliating slavery we can possibly imagine. Well?" "How so?" "Is it true or not?" "That don't happen to me. A woman who would ask a thing like that from a man, is that really possible? Can it happen?" "Well, there you read it." "Well, that's going a bit strong. Just let 'em come and try anything like that on me."

Franz reads the sentence again in amazement, then he gives a start, and shows something to the old man: "Well, and look what it says *here:* I would like to give an example from the work of d'Annunzio, *Lust,* now watch out, d'Annunzio's the name of that super-swine, he's a Spaniard or Italian or from America, maybe. Here the thoughts of the man are so full of his distant sweetheart that, during a night of love with a woman who serves as substitute, the name of his true love escapes him against his will. That beats everything. No, sirree, I won't have anything to do with things like that." "Hold on, where's that, lemme see it." "Here. Serves as substitute. Artificial rubber in place of rubber. Turnips instead of a real meal. Did you ever hear anything like it, a woman, a girl, for a substitute? He takes another one, just because he hasn't got his own, and the new one notices something, and that's the end, and I suppose she's not to peep? He gets that printed, the Spaniard! If I was a printer, I wouldn't print it." "Well, cut out that rot! Y' mustn't think you can understand everything with your little brain, what a fellow like that means, a real writer, and a Spaniard or Italian at that, right here in the crowd on the Hackesche Market."

Franz continues reading: "A great emptiness and silence then filled her soul. That's enough to make you climb trees. Nobody'll make me believe that. I don't care who he is. Since when, emptiness and silence? I can talk about that, too, just like that fellow, and the girls probably ain't any different there than anywhere else. Once I had one of 'em, and she noticed something, an address in my notebook, well, boy: she notices something, and then silence? Maybe you think so, heh, but then you don't know anything about women, old feller. You shoulda heard 'er. The whole house shook and roared. That's how loud she bawled. I couldn't tell 'er what it was all about. She kept on going, as if she was on a hot griddle. People came running. I was glad when I got outside." "Say, there's two things you don't seem to notice?" "Which are?" "When anybody takes a paper from me, he buys it and he keeps it. If there's any tripe in it, it don't matter either, he's only interested in the pictures, anyway." Franz Biberkopf's left eye disapproved of that. "And then here we got: *Woman's Love* and *Friendship*, and they don't talk any bunk, I'm tellin' you, they fight. Yes, sir, they fight for human rights." "Why, what's the matter with 'em?" "Penal Code, Section 175, if you don't know it." There just happens to be a lecture in Landsberger Strasse, Alexanderpalais, tonight, Franz might hear something about the wrong done to a million people in Germany every day. It's enough to make your hair stand on end. The man pushed a bunch of old papers under Franz's arm, Franz sighed, looked at the package under his arm: all right, he'll probably be there. What'll I do there, anyway, shall I really go, wonder if it's worth while handling magazines like that? The pansies; he just gives me this stuff and expects me to carry it home and read it. A fellow might feel sorry for those boys, but they're none o' my business.

He left in a great pother, the whole thing seemed to him so far from kosher that he didn't say a word to Lina and got rid of her in the evening. The old news-vender pushed him into a little hall, where there were almost nothing but men, mostly very young, and a few women, who sat apart in couples. Franz didn't say a word for an hour, but grinned a lot behind his hat. After ten o'clock, he couldn't stand it any longer, he had to beat it, the whole thing, and those funny people, it was too ridiculous for words, so many fairies in a bunch, and he right among 'em, he got out quickly, and laughed until he came to Alexanderplatz. As he was leaving, he heard the lecturer talking about Chemnitz and the police ordinance of November 27. This forbids all inverts to go on the streets or use the comfort stations, and, if they are caught, it costs them 30 marks. Franz looked for Lina, but she had gone out with her landlady. He went to sleep. In his dream he laughed and swore a lot, he had a fight with a silly old driver who kept driving him around and around the Roland fountain in the Siegesallee. The traffic cop, too, was running after the car. At last Franz jumped out, and the auto drove like mad around the fountain and around him in a circle, and this went on and on without stopping, and Franz was always standing around with the copper while they consulted together: what are we going to do with him, he's crazy?

Next morning he waits for Lina in the café as usual, he has the magazines with him. He wants to tell her what boys like that really have to suffer, Chemnitz and the article of the law with the 30 marks, at the same time it's not his business, and they can bother about their articles themselves. And then Meck might come too, trying to get him to do something for the cattle drivers. Nope, all he wants is peace, they can go soak their heads.

Lina sees right away that he has slept badly. Hesitantly he pushes the magazines towards her, the pictures on top. Frightened, Lina claps her hand over her mouth. Then he starts talking again about mind. Looks for yesterday's beer puddle on the table, but there isn't any. She moves away from him: Suppose there's something wrong with him like the kind here in the papers. She doesn't understand, up to now he certainly wasn't like that. He fiddles around, draws lines on the bare wood with his dry finger, then she takes the whole package of papers from the table and throws it down on the bench. At first she stands there like a mænad, and they stare at each other, he looking up at her like a little boy, then she waltzes off. And there he sits with his papers, now he can think about the fairies.

A baldpate goes walking one evening in the Tiergarten, he meets a pretty boy, who hooks onto him at once; they have a lovely stroll together for an hour, then the baldpate has the notion—the instinct, oh the desire, immense at that moment—to be very nice to the youngster. He is a married man, he has often noticed these things before, but now it has to be, ah, it's really marvelous. "You're my sunshine, you're my darling."

And the lad is so gentle. To think that such things exist: "Come on, let's go to a litle hotel. You can give me five marks, or ten. I'm quite broke." "Anything you want, my sunshine." He gave him his whole pocketbook. To think that such things exist. That's the nicest part of it all.

But in the room the door has peep-holes. The hotel-keeper sees something and calls his wife; she, too, sees something. And afterwards they say they won't allow such things in their hotel, they saw it all right and he can't deny it. And they would never permit such things, and he ought to be ashamed to seduce young boys like that, they are going to report him to the police. The porter and the chambermaid also come and grin. Next day the baldpate buys himself two bottles of champagne: Asbach Uralt, and leaves on a business trip. He wants to go to Heligoland, to end it all by drowning while plastered. He gets drunk all right, and takes a boat, but comes back two days later to the old girl; at home nothing has happened.

Nothing at all happens throughout the month, the whole year. Just one thing: he inherits $3,000 from an American uncle and is able to treat himself a bit. Then one day, while he's off at the seashore, a court summons arrives which the old lady has to sign for him. She opens it, and everything's there about those peep-holes and that pocketbook and the dear little boy. And when baldpate gets back from his holiday, they're all weeping around him, the old lady and his two grown daughters. He reads the summons, why, that's all dead and buried, that's bureaucracy and a lot of red tape dating back to Charlemagne, and now it has got to him, but it's true, all right. "What have I done, Judge? Why, I didn't offend anybody's feelings. I went to a room, locked myself in. Is it my fault if they have those peep-holes? Nothing illegal really happened." The boy confirms his story. "Now what is it I've done?" Baldpate weeps into his fur coat: "Did I steal anything? Did I commit a burglary? I only broke into a dear boy's heart. I said to him: my sunshine. And so he was."

He is acquitted. At home the family all keep on crying.

"Magic Flute," dance-hall, with an American Dance-Hall on the ground floor. The Oriental Casino available for private entertainments. What Christmas gift shall I give my best girl? Inverts: after many years of experiment I have at last found a radical antidote against the growth of the beard. Every part of the body can be depilated. Furthermore I have discovered the means of developing a truly feminine breast within an astonishingly short time. No medicines, absolutely safe and harmless. As proof: myself. Liberty for Love all along the front.—

A star-clear sky looked down upon the dark realms of mankind. The castle of Kerkauen lay in deep nocturnal quiet. But a fair-haired woman buried her head in the pillows and found no sleep. Tomorrow, tomorrow, her love, the dear love of her heart, would leave her. A whisper went (ran) through the sable, impenetrable (dark) night: Gisa, stay with me, stay with me (don't go away, don't go off on a voyage, don't fall down, take a seat please). Forsake me not. But the cheerless silence had neither ear nor heart (nor foot nor nose). And yonder, separated only by a few walls, there lay a pale slender woman with wide open eyes. Her dark, heavy hair lay in confusion on the silk of the bed (Castle Kerkauen is famous for its silk beds). A shiver of cold shook her. Her teeth chattered, as though she were deeply chilled, full stop. But she did not move, comma, she did not pull the coverlet closer over herself, full stop. Motionless her slender, ice-cold hands lay (as if deeply chilled, cold-shuddering, a slender woman with wide open eyes, famous silk bed) on it, full stop. Her luminous eyes roamed blazing through the darkness, and her lips trembled, colon, quotation marks, Eleanore, dash, Eleanore, dash, quotation marks, quotation francs, quotation dollars—going, going, gone!

"Nope, nope, I won't go with you, Franz. You're off my calling list. You can make yourself scarce." "Come on, Lina, I'm going to hand him back his junk." And as Franz took his hat off and placed it on the chest of drawers—it was in her room—and made a few convincing gestures towards her, she first scratched his hand and wept, then she went off with him. They each took some of the magazines in question and approached the battlefront on the line Rosenthaler Strasse, Neue Schönhauser Strasse, Hackesche Market.

In the fighting zone, Lina, the hearty, sloppy, unwashed, weepy little girl, made an offensive of her own à la Prince of Homburg: My noble uncle Friedrich von der Mark! Natalie! Let be! Let be! Oh God, Oh God, he is undone, so be it, so be it! She dashed post-haste and fast-paced to white-head's newsstand. Franz Biberkopf, noble sufferer, found it expedient to stay in the background. He stood backgrounded in front of the cigar-store of Schröder Import Export and from there observed, slightly impeded by fog, street-cars and passers-by, the progress of the action just engaged. The heroes had figuratively contacted each other. They skirmished for each other's weak and vulnerable points. And so Lina Przyballa of Czernowitz, the farmer Stanislaus Przyballa's only legitimate daughter—following two miscarriages which only half developed, both of which were to have been called Lina—pitched the package of papers down with a peppery gesture. The rest got lost in the noise of the street traffic. "What a wench! What a wench!" Franz, the joyously impeded sufferer, groaned in admiration. He approached, in his capacity of reserves, the center of the fighting zone. Already in front of Ernst Kümmerlich's beer-shop, Miss Lina Przyballa, heroine and conqueror, threw a smile at him, and sloppy, but joyful, she shrieked: "I gave it to him, Franz."

Franz knew it. In the café she forthwith sank *stante pede* to that part of his anatomy below his woolen shirt which she took for his heart, but which was in more exact terms his sternum and the upper lobe of his left lung. She was triumphant as she poured down her first Gilka: "And now he can pick up his rubbish in the street."

Oh immortality, thou art my very own, beloved what sheen is now outspread, hail, all hail, to the Prince of Homburg, victor in the battle of Fehrbellin, all hail! (Court ladies, officers, and torches appear on the castle terrace.) "Waiter, how 'bout another Gilka."

Hasenheide, Neue Welt, Life's one damned Thing after Another, we shouldn't make Life harder than it is

And Franz sits with Miss Lina Przyballa in her room, laughing: "Lina, y'know what a stock-girl is?" He gives her a poke in the ribs. She gapes: "Well, that Fölsch girl, now, isn't she a stock-girl, she gets out the phonograph records at the music-store." "That's not what I mean. When I give you a shove and you're lying on the sofa, and me next to you, then you're a stuck-girl and I'm a stock-man." "You're a nice one, all right." She squealed.

So once again, and once again lets umptidumtididdlediddledee, roll along, roll along, merrily we roll along, tidumtididdledee, and once again merrily we roll along, roll along, roll along.

And they get up from the sofa—you're not sick, sir, are you? If so, you'd better visit Uncle Doctor—and merrily stroll towards the Hasenheide into Neue Welt, where the high-steppers go, where bonfires blaze, prizes for the slimmest calves. The musicians sat on the stage in Tyrolese costumes. Soft music: "Drink, drink, brother, let's drink, Leave all your worries at home, Shun all trouble and shun all pain, Then life's a happy refrain, Shun all trouble and shun all pain, Then life's a happy refrain."

It got into their bones, with every measure and between beer-mugs, they tittered and smirked, they hummed with the music, moved their arms in rhythm; Booze, booze, guzzle and booze, Leave all your trouble at home, Booze, booze, guzzle and booze, Leave all your trouble at home, Shun all trouble and shun all pain, Then life's a happy refrain.

Charlie Chaplin was there in person, he whispered in northeastern German dialect, waddled about up there on the balustrade in his wide pants with the giant shoes, pinched the leg of a not too young lady, and raced with her down the coaster. Numerous families gobbled up food around a table, leaving a lot of dirt. You may buy a long stick with a paper tuft on top for 50 pfennigs and establish any connection with it you want, the neck is sensitive, so is the knee cap, afterwards you move your leg and turn around. Who is here anyway? Civilians of both sexes, then a handful of soldiers from the Reichswehr with feminine accompaniment: Drink, drink, brother, let's drink, Leave all your worries at home.

The air is thick, full of clouds from pipes, cigars, and cigarettes, the whole huge hall is enveloped in fog. The smoke, when it finds it is getting too smoky, tries to escape upwards because of its light weight, and, as a matter of fact, finds slits, holes, and ventilators ready to push it along. But outside, outside it is dark night and cold. Then the smoke repents of its levity, resists its constitution, but it can't find the way back, for the ventilators all turn to one side. Too late. It finds itself surrounded by physical laws. The smoke doesn't know what's happened, it grasps its brow, and has no brow, it wants to ponder—but in vain. The wind, the cold, the night have seized it; 'twas never seen again.

At a table sit two couples, looking at the passers-by. The gentleman in the salt-and-pepper suit, his mustache bent over the prominent bosom of a dark, stout woman. Their tender hearts tremble, their noses sniffle, he leans over her bosom, she over the pomade-covered back of his head.

Beside them, a woman in a yellow-checked dress sits laughing. Her gentleman friend puts his arm around her chair. She has prominent teeth, a monocle, her open left eye seems blind, she smiles, puffs, shakes her head: "What funny questions you ask." A young chicken with blond water-waves is sitting at the next table, or rather she covers, with her powerfully developed, though concealed backside, the iron seat of a low garden chair. She hums happily through her nose to the music, the after-effect of a beefsteak and three glasses of light beer. She chatters and babbles, lays her head on his neck, on the neck of the second fitter of a firm in Neukölln, this chicken being his fourth affair this year, while, on the other hand, he is her tenth, or rather eleventh this year, if we figure among them also her first cousin, who, be it said, is her official fiancé. She opens her eyes suddenly, for Chaplin might fall down up there any moment. The fitter grabs with both hands after the coaster, where something seems to be happening sure enough. They order salted pretzels.

A gentleman, 36 years old, part-owner of a little provision business, buys himself six big balloons at 50 pfennigs each, lets one after another go up in the aisle in front of the band, by which means he succeeds, because of his lack of other charms, in attracting attention to himself from girls, women, virgins, widows, divorcees, adulteresses, and other unfaithful lassies, who are wandering about alone or in couples, and so he finds company without much difficulty. You pay 20 pfennigs in the adjoining gangway for weight-lifting. A glance into the future. You dab, with your finger well wetted, on the chemical preparation in the circle between the two hearts and then smear it a few times on the empty page above, whereupon the picture of the future sweetheart will appear. You have been on the right road since childhood. Your heart knows no deceit, but, nevertheless, with fine sensitiveness, you scent every trap that envious friends would like to set for you. Continue to have confidence in your art of living, for the star under the light of which you stepped into this world, will be your constant guide and help you to find a life companion who will make your happiness perfect. This companion in whom you may have confidence has the same character as you yourself. He will not woo you impetuously, but your silent happiness at his side will be the more constant for that.

Near the cloak-room in another hall a band was playing on a balcony. The members of this band wore red waistcoats and kept yelling they had not enough to drink. Below them there stood a corpulent man of upright mien, in a frock-coat. He had on a curiously striped paper cap and wanted to put a paper carnation into his buttonhole while singing, an occupation in which, however, as a result of eight light beers, two punches, and four cognacs, he was not successful. In the tumult he sang up towards the band, then hopped, skipped, and jumped in a waltz with an old, tremendously bulbous person with whom he drew wide circles like a merry-go-round. While dancing, the person in question grew more and more diffuse, but she had enough instinct left to sit down on three chairs shortly before her explosion.

Franz Biberkopf and this man in the frock-coat met during an inter-mission, below the balcony, on which the band was still crying for beer. And a beaming blue eye stared at Franz, lovely moon thou roam'st so silently, his other eye was blind, they raised their white beer-mugs, this veteran croaked: "You're a traitor too, ain't you, the others are sitting around the feedbin." He gulped: "Don't look at me so hard, tell me, where did you serve in the army?"

They drank each other's health, flourish of trumpets by the band, we have nothing to drink, we have nothing to drink. Hey there, cut that out, cheer up, perk up, three cheers for good old Gemütlichkeit. "Are you a German, are you German to the bone? What's your name?" "Franz Biberkopf. Say, Fatty, he don't know me." The veteran whispered, his hand before his mouth, he belched: "Are you a German, honest and true? If you run with the Reds, you're a traitor. He who is a traitor isn't my friend." He embraced Franz: "The Poles, the French, the fatherland for which we bled, that's the nation's gratitude." Then he pulled himself together, danced again with that expansive person whom he had collected once more, the same old waltz, no matter what the tune. He staggered, seemed to be looking for something. Franz shouted: "Over here." Lina went and got him, then he danced with Lina, arm in arm they appeared before Franz at the bar: "Excuse me, with whom have I the pleasure, the honor? Your name, if I may ask." Drink, drink, brother, let's drink, Leave all your worries at home. Shun all trouble and shun all pain, Then life's a happy refrain.

Two pig's knuckles, one corned-beef, the lady had horse-radish, yes, where did you leave your things, there are two cloak-rooms here, by the way, are prisoners held for examination allowed to wear their wedding rings? I say, no. The boat-club affair lasted until four o'clock. The automobile roads there, why, they're something awful, a man bumps right against the roof of the car, might as well be diving.

Arm in arm the cripple and Franz sit at the bar: "Say, lemme tell you, they reduced my pension, they did, I'm gonna join the Reds. The fellow who drives us out of Paradise with a flaming sword is the archangel, and so we won't go back there. And there we are sitting up on the Hartmannsweilerkopf, says I to my captain, he's from Stargard like me." "Storkow?" "No, Stargard. Now I've lost my carnation no, there she is." He who has kissed by the beautiful sea, while the billows listened and rippled with mirth, knows surely what life's greatest charm can be, he has chatted with love upon this earth.

*

Franz now peddles racist, pro-Nordic papers. He is not against the Jews, but he is for law and order. For law and order must reign in Paradise; which everyone should recognize. And the *Steel Helmet*, he's seen those boys, and their leaders, too, that's a great thing. He stands by the subway exit, at Potsdamer Platz, in the Friedrichstrasse arcade, under the Alexanderplatz station. He shares the opinion of the cripple out there in the Neue Welt, the fellow with the one eye, the man with that fat madam.

To the German people on the First Sunday in Advent: Destroy your illusions once and for all and punish those who lull you to sleep with their juggling wiles! For the day will come when truth will rise from the battlefield with her sword of right and her unstained shield to conquer every foeman's guiles.

"While these lines are being written, there is in progress the trial of the Knights of the Reichsbanner, the Knights who, thanks to a superiority of about from 15 to 20 times, were able to express their programatic pacifism as well as the courage of their convictions by attacking a handful of National-Socialists, knocking them down and killing our party member Hirschmann, in a most bestial manner. Even from the testimony of the accused, who have the legal right, and, we suspect, their party's command, to lie, it is obvious with what premeditated brutality, so characteristic of their party principles, they acted."

"True federalism is anti-semitism, the struggle against Jewry is also the struggle for the autonomy of Bavaria. Long before the time set for the opening, the big Mathäser banquet hall was crowded, and the public continued to pour in. Up to the time of the opening of the meeting, our crack S.A. band entertained us with a smart rendition of sprightly marches and melodies. At half-past eight, our party member, Oberlehrer, opened the meeting with cordial greetings and then our party member, Walter Ammer, began his speech."

In the Elsasser Strasse the boys laugh themselves sick when he makes his appearance in the café at noon, his arm-band discreetly tucked in his pocket; they pull it out. Franz talks them down.

Turning to the jobless young locksmith, who puts down his big mug in amazement, he says: "So you're laughing at me, Richard, what for, I'd like to know? Because you're married? You're twenty-one and your wife is eighteen, and what do you know about life? Zero minus three. I tell ye, Richard, while we're at it, talking about the girls, seeing you got a little boy, I'll let you have your way on account of that bawling brat. But what else? Heh?"

Georg Dreske, the polisher, 39 years old, locked-out at present, plays with Franz's arm-band. "Take a peep at it, Georgie, there's nothing on that band I can't account for. I skidooed out there, old man, the way you did, I'll tell the world, but what came out of it afterwards? Whether a fellow has a red belly-band on his cigar or a gold band or a black-white-red band, the cigar won't taste any better for it. It depends on the tobacco, old fellow, wrapper, filler, and properly rolled and dried, and where it comes from. That's what I say. What did we do anyhow, Georgie, tell me that."

The latter quietly lays the band on the bar-counter in front of him and gulps down his beer, talking very hesitatingly with an occasional stutter and wetting his gullet frequently: "I'm only looking at you, Franz, and I'm only telling you, haven't I known you for ages—since Arras and Kovno— yes, they certainly did put one over on you." "On account of the band, you mean?" "Oh everything. Leave that stuff alone. You needn't do that, running around in the crowd that way."

Now Franz gets up, pushing aside young Richard Werner, the locksmith with the big Schiller collar, just as the latter is about to ask him something: "Nope, nope, Dick, you're a nice enough kid, but this is a man's job. Simply because you got the vote, don't think you can join in the talk between Georgie and me any time you want to." He stands for a while meditatively beside the polisher at the bar, while the proprietor in the big blue apron waits attentively inside, in front of the liqueur-shelf opposite them, his fat hands in the sink: "Well, Georgie, what was that about Arras?" "What do you mean? Don't you know that yourself? And the reason you skidooed. And about the band. Listen, Franz, old man, I'd rather hang myself with that. They certainly have soft-soaped you."

Franz stares with a very steady gaze at the polisher, who begins to stutter, throws his head back, and gazes straight into his eyes: "I want to hear about Arras. We'll find out if you were in Arras." "You must be having pipe-dreams, Franz, I didn't say anything. You must be tight." Franz waits and thinks to himself. I'll make him eat his words, he acts as if he didn't understand anything, he's playing the fool. "Why, of course, Georgie, we were certainly together at Arras, with Arthur Böse and Bluhm and the little non-com., what was his name, he had a funny name." "I forget." Let him talk, he's tight, the others notice it, too. "Wait a minute what was his name, Bistra or Birska, or something like that, that little fellow." Let him talk, I won't say anything, he'll get himself all tangled up, then he won't say anything more. "Yes, we know 'em all. But I don't mean that. Where we stayed afterwards, at Arras, after it was all over, after '18, when that other junk started, here in Berlin and in Halle and Kiel and . . ."

Georg Dreske declined with determination, that's too silly for me, I'm not going to stand around a saloon for such a lot of bunk. "Nope, cut it out, I'll be going. Tell it to little Richard. Here, Richard." "He's trying to act big in front of me, the Baron. He only goes with Barons now. I'm surprised he still hangs around with us in the café, this gentleman." Clear eyes bore into Dreske's unsteady eyes: "Well, that's what I mean, that's it exactly, Georgie, when we were stationed at Arras after '18, Field Artillery, or Infantry or the Signal Corps or the Labor Battalion or whatever you call it. And when peace came afterwards, you know?" Now I getcha, wait a minute, m'boy, you shouldn't touch on that subject, now should you? "Well, now, I'm just going to empty my mug, and you, Franz, old kid, you might look that up in your papers, if you happen to have any—I mean look up where you were later on, where you hung around or didn't hang around, also where you stood or where you sat, yes, sir. A peddler ought always to have his papers about him." Well, did you get me that time, the bull-pen, remember that. Calm eyes into Dreske's cunning ones: "Four years after '18 I was in Berlin. The whole war didn't last any longer than that, now did it? I was going around and you were going around, Richard here was still at his mother's apron-strings. Well, did we notice anything here like Arras, or did you maybe? We had inflation, paper bills, millions and billions of them, no meat, no butter, worse than before, we saw all that, and you too, Georgie, and where Arras was, you can just figure that out on your own fingers. There was nothing there, was there? All we did was to bum around and swipe the farmers' potatoes."

Revolution? Unscrew the flag-staff, wrap the bunting in the oil covers, and put the thing in the clothes-chest. Let the old lady bring you your house-slippers and untie your fiery red necktie. You always make revolutions with your mugs, your republic—nothing but an industrial accident.

Dreske thinks to himself: He's going to turn out to be a dangerous fellow. Richard Werner, that young duffer, opens his mouth again: "Maybe you'd like it better, Franz, if we'd started a new war, maybe you'd like to shove it on our backs. Merrily we'll conquer France! But you'll tear a big hole in your pants with that." Franz is thinking: What a monkey, regular ape, nigger heaven. All he knows about war is through the movies, a whack on his head and down with him.

The proprietor dries his hands on his blue apron. A green prospectus lies in front of the polished glasses, he pants heavily as he reads: Hand Assorted Come-Back Roast Coffee is unrivaled. People's Coffee (second quality and roast coffee); Pure Unground Bean Coffee, 2.29; Santos, guaranteed pure; first-class Santos Household Mixture, strong and economical; Van Campina's Strong Mixture, pure flavored; Mexico Mixture, exquisite, best value in Plantation coffee, 3.75; assortment of merchandise by railroad, 36 pounds minimum. A bee, a wasp, a bumblebee circles up there on the ceiling near the stove-pipe, in winter a perfect miracle of nature. Its tribal companions, companions of its own species, sentiment, and gender are dead and gone or else not yet born; this is the Ice Age which the lonely bumblebee endures without knowing how it came about or why this particular bee. But that sunlight which spreads silently over the table in front and on the floor, divided into two masses of light by the sign: Löwenbräu Patzenhofer, is age-old and makes all else seem perishable and unimportant, when you see it. It comes from over x miles away, it shot past the star y, the sun has been shining for millions of years, since long before Nebuchadnezzar, before Adam and Eve, before the ichthyosaurus, and now it shines into the little beer-shop through the window-pane, divided into two masses by a tin sign: Löwenbräu Patzenhofer, spreads out over the table and on the floor, imperceptibly gaining ground. It spreads over them, and they know it. It is winged, light, over-light, light-light, from heaven high I come to you.

Two big grown-up animals in clothes, two human beings, two men, Franz Biberkopf and Georg Dreske, a newsvender and a locked-out polisher, however, stand at the bar, hold themselves perpendicular on their pants-covered lower extremities, lean on the wood with their arms stuck in thick tubes of overcoats. Each of them thinks, observes, and feels, each something different.

"Then you might as well know this and remember it, there never was any Arras, Georgie, we simply didn't do anything, might as well confess, not us. Neither you or the ones who were there. There wasn't any discipline, wasn't anybody in command, always one against the other. I beat it out of the trenches and you, too, and Öse, too. Well, and here at home, when it started, who was it skidooed? The whole lot of 'em. Wasn't anybody to stick around, you saw that, didn't you, a handful, maybe, a thousand. You can have 'em." So that's his game and him such a bonehead, and he let 'em fool him. "Because they betrayed us, the big guys, in '18 and '19, Franz, and they killed Rosa and Karl Liebknecht too. How can people stick together that way and do anything? Take a look at Russia,

Lenin, there they stick together, like putty. But just wait and see." Blood must bubble, blood must bubble, in muggy currents thick. "I don't care. The world's going to the dogs and you, too, while you wait. I won't bother about bunk like that. Here's my proof: they couldn't accomplish anything and that's enough for me. Not the slightest thing was done, like on that Hartmannsweilerkopf, which a fellow is always preaching to me about, the veteran, he was up there, you don't know him, well, not a thing. And so—"

Here Franz gets up, takes his band from the table, stuffs it into his overcoat, waves back and forth horizontally with his left arm, slowly walking back to his table: "And then I say what I always said, you understand, Krause, you might remember this, too, Richard: there ain't nothing can come out of that business of yours. Not that way. Don't know if there's anything going to come out of the fellows with this band here. And I didn't say it either, but it's something else. Peace on earth, as they say, that's all right, and whoever wants to work, let him work and we're too good for that bunk."

And he sits on the window-sill and wipes his cheek, squints into the bright room and plucks a hair from his ear. The car grinds around the corner, No. 9, Ostring, Hermannplatz, Wildenbruchplatz, Treptow Depot, Warschauer Brücke, Baltenplatz, Kniprodestrasse, Schönhauser Allee, Stettiner Bahnhof, Hedwigkirche, Hallesches Tor, Hermannplatz. The proprietor leans on the metal beer-tap, sucks and lolls his tongue over the new filling in his lower jaw, tastes like a drug-store, little Emilie has got to go to the country again this summer or to Zinnowitz with the vacation colony, the child's ailing again, his eyes fall on the green prospectus, it's lying crooked, he straightens it out, a bit anxious about it, can't see anything lie around crooked. Marinated bismarck herring with first-class sauce, delicious boneless meats, rollmops in extra fine marinade sauce, delicious with pickle inside, herring in jelly, large chunks, delicious fish, roast herring.

Words, resounding waves, noise-waves, full of content, rock to and fro through the room, from the throat of Dreske, the stutterer, who smiles at the floor: "Well, Franz, good luck to you, as the sky-pilot says, on your new path of life. When we march out to Karl and Rosa in Friedrichsfelde next January, you're not going to be with us then, are you?" Let him stutter away, I'll sell my papers.

When they are alone, the proprietor gives Franz a smile. The latter stretches his legs comfortably under the table: "Why are they beating it,

Henschke, that gang? On account of my arm-band? I suppose they're going to get reinforcements." That fellow won't let up. Some of these days they're going to kick him out of here. Blood must bubble, blood must bubble, in currents muggy and thick.

The proprietor tastes his filling, I've got to push the goldfinch nearer the window, a wee little animal like that needs a little light. Franz helps him, drives a nail into the wall behind the bar, the proprietor carries the bird-cage with the fluttering little animal from the other wall: "It's certainly dark today. The houses are too high." Franz stands on the chair, hangs the cage up, steps down, whistles, raises his index finger and whispers again: "I hope nobody'll come near it now. It'll get used to it. It's a goldfinch, a she." Both are silent, nod to each other, look up and smile.

Franz is a Man of Form, he knows what he owes to himself

In the evening, sure enough, Franz is kicked out of Henschke's. He comes tripping along at nine, takes a look at the bird, it's got its head under its wings already and is sitting on the perch in the corner, funny, why is it a tiny animal like that doesn't fall off when it sleeps? Franz whispers to the proprietor: "What do ye say to that, the little animal sleeps right through all this racket, what do ye say to that, it's great, ain't it, it sure must be tired, wonder if all this smoke is good for it, for small lungs like that?" "It's never known anything else at my place, there's always smoke here, in the café, you know; at that, it's quite thin today."

Then Franz sits down: "Well, I'm not going to smoke today, it may get too thick otherwise, and we'll open the window a bit afterwards, there won't be any draft." Georg Dreske, young Richard, and three others sit at a separate table opposite. Two of them Franz does not know. There is nobody else in the room. When Franz came in, there was a big row going on and a lot of loud talking and swearing. As soon as he opens the door, they lower their voices, the two new ones look frequently in Franz's direction, bend over the table, then lean back impudently in their seats and drink each other's health. When lovely eyes begin to wink, when full glasses gleam and clink, there comes once more, once more, the call to drink. Henschke, the bald-headed proprietor, busies himself with the tap and the dish-washing; contrary to his custom he does not leave the place but manages to keep bustling and fussing around.

Then all of a sudden the conversation at the next table grows very loud, one of the newcomers leads in the chorus. He wants to sing, it's too quiet for him here, and there's no piano-player here, either; Henschke calls over to him: "Why should I get one, my business wouldn't pay for it." Franz knows what they want to sing, either the "Internationale" or "Brother, to light and liberty," unless they've got something new. There they go. They're singing the Internationale.

Franz chews, thinks to himself; they mean me. All right with me, if only they wouldn't smoke so much. When they sing, they don't smoke, it's bad for the little bird. That old Georg Dreske should be sitting with such young oafs, and don't even come over to join him, well, he never would have thought that possible. The old fool, married at that, an honest old fool, sitting with those kids and listening to them cackling away. One of the newcomers calls over to him: "Well, comrade, did you like the song?" "Me, fine, you got good voices." "Why don't you join in?" "I'd rather eat. When I get through eating, I'll sing with you, or else sing something myself." "All right."

They go on talking with each other, Franz eats and drinks at his ease, thinks of Lina, and that the little bird don't plump down while it's asleep, and looks across the room, who is that fellow smoking his pipe? Business was good today, but it was cold. There are always a couple of 'em over there watching him eat. Probably afraid I'm going to swallow the wrong way. Once there was a fellow ate a sausage sandwich and when it reached his stomach, it thought the thing over and came back up in his throat and said: you forgot the mustard; and then it went down the proper way. That's what a real sandwich of respectable parents does. And the moment Franz has finished and pours his beer down, rightaway that fellow calls across to him: "Well, how about it, comrade, are you going to sing us something now?" Maybe they're organizing a singing club over there, we might join 'em; if they sing they won't smoke. But I'm not in a hurry, when I promise anything, I keep my word. And he meditates, wiping his nose; it drips, when you get into a warm room, no use pulling it; he thinks, wonder where Lina's keeping herself, and I might as well treat myself to a coupla wienies, but I'm getting a bit stout, what'll I sing for 'em, they don't understand nothing about life, anyway, but a promise is a promise. And suddenly through his head there strays a phrase, a line, a poem he had learned in prison, they often recited it, it went from cell to cell. He remains under the spell of the moment, his head is warm and flushed from the heat, it sinks on his chest, he grows serious and thoughtful. With his hand on his mug, he says: "I know a poem, from prison, it's by a prisoner, his name was, wait a minute, what was his name, Dohms, that's it."

Right. Now it's out, but it was a fine poem. He sits alone at his table. Henschke, from behind his sink, listens along with the others, nobody comes in, the tile stove crackles. Franz, his head resting on his hand, recites a poem which Dohms composed, and he sees the cell, the courtyard, he can stand it now, wonder what young fellows are there now: he himself is walking in the prison courtyard, that's more than these guys know, what do they know about life, anyway?

He says: "If on this earth you want to be, a creature, male and full of glee, be careful and weigh everything, before you let the midwife fling you towards the daylight, there to grow: Earth is a nest of grief and woe. Believe the poet of these verses, who often pines and often curses, while chewing on this iron crust—quotation pinched from Goethe's Faust: Man only relishes life's glow, in general, as an embryo! . . . There is the good old father State, he rags and irks you soon and late. He pricks and pesters you—you're bled—with laws and codes: 'Prohibited!' His first commandment: Man, shell out. His second: Hold your dirty snout. And thus you live in adumbration, your state is that of offuscation. And if you seek to drown your queer, rough anger at some pub with beer, or with some wine, respectively, a headache promptly trails the spree. Meanwhile the years knock at the gate, the moths erode the hair, elate. Suspiciously the rafters creak, the limbs grow flabby, blighted, weak: gray matter sours in the brain, and thinner grows the good old strain. In short, you see fall coming nigh, you put the spoon down and you die. And now I ask you, friend, a-quiver: just what is man, what is life's river? Did not our great poet Schiller confess: 'It's not the highest men possess.' But I say: it's a chicken-ladder at best, up and down and all the rest."

They are all silent. Franz opines: "Yes, that's what he composed, came from Hannover, but I memorized it. Nice, heh, it's something for life, but bitter, too."

From across the way: "Well, you'd better keep it in mind, that stuff about the State, the good old father State, who rags and irks, the State. To memorize it, comrade, that's not all." Franz still has his head in his hand, the poem is still there: "Yes, they haven't got any oysters or caviar, and neither have we. To have to earn his bread, must be hard for a poor devil. Still a man should be glad he can walk about, and is out of it all." The men across the way start shooting again, the fool's going to wake up yet. "A man can earn his bread in many ways. Why, they used to have spies in Russia in the old days, they earned a lot of money with that." The other newcomer trumpets: "And there's other fellows here, too, who sit up there by the feed trough; they betrayed the working man to the capitalist, and what's more, they're paid for it." "They're no better than whores." "Worse."

Franz thinks about his poem and wonders what those nice boys are doing out there, they probably got some new ones by now, patrol wagons come and go every day; but then they shout: "Let her go! What about our song? We got no music, you're a man of your word, ain't you?" Another song, well, I'll give it to 'em. I'll keep my promise. First I'll wet my whistle.

And Franz orders a fresh mug, takes a nip, what'll I sing? For the moment he sees himself standing in the courtyard, bellowing something at the walls, funny things a fellow thinks about, now what was it? And calmly and slowly he sings, it flows forth: "I once had a faithful comrade, Never better could there be, The trumpet echoed wihidely, He firmly marched besihide me, There step for step with me, There step for step with me." Rest. He sings the second stanza: "One ball wing'd by death came flying, Is it sent for me or thee? Torn away from life and dyhying, As at my feet he's lyhying, He seems a part of me, He seems a part of me." And loudly the last stanza: "His hand he strives to give to me, I meanwhile my gun must load, No time have I to grahasp it, Until again I clahasp it, In yon eternal abode, In yon eternal abode."

At the end he sings loudly, solemnly, leaning back; boldly he sings and with a sense of satiety. Towards the close the fellows across the way have conquered their amazement, they howl with him and beat on the table, and scream and start acting the fool: "Until again I clahasp it." But while he was singing, Franz remembered what he really wanted to sing. He had been standing in the courtyard, he's satisfied now that he's found it, he doesn't care where he is; he's in the midst of singing now, out with it, he has got to sing the song, the Jews are there, they begin to quarrel, what was the Pole's name, what was that fine old gentleman's name; tenderness, gratitude; he blares it into the café: "There comes a call like thunder's peal, Like billow's roar and clash of steel, The Rhine, the German Rhine so free, Yes we will all thy guardians be, Dear Fatherland, be comfort thine, Dear Fatherland, be comfort thine, Firm stands and true the watch, the watch on the Rhine, Firm stands and true the watch, the watch on the Rhine." That's over with now, we know that, and here we sit, and life's nice, nice, everything's nice.

Then they grow quite silent, one of the newcomers calms them down, they let this pass; Dreske sits humped together and scratches his head, the proprietor steps up from behind the bar, sniffles and sits down at the table beside Franz. Franz at the end of his song salutes the whole of life, he swings his mug: "Cheerio," beats on the table, beams, everything's all right, he has eaten his fill, wonder where Lina's gone to, he pats his full face, he's a strong man, plenty of flesh with a touch of fat. Nobody answers. Silence.

One of the men across the way swings his leg over his chair, buttons his coat up, tightens his belt, a tall erect fellow, one of the newcomers; the applecart's upset all right. He goose-steps towards Franz, who'll get a crack on the head, that is, if the newcomer can reach him. With a hop he straddles Franz's table. Franz looks on, waiting: "Look here, there must be other chairs in the place." But he points down at Franz's plate: "What you been eatin'?" "Didn't I tell you, there must be other chairs in the place, if you only use your eyes. Say, your mother musta given you a bath that was too hot for you when you were a kid, didn't she?" "That's not the point. I want to know what you been eating." "Cheese sandwiches, you jackass. Don't you see the rind, you numbskull. Now you get down from this table, if you got no manners." "They were cheese sandwiches all right, I can smell that for myself. Only where from?"

But Franz leaps up with flushed ears, the men at the other table do the same. Franz has grabbed his table, tipped it over, and the newcomer, with plate, mug, and mustard pot, falls plump down on the floor. The plate is broken. Henschke expected that, and stamps on the pieces: "Nothing doing, no brawls in my place, no scrapping here, if you don't keep quiet, you'll get thrown out." The long-legged chap is on his feet again, shoves the proprietor aside: "Just leave us alone here, Henschke, there ain't going to be any fight. We're settling accounts. If anybody breaks anything, he'll have to pay for it." With heart and with soul, thinks Franz, who has squeezed himself against the window in front of the blinds, here goes, if those fellows only don't touch me, boy, if they only don't touch me: I feel kind towards everybody, but there's going to be trouble, if that fellow's silly enough to touch me.

The tall man pulls up his trousers, well, he's off. Franz sees there's something coming, what's Dreske going to do now, I wonder, he's just standing there and looking on. "Georgie, what kind of a cheap guy is this anyway, where did you pick up this louse you're dragging round here?" The tall man was fussing with his trousers, they're slipping down most likely, ought to get some new buttons sewed on. He gibes at the proprietor: "Just let 'em talk. We let Fascists talk, too. Whatever they say, they get freedom of speech from us." And Dreske signals towards the back with his left arm. "Nope, Franz, I didn't mix in this, the trouble you get yourself into with your songs, and everything, nope, I won't mix in it, we never had that kind of thing here before."

There comes a call like thunder's peal, aha! that song I sang in the courtyard, they want to razz me about that, they'd like to say something about that, too.

"Fascist, bloodhound." The tall fellow roars at Franz: "Gimme that arm-band! And be quick about it."

Now it's going to start, the four of 'em want to get at me, I'll stand with my back to the window, first of all let's get a chair. "Lemme have that arm-band. I'll pull it out of his pocket. I want to get that band from this guy." The others are with him. Franz has the chair in his hands. First get hold of him. Hold him first. Then I'll pull it out.

The proprietor holds onto the tall chap from behind, and pleads: "Now Biberkopf, you better go, right away, just get out." He's worrying about his premises, probably hasn't had his panes insured, well, it's all right with me. "Henschke, of course, there's plenty other saloons in Berlin, I was only waiting for Lina. So you're going to help those fellows? Why do they want to push a man out, when I come here every day and those fellows are here for the first time?" The proprietor has pushed the tall chap back, the other, the newcomer, spits out: "Because you're a Fascist, you got that band in your pocket, you're a swastika man."

"So I am, I told Georgie Dreske all about it, too. And why? You don't understand and that's why you holler." "No, it was you who hollered, the Watch on the Rhine." "If you start a row, like you did just now, and one of you sits down on my table, you'll never get any peace in this world that way. Not that way. And there's got to be peace so we can work and live. Factory hands and tradespeople and everybody, and some kind of order, otherwise you can't work. And how do you want to make your living, you big-mouthed slobs? What you do is to get soused on talking. All you know is how to start a row and bait other people till they get mad and land you one. Are you going to let anybody step on your toes?"

Suddenly he begins to shout, what's come over him, something bubbles up in him, something's been released, his eyes become bloodshot: "You criminals, you, you lousy fools, why, you don't know what you're doing, somebody has got to beat hell out of you, you ruin the whole world, just watch out you don't get into trouble, you blood-spillers, you crooks, you."

He is bubbling over, he's done time in Tegel, life is awful, what kind of a life is this, the fellow who wrote that song is right, I mustn't think about what happened to me, Ida.

And he goes on shouting with a feeling of horror, what's going to happen there, he wards it off, he steps on it, he must bellow, bellow it down. The café roars, Henschke stands before him at the table, dares not come near him, standing there like that with that roaring coming out of his throat all topsy-turvy and foaming: "And none of you's got anything to say to me, not one of you can tell me anything, not a single one of you, I know all that better than you do, I didn't go to the front and lie in the trenches for this, so you could bait me, you agitators, we've gotta have order, order, I'm telling you, order—and put that in your pipes and smoke it, order and nothing else" (yes, that's it, here we are, that's just it), "and if anybody comes and starts a revolution now and don't give us order, they ought to be strung up all along the street" (black poles, telegraph poles, a whole row on the Tegel Road, I know all about that) "then they'll get theirs, when they swing, yes, sir. You might remember that whatever you do, you criminals." (Yes, then we'll have order, then they'll be quiet, that's the only thing to do, we'll find that out.)

A frenzy, a numbness comes over Franz Biberkopf. Blindly he croaks in his throat, his eyes are glassy, his face blue, bloated, he spits, his hands burn, the man's out of his mind. His fingers claw the chair, but he manages to hold on to it. Soon he will take the chair and haul out.

Danger ahead, clear the streets, load, fire, fire, fire.

At the same time this roaring man hears his own voice, from far away, is looking at himself. The houses, the houses threaten to cave in again, the roofs to smash over him, this won't do, no, they can't get away with that, those criminals won't succeed, what we need is order.

Something buzzes inside him: it's going to start soon and I'm going to do something, grab a throat, no, no, I'm about to topple over, fall down, another moment, just one moment more. And me thinking the world is quiet, there is law and order. In his twilight state he is frightened: something is out of gear with the world, the others seem so terrible to him, he experiences it with a sort of clairvoyance.

But once in Paradise there lived two beings, Adam and Eve. Paradise was the wonderful garden of Eden. Birds and animals played about.

Well, if that fellow isn't crazy. They're not moving, the tall one, too, is puffing away back there through his nose and blinking at Dreske; we'd better sit down at the table, then we can talk about something else. Dreske stutters during the calm: "Well, Franz, you'd better be going, you might let go of that chair, too, you've talked enough now." Things are calming down inside Franz, the cloud is passing over. Passing over. Thank God, passing over. His face grows paler and paler, becomes less tense.

They stand at their table. The tall fellow is seated drinking. The wood-manufacturers boast about their receipts, Krupp lets his pensioners starve to death, a million and a half unemployed, an increase of 226,000 in two weeks.

The chair has fallen from Franz's hand, his hand has become soft, his voice sounds as usual, he still holds his head bowed, they don't excite him any more: "I'll go then. The pleasure is all mine. What's in your heads is none of my business."

They listen without replying. Let those contemptible scoundrels, belonging to a renegade clique, slander the Soviet constitution with the approval of the bourgeoisie and the social chauvinists. It but hastens and deepens the rupture of the revolutionary workers of Europe with the Scheidemen, and their likes. The masses of the oppressed classes are with us.

Franz picks up his cap: "I'm sorry, Georgie, for us to separate like this." He holds out his hand, Dreske does not take it, sits down on his chair. Blood must bubble, blood must bubble, in currents muggy and thick.

"All right then, I'll go. How much do I owe, Henschke, and don't forget the glass and the plate."

That's his kind of order. For 14 children a china cup. A charity edict by Hirtsiefer, the Centrist minister: Publication of this edict shall be omitted. But because of the paucity of the means put at my disposal only those cases can be considered where not only the number of children has reached a very high figure—let us say 12—but also where the careful education of the children with respect to economic conditions involves a special sacrifice and is nevertheless carried out in an exemplary manner.

One of the fellows shouts after Franz: "Greet you in victory, hail—potatoes with a herring's tail." Ought to wipe the mustard off his backsides, the louse. Too bad I didn't get my claws on him. Franz has his cap on. He is thinking about the Hackesche Market, the fairies, the white-head's stand with the magazines, and he didn't want to do it, he hesitates, he leaves.

He is outside in the cold. Lina, who happens to be just arriving, is standing directly in front of the café. He walks slowly. He'd give anything to go back and tell those fellows how crazy they are. They sure are crazy, they get all boozed up, they're not really all like that, not even the tall, nervy fellow who flopped down on the floor. Only they don't know what to do with all that blood, yes, sir, their blood's hot, if they were out in Tegel, or had something behind them, they'd find out a thing or two, maybe a hundred things.

He takes Lina's arm, looks around the dark street. It wouldn't hurt to have a few more street-lamps. What do those people want anyway, first the fairies, who don't concern me, and now the Reds? What have I got to do with all this, let 'em clean up their own dirt. Ought to leave a fellow be; you can't even finish your beer in peace. What I really would like to do would be to go back and smash Henschke's whole outfit into smithereens. Something flares and flickers again in Franz's eyes, his forehead and nose become thick. But that passes, he sticks close to Lina, he scratches her wrist, she smiles: "That's all right, Franzeken, that's a nice li'l scratch you gave me."

"Let's go shake a foot, Lina; and not go into a pig-pen like that again. I've had enough of it, they smoke and smoke, and there's a little goldfinch in there and it could easily pass out, for all they care." And he explains to her how entirely right he had been just now, and she agrees. They take the street-car and ride down to the Jannowitz Brücke to Walterchen's dance-hall. He is going just as he is and Lina, even, is not to change her dress, she is nice enough like that. In the car stout Lina takes a little rumpled paper out of her pocket. She brought it along to show him, it's a Sunday paper, the *Peace Messenger*. Franz remarks he doesn't handle that paper, he squeezes her hand, admires the nice title and headline on the first page: "From Misfortune to Happiness."

With our little hands we go clap, clap, with our little feet we go tap, fish, fowl, all day long, paradise.

The car jolts along. With their heads together, they read by the dim light the poem on the first page which Lina had marked with a pencil: "Walking is best when we're two," by E. Fischer: "When we walk alone, it's a walk of woe, The foot oft stumbling, the heart bowed low: Walking is best when we're two. And if you fall, who'll take your arm, If weary, who'll ward off all harm? Walking is best when we're two. You silent rover through space and time, Take Jesus as your mate sublime. Walking is best when we're two. He knows the road, he knows the lane, with word and deed he heals your pain, Walking is best when we're two."

At that I'm still thirsty, thinks Franz in the meantime, as he reads, two glasses wasn't enough, and talking so much dries your throat. And then he remembers his song, he feels at home, and presses Lina's arm.

She scents the morning air. On the way through Alexanderstrasse to Holzmarktstrasse she softly clings to him: How about getting properly engaged soon?

Dimensions of this Franz Biberkopf. He is a Match for old Heroes

This Franz Biberkopf, formerly a cement-worker, then a furniture-mover, and so on, and now a newsvender, weighs around two hundred pounds. He is strong as a cobra and has again joined an athletic club. He wears green putties, hobnail boots, and a leather jacket. As far as money is concerned, you won't find a great deal on him, his current income arrives always in small quantities, but just let anyone try to get near him.

Is he hounded by things in his past, Ida and so on, by conscientious scruples, nightmares, restless sleep, tortures, Furies from the day of our great-grandmothers? Nothing doing. Just consider the change in his situation. A criminal, an erstwhile God-accursed man (where did you get that, my child?), Orestes, killed at the altar Clytemnestra, hardly pronounceable that name, eh? anyhow, she was his own mother. (Which altar do you really mean? Nowadays you could run around a long time looking for a church that's open at night.) I say, times are changed, up and at him, hey, terrible brutes, trollops with snakes, then dogs without muzzles, a whole repulsive menagerie, they snap at him, but don't get near him, because he stands at the altar, that's a Hellenic conception, and the whole pack of them dancing angrily around him, the dogs amongst them. Without harps, as the song says, the Furies dance, they wind themselves about the victim in a mad frenzy, a delusion of the senses, a preparation for the booby-hatch.

But they don't hound Franz Biberkopf. Let's admit it, here's how, with his arm-band in his pocket he drinks one mug after another at Henschke's or somewhere else, and in between a Doornkaat, and his heart grows warm. Thus our furniture-mover, newsvender, etc., Franz Biberkopf, of Berlin N. E., differs from the famous old Orestes in the end of 1927. Who would not rather be in whose skin?

Franz killed his fiancée, Ida, the family name does not matter, in the flower of her youth. This happened during an altercation between Franz and Ida, in the home of her sister Minna, where, first of all, the following organs of the woman were slightly damaged: the skin on the end of her nose and in the middle, the bone and the cartilage underneath, a fact, however, which was noticed only after her arrival at the hospital and later played a certain rôle in the court records, furthermore the right and left shoulder sustained slight bruises, with loss of blood. But then the discussion became lively. The expressions "son of a bitch" and "whore-chaser" were extremely upsetting to Franz Biberkopf who, albeit very dissipated and at that time excited for other reasons, was nevertheless very sensitive about his honor. His muscles jiggered up and down. All he had taken in his hand was a small wooden cream-whipper, for he was in training then and had recently wrenched his hand. And with a twice repeated, terrible lunge, he had brought this cream-whipper with its wire spiral, in contact with the diaphragm of Ida, who was the second party to the dialogue. Up to that day Ida's diaphragm had been entirely intact, but that very small person, who was very nice to look at, was herself no longer quite intact—or rather: the man she was supporting, suspected, not without reason, that she was about to give him his walking papers in favor of a man recently arrived from Breslau. The diaphragm of this dainty little girl, at any rate, was not adapted to contact with cream-whippers. At the first blow she cried "ouch" and no longer called him "you dirty bum," but "oh, man," instead. The second encounter with the cream-whipper occurred with Franz holding an upright position after a quarter turn to the right on Ida's part. Whereupon Ida said nothing at all, but merely opened her mouth, pursing her lips curiously, and jerked both arms in the air.

What happened to the woman's diaphragm a second before, involves the laws of statics, elasticity, shock, and resistance. The thing is wholly incomprehensible without a knowledge of those laws. We shall therefore have recourse to the following formulæ:

Newton's first law which says: Every body perseveres in its state of rest or of moving uniformly in a straight line, except so far as it is made to change that state by external force (this applies to Ida's ribs). Newton's second law of motion: Change of motion is proportional to the impressed force, and takes place in the direction in which the force is impressed (the impressed force is Franz, or his arm, and his fist, together with the contents thereof). The magnitude of the force is expressed by the following formula:

$$f = c \lim \overline{\frac{\Delta v}{\Delta t}} = cw.$$

The acceleration effected by the force, that is, the degree of the disturbance of rest thus effected, is expressed by the following formula:

$$\overline{\Delta v} = \frac{1}{c} f \, \Delta t.$$

The natural and actual result is as follows: the spiral of the cream-whipper is pressed together and the wooden part encounters something. On the other side, the side of inertia and resistance: fracture of the 7th and 8th ribs in line with the left shoulder-blade.

Thanks to such timely consideration, we can dispense entirely with Furies. We can follow, step by step, what Franz did and what Ida suffered. There is no unknown quantity in the equation. There remains only to enumerate the continuation of the process which was thus inaugurated: We have the loss of the vertical position on Ida's part, a transition to the horizontal, this being the effect of the rude shock received, at the same time, respiratory impediment, violent pain, terror, and physiological disturbance of the equilibrium. Franz would nevertheless have killed this damaged person, whom he knew so well, like a roaring lion, if her sister had not come bouncing in from the next room. Before this woman's abusive talk he retreated, and in the evening they nabbed him during a police raid in the vicinity of his home.

"Up and at him, whoa," shriek the old Furies. Horror, oh, horror, to see a God-accursed man at the altar, his hands dripping with blood! How they snort: Dost thou sleep? Thrust slumber away. Up, up. Agamemnon, his father, had started many years ago from Troy. Troy had fallen, and thence shone the signal fires, from Ida over Athos, oil-torches constantly blazing towards the Cytherean forest.

How splendid, be it said in passing, this flaming message from Troy to Greece! Isn't that grand, this march of fire across the sea, this is light, heart, soul, happiness, rejoicing!

The dark-red fire, flaming red over the Gorgopis lake is seen by a watchman who shouts with joy, ah, that's life, and fresh fires are lighted to pass on the news, the excitement and joy, everything together, and with a leap over a gulf, in a stormy race to the heights of Arachneon, this outcry continues, this madness, which you see, flaming red: Agamemnon is coming. We can't compare ourselves with this way of doing things. Here again we're inferior.

Let us use for purposes of information a few results from the experiments of Heinrich Hertz, who lived in Karlsruhe, died at an early age, and who, at least in the photo of the Munich Graphic Collection, wore a full beard. We telegraph by wireless. We produce high frequency alternating currents through transmitters in big stations. We produce electric waves by oscillations of a vibrating circle. The vibrations spread out spherically, as it were. And then there is also an electron-tube of glass and a microphone the disk of which vibrates in alternating degrees, thus reproducing tones, precisely as when they entered the machine, and that is astonishing, clever, tricky. It's hard to get enthusiastic about all this; it functions, and that's all.

Quite different the oil-torch with its message of Agamemnon's return.

It burns, it blazes, it speaks, it feels, at every moment, in each place, and the joy is general: Agamemnon is coming. A thousand men are aglow in each place: Agamemnon is coming, and now there are ten thousand, across the bay, a hundred thousand.

And then, to get to the point, he arrives home. Things change. Things change considerably. The disk turns. When the wife gets him home, she sticks him into the bath. She shows then and there that she is the worst bitch on record. She plunks a fish-net over him in the water, so that he can't do anything, and she has brought an ax along, presumably to chop wood. He groans heavily: "Woe is me, I am undone!" Outside they ask: "Who is bemoaning himself?" "Woe is me, and again woe." The Hellenic beast finishes him off, without batting an eye, and outside she even has the nerve to yelp: "I have achieved it, I threw a fish-net over him, and struck twice, and with two sighs he was laid out. Then, with yet a third blow, I sent him to Hades." Whereupon the senators are grieved, but nevertheless they remark appropriately: "We bow before the boldness of your speech." It was this woman then, this Hellenic beast, who, as the result of conjugal amusement with Agamemnon, had become the mother of a boy who was called Orestes at his birth. She was subsequently killed by this fruit of her joys, after which he was tortured by the Furies.

Our Franz Biberkopf, however, is in a different position. Five weeks later his Ida, too, is dead in the Friedrichshain hospital, complicated fracture of the ribs, rupture of the pleura, small rupture of the lung, with the resultant empyema, pleurisy, pneumonia, the dickens the fever won't go down, how badly you look now, get a mirror, baby, you're done for, you're finished, you can pack up and go. They dissected her, put her in the earth in the Landsberger Allee, three yards under ground. She died with a feeling of hatred against Franz, he was stinkin' mad at her even after her death, her new friend, the one from Breslau, paid her a visit before she died. Now she lies below, five long years already, horizontally on her back, the planks are beginning to rot, she is dissolving in manure-juice, she who once danced in white canvas shoes with Franz in the Paradiesgarten of Treptow, who loved and gadded about, now she lies quite still, she is no more.

But he has done his four years. He who killed her is walking about, alive and flourishing, boozing, swilling, spilling his semen, continuing to disseminate life. Even Ida's sister did not escape him. He'll get it in the neck, too, some day. For didn't what's-his-name die? But that's a long time off. He knows that. In the meantime, he will go on breakfasting in the cafés and praising the sky over the Alexanderplatz in his own sweet way: Since when does Grandma play the trombone, and: My parrot don't eat hard-boiled eggs.

And where is now the red prison wall of Tegel, which had made him so afraid that he could hardly get his back away from it? The guardian stands at the black iron gate, which once excited such abhorrence in Franz, it is still hanging on its hinges, it does not bother anybody, there is always a good draft there, at night it is closed, as is the case with every good gate. Now in the morning the guardian stands in front, smoking his pipe. The sun shines, it is always the same sun; you can predict exactly when it will reach a given place in the sky. Whether it shines or not depends upon the cloud formation. A few persons are just leaving car No. 41, they are carrying flowers and small parcels, they are probably going to the sanatorium, straight ahead to the left, down the Chaussee, all of them well-nigh freezing. The trees stand in a black row. Inside, the convicts are still cowering in their cells, bustling about in the work-rooms, or marching in goose-step on the promenade grounds. Strict orders to appear during recreation hour with shoes, cap, and muffler only. Inspection of cells by the old man: "How was the soup last night?" "It could have been better and a bit more wouldn't hurt." Doesn't want to hear that, pretends to be deaf: "How often do you get clean bed-linen?" As if he didn't know.

One of the convicts in solitary confinement has written: "Let sunlight in. This is the call that resounds throughout the world today. Only here, behind prison walls, it has not found an echo. Don't we deserve to have the sun shine on us? The penal institutions are so constructed that certain wings do not receive the rays of the sun during the entire year, on the northeast frontage. Not a ray of sun strays into these cells to bring greetings to their occupants. Year in, year out, these people have to work and wither without the vivifying light of the sun." A commission is about to inspect the building, the guardians run from cell to cell.

Another prisoner: "To the District Attorney. During my trial before the High Criminal Bench of the District Court, the President, Director of the District Court, Dr. X, informed me that an unknown person removed various articles from my home, 76 Elizabethstrasse, after my arrest. This fact has been established by court records. Since this has been established by court records, a perquisition must necessarily have been made by the police or the district attorney's office. I was not informed in any way about the theft of my articles after my arrest until I learned it at the trial. I beg the district attorney to inform me about the result of the inquiry, or else to send me a copy of the report as recorded, in order that I may subsequently start a suit for damages, if my landlady has acted with negligence."

And as regards Frau Minna, Ida's sister, she is doing well, thank you for asking. It is now 11.20, she is just leaving the Ackerstrasse Market, a yellow municipal building, which has also an exit on the Invalidenstrasse. But she chooses the Ackerstrasse exit because it is nearer for her. She is carrying cauliflowers and pig's-head, also some celery. In front of the market she buys something else from a wagon: a big fat flounder and a bag of camomile tea, you never can tell, you may need it any day.

THIRD BOOK

Here Franz Biberkopf, who is a respectable, good-natured man, suffers his first blow. He is deceived. The blow carries.

Biberkopf has vowed to become respectable and you have seen how he stayed straight for many a week, but it was only a respite, so to speak. In the end life finds this going too far, and trips him up with a wily jar. To him, Franz Biberkopf, however, this doesn't seem a very sporting trick, and, for a considerable time, he finds this sordid, draggle-tailed existence, which contradicts his every good intention, a bit too thick.

Why life acts this way, he does not understand. He still has a long way to go before he will see it.

Yesterday upon proud Steeds we rode

With Christmas coming on, Franz makes a change, doing business in all kinds of occasional articles. He gives a few hours in the morning or the afternoon to shoe-laces, first by himself, then later with Otto Lüders. The latter has been out of work for two years, and his wife takes in washing. Stout Lina got them together, Otto being Fatty's uncle. In the summer he had worked for a few weeks as a Rüdersdorfer Peppermint Man with a plumed hat and a uniform. Franz and he do the streets together, enter houses, ring bells, then meet afterwards.

One day Franz Biberkopf arrives at the café. Fat Lina is also there. He is in an especially good humor. He gulps the fat girl's sandwiches down and while still chewing away, gives another order for pig's ears and peas for the three of them. He squeezes fat Lina so hard that she waddles off after the pig's ears with her face flaming red. "Good thing Fatty's going, Otto." "She's got a place of her own, hasn't she? Always traipsing around after you."

Franz leans over the table, looks up at Lüders: "Say, Otto, what do you think has happened?" "Well, what?" "Well, shoot." "Well, what is it?"

Two light beers and a lemonade. A new customer comes puffing into the place, wipes his nose on the back of his hand, coughs: "Cup of coffee." "With sugar?" The proprietor rinses the glasses. "Nope, but make it quick."

A youngster with a brown sport cap walks through the place looking for somebody, warms himself at the big stove, looks around at Franz's table, then at the next one: "Have you seen a man with a black overcoat, brown collar, fur collar?" "Here often?" "Yep." The older man at the table turns his head to the pale man next to him: "Brown fur?" The latter gruffly: "Lots of 'em come here with brown fur on." The gray-haired man: "Where do you come from? Who sent you?" "What difference does that make? As long as you didn't see him." "Lots of men come here with brown fur coats. We have to know who sent you." "But I don't have to tell you my business." The pale man gets excited: "If you ask a man if somebody's been here, can't he ask you who sent you here?"

The customer is already standing at the next table: "If I ask him, it's none of his business who I am." "All right, if you ask him, he certainly can ask you back. You don't have to ask him, do you?" "I don't have to tell him what kind of business I'm in." "Then he don't have to tell you if anybody was here."

The customer goes to the door, turns around: "If you're that clever then just stay that way." He turns around, opens the door brusquely, is gone.

The two at the table: "Do you know him? I don't know him at all." "He never comes here. Who knows what he wants?" "A Bavarian." "That chap? A Rhinelander. From the Rhineland."

Franz grins at the wretched, shivering Lüders: "So you can't guess. Well, supposing I had some money?" "Well, have you got any?"

Franz has his fist on the table, he opens it, grins proudly: "All right, how much?" Poor, wretched little Lüders is leaning forward, sucking a hollow tooth: "Two tens, the deuce you say." Franz plunks them on the table. "How about that? Did that in fifteen, in twenty minutes. No longer. Betcha." "Say, boy." "Nope, not what you think either, nothing underhanded, nothing shady, no, it ain't that. Honestly, Otto, I got it decent, in a proper way, you get me."

They start whispering, Otto Lüders moves closer to him. Franz had stopped in at a woman's house: Makko shoe-laces, do you need anything for yourself, for hubby, for your little kiddies, she looked at them, then she looked at me, she's a widow, still in good condition; we were talking in the hallway, then I asked her if I couldn't get a cup of coffee, terribly cold this year. I drank some coffee, she did too. And then a little bit more. Franz blows through his hand, laughs through his nose, scratches his cheeks, pushes his knee against Otto's. "I left my whole caboodle with her. Did she notice anything?" "Who?" "Well, the fat girl, of course, who else, because I didn't bring anything back with me." "What if she did notice anything, you sold everything, where was it?"

And Franz whistles: "I'll go there again, but not right away, it's behind Elsasser, she's a widow, twenty marks, that's business for you." They eat and drink till three, Otto gets a fiver, but doesn't become any livelier for that.

Who is that slinking through the Rosenthaler Tor next morning with his shoe-laces? Otto Lüders. He waits at Fabisch's on the corner, till he sees Franz ambling down Brunnenstrasse. Then quickly he goes down Elsasser. Righto, that's the number. Maybe Franz has been upstairs already. How quietly people walk down the street! I'll stand in the hallway a bit first. If he comes, I'll say, what'll I say, I've got heart palpitations. People worry you all day long, and no profit, the doctor don't find anything the matter, but I've got something all right. A fellow gets down and out, in rags like this, always the same old outfit, from the war. Up the stairs he goes.

He rings: "Want some Makko shoe-laces, madam? Nope, just wanted to find out. Say, won't you listen to me a minute." She tries to push the door shut, he jams his foot between. "As a matter of fact, I didn't come for myself, my friend, you know, he was here yesterday, he left his stuff here." "Oh, Lord." She opens the door, once inside, Lüders quickly pulls the door to behind him. "Good Lord, what's the matter?" "Nothing at all, lady. What makes you so dithery?" He's dithery himself, he got in so suddenly, things are moving, whatever happens, it'll go all right. He ought to be tender, but his voice fails him, in front of his mouth and under his nose he has a wire netting, that spreads out over his forehead, and his cheeks. If my cheeks get stiff, it's the end of me. "I just came to get the stuff." The nice little woman runs into the room, starts to get the package, but he is already in the doorway. She chews and stares: "Here's the package." "Thanks, thank you. What makes you so dithery, lady? Why, it's nice and warm here! It's real nice and warm here! Can't you lemme have a cup of coffee, too?" Just remain standing, keep on talking, mustn't get out, strong as an oak tree.

The woman, who is thin and neat, stands before him, her hands clasped over her abdomen: "Did he tell you anything else? What did he tell you?" "Who, my friend?" Keep on talking, talking all the time, the more you talk, the warmer you get, the netting only tickles now in front, under the nose. "Oh nothing else, nope, what else was there to tell? Why should he talk about the coffee? I got the goods anyway." "I'm just going into the kitchen." She's afraid, what do I care about her coffee, I can make it much better myself, I can get it quicker in the café, she's trying to back out, just wait, we're not gone yet. But it's a good thing I'm inside, I slipped in like lightning. But Lüders is afraid, nevertheless, and listens towards the door, the stairs, upstairs. He steps back into the room. Slept damned badly last night, the brat's always coughing, all night long, I believe I'll sit down. And he sits down on the red plush sofa.

Here's where she did it with Franz, now she's making coffee for me, I guess I'll take off my hat, my fingers are cold as ice. "Here's a cup for you." But still she's afraid, she's a pretty little person, really tempts a fellow to try something. "Why don't you take some, too? To keep me company?" "No, no, my lodger will soon be here, this is his room." Wants to get rid of me, where does she keep her lodger, there ought to be a bed here. "Is that all? Forget that fellow. A lodger, he won't come back before noon, hasn't he got his work? Well, that's all my friend told me. I'm just supposed to get his stuff."—He leans forward and contentedly laps up the coffee.— "Nice and hot, it's cold today, what do you think he told me anyway? That you're a widow—that's true, ain't it?" "Yes." "What about your husband, dead? Killed in the war?" "I'm busy now, must get at my cooking." "Go ahead, and let me have another cup. Why be in a hurry like that? We'll be older the next time we see each other. Have you got any children?" "If you'd only go, you got your things, I got no time." "Now don't get nasty, I suppose you're going to get the police, you won't need 'em for me, I'll go, but can't I finish my coffee? You got no time all of a sudden. The other day you had lots of time, you know what I mean. All right, here's how, I'm not like that, I'm off."

He planks his hat on his head, gets up, shoves the little package under his arm, ambles slowly to the door, has already passed her, then he turns quickly around: "All right now, let's have the small change." His left hand stretched out, the index-finger coaxing. She holds her hand before her mouth, little Lüders is close upon her. "You better not yell. I suppose you only give something when you've had what you want out of a fellow, you see I know all about that. There's no secrets among friends." Damned swinishness, she's an old sow, with her black dress, I'd really like to box her ears for her, she's no better than my old woman. The woman's face is flushed, but only on the right side, the left is snow-white. She has her purse in her hand, rummages in it, but looks at little Lüders with scared eyes. Her right hand offers him several pieces of money. Her expression is strained. His index-finger goes on coaxing. She pours the contents of her purse into his hand. But suddenly he goes back to her room, and snatches up the red embroidered cover from the table. She groans, but otherwise does not let out a sound; she can't get her mouth open any further and stands quite still in the doorway. He grabs two sofa cushions, then rushes into the kitchen, pulls open the cupboard, searches it. A lot of old junk, gotta run, otherwise she'll start yelling. There she's toppling over, let's get out o' here.

He crosses the hallway, pulls the door slowly to, down the stairs, into the neighboring house.

In my Breast today a Bullet's Load

Once there was a wonderful Paradise. The waters teemed with fish, out of the soil there sprouted trees, animals played about, beasts of the earth, of the sea, and birds.

A tree rustled. A serpent, serpent, serpent stuck out its head, a serpent dwelt in Paradise, more cunning than all the beasts of the field, and began to speak, to speak to Adam and Eve.

A week later as Franz Biberkopf slowly walks up the stairs with a bouquet wrapped in oiled paper, he thinks of fat Lina and reproaches himself, but not very seriously, stops, she is true as gold, that girl, what are you worrying about, Franz, pshaw, it's business, business is business. He rings the bell, smiles in anticipation, smirks contentedly, warm coffee, a little doll. There's somebody walking in there, it's she. He throws out his chest, presents the bouquet at the wooden door, the chain is put back in place, his heart beats, how's my necktie, her voice asks: "Who's there?" He giggles: "The postman."

Small black door slit, her eyes, he leans tenderly down, smirks happily, wags the nosegay in her direction. Crash. The door is shut, slammed shut. RRRrrr, bolted. The devil! The door is shut. What a nerve! There you got it. That woman must be crazy. Wonder if she recognized me. Brown door, door-frame, here I stand on the staircase, my tie's all right. That's unbelievable. Shall I ring again, or not? He looks at his hands, a bouquet just bought at the corner, for a mark, with oil paper wrapping. He rings again, twice, very long. She's probably still standing at the door, just shut it, she doesn't move, holds her breath and let's me stand here. And then she still has my shoe-laces, the whole stock, maybe three marks' worth, I've gotta get 'em. There's someone walking inside, now she walks away, she's in the kitchen. What a——

I guess I'll go downstairs again. Then up again: I'll ring again, must find out about that, she couldn't 'a' seen me, or maybe she took me for someone else, for a beggar, lots of 'em come here. But when he stands in front of the door, he does not ring. He has no sensations. He only waits, stands there. Well, she's not going to open the door, I just wanted to know. I won't sell anything in this house any more, what'll I do with my bouquet, it cost me a whole mark. I'll throw it into the gutter. Suddenly he rings once more, as if on command, waits calmly, all right, she don't even come to the door, she knows it's me. Suppose I leave a note with the neighbors, I must get my stuff again.

He rings next door, nobody there. All right, let's write a note. Franz goes to the window of the hallway, tears off the white corner of a newspaper and writes with a small pencil: "Since you don't open, I want my stuff back, to be left at Klaussen's, corner Elsasser."

Say, you bitch, if you knew who I am, what one of 'em got from me once, you wouldn't. Well, we'll fix that. I ought to take a hatchet and smash the door open. Softly he slips the note under the door.

Franz remains sullen all the following day. Next morning, before his meeting with Lüders, the saloon-keeper gives him a letter. That's her. "Anything else left with it?" "No, what else?" "A package, with stuff in it?" "No, a boy brought this last night." "Well, I'll be darned, maybe I'm supposed to fetch the stuff myself."

Two minutes later Franz walks over to the show-window, sinks down onto a wooden footstool, holds the letter in his slack left hand, pinches his lips together, stares across the table-top. Poor little Lüders comes in, sees Franz, notices how he's sitting, there's something wrong with him, and off he goes.

The proprietor steps up to the table: "What's Lüders running away like that for, he hasn't got his stuff yet." Franz sits and sits. Did anybody ever see the like of it? My legs feel like they'd been hacked off. Did anybody ever see the like o' that? That never happened before. Can't get up. Let Lüders run, he's got legs, he can run. That's some fellow, unbelievable.

"Want a cognac, Biberkopf? Have you had a death in your family?" "No. No." What's he talking about, don't hear very well, cotton in my ears. The proprietor does not leave. "What's Lüders running away for? Nobody's goin' to hurt him. As if somebody was after him." "Lüders? Oh, he's probably got something to do. Yes, gimme a cognac." He pours it down, his thoughts become scattered again. The devil, that's funny about that letter. "Here, you dropped your envelope. Maybe you want to read the morning papers." "Thanks." He goes on brooding: Really I'd like to know what it's all about, this letter, writing things like that. Lüders is a sensible fellow, has got children. Franz puzzles how this could have happened till his head grows heavy and falls forward, as though he were asleep; the proprietor believes he is tired, but it's his pallor, space and emptiness, his legs slide from under him, he plops right into it and turns once to the left, now down, straight down.

Franz sprawls his chest and head over the table, he looks obliquely under his arm across the table-top, blows the dust off the table and holds his head: "Has Fatty Lina been here already?" "No, she never gets here till twelve." You're right, yes, it's only nine, haven't done anything yet, Lüders is gone, too.

What is a man to do? And then something surges through him, and he bites his mouth shut: That's the punishment, they let me out, the others are still peeling potatoes behind the prison by the big rubbish dump, and I have to take the street-car, damn it, it was pretty nice there after all. He rises, got to get out in the street, must get rid of this, only don't get scared, I'm standing straight on my legs, nobody's going to come near me, nobody. "When Fatty comes, tell her I have a death in my family. News of a death, uncle or something like that. I won't come at noon today, nope, she needn't wait for me. Well, how much?" "As usual." "Here you are." "And you'll leave the package here?" "Which package?" "Well, it certainly did hit you hard, Biberkopf. No nonsense now, hold onto yourself. I'll keep the package for you all right." "Which package?" "Well, you better go get some fresh air."

Biberkopf is outside. The proprietor watches him through the window-pane: "They'll probably bring him back right away. That's certainly queer. Such a strong man, too. Fatty sure will open her eyes wide."

A pale, small man stands in front of the house, he has his right arm in a bandage, his hand in a black leather glove. He's been standing there an hour in the sun and does not go upstairs. He has just left the hospital. He has two grown daughters, a boy came later, he was four years old, he died in the hospital yesterday. First it was only inflammation of the throat. The doctor said he'd be back right away, but he didn't come till night, and then he says at once: Hospital, possible diphtheria. The boy lies there four weeks, he was quite all right again, then he gets scarlet fever, too. And two days later, yesterday, he's gone, weak heart, the medical director said.

The man stands in front of the door of his house, upstairs his wife will cry and moan as she did yesterday and all night long and reproach him for not taking the boy out three days ago, he was certainly all right then. But the nurses said, he still has germs in his throat and when there are other children at home, a thing like that is dangerous. The woman did not want to believe it right away, but it is really possible, that something might have happened to the other children. There he stands. Children shout and play in front of the house next door. Suddenly he remembers that they asked him in the hospital when he took the child there, if it had received the serum injection. No, it had not. He had waited all day for the doctor to come, not till night, and then he said: Must be moved at once.

And right away the war veteran starts out on the trot, across the street, along the street, up to the corner, to the doctor, who they say is not at home. But he shouts, it is morning, the doctor must be at home. The door of the consulting-room opens. The bald-headed, corpulent gentleman looks at him, pulls him into his office. The man stands there talking about the hospital, the child is dead, the doctor presses his hand.

"But you let us wait all day Wednesday, from morning till six o'clock in the evening. We sent for you twice. You did not come." "But I did come in the end." Again the man starts shouting: "I am a cripple, we gave our blood at the front, and now they make us wait, anything is good enough for us." "Now just sit down, calm yourself, please. The child did not die of diphtheria. Such infections sometimes occur in hospitals." "Always trouble, always trouble," he keeps on shouting. "They keep us waiting, we're nothing better than coolies, our children can croak, the way we croaked."

Half an hour later he walks slowly down the stairs, takes a turn in the sun, goes upstairs. His wife is busy in the kitchen. "Well, Paul?" "Well, mother." They take each other's hands, they drop their heads. "You haven't eaten yet, Paul. I'll get something ready at once." "I went over to the doctor, told him he didn't come on Wednesday. I told him a thing or two." "But he didn't die of diphtheria, our little Paul." "Doesn't matter. That's what I told him. But if he had gotten a serum injection right away, he wouldn't have had to go to the hospital. Not at all. But he didn't come. I gave him a piece of my mind. One has to think of other people too when a thing like that happens again. That may happen every day, who knows?" "You'd better eat something now. What did the doctor say?" "He is a kind man. He's not a youngster any more, he's busy and has to hustle a lot. I know all that. But if something happens, it happens, that's all. He gave me a glass of cognac and told me to calm myself. And his wife came in, too." "I suppose you shouted a lot, Paul?" "No, not at all, only in the beginning, afterwards everything went quietly. He admitted it himself: someone had to tell him. He's not a bad sort, but somebody has got to tell him."

He trembles violently as he eats. The woman is crying in the next room, then they drink their coffee together by the stove. "Real coffee, Paul." He sniffs over his cup: "Can smell it."

And at Dawn the cool, cool Grave, but we'll manage to control our Feelings

Franz Biberkopf has disappeared. On the afternoon of the day when he got the letter, Lina goes to his room. She wants to leave a brown knitted sweater which she has made as a surprise for him. Just imagine, there he is, sitting at home, when he usually goes peddling every day, particularly now it's Christmas. He's sitting on his bed, beside his table, monkeying around with his alarm clock which he has just taken apart. At first she's frightened, because he's there and may have seen the sweater, but he hardly looks at her, only looks at the table and his clock. She finds that quite all right, and manages to hide the sweater by the door. But then he talks so little, what's the matter with him anyhow, he's got a hang-over and what a face he's making, I don't recognize him like that, and there he is monkeying around with the old alarm clock, he acts like he's off his bat. "The alarm clock was all right, Franz." "No, no, it wasn't all right, let me alone, it's always making a funny noise, it don't ring right, I'll find out why." And he goes on monkeying with it and leaves it lie around again and picks his teeth, he doesn't even look at her. She does a fade-out, she's feeling a bit anxious, he ought to take a good nap. And when she comes back in the evening, the man's gone. Paid up, packed his things, taken everything along and gone. The landlady knows only that he has paid up, and she is supposed to write on the police card: Traveling. Probably has to make himself scarce, what?

Then Lina passed twenty-four terrible hours, until finally she found Gottlieb Meck to help her. He, too, had moved, she ran around in the afternoon from saloon to saloon; finally she nabbed him. He knows nothing about it, what can have happened to Franz, the fellow has got muscles or hasn't he, and he's clever too, he can stay away a while if he wants to. Suppose he's in trouble for something or other? Out of the question with Franz. Maybe they had a row, Lina and Franz. But no, not at all, how could we, didn't I bring him a sweater? Next morning Meck goes to the landlady, Lina keeps after him. Yes, Biberkopf left helter-skelter like that, there was something wrong, he's always been in a good humor, and that morning, too, there must have been something in the wind, you can't convince me otherwise; he took everything along, he didn't leave a single one of his things, come and see. Meck then says to Lina, Lina must calm herself, he'll look into the matter. He reflects, and being an old peddler himself, he gets a hunch and goes to find Lüders. The latter is at home with his brats, where is Franz? Well, says he, obdurately, he gave me the slip, even left without paying what he owed me, Franz forgot to settle with me. But Meck doesn't believe that at all, they talk together for over an hour, can't get anything out of the man. In the evening, Meck and Lina find him in the café opposite. And then things come to a head.

Lina talks and howls. But he must know where Franz is, weren't they together in the morning, Franz certainly did say something, a single word. "No, he didn't say anything." "Something must 'a' happened to him." "To him? He probably had to skedaddle off, what else would he do?" No, he hasn't pulled anything funny, Lina won't listen to anything like that, he didn't do anything, she'd put her hand in the fire for that, maybe it would be best to go and ask the police. "You think maybe he's got lost and they ought to send out a general alarm for him?" Lüders laughed. The grief of that little fat thing! "What are we going to do, what on earth are we going to do?" Until Meck, who has been sitting there, thinking his bit, has enough of all this and gives Lüders a sign with his head. He'd like to talk with Lüders alone, this is no good. Whereupon Lüders goes outside. They walk along Ramlerstrasse up to Grenzstrasse, talking hypocritically the while.

And there in the pitch darkness Meck jumped unexpectedly upon little Lüders. He gave him a terrible thrashing. While Lüders was lying on the ground yelling, Meck took a handkerchief from his pocket and plunked it over his mouth. Then he let him get up and showed the little fellow his open knife. They were both out of breath. Then Meck advised Lüders, who had not yet come to, to beat it and to look for Franz tomorrow. "How you find him, bo, don't matter to me. If you don't find him, you'll see what you'll get. We'll find you all right. And your old woman, too, if we have to."

Pale and silent, little Lüders, at a wink from Meck stepped out of the café next evening and they went into the private room. It was some time before the proprietor lighted the gas. There they stood. Meck asked: "Well, didja go?" The other nodded. "You see? Well, and . . .?" "There ain't no And." "What did he say, how can you prove you were there?" "You think, Meck, he'd have to beat holes into my head like you did? No, I was ready for that." "Well, what about it now?"

Lüders came nearer: "Look out, Meck, listen to me. Just you listen to me: I want to tell you, if Franz is your friend, you needn't have talked to me like that yesterday on his account."

Meck stared at him, he'll soon get another biff in the jaw, and then they can all come in, as far as he's concerned. "No, why he's crazy! Didn't you ever notice it, Meck? There's something's wrong in his upper story." "No, now cut out that nonsense. He's my friend, say, for God's sake, my legs are shaking." Then Lüders starts telling his story, Meck sits down.

He had met Franz yesterday between five and six: he was lodging right near his old home, three houses beyond, he was seen to go in with his cardboard box and a pair of shoes in his hand, and then they led him in right upstairs to a room in the courtyard building. When Lüders knocks and goes in, Franz is lying on the bed, his feet with his shoes on hanging over the side. He recognizes Lüders, a light is burning overhead, that's Lüders, there he comes, the scoundrel, but what's the matter with him? Lüders keeps his hand on an open knife in his left pocket. In the other one he has money, a few marks, he puts them down on the table, talks about all sorts of things, turns round and round, his voice is hoarse, he shows the bumps on his head which Meck gave him, his swollen ears, he's about to bawl with anger and rage.

Biberkopf sits up, his face growing very hard at times, the little pouches of flesh in his face a-quiver. He points to the door and says softly: "Get out o' here." Lüders has put down his few marks, he is thinking of Meck and how they would be lying in wait for him, and asks for a note saying he was there, or if Meck could come up himself, or Lina. Then Biberkopf stands up and Lüders quickly slips towards the door, his hand on the latch. But Biberkopf edges away to the wash-stand, takes the basin and—whatcha think—with a single lunge he hurls the water across the room at Lüders' feet. Dust thou art, to dust returnest. Lüders opens his eyes, ducks to one side, presses the latch. Biberkopf takes hold of the water pitcher, there was still some water in it, we still have lots left, we're going to clean things up, dust thou art. He pours it over him at the door, it squirts against his throat and mouth, ice-cold water. Lüders slides out, he's gone, the door is shut.

In the café he whispers venomously: "He's crazy, don't you see, there you have it." Meck asked: "What number was it? Who does he live with?"

Afterwards Biberkopf threw load after load into the room. He splashed water with his hand through the air: Everything's gotta be clean, everything must go; now let's open the window and get some air, we got nothing to do with all that. (No houses collapsing, no sliding of roofs, all that's behind me. Once and for all. Behind me.) It began to grow cold as he stood by the window staring at the floor. Ought to wipe it off, it's dripping on their heads down there, it's making stains. He shut the window and lay down flat on the bed. (Dead. Dust thou art, to dust returnest.)

Our little hands go clap clap clap, our little feet go tap tap tap.

That evening Biberkopf no longer lived in that room. Meck could not find out where he had moved to. He took little Lüders, who was malignantly determined, into his café with the cattle dealers. They were to question Lüders about what had happened and what about that letter which the saloon-keeper had received. Lüders remained obstinate, he looked so spiteful, that they let the poor devil go. Meck said himself: "He's got his all right."

Meck ruminated: Franz, well, maybe Lina had deceived him, or he had got mad at Lüders, or something else. The cattle dealers said: "That fellow Lüders is a sharper, whatever he tells you there isn't a word of truth in it. Maybe Biberkopf is crazy. Remember when he had those notions about that permit, when he didn't even have any goods to sell. That's the way they act when their dander's up." Meck insisted: "That might affect your gall but not your bean. Bean's entirely out of the question. Why, he's an athlete, a day-laborer, he was a first-class furniture-mover, pianos and so on, a fellow like that wouldn't have any trouble with his head." "He's just the kind it does hit on the head. He's sensitive, that one. It's because his head works too little, and if it does work, off it goes." "Well, and what about you fellows and your law-suits? Everything going all right?" "A cattle dealer has a hard skull. Believe me. If they once start getting mad at things, they could all go to the Herzberge Asylum. We don't get mad at all. Ordering goods and then getting the slip or not getting paid, that happens to fellows like us every day. Folks simply never seem to have any money." "Or no ready cash." "That, too."

One of the cattle dealers looked at his dirty vest: "You know at home I drink coffee out of a saucer, tastes better, but it spills." "Ought to tie a napkin around you." "So my old woman could have a laugh. No, my hands get shaky, just look."

Meck and Lina can't find Franz Biberkopf. They run all around, through half of Berlin but they don't find him.

FOURTH BOOK

Franz Biberkopf has not really met with an accident. The ordinary reader will be astonished and ask: What happened then? But Franz Biberkopf is no ordinary reader. He feels that his principle, simple though it be, must be defective somewhere. He does not know where, but the feeling that this is so plunges him into uttermost gloom.

Here you are going to see our man boozing, almost giving himself up for lost. But it wasn't so bad after all, Franz Biberkopf is being spared for a harder fall.

A Handful of Men around the Alex

On the Alexanderplatz they are tearing up the road-bed for the subway. People walk on planks. The street-cars pass over the square up Alexanderstrasse through Münzstrasse to the Rosenthaler Tor. To the right and left are streets. House follows house along the streets. They are full of men and women from cellar to garret. On the ground floor are shops.

Liquor shops, restaurants, fruit and vegetable stores, groceries and delicatessen, moving business, painting and decorating, manufacture of ladies' wear, flour and mill materials, automobile garage, extinguisher company: The superiority of the small motor syringe lies in its simple construction, easy service, small weight, small size.—German fellow-citizens, never has a people been deceived more ignominiously, never has a nation been betrayed more ignominiously and more unjustly than the German people. Do you remember how Scheidemann promised us peace, liberty, and bread from the window of the Reichstag on November 9, 1918? And how has that promise been kept?—Drainage equipment, window-cleaning company, sleep is medicine, Steiner's Paradise Bed.—Book-shop, the library of the modern man, our collected works of leading poets and thinkers compose the library of the modern man. They are the great representatives of the intellectual life of Europe.—The Tenants' Protection Law is a scrap of paper. Rents increase steadily. The professional middle-class is being put on the street and strangled, the sheriff has a rich harvest. We demand public credits up to 15,000 marks for the small tradesman, immediate prohibition of all public auctions in the case of small tradesmen.—To face her hour of travail well prepared is the desire and duty of every woman. Every thought and feeling of the expectant mother revolves around the unborn. Therefore the selection of the right drink for the mother-to-be is of especial importance. Genuine Engelhardt Stout and Ale possess, above all other drinks, the qualities of palatability, nutritiousness, digestibility, tonic vigor.—Provide for your child and your family by contracting a life insurance with a Swiss life insurance company, Life Annuities Office, Zürich.—Your heart is light! Your heart is light with joy, if you possess a home equipped with the famous Höffner furniture. Everything you have dreamed of with regard to pleasant comfort is surpassed by an undreamed-of reality. Although the years may pass, it will always look well and its durability and practical wear will make you enjoy it continuously.—

The Private Protective Agencies watch everything, they walk around buildings and through buildings, they look into buildings, control clocks, Automatic Alarms, Watch and Safeguard Service for Greater Berlin and environs, Germania Protective Agency, Greater Berlin Protective Agency, and former Watch and Ward Division of the Café Proprietors' Association of the Society of Berlin House-Owners and Landlords, Associated Management, West Side Central Watchmen's Service, Watch and Protection Company, Sherlock Company, collected works on Sherlock Holmes by Conan Doyle, Watch and Protection Company for Berlin and adjacent towns, catch it in time, Watch on the Rhine, wash on the line, washing eliminated, Apollo Linen Renting Agency, Adler's Wet-Wash Service, handles all household and body linen, specialty of fine gents' and ladies' washing.

Above and in back of the shops, however, there are dwellings, behind which there are courtyards, side-wings, cross-buildings, out-houses, garden-houses. Linienstrasse, there is the house where Franz Biberkopf sneaked off after the trouble with Lüders.

In front there is a nice shoe-business with four brilliant show-windows, six girls serve the customers, that is, when there are any, they receive around 80 marks per head and nose, and at the most, after they become gray, they get 100. This nice big shoe-business belongs to an old woman, who married her business manager, and since that time sleeps in the back, and things are going badly for her. He is a dashing man, has made the shop flourish, but he is under forty and that's the trouble. When he comes home late, the old woman is still awake and unable to sleep for rage.—On the first floor, the gentleman of the law. Does the wild rabbit in the Duchy of Saxe-Altenburg fall under the heading of hunting-game? The defense contumaciously disputes the finding of the District Court that the wild rabbit in the Duchy of Saxe-Altenberg may be numbered among the game animals. The issue concerning which animals are subject to the Game Laws and which may be hunted without permit has been decided differently in Germany in the various provinces. In the absence of special rulings the law of custom decides it. In the bill for the game-control law of Feb. 24, '54, the wild rabbit had not yet been mentioned.—At six at night a charwoman begins her work in the office, sweeps, scrubs the linoleum in the reception-room. The lawyer hasn't enough money for a vacuum-cleaner, the stingy old thing, particularly as he is not even married, and Frau Zieske, who rants about being the houselady ought to know that. The charwoman scrubs and cleans with might and main, she is grotesquely thin, but supple, she slaves for her two children. The importance of fats for nutrition: fat covers the bone promontories and protects the underlying tissue against pressure and shocks, highly emaciated persons complain therefore of a pain in the sole while walking. But this is not the case with this charwoman.

At seven o'clock in the evening, Herr Löwenhund, Attorney at Law, is seated at his writing-desk, working by two lighted table-lamps. It so happens that the telephone is not busy. In the criminal case Gross A 8 780–27, I assume authority to act on behalf of the accused, Frau Gross, under the circumstances. I request that I may be authorized to enter into personal communication with the said accused.—To Frau Eugenie Gross, Berlin. Dear Frau Gross: It had been my intention for a long time to pay you another visit. Pressure of work and my indisposition have, however, made this impossible. I have every hope that I may be able to visit you next Wednesday and I beg you until then, to be patient. Faithfully yours. Letters, money-orders and parcel-post should bear the personal address as well as the prisoner's number. As destination give Berlin N.W. 52, Moabit 12a.

—To Herr Tollmann. In your daughter's affair, I feel obliged to ask for an additional fee, the sum of 200 marks, I leave you the choice of payment by installments. Secondly: resubmit.—My dear Attorney, as I desire to visit my unfortunate daughter in Moabit, but do not know to whom to apply, I ask you to be so kind as to arrange when I can go there. And also to arrange for me to send her a package of foodstuffs every fortnight. I await a reply by return mail, preferably at the end of this or the beginning of next week. Frau Tollmann (mother of Eugenie Gross).—Lawyer

Löwenhund gets up. With a cigar in his mouth he looks through the curtain slit down upon the lighted Linienstrasse and thinks, shall I telephone her or not? Venereal diseases, a deserved misfortune, Superior District Court, Frankfurt 1, C. 5. One may think less severely of the moral delinquency of sexual intercourse on the part of unmarried men and yet admit that in a legal sense an offense is incurred, that extra-conjugal sexual intercourse, as Staub says, is a dangerous excess, and that he who indulges in such excesses must bear their consequences. And Plank, too, following this decision, regards a sickness caused by extra-conjugal sexual intercourse in the case of a man liable to military service as a malady due to gross negligence.—He takes off the receiver, Neukölln Office, please, ah, the number is changed to Bärwald.

Second story: The manager and two stout couples, a brother with his wife and a sister with her husband, also a sick girl.

Third story: A man 64 years old, a furniture-polisher with a bald spot on his head. His daughter, a divorcee, keeps house for him. He crashes down the stairs every morning, his heart is bad, he will soon have himself put on the sick-list (*Coronarsclerosis, Nyodegeneratio cordis*). He was formerly a crack oarsman, what can he do now? Read papers in the evening, light his pipe, while the daughter, of course, stands gossiping in the hallway. His wife is not there, died at 45, she was alert and hot-blooded, could never get enough, you know what I mean, and so one day she went all to pieces, but said nothing; next year she probably would have had her change of life anyway, off she goes to one of them women, then to the hospital, and that's the last of her.

Next-door a turner, around thirty, he has a little boy, a room, and a kitchen; his wife, too, is dead, consumption, he also coughs, the boy is in a day-nursery during the day, at night the man fetches him. When the boy has gone to sleep, the man prepares his weak tea, potters till late at night with his radio, is foreman in the radio union, cannot fall asleep until his tinkering has succeeded.

Then a waiter with a woman, room and kitchen nicely arranged, gaschandelier with glass pendants. The waiter is at home all day till two, he sleeps till then, and plays the zither, while lawyer Löwenhund in a black gown dashes around the District Court 1, 2, 3, through the halls, from one lawyer's room to another, from one court to another, the case is postponed, I pray for a judgment for failure to appear against the defendant. The waiter's girl-friend is supervisor in a department store. So she says. This waiter, during his married life, was disgracefully deceived by his wife.

But she was always able to console him until he finally walked out. He was nothing more than a bed-fellow, always running back to the woman, and was nevertheless finally declared the guilty party in the divorce trial, because he couldn't prove anything and had shamefully deserted his wife. Then he got to know the present one in Hoppegarten, where she was out man-hunting. The same brand of woman as the first, only a bit cleverer. He doesn't notice anything when his girl-friend goes off every few days on a so-called business trip, since when does a supervisor have to travel, well, it's a confidential post. But now he is sitting on the sofa, with a wet towel on his head; he is crying and she has to wait on him. He slipped in the street and couldn't get up. So he says. Somebody had pushed him. She doesn't go to her so-called business. If he noticed anything it would be too bad, he's certainly a nice, sweet boob. We'll fix him up all right.

At the very top a tripe butcher, where of course there's a bad smell and also the howling of children and alcohol. Next-door a baker's apprentice with his wife, an employee in a printing-shop, she has inflammation of the ovaries. Wonder what those two get out of life? Well, first of all, they get each other, than last Sunday a vaudeville and a film, then this or that social meeting and a visit to his parents. Nothing else? Well now, don't drop dead, sir. Add to that nice weather, bad weather, country picnics, standing in front of the stove, eating breakfast and so on. And what more do you get, you, captain, general, jockey, whoever you are? Don't fool yourself.

Biberkopf in a Stupor. Franz sneaks off, Franz doesn't want to look at Anything

Franz Biberkopf, watch out, how's all this boozing going to end! Always lying around the dump, doing nothing but drinking and moping and moping!—

Whose business is it what I'm doing? If I want to mope, I'll mope in one spot till doomsday. He nibbles at his nails, groans, moves his head on the sweaty pillow, blows through his nose: I'll lie like this till doomsday, if I want to. If that woman would only heat the room a bit. She sure is lazy, thinks about nothing but herself.

He turns his head away from the wall, there's a mushy something on the floor, a puddle.—Puked. Must 'a' been me. The stuff a man carries around with him in his stomach. Phew! Spider webs in the gray corner, they can't catch any mice. I'd like a drink of water. Whose business is that? My spine hurts too. Just come in, Frau Schmidt. Between the spider webs up above (black dress, long teeth). Some slut that one (comes from the ceiling). Phew! A fool says to me, why do you stay at home? In the first place, says I, you fool, what right have you to ask me that, and in the second place, if I stay here from 8–12. And then in that stinking dump. He says he was joking. Nope, that's no joke. Kaufmann also said, he can ask him, then. Maybe I can arrange it, so in February, in February or March I could, March is right—

—Did you lose your heart in nature? That's not where I lost my heart. To be sure, it seemed to me as if the essence of the primal spirit was about to carry me away while I was standing opposite the alpine giants or lying on the beach by the roaring sea. Yes, something also bubbled and boiled in my bones. My heart was shaken, but I did not lose it, neither where the eagle nests, nor where the miner digs for the hidden ore-veins of the deeps.—

—Then where?

Did you lose your heart in sport? In the roaring stream of the youth movement? In the turmoil of political struggle?—

—I did not lose it there.—

—Didn't you lose it anywhere?

Do you belong to those who lose their heart nowhere, but keep it for themselves, to conserve it nicely and mummify it?—

The road to the supernatural world, public lectures. All Souls Day: Does Death really end everything? November 21, 8 p.m.: Can we still believe today? Tuesday, November 22: Can man change? Wednesday, November 23: Who is just before God? We call your special attention to the development of the Declamatorium, "St. Paul."

Sunday, quarter to eight.

Howdy, Preacher, why, my name's Franz Biberkopf, I'm a handy-man. Used to be a furniture-mover, now out of work. You see I wanted to ask you something. Why, what can a fellow do for stomach trouble? I've got that sour feeling. Ouch, there it is again. Phew! Poison gall. Of course, comes from drinking too much. If you please, beg pardon, for gassing at you like this right out in the street. It's interfering with your duties. But what on earth am I going to do for gall poison? One Christian man has got to help another. You're a good man. I won't get to heaven. Why? Just ask Frau Schmidt who always comes out of the ceiling up there. She comes and goes, and is always after me to get up. But nobody can tell me any-thing. If there are criminals though, then it's me who can talk about 'em. In honor true. We swore it to Karl Liebknecht, to Rosa Luxemburg we gave our hand. I'll go to Paradise when I'm dead, and they'll bow before me and say: That's Franz Biberkopf, in honor true, a true-blue German, a handy-man, in honor true, high waves the banner black-white-red, but he kept it for himself, he didn't become a criminal like the others, who want to be Germans and deceive their fellow-men. If I had a knife, I'd run it into his guts. Yes, I would. (Franz tosses about in bed, swings his arms in the air.) Now you want to run to the preacher, old kid. Little old kid, eh! Go ahead, if you like it, if you can still squawk! In honor true, I'll keep my hands off o' that, Preacher, yes, it's too good for that, scoundrels shouldn't even be in prison; I was in prison, I know it like a book, first-class affair, first-class merchandise, no use talking, scoundrels don't belong there, especially when they're like the one who's not even ashamed before his wife, which he ought to be, and before the whole world, as well.

2 times 2 is 4, no use talking.

Here you see a man, excuse me, you're a busy man. I've got such awful stomach trouble. I'll know how to get hold of myself. A glass of water, Frau Schmidt. The bitch has got to stick her nose into everything.

Franz in Retreat. Franz blows a Farewell March to the Jews

Franz Biberkopf, strong as a cobra, but shaky on his legs, got up and went to the Jews in Münzstrasse. He didn't go there directly, he took a round-about way to get there. The fellow wants to be done with everything. The fellow wants to get things straightened out. There we go again, Franz Biberkopf. Dry weather, cold, but crisp, who would want to stand in the hallway now, be a street-vender, and freeze his toes off? In honor true. Lucky a fellow's out of the room and can't hear the squealing of the dames any more. Here is Franz Biberkopf, he's walking along the street. All the bar-rooms empty. Why? The bums are still snoozing. The saloon-keepers can drink their manure-juice alone. Dividend juice. We're not jus' in the mood for it. We drink rum, by gum.

Franz Biberkopf quietly shoved his body in the gray-green army coat through the crowd and watched the little women buying vegetables, cheese, and herring from the push-carts. Somebody was hawking onions.

People do what they can. Have children at home, hungry mouths, bird beaks, clap open, clap shut, clap open, clap shut, shut, open, shut, open, shut.

Franz walked faster, stamped around the corner. That's it, fresh air. He slowed up in front of the big show-windows. What do shoes cost now? Patent-leather shoes, dance slippers, must look swell on the foot, how about a nice li'l girl, with dance slippers on. That dumbbell Lissarek, the Bohemian, the old fellow with the big nostrils out there in Tegel, got his wife, or whatever she pretended to be, to bring him a pair of nice silk socks every three weeks, a pair of new ones and a pair of old ones. Makes me giggle. And if she had to steal 'em, he was bound to have 'em. Once they caught him with the socks on his dirty legs, what a fool, and now he pipes his legs and gets all worked up looking at 'em, and his ears get all red, the fellow makes me giggle. Furniture on the installment plan. Kitchen furniture in twelve monthly installments.

Biberkopf continued walking in a happy mood. Only here and there was he obliged to look at the pavement. He examined his steps and the nice firm asphalt. But then his glance slipped with a jerk up the house-fronts, examined them, made sure they were standing still and did not stir, although really a house like that has lots of windows and could easily bend forward. That might get the roofs started, carry them along with it; they are liable to start rocking. They might begin to shake, to rock, to jolt. The roofs could slide down, obliquely like sand, like a hat falling down from a head. Why, they're all, yes, all of them, standing obliquely over the roof-tree, along the whole row. But they're nailed down fast, strong beams below and then the roofing, the tar. Firm stands and true, the watch, the watch on the Rhine. Good morning, Franz Biberkopf, here we are walking erect, chest out, back straight, old boy, along the Brunnenstrasse. God has mercy on all men, we are German citizens, just like the prison director said.

A man with a leather cap and a flabby white face scratched a little boil on his chin with his index-finger, his lower lip hanging out the while. Another man with a broad back and baggy pants-bottom stood leaning over beside him; they barricaded the way. Franz walked around them. The one with the leather cap poked into his right ear.

He noticed with satisfaction that people were quietly walking along the street, the drivers were unloading, the authorities were inspecting the houses, there comes a call like thunder's peal, well then, we can walk here, too. A poster kiosk at the corner, on yellow paper there stood in black Roman letters: "Have you lived on the beautiful Rhine." "The King of Football Centers." Five men stood in a little circle on the asphalt, swung hammers, split the asphalt, we know the one in the green woolen jacket, that's sure, he's working all right, we can do that, too, later on maybe, you hold it tight with your right hand, lift it up, grasp it; then bang, down with it. That's us, the working men, the proletariat. Right high, left swing, heave, right high, left swing, heave. Danger. Building site. Stralau Asphalt Company.

He was walking leisurely along the rattling trolley-line, look out, don't get off while the car is in motion! Wait till the car stops! The cop regulates the traffic, a letter-carrier wants to get across quickly. I'm not in a hurry, just want to go to the Jews. They'll still be there. What a lot of dirt you get on your shoes, but then they weren't shined anyhow, for who's going to shine 'em, that Schmidt woman perhaps, she doesn't do anything (spider webs on the ceiling, sour heartburn, he sucked his palate, turned his head towards the window-panes: Gargoyle Mobiloil Vulcanizing, Bobbed Hair Shop, Water Waves, against a blue background, Pixavon, refined tar product.) Wonder if stout Lina could shine his shoes? Now he had already acquired a speedier tempo.

That crook Lüders, the woman's letter, I'll box you a knife in the guts. OLORDOLORD, say, leave that alone, we'll take care of ourselves, you bums, we won't do anybody dirt, we've already done time in Tegel. Let's see: custom tailoring, gent's furnishings, that first, then in the second place, mounting rims on carriage wheels, automobile accessories, important, too, for quick riding, but not too fast.

Right foot, left foot, right foot, left foot, marching slowly in step, don't crowd, Miss. Careful! Cop and a crowd! What's that? Make haste and you get laced. Hoohoohoo, hoohoohoo, the roosters crow. Franz was happy, the faces all looked nicer.

Joyously he meditated on the street. A cold wind was blowing, mixed, according to the houses, with warm cellar smells, native and Southern fruits, gasoline. Asphalt doesn't smell in winter.

At the Jews' Franz sat on the sofa for a whole hour. They talked, he talked, he was wondering, they were wondering, a whole long hour. What was he wondering about, sitting on the sofa, while they were talking and he was talking? That he was sitting here and talking and they were talking, and above all he was wondering at himself. Why was he wondering at himself? He knew and noticed it himself, he established it as an accountant does a miscalculation. He established something in his mind.

It was decided, he was wondering at the decision which he had arrived at. This decision said, while he looked into their faces, smiled, questioned, answered: Franz Biberkopf, they may say what they please, they've got the preacher's outfit, but they're not preachers, it's a caftan; they're from Galicia, near Lemberg, they're clever, but they can't tell me anything. I'm sitting here on the sofa and I won't do business with 'em. I've already done what I can.

The last time he had been here he had sat with one of them on the carpet below. Git, skidoo, I'd like to try it. But not today, that's all over. We sit here nailed on our bottoms and look at the ole Jews.

Man can't give any more, he's not a machine. The eleventh commandment says: Don't let 'em bluff you. A nice place, these guys have, simple, in bad taste, and no show. They won't knock Franz flat with that. Franz can hold his own. That's over with. To bed, to bed, if you've got one, or if you haven't, you must all go to bed, to bed. We won't work any longer. The old boy's gone on a strike. When the pump gets stuck in the sand you can work on the old thing as much as you want. Franz gets a retiring allowance without pension. How's that, he thought maliciously, and looked down the edge of the sofa. Retiring allowance without pension.

"And when a man has the strength you have, a strong fellow like you, he should thank his Creator. What can happen to him? Does he have to drink? If he isn't doing one thing, he's doing another. Goes to the public market, stands in front of the shops, stands around the railroad station: what do you think one of those fellows took from me the other day when I came back from Landsberg, I was away one day, and what do you thind he took from me? Just guess, Nachum, a man as big as that door, a Goliath, God save me. Fifty pfennigs. Yes sir, fifty pfennigs, I'm telling you, fifty pfennigs. For a small trunk from here to that corner. I didn't want to carry it myself, it was Shabbes. To think that fellow took fifty pfennigs from me. But I gave him a look. Well, you could also— I know something for you. Isn't there something open at Feitel's, the grain dealer's, say, you know Feitel, don't you?" "Not Feitel, his brother." "Well, he carries grains, too. Who is his brother?" "Feitel's brother, told you." "Do I know everybody in Berlin?" "Feitel's brother. A man with an income that's . . ." He shook his head in despairing admiration. The red-haired man raised his arm, ducked his head. "You don't say so? And from Czernowitz." They had forgotten all about Franz. They both were thinking intensely about the wealth of Feitel's brother. The red-haired man walked around in great excitement, then gave a snort. The other one purred, streamed delight, smiled sardonically behind him and clicked with his nails: "Yep." "Great. You don't say so!" "Everything that family touches is gold. Gold is not the word. GOLD." The red-haired fellow wandered around, then sat down by the window, deeply moved. What he saw going on outside filled him with contempt, two men in their shirt-sleeves were washing a car, an old car. One of them had his suspenders hanging down, they dragged along two pails of water, the courtyard was streaming with water. With a meditative look, dreaming of gold, he contemplated Franz: "What do you think of that?" What can he say, he's a poor, half-crazy fellow, what does a poor devil like that understand about Feitel's money in Czernowitz? He wouldn't let that one clean his shoes. Franz answered his look. Good morning, Preacher, the trolleys keep on tinkling along, but we know what that means, a man can give only so much. They're not working any more, and even if all the snow melts, we won't lift a finger, we'll make ourselves scarce.

The serpent had rustled down from the tree. Thou art cursed above all cattle, upon thy belly shalt thou go and dust shalt thou eat all the days of thy life. And I will put enmity between thee and the woman. In sorrow thou shalt bring forth children, Eve. Adam, cursed is the ground for thy sake, thorns also and thistles shall it bring forth to thee, and thou shalt eat the herb of the field.

We won't work any more, no use, and even if all the snow melts, we won't lift a finger.

It was the iron crowbar which Franz Biberkopf held in his hands, with which he sat and went through the door later on. His mouth said something or other. Hesitatingly he had sneaked in, he had been discharged from Tegel prison a few months before, he had been riding in the trolley, sh-sh-sh-along the streets, past the houses, the roofs slipping by, he had eaten with the Jews. He got up, let's move on, I went to see Minna that time, what's keeping me here, let's go see Minna, let's look at everything accurately and just the way it was.

Off he went. He trailed up and down in front of Minna's house. Li'l Mary sat upon a stone, all alone, on a stone. What do I care about her? He snooped around the house. Let her be happy with her old man. Sauerkraut with beets, they drove me away, if mother had only cooked meats, I would have stayed all day. The cats here don't stink any different from other places. Li'l rabbit beat it, yes, like the sausage in the press. Am I going to stand around here with the blues looking at the house. And the whole bunch hollering cock-a-doodle-doo.

Cock-a-doodle-doo. Cock-a-doodle-doo. Thus spake Menelaus. And, without meaning to, he made Telemachus's heart so sad that the tears rolled down his cheeks, so that he had to draw his purple mantle with both hands firmly before his eyes.

In the meanwhile Princess Helen strolled from out the women's apartments, like unto a goddess in beauty.

Cock-a-doodle-doo. There are many kinds of chickens. But if anyone asks me, on my honor and conscience, which I like best, I answer freely and frankly: Broiled chickens. Pheasants also belong to the gallinaceous birds, and in Brehms's Animal Life it says: The little dwarf moor-hen differs from the little prairie-hen, apart from its smaller size, through the fact that both sexes in spring wear an almost identical coat. Explorers in Asia know also the monial or monal, which is called by the scientists glossy pheasant. It is difficult to give a description of the splendor of its coloring. One hears it call, a long plaintive note, in the woods at all hours of the day, most frequently before daybreak and toward evening.

But all this takes place very far away, between Sikkam and Bhutan in India, and is a rather sterile bit of library knowledge for Berlin.

For it happens alike with Man and Beast; as the Beast dies, so Man dies, too

The slaughter-house in Berlin. In the northeast part of the city, from Eldenaer Strasse across Thaerstrasse across Landsberger Allee as far as Cotheniusstrasse along the Belt Line Railway, run the houses, halls, and stables of the slaughter- and stock-yards.

They cover an expanse of 47.88 hectares, equal to 118.31 acres. Not counting the structures behind Lands-berger Allee, 27,083,492 marks were sunk into this construction, of which sum the cattle-yards cost 7,682,844 marks, and the slaughter-house 19,410,648 marks.

The cattle-yard, slaughter-house, and wholesale meat-market form an inseparable economic whole. The administrative body is the municipal committee for stock-yards and slaughter-houses, and consists of two members of the city administration, a member of the district office, 11 councillors and three citizen-deputies. There are 258 employees in the organization: among them are veterinaries, inspectors, branders, assistant veterinaries, assistant inspectors, permanent employees and laborers.

Traffic ordinance of October 4, 1900: General Regulations governing the cattle-driving, delivery of fodder, scale of fees, market fees, boxing fees, slaughter fees, fees for the removal of fodder-troughs from the pork-market hall.

Along Eldenaer Strasse run the dirty-gray walls topped with barbed wire. The trees outside are bare, it is winter, the trees have sent their sap into the roots, to wait for spring. Slaughter wagons roll up at a smart gallop, with yellow and red wheels, prancing horses in front. A skinny horse runs along behind a wagon, from the sidewalk somebody calls "Emil," they bargain about the old nag, 50 marks and a round for the eight of us, the horse turns, trembles, nibbles at a tree, the driver tears it away, 50 marks and a round, Otto, otherwise we'll let it drop. The man on the sidewalk slaps the horse: All right!

Yellow administration headquarters, an obelisk for the war dead. And to the right and left longish halls with glass roofs, these are stables and waiting-rooms. Outside black signboards: property of the Berlin Union of Wholesale Butchers, Incorporated. No bill posting without proper authority. The Board of Directors.

In the long halls there are doors, black openings through which the animals are driven, numbered 26, 27, 28. The cattle-hall, the pork-room, the slaughter-rooms: death tribunals for the animals, swinging hatchets, you won't get out of here alive. Peaceful streets nearby, Strassmann-strasse, Liebigstrasse, Proskauer, Public Gardens in which people are strolling about. They dwell snugly side by side, the doctor comes running when one of them gets sick and has a sore throat.

But on the other side, the tracks of the Belt Line Railway stretch over a distance of 10 miles. Live-stock comes rolling up from the provinces, specimens of the genus sheep, hog, ox, from East Prussia, Pomerania, Brandenburg, West Prussia. They bleat and low over the railings of their pens. The hogs grunt and sniff the ground, they can't see where they're going, the drivers follow them with sticks. They lie down in the stables, white and fat, side by side, snorting and sleeping. They have been driven a long time, then well shaken up in the cars; now there's nothing vibrating beneath them, only the flagstones are cold. They wake up and huddle close together. They lie piled one on top of the other. Two of them are fighting, there is room in the pen, they butt their heads together, snap at each other's necks and ears, turn around in a circle, snort, then at times become quite still, just biting each other. One of them grows afraid and climbs over the bodies of the others, its adversary climbs after it, gives a snarl, and while those underneath grub themselves up again, the two plump down, looking for each other.

A man in a linen smock ambles through the corridor, the pen opens, he steps in between the animals with a stick; then, once the door is open, they rush out, squealing, grunting, and screaming. They crowd along the corridors. Across the courtyards, between the halls, he drives them up, those funny bare creatures with their jolly fat hams, their jolly little tails, and the green and red stripes on their backs. Here you have light, dear little pigs, and here you have dirt, just give a sniff, go ahead and grub a while, for how many minutes longer will it be? No, you are right, one should not work by the clock, just go on sniffing and grubbing. You are going to be slaughtered, there you are, take a look at the slaughter-house, at the hog slaughter-house. There exist old houses, but you get a new model. It is bright, built of red brick, from the outside you might take it for a locksmith's workshop, for a machine-shop, an office-room, or a drafting-room. I am going to walk the other way, dear little pigs, for I'm a human being, I'll go through this door, we'll meet again, inside.

A push against the door, it rebounds, swings to and fro. Whew, what a lot of steam! What are they steaming? It's like a bath, all that steam, the hogs are taking a Turkish bath, perhaps. You can't see where you're walking. Your glasses are covered with vapor, you could go naked, sweat out your rheumatism, cognac alone won't do, the slippers go clattering about. Nothing can be seen, the steam is too thick. But a continuous noise of squealing, snorting, clattering, men's voices calling back and forth, tools being dropped, slamming of lids. Somewhere around here are the hogs, they came in from across the way, from the door at the side. This thick white steam! Here they are, the hogs, some of them are hanging up, already dead, they've been cut up, almost ripe for guzzling. A man with a hose is squirting water on the white halves of the hogs. They are hanging on iron posts, head downward: some of the hogs are still whole, their legs are locked in a cross-beam above, a dead animal can't do anything at all, nor can it run. Pigs' feet, hacked off, lie in a pile. Two men arrive out of the fog carrying something, an animal on an iron bar, gutted and slit open. They lift the bar up and put it through the rings. Many of its comrades are dangling there, staring at the flagstones.

You walk through the room in a fog. The flagstones are grooved, damp, covered with blood. Between the posts are rows of white eviscerated animals. Behind there must be the slaughter-pens, there is a sound of smacking, clattering, squealing, screaming, rattling, grunting. Steaming boilers and vats send vapor into the room. The dead animals are dipped in the boiling water, then scalded and taken out very white, a man scrapes off the epidermis with a knife, the animal grows whiter still, becomes quite smooth. Quite soft and white, relaxed as though after a tiring bath, after a successful operation or a massage, the hogs lie in rows, on benches or planks, they lie quite still in their replete tranquillity, in their new white shirts. They all lie on their sides, on some of them can be seen a double row of teats, a sow has many breasts, they must be fertile animals. But they all have a straight red slit at their throats right down the middle, that's very suspicious.

The cracking sound starts up again, a door is opened in back, the vapor vanishes, they drive in a new lot of hogs, there you run while I walk in front through the sliding door, funny rosy creatures, jolly hams, jolly little curly tails, backs with motley colored stripes. And they sniff in the new pen. It's cold as the old one, but there is still something wet on the floor, something unknown, a red lubricity. They sniff at it with their snouts.

A pallid young man with slick blond hair has a cigar in his mouth. Look here, that's the last man who will occupy himself with you. Don't think ill of him, he is doing his official duty. He has to settle an administrative matter with you. He is dressed only in his boots, trousers, shirt and suspenders, the boots come up over his knees. That's his official garb. He takes his cigar out of his mouth, lays it on a shelf on the wall, takes a long hatchet from out the corner. It is the sign of his official dignity, of his rank over you, like the brass badge of a detective. He'll soon flash it at you. The young man takes a long wooden pole, lifts it up to the height of his shoulders over the squeaking little pigs which are rooting, sniffing and grunting undisturbed down below. The man walks around, looking down, searching, searching. The problem at stake is an inquiry against John Doe, John Doe in the case of X *vs.* Y.—Bing, one of them has run in front of his feet, bing, another one. The man is quick, he has given an account of himself, the hatchet has whizzed down, plunged into the lot of them with its blunt side, first on one head, then on another. That was a great moment! Kicking, writhing. Flinging from side to side. No longer conscious. Just lying there. What are those legs and heads doing? But the pig isn't doing that, it's the legs that do it, on their own, you might say. And already two men have begun to look across from the scalding room; it's time for them now, they lift a slide onto the killing-pen, drag out the animal, they sharpen their long knives on the stone and kneel down, slash, slash, they thrust them into the throat, zzing, a long slit, a very long slit in the throat, the animal is opened up like a bag, deep, plunging cuts, the animal twitches, kicks, thrashes about, it is unconscious, no more than unconscious now, more's to come, it squeals, and now for the opening of the veins in the throat. It is profoundly unconscious, we have stepped into metaphysics, into theology, my child, you no longer walk on earth, we're wandering now on the clouds. Hurry up with the pan now, the black warm blood streams into it, foams and bubbles in the pan, stir it quickly. The blood coagulates in the body, forms clots and stops up wounds. Now it has left the body, and it still wants to coagulate. Like a child that keeps on crying Mama, Mama, when it lies on the operating table, but there is no question of Mama, and Mama does not come, but it's suffocating under the mask with the ether, it goes on crying till it can cry no longer: Mama. Zzing, zzing, the veins, right and left. Stir it quickly. That's it. Now the twitching stops. Now you are still. We are through with physiology and theology, physics begins.

The man who was kneeling gets up. His knees hurt him. The pig has to be scalded, gutted, then hacked up; this is done step by step. The boss, looking well-fed, wanders up and down through the steam, puffing at his pipe, glancing from time to time at an open belly. On the wall next to the swinging door hangs a poster: Annual Ball, First Section of Live-Stock Shippers, Saalbau, Friedrichshain, Kermbach Orchestra. Outside are posters announcing boxing matches. Germania Halls, Chausseestrasse 110, Entrance from 1.50 to 10 marks, 4 Qualification Matches.

Supply at the cattle-market: 1399 steers, 2700 calves, 4654 sheep, 18,864 hogs. Market conditions: prime steers firm, otherwise quiet. Calves firm, sheep quiet, hogs opening firm, closing weak, overweights lagging.

The wind blows through the driveway, it is raining. The cattle bleat as several men drive a big, roaring, horned herd into the place. The animals close in on each other, they stop in their tracks, then run in the wrong direction while the drivers chase them with sticks. A bull jumps up on a cow in the middle of the bunch, the cow runs right and left, the bull is after her, hugely he rises up on her again and again.

A big, white steer is driven into the slaughter-hall. Here there is no vapor, no pen like they have for the swarming pigs. The big strong animal, the steer, steps in alone, between its drivers through the gate. The blood-bespattered hall lies open before it with the chopped-up bones, and the halves and quarters hanging about. The big steer has a broad forehead.

With sticks and thrusts it is driven up to the butcher. In order to make it stand still, he gives it a slight blow on the hind leg with the flat part of the hatchet. One of the drivers seizes it from below around the neck. The animal stands for a moment, then yields, with a curious ease, as if it agreed and was willing, after having seen everything and understood that this is its fate, and that it cannot do anything against it. Perhaps it thinks the gesture of the driver is a caress, it looks so friendly. The animal follows the tug of the driver's arms, turns its head obliquely to one side, mouth upward.

But then the butcher stands behind it with his hammer uplifted. Don't look around! The hammer lifted by the strong man with both his fists is behind you, above you, and then: zoom, down it comes! The muscular force of a strong man like an iron wedge in its neck! And a second later—the hammer has not yet been lifted—the animal's four legs give a spring, the whole heavy body seems to fly up with a jerk. And then as though it had no legs, the beast, the heavy body, falls down on the floor with a thud, onto its rigidly cramped legs, lies like this for a moment, drops on its side. The executioner walks around the animal from left to right, cracks it over the head, and on the temples, with another mercifully stunning blow: you will not wake up again. Then the other man beside him removes the cigar from his mouth, blows his nose, sharpens his knife, it is half as long as a sword, and kneels behind the animal's head; its legs have already stopped their convulsive movements. With short twitching jerks it tosses the hind part of its body back and forth. The butcher searches for something on the floor and before using the knife, he calls for the basin to catch the blood. The blood is still circulating quietly inside, little disturbed, under the impulses of a mighty heart. To be sure, the spine is crushed, but the blood still flows quietly through the veins. The lungs breathe, the intestines move. Now he applies the knife, the blood will gush out, I can see it now, in a stream as thick as your arm, black, beautiful, jubilating blood. Then the whole merry party will leave the house, the guests will dance out into the open, a tumult, and gone are the happy pastures, the warm stable, the fragrant fodder, everything gone, blown away, an empty hole, darkness, a new cosmos emerges! Haha! Suddenly we see a gentleman who has bought the house, new streets being laid out, better business conditions, going to tear down everything. They bring the big basin, shove it up to him, the huge animal throws its hind legs in the air. The knife is thrust into its neck near the gullet, look carefully for the veins, they are covered with a tough skin, well safeguarded. And now it's open, another one too, it spurts forth, hot steaming blackness, black red, the blood bubbles out over the knife, over the butcher's arm, jubilant blood, hot blood, the guests are coming, the transformation act proceeds, from the sun came your blood, the sun hid in your body, now it surges forth again. The animal breathes with huge efforts, it amounts to suffocation, a huge irritation, it snorts and rattles. Yes, the beams are cracking. The flanks heave so fearfully that one of the men helps the beast. If you want a stone to fall, give it a push. A man jumps on top of the animal, on its body, with both legs, he stands up there, bouncing, steps on the entrails, bobs up and down, the blood should come out more quickly, all of it. And the snorting grows louder, it is a long drawn-out panting, panting away, with light defensive blows of the hind legs. The legs quiver gently. Life is going out with a snort, the breathing begins to die down. The hind quarters turn over heavily. That's the earth, that's gravity. The man bobs upward. The other man underneath is already preparing to turn back the hide of the neck.

Happy pastures, damp warm stable.

The well-lighted butcher shop. The lighting of the store and that of the show-window should be made to harmonize. Predominantly direct or semi-indirect lighting should be used. In general, fixtures for predominantly direct lighting are practical, because store, desk, and chopping-block, above all, should be well lighted. Artificial daylight obtained by the use of blue-filter lamps, cannot be considered for butcher shops, because meat always demands lighting under which the natural meat color does not suffer.

Stuffed pig's feet. After the feet have been well cleaned, they are split lengthways, so that the rind remains whole; then they are laid together and tied with a thread.

—Franz, for two weeks you haven't stirred out of your wretched room. Your landlady is soon going to give you the air. You can't pay her, the woman doesn't rent rooms for the fun of it. If you don't pull yourself together soon, you'll have to go to the poor-house. And then what: well, what? You don't let any air into your hole, you won't go to the barber, you're getting a full brown beard, you certainly could dig up the necessary 15 pfennigs from somewhere.

Conversation with Job, it's up to you, Job, you don't want it

After Job had lost everything, everything men can lose, neither more nor less, he was lying one day in the cabbage garden.

"Job, you are lying in the cabbage garden, by the dog-kennel, just far enough away so that the watchdog cannot bite you. You hear the gnashing of its teeth. The dog barks at every approaching step. When you turn around, when you want to rise up, it growls, lunges forward, tears at its chains, jumps up, slavers and snaps.

"Job, there is the palace, and these are the gardens and the fields you yourself once possessed. You did not even know this watchdog, this cabbage garden, into which you have been thrown; you did not even know them, nor did you know the goats which are driven past you in the morning and which pull at the grass as they pass by and chew on it and stuff their cheeks full. They belonged to you.

"Job, you have lost everything. You are allowed to creep into the barn at night. People are afraid of your sore boils. You rode in splendor over your estate and they crowded about you. Now you have a wooden fence in front of your nose, with little snails creeping up on it. You may also study the earthworms. They are the only creatures which are not afraid of you.

"Only at times do you open your scale-covered eyes, O heap of misfortune, O living morass, that you are.

"What tortures you most, Job? That you have lost your sons and daughters, that you do not possess anything, that you freeze in the night, your sore boils in your mouth, or on your nose? Which is it, Job?"

"Who is asking?"

"I am only a voice."

"A voice comes out of a throat."

"You think I must be a human being?"

"Yes, and that's why I do not want to see you. Go away."

"I am only a voice, Job, open your eyes, as wide as you can, you will not see me."

"Ah, I am raving. My head, my brain, I am now being driven crazy, too, now even my thoughts are to be taken from me."

"And if this happens, will it matter?"

"I don't want it to happen."

"Although you suffer so, and although you suffer so through your thoughts, you don't want to lose them?"

"Don't ask questions, go away."

"But I shan't take them away from you. I only want to know what tortures you most."

"That's nobody's business."

"Nobody's but your own?"

"Yes. Yes. Not yours."

The dog barks, snarls, bites. The voice comes back after a while.

"Is it for your sons you lament?"

"Nobody need pray for me when I am dead. I am poison for the earth. Men must spit after me. Job must be forgotten."

"For your daughters?"

"The daughters, ah. They are also dead. They are well off now. They were wonderful women. They would have given me grandchildren, and now they have been carried off. One after the other they fell, as if God had taken them by their hair, lifted them up, and thrown them down so that they broke in two."

"Job, you are unable to open your eyes, they are glued together, they are glued together. You lament because you are lying in the cabbage garden, and the dog-kennel is the last thing left to you, and your illness."

"That voice, O voice, whose voice are you, and where are you hiding?"

"I don't know the cause of your lamentation."

"Oh, oh."

"You groan and you don't know it either, Job."

"No. I have—"

"I have?"

"I have no strength. That's it."

"That's what you would like to have."

"No more strength to hope, no desire. I have no teeth. I am soft. I am ashamed of myself."

"That's what you said."

"And it is true."

"Yes, you know it. That's the most terrible thing about it."

"So it is already written on my brow. To such tatters have I fallen."

"That's it, Job, that's what you suffer from most. You do not like to be weak, you would like to be able to resist, or rather be full of holes, your brain gone, your thoughts gone, and then become like a beast of the field. Make a wish."

"You have asked me so many questions, O voice, now I believe you may question me. Heal me, if you can. Whether you be Satan or God, angel or man, heal me."

"So you are ready to be healed by anybody?"

"Heal me."

"Job, think it over carefully, you cannot see me. If you open your eyes, perhaps you will be frightened by me. Perhaps I demand a high and terrible price."

"We shall see everything. You talk as though you were in earnest."

"But suppose I should be Satan or the Evil One?"

"Heal me."

"I am Satan."

"Heal me."

Then the voice retreated, grew weaker and weaker. The dog barked. Anxiously Job listened: He is gone, I must be healed, or else I must die. He screamed. A ghastly night fell. The voice came back once more.

"And suppose I am Satan, how are you going to dispose of me?"

Job screamed: "You don't want to heal me. Nobody wants to help me, neither God, nor Satan, nor angel, nor man."

"And you yourself?"

"What of me?"

"But you don't want it."

"What?"

"Who can help you, if you yourself don't want it?"

"No, no," Job stammered.

The voice facing him: "God and Satan, angels and men, all want to help you, but you don't want it. God, for love, Satan, in order to seize you later, the angels and men, because they are the helpmeets of God and Satan, but you don't want it."

"No, no," Job stammered, and shouted, and threw himself about. He screamed the whole night long. The voice called incessantly: "God and Satan, the angels and men, want to help you, you don't want it." Job incessantly: "No, no." He sought to choke the voice, it grew in intensity, grew still more in intensity, it was always ahead of him one degree. All night long. Towards morning Job fell on his face. In silence lay Job.

That day his first sores began to heal.

And they all have the same Breath, and Men have no more than Beasts

Cattle-market supply: Hogs 11,543, Beef 2016, Calves 1920, Mutton 4450.

But what is this man doing with the cute little calf? He leads it in alone by a rope; this is a huge hall in which the bulls roar; now he takes the little animal to a bench. There are many benches side by side, next to each one there is a wooden club. He lifts the delicate little calf with both arms, puts it on the bench, it does not protest as he lays it down. Then he grasps the animal from underneath, takes hold of one hind leg with his left hand so it can't kick. Now he grabs the rope with which he led the animal in, and ties it firmly to the wall. The animal is patient and still, there it lies, it does not know what is going to happen, it is lying uncomfortably on the wood, it bumps its head against a stick and does not know what it is: but it is the end of the club which is standing on the ground and with which it will soon receive a blow. That will be its last encounter with this world. And sure enough, the man, the simple old man, who stands there all alone, a gentle old man with a soft voice—he talks to the animal—takes the butt-end, lifts it lightly, it does not require very much strength for such a delicate creature, and gives the gentle animal a blow in the neck. Quite calmly, in the same way in which he had brought the animal here and said: Now lie still, he gives it a blow in the neck, without anger, without great excitement, but also without melancholy, no, that's the way it is, you're a good animal, you know, of course, that's the way it has to be.

And the little calf: prr-prr, quite, quite stiff and rigid, its little legs stretched out. The black velvet eyes of the little calf grow suddenly very big, stand still, are edged with white, now they turn towards the side. The man knows all about that, well, that's the way animals look, but we still have lots to do today, we must be getting on, and he looks under the little calf on the bench, his knife is lying there, with his foot he pushes the receptacle for the blood into place. Then zzing, the knife is drawn straight across the neck, through the throat, through all the cartilage, the air escapes, the muscles are slashed sidewise, the head is entirely severed, then clatters downward towards the bench. The blood spurts, a dark, red, thick, bubbling liquid. Well, that's over with. But he keeps on cutting calmly and more deeply, his peaceful expression unchanged, he seeks and gropes in the depths with his knife, pushes through between two vertebræ, it is a very young, soft tissue. Then he takes his hand off the animal, the knife clatters down onto the bench. He washes his hands in a pail and goes off.

And now the animal lies alone, wretchedly, on its side, just the way he tied it. All over the hall there is gay noise, people are working, dragging things around, calling to each other. The severed head hangs frighteningly by the hide, between the two table-legs, running over with blood and saliva. The tongue, thick-blue, is squeezed between the teeth. And terribly, terribly, the animal rattles and groans on the bench. The head quivers on the hide. The body on the bench becomes convulsive. The legs palpitate, jerk; childishly thin, knotty legs. But the eyes are quite fixed, blind. They are dead eyes. This is a dead animal.

The peaceful old man stands by a pillar with his little black notebook, looks across at the bench, and writes down figures. Living's expensive these days, difficult to calculate, hard to keep going, what with all the competition.

Franz's Window is open, funny Things, too, happen in the World

The sun rises and sets, there come bright days, the baby-carriages roll along the street, it is February 1928.

Franz Biberkopf, with his loathing of the world and his disgust, boozes right into February. He spends everything he has on drink, doesn't care what's going to happen. He had wanted to be respectable, but there are rascals and skinflints and four-flushers in the world, and so Franz Biberkopf no longer wants to see and hear anything of the world, and even if he should get to be a real bum, he is going to booze until he's spent his last pfennig.

February finds Franz Biberkopf still raging, and then one night he is awakened by a noise in the courtyard. In the back there is a wholesale house. He looks down in his woozy condition, opens the window, and shouts across the courtyard: "Get the hell away from there, you saps, you jackasses!" Then he lies down, thinks no more about it, the fellows back there have left in a flash.

A week later, the same thing happens. Franz is about to pull the window open and throw down a chunk of wood, when he remembers: it's one o'clock now, he'll take a good look at those boys. What on earth are those birds doing there at one in the morning? What are they up to, do they really belong in the house, let's have a peep at this!

Yes, that's it; there is a lot of cautious hustling back and forth going on down there, they glide along the wall, up above Franz is craning his neck. One man is standing at the courtyard door, he's the look-out, they're getting ready to pull off a job, they're tinkering with the big cellar door. Three of them are at it. Funny, they're not afraid of being seen. Now there's a creaking sound, the door's open, they've swung it, all right, one of them stays in the courtyard, in the doorway; the other two have gone down in the cellar. It's mighty dark here, that's what they wanted.

Franz gently shuts his window. The air has cooled his head off. That's the kind of thing people do, all day long and even at night, that's the way they go about their crooked business, I ought to take a flower-pot and lam it down into the courtyard. What business have they got in the house I live in? None at all.

Everything is quiet, he sits down on his bed in the darkness, then he has to go back to the window and look down: what are those fellows after in my house, anyway? He lights a candle, looks for the brandy bottle, and, when he finds it, does not drink. One ball wing'd by death came flying, is it sent for me or thee?

But when noon comes around, Franz goes down into the courtyard. A lot of people are standing around. Gerner, the carpenter, is also there, Franz knows him, they talk together: "They've been hooking something again." Franz nudges him: "I saw the rats, I won't give 'em away, but if they come again to this courtyard where I'm living and sleeping and where they got no business, I'll come down and as sure as my name's Biberkopf they'll have to pick up the pieces, even if they're three of 'em." The carpenter clings to Franz: "If you know anything, there are some detectives here, go ahead and talk to 'em, you might earn something." "Leave me alone with those fellows. I ain't never squealed on anybody. Let 'em do their own work, ain't they paid for it?"

Franz beats it. While Gerner is still standing there two detectives come up to him and insist on knowing where Gerner lives, that is to say, himself. I'm scared stiff. The man turns pale down to his corns. Then he says: "Let's see, Gerner, he's the carpenter, ain't he, I can show you." And says not a word, rings his own door-bell, the wife opens the door, the whole bunch piles in after him. Finally Gerner pushes his way through, gives his wife a shove in the ribs, a finger on his lips, she doesn't know what's the matter, he mixes in with the others, his hands in his trousers pockets. There are two other men in the party, gentlemen from the insurance company, they take a good look at his home. They want to know how thick the walls are here and how about the floor, they knock on the walls and measure and take notes. As a matter of fact, it's getting to be a bit thick, these burglaries in this wholesale house, these crooks have some nerve, they tried to break through the wall, because there's a bell system by the door and on the stairs, they knew that all right. Yes, the walls are dreadfully thin, the whole structure is ramshackle, a kind of magnified Easter egg.

They march back to the courtyard, Gerner, playing the dumbbell, sticks by them. Now they study the two new iron doors in the cellar, Gerner standing nearby. And then, as chance would have it, he steps back a pace, he wants to make room for somebody, but, chance would have it, he steps on something, something overturns, and as he makes a quick grab for it, it turns out to be a bottle, but it happens to have fallen on some paper, so nobody has heard anything. There's a bottle standing here in the court-yard, they must have left it behind, we'll take it along, why not, the big fellows won't lose anything by that. And he leans down, as if he wanted to lace his shoes, with that he grabs the bottle along with the paper. And thus Eve gave Adam the apple, and, if the apple had not fallen from the tree, Eve would not have touched it, and the apple would not have reached Adam's address. Later, Gerner puts the bottle under his coat, and off with it across the courtyard, to the old lady at home.

Whatcha say, old lady? She beams: "Where did ye get that, August?" "Bought it when nobody was there." "You don't say so!" "Danziger Goldwasser, whatcha say to that?"

She beams and beams, as if she came from Beamville. She pulls the curtains to: "Man alive, some of 'em are still standing over there, you got it from over there, didn't ye?" "Found it standing by the wall, those fellows would have taken it along with 'em." "You'll have to give that back." "Since when does a man have to give up Goldwasser when he finds it? When did we ever treat ourselves to a bottle of cognac, old lady, with times as bad as they are? That would be a fool trick wouldn't it, old lady?"

In the end that's her opinion, too, she's not that kind, a bottle, a little bottle, what difference does it make with such a big firm and then, old lady, when you get down to it, it doesn't belong to the firm anyway, it belongs to the burglars, and do you expect me to throw it after 'em? That would be a criminal offense. And they take a nip, then they tipple, another little nip, yes, you have to keep your eyes open in this world, not everything has to be made of gold; silver, too, has its value.

On Saturday the burglars come and a funny thing happens. They notice a stranger sneaking around in the courtyard, or rather the one who is standing by the wall notices it, and already the others, with dark lanterns, like gnomes from a pit, make full speed ahead towards the courtyard door. But there stands Gerner, and they leap like greyhounds over the wall to the next-door yard. Gerner runs after them, they rush off. "Cut it out, I won't do anything to you, God, what saps." He watches them climb over the wall, his heart is near breaking, two have already made their get-away: "Fellers, don't act like fools." Only the last man, astride up there on the house-wall, turns his dark lantern on his face: "What's the matter with you?" A rival, maybe, gummed the game for us. "Why, I'm with ye," says Gerner. What's the matter with him anyway? "Of course, I'll work with you, why do you beat it?"

And after a while he creeps down from the wall, alone, takes a look at the carpenter, that man looks tight. But old Fatty is courageous, because the carpenter is fuddled and smells of hooch. Gerner gives him his hand. "Shake, pard, coming along?" "Is this a frame-up?" "How's that?" "Maybe you think I'm goin' to bite?" Gerner is insulted, grieved, the other does not take him seriously, if he only doesn't run off, that Goldwasser was really too good, his wife would give him the deuce, Lord, wouldn't she now, if he came home looking like a damned fool. Gerner starts begging: "Ah, say, what do you mean, go on in, here's where I live." "Who?" "Why, man, I'm the Superintendent here, can't something come my way once in a while?" Then the thief reflects; he finds that O. K., that would really be great, if the other fellow were in on it, if it's only not a trap, well, we've got a gun with us.

And he leaves his ladder standing against the wall, walks off with Gerner across the courtyard, the others have already made their get-away, probably think I've hit a snag. Gerner then rings the down-stairs bell. "Heh, whatcha ringing for, who lives here?" Gerner proudly: "Me. Watch it." Then he lifts the latch and opens the door noisily: "Well, is it me or not?"

And he switches on the light, his wife's already at the kitchen door, trembling. Gerner jovially makes the introductions: "This is my wife, and here's a pal of mine, Gusta." She shakes in her shoes, stays inside, suddenly she nods solemnly, smiles, why, that's a nice man, ain't that a young, handsome lad! Then she comes out, there she is: "But, Paul, you can't let the gentleman stay out here in the hallway, won't you kindly step up, sir, and take your cap off."

The stranger would like to beat it, but the other two won't give in, he is astonished, can this be possible, why those are respectable people, in bad straits probably, the lower middle-class is hard hit, inflation and so on. The little woman keeps looking at him lovingly, he gets warmed up on punch, then off he goes, never quite sure what it's all about.

At any rate, this youngster, obviously sent by his gang, comes to Gerner's next morning after breakfast, and inquires minutely as to whether he had left anything there. Gerner is not home, only his wife, who receives him amiably, almost humbly in fact, even offers him a brandy, which he deigns to accept.

To the regret of the carpenter, the burglars stay away the whole week. A thousand times Paul and Gusta discuss the situation, whether they hadn't scared the boys off maybe, but neither can find anything to cause self-reproach. "Maybe you were too rough with 'em, Paul, you sometimes have a funny way with you." "Nope, Gusta, it's not my fault, it's more likely yours, you made a face as if you were the preacher himself, and that drove him off, they don't feel at home with us, it's terrible, what are we going to do about it?"

Gusta has begun crying; if only one of them would come again; to think she should have to go on listening to these reproaches, and, really, it wasn't her fault.

But sure enough, Friday is the great moment. There's somebody knocking. I think there's somebody knocking. And as she opens, even though she does not see anything as yet, because in her excitement she forgot to switch on the light, she knows at once who it is. And it is the tall fellow, who always plays the gentleman, he wants to talk to her husband, and he is very serious and cool. She is frightened, has anything happened? He reassures her: "No, it's purely a matter of business." Then he talks about different places and how nothing can come out of nothing, and so on. They sit in the sitting-room, she is happy, now she has got him inside, and Paul can no longer say that she chased him, and she says, that's what she always said, and the opposite is right, from nothing, nothing can come. Follows a long debate over this problem, and it turns out that both have at their disposal quite a few sayings from their parents, grandparents, uncles, and aunts to this same effect: from nothing, nothing can come, never, you can always take an oath on it, it's that sure, and they were of the same opinion. They brought up one example after another, from their own past, from the neighborhood, and were still right in the midst of it, when the bell rang and two men stepped in, who turned out to be detectives, accompanied by three insurance officials. One of the officials addressed the visitor without much ado: "You are Herr Gerner, you'll have to help us a bit, it's with regard to all those burglaries over there, I would like you to join us in a special surveillance. The gentlemen of the wholesale firm, as well as the insurance company, will, of course, pay your expenses." They talk for ten minutes, the woman listens to everything, at twelve they leave. And the two who stayed behind became so excited and gay that around one o'clock something unspeakable happened between them, beggaring description, something of which both were indeed ashamed. For the woman was thirty-five and he perhaps twenty or twenty-one. But it was not only the difference in their ages—and he being 6 feet 3 inches and she just 5 feet—but that such a thing could happen, it somehow developed between their talk and the excitement and their mocking at the policemen, and on the whole it was not so bad, only embarrassing afterwards, at least for her, nevertheless, it will pass over. At any rate, at two o'clock Herr Gerner found a situation confronting him and a general coziness that were indescribable, he had never imagined anything so nice. So he sat down with them at once.

They were still sitting together at six o'clock, and he listened quite enraptured, as did also his wife, to everything the tall fellow told them. Even if it were only partly true, they were first-class lads, and he was astonished to hear such reasonable ideas about life from a young man of today. He himself was already a decrepit old thing, the scales fell from his eyes by the pound. Yes, after the youngster had gone and they had hit the hay around nine, Gerner said he didn't know how such bright boys could have anything to do with him—there must be something, Gusta would have to admit it, there surely must be something about him, he certainly had something to offer. Gusta was of the same opinion, and the old boy stretched himself contentedly.

And early in the morning, before he got up, he said to her: "Gusta, my name's Jake if I go back to work as a polisher. I had a business of my own and now it's gone and that's no work for a man who has been his own boss, and they would like to kick me out, anyway, because I'm too old. And why shouldn't I make something out of the wholesalers back there. Just look how clever the boys are. If you're not clever today, you go under. That's what I say. What do you say?" "Always said that myself." "You see, I'd like to live like a prince and not freeze my toes off." She embraced him happily, grateful for everything he offered her, and would offer her. "You know what we ought to do, old lady, you and me?" He pinched her legs till she cried out. "You'll lend us a hand, old lady." "Nope, nothin' doin'." "And I say, yes. You mean we can get along just as well without you, old lady?" "Being as you are five already, all strong men." And how strong! "Want me to be a look-out?" she continues jabbering. "Can't do it. I got varicose veins."

"And help you, what could I do?" "Are you afraid, old gal?" "Afraid, what do you mean? Suppose *you* had varicose veins and then tried to run? Why a dachshund could outrun you! And if they catch me, you certainly would get into trouble, 'cause I'm your wife." "Is it my fault you're my wife?" He pinched her leg, with emotion. "You better stop, Paul. It gets you all excited." "You see, old lady, you'll be a different woman once you get out of this damned hole here." "Why, I'd like to all right, ain't my mouth waterin' for it?" "Just you wait, old lady, that small stuff, that wasn't nothing, take the cotton out of your ears. I'll work the game alone." "Sakes alive. And the others?" What a fright.

"Why, that's just it, Gusta. We'll ditch 'em. Y'know, partnership never works in business, that's an old saw. Well now, am I right or not? I'm goin' to be my own boss. After all, we're the first-comers, living here on the ground-floor, and the courtyard belongs to our house, don't it?" "But I can't help you there, Paul, I really got varicose veins." And it was also too bad in other respects. The old girl agreed bitter-sweetly with her lips, but inside, where the feelings are, she says: No, and keeps saying: No.

And in the evening, since all the firm had left the basement at two o'clock and Gerner had let himself be locked up there with his wife, and it is now nine, and nothing is stirring in the house, and he is just about to start working, and the watchman is probably now patrolling before the house-door, what happens? There is a knock at the basement door. A knock. I think there's a knock. Who could be knocking here anyway? I don't know, but there was a knock. Nobody has any business knocking here now. The store is closed. Somebody knocked. Another knock. Both of them dead silent, not stirring, not saying a word. Again there's a knocking. Gerner nudges her: "Somebody knocked." "Yes." "What is it anyway?" Curiously enough she is not at all afraid, but says: "Likely it isn't anything, they're not goin' to kill us." Nope, he won't kill us, the chap who's coming, I know him, he won't kill me, he's got two long legs and a wee bit of a mustache, and if he comes, I'd be glad, I would. But then the knocking grows insistent, though soft. For Lord's sake, that's a signal. "That's somebody who knows us. That's one of our boys. Been thinkin' that for a long time, old lady." "Then why don't you say so?"

Hello! Gerner's already on the stairs, how did those chaps find out we're here anyway, they've surprised us: the man outside whispers: "Open that door, Gerner."

And whether he wants to or not, he has to open it. It's a lousy trick, goddamned swinishness, I could smash the whole world to smithereens. He has to open the door, it's the tall fellow, alone, her beau. Gerner notices nothing, she has double-crossed him, after all she would like to show her gratitude to her beau. She beams on him once he's downstairs, she can't help it, her husband looks like a bulldog, he curses: "Whatcha grinning for, you?" "Why, I was so afraid it might 'a' been somebody in the house or the watchman." Now lets get to work and divvy up, cursing won't change things either, damned swinishness.

When Gerner tries it for the second time, and leaves the old woman outside, growling that she brings him bad luck, there comes a knocking again, but now there are three of them and they even act as if he had invited them, and there's nothing to be done about it; a fellow is not even master in his own house, nothing doing against foxy lads like that. Then Gerner says to himself, checkmated, stinking mad: For today I'll work with them, caught together, hanged together, but tomorrow nothing doing, if those dirty fools come again into my house where I'm the superintendent, and mix up in my affairs, then they'll find out how fast the coppers'll get here. Regular profiteers they are, blackmailers!

So they work and work in the basement for two whole hours, carrying most of the stuff into Gerner's place, everything in bags, coffee, dried currants, sugar, they make a clean sweep of things, then cases of alcohol; all kinds of brandy and wine, they drag away half the stock. Gerner is raging that he has to divide all this up with them. At home the old woman pacifies him: "Why I wouldn't 'a' been able to carry so much, me with my varicose veins." He's in a poisonous rage, they're still carrying things over: "Your varicose veins, you should have bought yourself rubber stockings long ago, that's what comes from saving, always saving and scraping in the wrong place." But Gusta keeps looking at her big boy, and the latter is mighty proud of her in front of the other boys, that's his department, he's smart at that sort of thing.

After they're gone, having worked like brutes, Gerner closes the door of his lodgings, locks himself in and starts to booze with Gusta, that's the least he can have. He can't help trying all the various specimens, the best brands he is going to pass on to a few shopkeepers tomorrow, and both of them are happy at the idea, Gusta too, isn't he her good husband and after all he is her husband, she'll help him do it. From two till five they both sit there trying out all the various kinds, methodically, according to a plan. Deeply contented with the night's work they collapse, both of them, tight to the gills, and fall over flat as logs.

Towards noon they are supposed to open the door. There's a ringing, a tinkling, a pealing of bells. But the Gerners are the very ones who don't open. How can they open in their stupor? But the people outside won't give up, they bang at the door, and then Gusta suddenly notices something, sits up and begins to hammer away on Paul: "Paul, there's someone knockin' outside, you got to open up." First he says: "Where?" Then she pushes him out, they are smashing in the whole door, maybe it's the postman. Paul gets up, puts on his trousers, opens the door. And then they march past him, three men, a whole gang, what do they want, have the boys come to get their stuff already, nope, these aren't the same people. These are bulls, detectives, and they have an easy job, they're astonished, they're astounded, Herr Gerner, the superintendent, and here's everything stacked up on the floor, in the hallway, in the room, bags, cases, bottles, straw, all jumbled up in a heap. The chief detective says: "I never saw such a beastly thing in all my life."

And what has Gerner got to say for himself? What's he going to say? He doesn't say a word. He only stares at the bulls, he's feeling rotten, the bloodhounds, if I had a gun, they wouldn't get me out of here alive, the dirty bloodhounds. I suppose I ought to work all my life in a building shed, and let the profiteers put my money in their pockets? If they would only let me take another nip. But there's nothing doing, he has to get dressed. "I guess you'll let a man fasten his galluses before you take 'im out."

The woman blubbers and dodders: "But I don't know nothin' about it, chief, we're respectable people, somebody musta trapped us, those cases there, we were sleeping soundly, you musta noticed it, somebody from the house musta played a dirty trick on us, chief, sure enough, heh, Paul, what's this all about?" "You can tell all that at the station." Gerner interrupts: "This time, old girl, they broke into our place, too, during the night, the same gang as was there in the back, and that's why they tell us to go to the station." "You can tell that story at the station, or at headquarters, later on." "I won't walk to headquarters." "We're going to ride." "My God, Gusta, I didn't hear a sound when they broke in. I was sleeping like a beaver." "Neither did I, Paul."

Gusta tries to snatch two letters out of the chest of drawers, they're from the tall chap, but one of the detectives sees her. "Let's have a look. No, you can put them back. We'll search the house later."

She insists with mulish obstinacy: "Go ahead then, oughta be ashamed of yourselves, coming into a body's house like that." "All right, come along."

She cries, does not look at her husband, screams and makes a scene and throws herself on the ground; they have to lift her up. The man curses and swears, but they hold him tight. "Are you going to do violence to that woman now?" Those low-down criminals, those blackmailers, they're gone, and they left me to get caught with that stuff.

Gallop-a-Trot, Gallop-a-Trot, little Horsey starts trotting again

Franz Biberkopf, his hands in his pockets, his collar up over his ears, head and hat between his shoulders, did not take part in the conversation in the hallway or in the courtyard. He just listened and listened around in the crowd. Presently he looked on, as they all lined up on each side of the sidewalk, while the carpenter and his fat little wifie were being led through the hall to the street. Now they're off. Once I was marched off like that, too. But it was dark then. Look at 'em, the way they stare straight ahead. Ashamed. Yes, sir, just go on jibing, you fellows! You know all about how it feels inside a person! They're real stick-in-the-muds, they sit by their stoves, these crooks, but that sort's never caught. Hard to catch up with the smart tricks of them lads. Now they're opening the Black Maria. Well, hop right in, right in, me children, the li'l lady, too, she's probably stewed, and she's right I ain't blamin' her. All aboard, we're off.

The people put their heads together. Franz Biberkopf stood in front of the street-door, it was bitter cold. He looked at the door from the outside, looked across the street, what am I goin' to do now, what could he do? He stood first on one foot, then on the other. Damned cold, goddamned cold. I won't go upstairs. What'll I do now?

There he stood, moving back and forth—and did not realize he was so keenly alive. He had nothing to do with that jibing crowd. I'll go look somewhere else. Can't stand that bunch. And smartly he jogs off, down Elsasser Strasse, by the subway kiosk to the Rosenthaler Platz, just anywhere.

Thus it happened that Franz Biberkopf crept forth from his diggings. The man who had been made to run the gauntlet, the dumpy slightly tingled woman, the burglary, the Black Maria, all accompanying him. But when a saloon hove in sight, just before the corner of the Platz, things began to hum. His hands automatically went into his pockets, and no bottle to fill. Nothing. No bottle. Slipped his mind. Left it upstairs. On account of that nonsense. When the rumpus had started, into that overcoat was all he had thought, downstairs, forgetting the bottle. Damn it! Hoof it back? Then things started inside him. No, yes, yes, no. Such a lot of switching back and forth, swearing, giving in to it, shoving, well what is it, leave me alone, I want to go in there, such a thing hadn't come over Franz for an eternity. Shall I go in, shall I not go in, am I thirsty, but then mineral water will do, if you go in, all you want to do is to swill, old boy, yes, sir, I am hellishly thirsty, immensely, enormously thirsty, God, wouldn't I like to booze now, you better stay here, don't go into that dump, otherwise you'll soon be lying on your nose, and then you'll get stuck up at the old landlady's again. And then there came back the Black Maria and that carpenter couple and bang to the right, nope, we won't stay here, maybe somewhere else, farther on, keep moving, just keep moving.

Thus Franz, with 1.55 marks in his pockets, kept on walking as far as the Alexanderplatz, gulping down nothing but air, and running. Then he took hold of himself, and, though he hated it, had a meal in a restaurant, a good meal, ate really for the first time in weeks, veal stew with potatoes. Afterwards his thirst grew less intense, 75 pfennigs left, he rubbed them between his fingers. Shall I go to see Lina, what'll I do with Lina, don't want her. His tongue grew dull and bitter, his throat burned. I'll have to pour down another seltzer.

And then—just as he was gulping it down, swallowing the lovely cool water with the tickle of the soda—he knew where he wanted to go. To see Minna, he had sent her the cutlet, and she hadn't accepted the aprons. Yes, that's the thing.

Let's get up. Franz Biberkopf tidied himself in front of the mirror. But the man who wasn't at all edified, when he saw his pale sluggish pimply cheeks, was Biberkopf. What a mug that fellow has, welts on his forehead, wonder what the welts come from, from his cap, and that nose like a cucumber, boy, gee what a thick red smeller he's got, but that doesn't have to be on account of the booze, it's cold today, only those ghastly old goggle-eyes like a cow's, wonder where I got those calves' eyes from, and that vacant stare, as if I couldn't blink 'em. As if somebody had poured glue over 'em. But that doesn't make any difference to Minna. I'd better brush my hair a bit. That's that, he'll go to see her. She'll give me a few pfennigs till Thursday, and then we'll see what we'll see.

Out of the dump into the cold street! A lot of people. What a huge lot of people there are on the Alex, all busy! Seems they can't do without it. Now that Franz Biberkopf was stepping out, he cast his eyes right and left. Just like an old nag that has slid on the wet pavement and gets a kick in the belly with a boot, that's how Franz gets up, prances off and runs like mad. Franz had muscles, he was once a member of the athletic club; now he trotted through Alexanderstrasse and noticed the kind of steps he was taking, firm and solid, like a soldier of the Kaiser's Guard. Here we go, right in step with the others.

Weather forecast at noon today: Weather prospects are somewhat more favorable. To be sure, there is still a strong cold spell prevailing, but the barometer is rising. The sun is shining again, although intermittently. We may expect a rise in temperature in the immediate future.

All those who own an NSU 6-cylinder car and drive it themselves are enthusiastic about it. 'Tis there, 'tis there, beloved, with thee, my heart longs to roam.

And when Franz reaches her house and stands before the door, there is a bell. He tears his hat off with a jerk, pulls the bell, and who opens the door, who do you think—here we curtsy, when a girl has a man, well, who do you think—tickle, tickle—bing: a man! Her man! It's Karl. Karl, the locksmith. But it doesn't matter. Just go on looking glum, old boy, I don't care.

"So it's you, is it? Whassa matter?" "Well, you can let me come in, Karl, I won't bite anybody." And he is already inside. So here we are. What a dumbbell, this is a nice thing to happen to a fellow.

"Dear Honored Herr Karl, even if you are a master locksmith and I'm only odd-job worker, you needn't look so high and mighty. You might give me a howdy when I say howdy." "Whatcha want, you? Did I let you in? Whatcha mean by pushing through that door?" "Well, then, is your wife in? Maybe I can say howdy to her." "Nope, she's not in. And certainly not for you. Nobody's in for you." "Is that so?" "Yes, nobody." "Well—you're still in, Karl." "Nope, I'm not in, either. I only came to get myself a sweater, I've got to go down in the store right away." "Business going as grand as that?" "Yes, sir." "That means you're giving me the air, eh?" "Did I let you in? Say, what do you want here anyway? Ain't you ashamed to come up here and compromise me where everybody in the house knows you?" "Let 'em chatter, Karl. That ain't nothin' much to worry about. I wouldn't like to take a look into their rooms, either. Y'know, Karl, you needn't worry on account of those people. Why, today, they took one of 'em away in my house, the coppers did, a skilled carpenter and super-intendent of the house, he was. Imagine it. With his wife, too. And they pinched everything they could get hold of. Did I steal? Well, did I?" "Listen I'm going downstairs. Get out. What's the use of me standing here with you? If Minna gets a look at you, watch out, she'll take a broom and whack you one." Little does he know about Minna. So that old husband with his goat horns is trying to put me wise! I have to laugh myself sick. When a girl's got a man that she loves—ain't it gran'! Karl steps towards Franz. "What do you keep standing there for? We're no kin to you, Franz, none and more than none. And if you're out of the jug now, you'll have to look out for yourself, see?" "Did I ask anything from you?" "Nope, and Minna hasn't forgotten her sister Ida yet, a sister is a sister and to us you're the same man you were before. You're done for with us." "I didn't kill Ida. That could happen to anybody, a slip of the hand when he's mad." "Ida's dead, you'd better go on your way now, we're respectable people."

That dirty dog, with the horns on his head, a regular poison bag, I'd just as lief tell him all about it, I'll just take his wife out of his bed alive. "I've done my four years to the minute, so you needn't try to act any bigger than the law." "I don't care about your law. Now off with you. Once and for all. This house don't exist for you any more. Once and for all." Wonder what he's after, his honor the locksmith, maybe he's going to start something with me?

"I just wanted to tell you, Karl, I want to make my peace with you now that I've done my time. And I give you my hand on that." "Then I won't take it." "That's just what I wanted to know. (Quickly now, get hold of the fellow, grab him by the legs, fire him against the wall.) Now I know as good as if it was in writing." He put his lid on with the same flourish as before: "Then good-bye, Karl, Karl, the master locksmith, Esq. Give my best to Minna, tell her I was here, just called to see how's tricks. And you, you dirty cur, you're the lousiest bastard in the world. Write that behind your ears and take a good look at my fist if you want something, and don't you come near me. I'm sorry Minna's gotta put up with a hunk o' tripe like you."

Off. Quietly off. Slowly and quietly down the stairs. Let him follow me, bet he won't do it. And opposite the house, he took just one brandy, a hot cordial. And maybe he'll come after me, anyway. I'll wait. And Franz went his way contentedly. I'll get money somewhere else, don't worry. And he felt how thick his muscles were, and I'll get something in my belly again, never mind!

"You want to stop me on my way and throw me down. But I have a hand that can strangle you, and you are impotent against me. You crush me with your mockery, you want to pour contempt over me, no, not me, not me, I am very strong. I can ignore your sneer. Your teeth cannot penetrate my armor, against vipers I am charmed. I do not know who gave you the power to assail me. But I can resist you surely. The Lord has set mine enemies against me with their necks.

"Go on talking. How well birds can sing once they have escaped the polecat! There are many polecats, but just let the birds keep on singing. You are still without eyes for me. You do not yet need to look at me. You listen to the babbling of men, to the noise in the street, the roaring of the street-cars. Just take a breath! Just listen! In addition to all these sounds, you will listen to me some day."

"To whom? Who is speaking?"

"I will not say. You shall see. You shall feel it. Gird up your heart, then I will speak to you. Then will you see me. Your eyes will give forth tears alone."

"You can go on talking like that for a hundred years. I only laugh at it."

"Don't laugh. Don't laugh."

"Because you do not know me. Because you do not know who I am. Who Franz Biberkopf is. He's not afraid of anything. I have my fists! Just look at what muscles I have!"

FIFTH BOOK

A quick recovery, our man stands again where he stood before, he has not understood anything, nor learned anything more. Now the first heavy blow falls on him. He is dragged into a criminal case, it's against his will, he defends himself, but the issue he must face.

Fiercely and bravely, with hand and foot, he tries to win the race, but it's no use, he's beaten, the issue he must face.

Rencounter on the Alex, cold as the Devil. Next Year, 1929, it'll be colder still

Boom, boom, the steam pile-driver thumps in front of Aschinger's on the Alex. It's one story high, and knocks the rails into the ground as if they were nothing at all.

Icy air, February. People walk in overcoats. Whoever has a fur piece wears it, whoever hasn't, doesn't wear it. The women have on thin stockings and are freezing, of course, but they look nice. The bums have disappeared with the cold. When it gets warmer, they'll stick their noses out again. In the meantime they nip a double ration of brandy, but don't ask me what it's like, nobody would want to swim in it, not even a corpse.

Boom, boom, the steam pile-driver batters away on the Alex.

A lot of people have time to spare and watch the pile-driver whacking away. Up on top there is a man who is always pulling on a chain, then there is a puff on top, and bang! the rod gets it in the neck. There they stand, men and women, especially youngsters, they love the way it works, as if it were greased, bang! the rod gets it in the neck. After that it grows small as the tip of your finger, but it gets another blow and it's welcome now to do whatever it pleases. Finally it's gone, Hell's bells, they've given it a nice drubbing, the people walk off satisfied.

Everything is covered with planks. The Berolina statue once stood in front of Tietz's, one hand outstretched, a regular giantess, now they have dragged her away. Maybe they'll melt her and make medals out of her.

People hurry over the ground like bees. They hustle and bustle around here day and night, by the hundreds.

The street-cars roll past with a screech and a scrunch, yellow ones with trailers, away they go across the planked-over Alexanderplatz, it's dangerous to jump off. The station is laid out on a broad plan, Einbahnstrasse to Königstrasse past Wertheim's. If you want to go east, you have to pass police headquarters and turn down through Kloster-strasse. The trains rumble from the railroad station towards Jannowitz Brücke, the locomotive puffs out a plume of steam, just now it is standing above the Prälat, Schlossbräu entrance a block further down.

Across the street they are tearing down everything, all the houses along the city railroad, wonder where they get the money from, the city of Berlin is rich, and we pay the taxes.

They have torn down Loeser and Wolff with their mosaic sign, 20 yards further on they built it up again, and there's another branch over there in front of the station. Loeser and Wolff, Berlin-Elbing, A-1 quality for every taste, Brazil, Havana, Mexico, Little Comforter, Lilliput, Cigar No. 8, 25 pfennigs each, Winter Ballad, package containing 25 at 20 pfennigs, Cigarillos No. 10, unselected, Sumatra wrapper, a wonderful value at this price, in boxes of a hundred, 10 pfennigs. I beat everything, you beat everything, he beats everything with boxes of 50 and cardboard packages of 10, can be mailed to every country on earth, Boyero 25 pfennigs, this novelty has won us many friends, I beat everything, but I never beat a retreat.

Alongside the Prälat there is lots of room, there are wagons standing there loaded with bananas. Give your children bananas. The banana is the cleanest of fruits, because it is protected from insects, worms as well as bacilli, by its skin. We except such insects, worms, and bacilli as are able to penetrate the skin. Privy Councillor Czerny emphatically pointed out that even children in their first years. I beat everything to pieces, you beat everything to pieces, he beats everything to pieces.

There is a lot of wind on the Alex, at the Tietz corner there is a lousy draft. A wind that blows between the houses and through the building excavations. It makes you feel you would like to hide in the saloons, but who can do that, it blows through your trousers pockets, then you notice something's happening, no monkey business, a man has got to be gay with this weather. Early in the morning the workers come tramping along from Reinickendorf, Neukölln, Weissensee. Cold or no cold, wind or no wind, we've gotta get the coffee pot, pack up the sandwiches, we've gotta work and slave, the drones sit on top, they sleep in their feather-beds and exploit us.

Aschinger has a big café and restaurant. People who have no belly, can get one there, people who have one already, can make it as big as they please. You cannot cheat Nature! Whoever thinks he can improve bread and pastry made from denatured white flour by the addition of artificial ingredients, deceives himself and the consumer. Nature has her laws of life and avenges every abuse. The decadent state of health of almost all civilized peoples today is caused by the use of denatured and artificially refined food. Fine sausages delivered to your house, liverwurst and blood-pudding cheap.

The highly interesting *Megazine*, instead of 1 mark, now only 20 pfennigs; *Marriage*, highly interesting and spicy, only 20 pfennigs. The newsboy puffs his cigarettes, he has a sailor's cap on, I beat everything.

From the east, Weissensee, Litchtenberg, Friedrichshain, Frankfurter Allee, the yellow street-cars plunge into the square through Landsberger Strasse. Line No. 65 comes from the Central Slaughter-House, the Grosse Ring, Weddingplatz, Luisenplatz; No. 76 from Hundekehle via Hubert-usallee. At the corner of Landsberger Strasse they have sold out Friedrich Hahn, formerly a department store, they have emptied it and are gathering it to its forebears. The street-cars and Bus 19 stop on the Turmstrasse. Where Jürgens stationery store was, they have torn down the house and put up a building fence instead. An old man sits there with a medical scale: Try your weight, 5 pfennigs. Dear sisters and brethren, you who swarm across the Alex, give yourselves this treat, look through the loophole next to the medical scale at this dump-heap where Jürgens once flourished and where Hahn's department store still stands, emptied, evacuated, and eviscerated, with nothing but red tatters hanging over the show-windows. A dump-heap lies before us. Dust thou art, to dust returnest. We have built a splendid house, nobody comes in or goes out any longer. Thus Rome, Babylon, Nineveh, Hannibal, Cæsar, all went to smash, oh, think of it! In the first place, I must remark they are digging those cities up again, as the illustrations in last Sunday's edition show, and, in the second place, those cities have fulfilled their purpose, and we can now build new cities. Do you cry about your old trousers when they are moldy and seedy? No, you simply buy new ones, thus lives the world.

The police tower over the square. Several specimens of them are standing about. Each specimen sends a connoisseur's glance to both sides, and knows the traffic rules by heart. It has putties around its legs, a rubber mace hangs from its right side, it swings its arms horizontally from west to east, and thus north and south, cannot advance any farther, east flows west, and west flows east. Then the specimen switches about automatically: north flows south, south flows north. The copper has a well-defined waist-line. As soon as he jerks around, there is a rush across the square in the direction of Königstrasse of about 30 private individuals, some of them stop on the traffic island, one part reaches the other side and continues walking on the planks. The same number have started east, they swim towards the others, the same thing has befallen them, but there was no mishap.

There are men, women, and children, the latter mostly holding women's hands. To enumerate them all and to describe their destinies is hardly possible, and only in a few cases would this succeed. The wind scatters chaff over all of them alike. The faces of the eastward wanderers are in no way different from those of the wanderers to the west, south, and north; moreover they exchange their rôles, those who are now crossing the square towards Aschinger's may be seen an hour later in front of the empty Hahn Department Store. Just as those who come from Brunnenstrasse on their way to Jannowitz Brücke mingle with those coming from the reverse direction. Yes, and many of them turn off to the side, from south to east, from south to west, from north to west, from north to east. They have the same equanimity as passengers in an omnibus or in street-cars. The latter all sit in different postures, making the weight of the car, as indicated outside, heavier still. Who could find out what is happening inside them, a tremendous chapter. And if anyone did write it, to whose advantage would it be? New books? Even the old ones don't sell, and in the year '27 book-sales as compared with '26 have declined so and so much per cent. Taken simply as private individuals, the people who paid 20 pfennigs, leaving out those possessing monthly tickets and pupils' cards—the latter only pay 10 pfennigs—are riding with their weight from a hundred to two hundred pounds, in their clothes, with pockets, parcels, keys, hats, sets of artificial teeth, trusses, riding across Alexanderplatz, holding those mysterious long tickets on which is written: Line 12 Siemensstrasse D A, Gotzkowskistrasse C, B, Oranienburger Tor C, C, Kottbuser Tor A, mysterious tokens, who can solve them, who can guess and who confess them, three words I tell you heavy with thought, and the scraps of paper are punched four times at certain places, and on them there is written in that same German in which the Bible and the Criminal Code are written: Valid till the end of the line, by the shortest route, connection with other lines not guaranteed: They read newspapers of various tendencies, conserve their balance by means of the semicircular canals of their internal ear, inhale oxygen, stare stupidly at each other, have pains, or no pains, think, don't think, are happy, unhappy, are neither happy nor unhappy.

Rrrr, rrr, the pile-driver thumps down, I beat everything, another rail. Something is buzzing across the square coming from police headquarters, they are riveting, a cement crane dumps its load. Herr Adolf Kraun, house-servant, looks on, the tipping over of the wagon fairly fascinates him, you beat everything, he beats everything. He watches excitedly how the sand truck is always tilting up on one side, there it is up in the air, boom, and now it tips over. A fellow wouldn't like to be kicked out of bed like that, legs up, down with the head, there you lie, something might happen to him, but they do their job well, all the same.

Franz Biberkopf has his knapsack on again and is selling newspapers. He has changed his beat. He has left the Rosenthaler Tor and is now on the Alexanderplatz. He is feeling entirely O. K. again, 5 feet 10½ inches tall, his weight is down, that makes it easier to carry. On his head he wears the official newspaper cap.

Danger of a crisis in the Reichstag, talk of March elections, probably April elections, which direction, Joseph Wirth? The Central German fight continues, they may appoint an arbitration commission, man attacked by bandits in Tempelherrenstrasse. He has his stand at the Alexanderstrasse subway exit, opposite the Ufa movie-house, on the same side where Fromm, the optician, has built a new business. Franz Biberkopf looks down Münzstrasse as he stands for the first time in a crowd and thinks to himself: Wonder how far it is to the two Jews', they don't live far from here, that was when I was having my first troubles, maybe I'll call on them one of these days, they might buy a copy of the *Völkischer Beobachter* from me. Why not, if they want it, I don't care, as long as they buy it. He grins foolishly at the thought, that very old Jew in those funny slippers was really too comical for words. He looks around, his fingers are stiff, next to him stands a little cripple with a crooked nose, probably broken. Talk of crisis in the Reichstag, No. 17 Hebbelstrasse evacuated owing to danger of collapse, murder on a fishing boat, mutineer or madman.

Franz Biberkopf and the cripple blow through their fingers. Business before noon is slack. A thin, elderly man, looking seedy and down at the heels, comes up to Franz. He has on a green felt hat and asks Franz how the paper business is going. Franz, too, had once asked that. "If it's for yourself, pardner, who can tell?" "Yes, I'm fifty-two." "Well that's just it, don't the rheumatiz start around fifty? When I was in the Prussian army, we had an old reserve captain, he was only forty, from Saarbrücken, a lottery-cashier—I mean, that's what he said, he was probably a cigar salesman—he had the rheumatiz at forty already, in the small of his back. But he pulled himself together, he did. He walked like a broomstick on roller-skates. He always had himself rubbed with butter. And when there was no more butter to be had, around 1917, only Palmin, first class plant-oil, and rancid at that, he had himself shot dead."

"What's the use? The factories won't take you any more either. And last year they operated on me, in Lichtenberg, Hubertus Hospital. One testicle is gone, it was supposed to be tubercular. I tell you, I still have pains." "Well, you better look out, otherwise the other one'll get it too. Maybe it's better to work sitting down, why not be a hack-driver." The Central German struggle continues, negotiations without results, attack aimed at the Tenants' Protection Law, Wake Up, Tenants, or they'll take the roof from over your head. "Yes, pardner, it's all right to sell newspapers, but you've gotta be able to get around, and you've gotta have a voice, how's the chest, robin redbreast, can you sing? Well, y'see, that's the main thing with us, we've gotta know how to sing and get around. We need good barkers. The loudspeakers do the best business. A bunch of tough birds, I'll tell ye. Look, how many groschen is that?" "Four, as far as I can see." "Righto, for you it's four. That's the point. For you. But when one of these chaps is in a hurry, and then looks around in his pockets, and he's got a half-groschen piece and a mark or ten marks, go ahead and ask those boys, yes, sir, they can all make change. Clever, I should say so, they're real bankers, they are, they understand all about making change, they deduct their own percentage, but ye don't notice anything, that's how fast they work."

The old man sighs. "Yes, you're fifty years old and rheumatiz along with it. If you can put up a bold front, old boy, you won't be by yourself, hire a couple o' youngsters, have to pay 'em of course, they get half maybe, but you'll have to mind the business, you can save your legs and your voice. You've gotta have connections and a good stand. When it rains, it's wet. For business to be good you must have prize fights and changes in government. At Ebert's death, they tell me, people grabbed the papers away from you. Don't make such a face, old fellow, things are only half as bad as they look. Just watch that pile-driver over there, imagine that falling on your head, then what's the use in worrying about all that?"

Attack aimed at the Tenants' Protection Law. Discharge for Zörgiebel. I resign from the party of traitors to their principles. British censorship concerning Amanullah, India must be kept in the dark.

Opposite, in front of the little Web Radio Store—till further notice free charging of batteries—there stands a pale young woman, her hat pulled down over her face, she seems to be thinking intensely. The chauffeur of the big black and white taxi standing nearby thinks to himself: Is she wondering now whether she ought to take a taxi, and if she has enough with her or is she waiting for somebody. But what she does is to twist about in her velvet coat as if her body were being wrenched, then she starts up again, she's unwell, that's all, and has the cramps, as usual. She is about to take her teacher's examination, today she would have liked to stay at home with a hot-water bottle, it'll go better tonight anyway.

For a long while Nothing, Rest Hour, back to a normal Basis

On the evening of February 9, 1928, when the Labor government fell in Oslo, and it was the last night of the six-day bicycle races in Stuttgart— the winners were Van Kempen—Frankenstein with 726 points, 2440 kilometers—the situation in the Saar Valley appeared more critical, on the evening of February 9, 1928, a Tuesday (one moment please, now you will see the mysterious face of the strange woman, the question asked by this beautiful woman concerns everybody, even you: do you smoke Garbaty Kalif?), that evening Franz Biberkopf stood on the Alexanderplatz before a poster column studying an invitation of the truck-gardeners of Treptow-Neukölln and Britz to a meeting of protest in Irmer's Assembly Hall, order of the day, the arbitrary notices of dismissal. Underneath was the advertisement: the torture of asthma and masks for rent, large assortment for ladies and gentlemen. Suddenly little Meck stood beside him. Meck, why we know that fellow. Up he comes a-shaking, long steps he is taking.

"Well, well, Franz, old boy." Meck was delighted, how delighted he was! "Franz, old fellow, who woulda thought it, seeing you again, you've been like a dead man. I'd 'a' sworn—" "Now what? Can imagine it all right—I've done something again. Nope, nope, old boy." They shook hands, shook each other's arms up to the shoulders, shook each other's shoulders down to the ribs, slapped each other on the shoulder-blades till their bodies began to wobble.

"That's the way it is, Gottlieb. We never see each other any more. Why, I'm in business around here." "Here on the Alex, Franz, you don't say, why, I should have run into you sometimes. Here I go past a fellow and don't see him." "That's true, Gottlieb."

And arm-in-arm they wander down the Prenzlauer Strasse. "Didn'cha once want to sell plaster heads, Franz?" "I ain't got the brains for plaster heads. You need culture for plaster, I ain't got that. I'm selling newspapers again. You can make a living out of that. And how about you, Gottlieb?" "I'm over there on Schönhauserstrasse peddling men's wear, leather jackets and pants." "And where do you get those things?" "Still the same old Franz, always gotta ask where from. That's what the girls ask when they want alimony." Franz toddled silently along beside Meck with a gloomy expression on his face: "You fellows will keep on swindling till you get it in the neck." "What do you mean get it in the neck, what do you mean by swindling, Franz, a fellow has to be a business man, he's got to know something about buying."

Franz did not want to walk along any farther, no, he didn't want to, he was recalcitrant. But Meck wouldn't give in, kept on gabbling and wouldn't give in: "You come along with me to the café, Franz, you might meet the cattle dealers, you remember 'em, don't you, the ones with the law-suit going on who were sitting with us at the table at the meeting when you got your membership card. They certainly got themselves in trouble with their suit. Now they've gotta take an oath and they've gotta get witnesses to take the oath. Boy, they're gonna get a nice fall, but with their heads first." "Nope, Gottlieb, I'd rather not come along."

But Meck did not give in, he was his good old friend and the best of them all at that, except of course Herbert Wischow, but he was a pimp, and he didn't want to have anything to do with him, nope, never again. And arm-in-arm, down Prenzlauer Strasse, the distillery, textile factories, candy, silk, silk, I recommend silk, something amazingly smart for the well-built woman!

When eight o'clock came around, Franz was sitting with Meck and another man who was mute and had to talk in signs, at a table in the corner of a café. And things went on in great style. Meck and the mute were astonished how completely Franz thawed out, with what joy he ate and drank, two pig's feet, then baked beans, one mug of Engelhardt after the other, and he paying for it. The three of them propped their arms one against the other so that no one could come near the small table and disturb them; only the thin proprietress was allowed to clear the table off and get things straightened up and bring the new orders. At the table next to them sat three men who from time to time stroked each other's bald heads. Franz, his cheeks bulging, smiled, the slits of his eyes roved towards the group. "What are they doing there, anyway?" The proprietress pushed the mustard towards him, his second pot: "Well, I guess they're in love." "Yep, I can believe that." And they laughed and guffawed, smacking their lips and gulping away, the three of them. Again and again Franz announced: "Gotta fill yourself up. A man must eat to be strong. If your belly ain't full, you can't do anything."

The animals come rolling along from the provinces, from East Prussia, Pomerania, West Prussia, Brandenburg. They moo and low as they run along the cattle gangway. The pigs grunt and sniff at the ground. In fog you walk. A pale young man takes a hatchet, bing, that was a great moment, it's all over with.

At nine they unlocked their elbows, stuck their cigars in their fat mouths and started belching to give up the warm effluvia of their meal.

Then something began to happen.

First a fresh youngster came into the café, hung his hat and overcoat on the wall and started to bang on the piano.

The place began to fill up. A few men were standing at the bar discussing things. Some sat down by Franz at the next table, elderly men with caps on, and a young man with a derby. Meck knew them, the conversation went back and forth. The younger man, who had black flashing eyes, a smart fellow from Hoppegarten, said:

"What they found when they got to Australia? First of all, sand and heather and fields and no trees and no grass and nothing. Just a desert of sand. And then millions and millions of yellow sheep. They grow wild there. Those are the ones the English lived off of at first. And they exported them too. To America." "That's where they *would* need sheep from Australia." "South America, of course." "That's where they have so many jackasses. Why they don't know what to do with 'em all." "But sheep, the wool. When there are so many Negroes in the country, and all of them freezing. Well, I guess the English know where to send their sheep, don't they? You needn't worry about the English. But what became of the sheep afterwards? Nowadays you can go to Australia, a fellow told me, as far as you can see, not a sheep. Everything smooth as a billiard ball. And why? Where are all the sheep?" "Wild animals." Meck shook his head: "What d'y mean wild animals? Epidemics. That's always the greatest misfortune for a country. They die off, and there you are." The youngster with the derby was not of the opinion that epidemics had been decisive. "It may have been epidemics. Where there are so many animals as that some of them die anyway, then they rot and diseases come. But that's not the reason. Nope, they all trotted into the ocean at a gallop, when the English came. The sheep, all over the country were scared to death, when the English came and began to catch them and put them in freight cars, so the poor beasts ran away by the thousands, into the ocean." Meck: "Let 'em be. That's all right. Let 'em run. Of course there were ships waiting for 'em. That's how the English saved railroad expenses." "Railroad expenses, that's how much you know about it. It went on like that a long time till the English began to notice something. They naturally sticking to the interior and catching and driving them around and right into the freight cars, such a big country too, and no organization, it's always like that in the beginning, and later on it's too late, too late. The sheep, of course, all skedaddled to the ocean where they swilled that dirty salt." "And then what?" "Whatcha mean, what? Suppose you're thirsty and nothing to eat and then swill dirty salt yourself like them sheep." "Drowned and dead as a doornail." "Why sure. They say they were lying in that there ocean by the thousands, and stinking away, and off they go." Franz agreed: "Animals are sensitive. With animals it's sort o' funny. A man's gotta be able to deal with 'em. If you don't get 'em right, better keep your hands off of 'em."

They all drank in their amazement, exchanging observations about wasted capital and the way things happen, how even in America they let the whole wheat harvest rot, all sorts of things can happen. "Nope," explained the man from Hoppegarten, the fellow with the black eyes, "there's nothing in the papers about it, and they don't write anything, can't say why, perhaps on account of the immigration, otherwise nobody'd go there, maybe. They say they got a kind of lizard, a regular antediluvian kind of lizard, several yards long, they won't even show it in the Zoo, the English wouldn't allow it. One of 'em was caught, by some sailors, they've been showing it around in Hamburg, but it was prohibited right away. Nothing doing. They live in pools, in stagnant water, no one knows what they live on. Once a whole automobile caravan sank, they didn't even dig for them, to see where they got to. Nothing. Nobody would dare go near 'em. Yep." "I'll be jiggered," observed Meck. "And how about gas?" The youngster reflected: "Might try that. Trying don't hurt." That seemed clear enough.

An elderly man sat down behind Meck, his elbows on Meck's chair, a short, under-sized fellow, fat face, red as a lobster, protuberant big eyes shiftily glancing here and there. They made room for him. And soon Meck and he started whispering together. He wore high shiny boots, carried a linen duster over his arm, and seemed to be a cattle dealer. Franz was talking across the table with the youngster from Hoppegarten, whom he liked. At that moment Meck tapped him on the shoulder, signaled to him with his head, they got up, the small cattle dealer, who was laughing good-naturedly, went along with them. The three of them stood away from the others near the iron stove. Franz thought it was on account of the two cattle dealers and their law-suit. He'd certainly like to keep out of that. But it was quite pointless really, their standing around like that. The small fellow only wanted to shake hands with him and know what business he was in. Franz tapped his newspaper case. Well, maybe he might occasionally want to do something in fruit; his name is Pums, he says, fruit dealer, and sometimes he might need a man to peddle with a wagon. Franz answered by shrugging his shoulders: "Depends on the profits." Whereupon they sat down. Franz thought how cleverly that small man talks: to be used with caution, shake after using.

The conversation continued, with Hoppegarten, as usual, in the lead; they were in America now. The Hoppegarten lad had his hat between his knees: "Well, that guy marries a woman in America and don't think much about it. And it's a Negress. 'What' says he, 'you're a Negress?' Bang, out she goes. Then the woman had to undress herself before the judge. In a bathing suit. Of course she don't want to at first, but they tell her to stop that bunk. Her skin was all white. Because she was a mestizo. The man says: 'She's a Negress, I'm telling you.' And why? Because her finger-tips are tinted brown instead of white. She was a mestizo, ye see." "Well, and what did she want? Divorce?" "Nope, damages. After all, he married her, and perhaps she lost her position. Nobody wants a divorced woman, anyway. She was snow-white, that woman, pretty as a picture. Descended from Negroes, maybe from the seventeenth century. Damages."

A fight was going on around the bar. The proprietress was hollering at an excited chauffeur. He was contradicting her: "I'd never take the liberty of monkeying with food." The fruit dealer yelled: "Keep quiet there." Whereupon the chauffeur turned around angrily, and looked at the stout chap, the latter smiled him out of countenance, however, and there followed a vicious silence around the bar.

Meck whispered to Franz: "The cattle dealers are not coming today. Got everything fixed up. They're all set for the next session. Take a look at that yellow chap, he's a big boy around here."

All evening Franz had been watching the yellow-faced man whom Meck had pointed out to him. Franz felt tremendously attracted by him. He was slim, wore a shabby army coat—wonder if he's a communist—and had a long, thin, yellowish face; what struck you most about him were the deep wrinkles on his forehead. Surely the man was only in his early thirties, but he nevertheless had gaping hollows on both sides of his face, from his nose to his mouth. Franz kept on looking intently at the man's nose; it was short, blunt, and planted in a very business-like way. His head was leaning on his left hand in which he held a burning pipe. He had high, black, upstanding hair. When he went over to the bar later on—he dragged his legs behind him as if his feet were sticking to something—Franz noticed that he wore miserable yellow shoes, and his thick gray socks were hanging overboard. Wonder if that fellow's a consumptive? He ought to be put in a hospital, Beelitz or somewhere, to think they let him run around like that. What's he doing anyway? The man came ambling along, his pipe in his mouth, in one hand a cup of coffee, in the other a lemonade with a big tin spoon. Then he sat down at the table, took one swallow of coffee and then of lemonade. Franz couldn't take his eyes off him. What sad eyes the fellow has! Probably been doing time. Say, look here, he probably thinks I've been doing time, too. So I did, Tegel, four years, now you know it, what about it?

Nothing else that evening. But Franz began to go to Prenzlauer Strasse more frequently now and soon he made up to the man in the old army coat. He was a fine fellow, only stuttered a lot, and it took a long time for him to get something out, that's why he had such big pathetic eyes. It turned out, however, that he had not yet done time, only he had been mixed in politics once, when he almost blew up a gas works. Somebody had squealed on the gang, but they didn't catch him. "And what are you doing now?" "Selling fruit and things like that. Helping around. If that doesn't bring it in, then the dole." Franz Biberkopf has got in with a suspicious bunch, funny, most of them here were selling fruit, doing well with it, too; the little man with the beet-red face supplied the stock, he was their wholesaler. Franz kept his distance, and so did they, as far as he was concerned. He couldn't quite make it all out. He said to himself: I'd rather sell papers.

Spirited White Slavery

One evening the man in the soldier overcoat, Reinhold was his name, got to talking, or rather stuttering, more freely, it went more quickly and even smoothly, he was damning the women. Franz laughed himself sick, the young man really took women seriously. He wouldn't have suspected that about the fellow; so he was cuckoo, too, they were all cuckoo in this place, one here, the other there, none of them was entirely right. The lad was in love with the wife of a helper on a beer-truck; she had already run away from her husband on account of him, and the trouble was, now Reinhold didn't want her any more, no, sir, not at all. Franz rattled through his nose with delight, this boy was really too funny: "Why, let 'er run!" The other stuttered, a terrible look came into his eyes: "That's what's so hard. These damned women don't understand anything, even if you give it to 'em in writing." "Well, Reinhold, did ye write her about it?" The latter stuttered, spat and turned around: "Told her a hundred times. She says she doesn't understand. I'm probably crazy. She just won't understand. So I suppose I'll have to keep her till I croak." "Maybe so." "That's what she says, too." Franz laughed heartily, Reinhold got angry: "Say, don't get foolish." No, Franz couldn't get that, a nice smart fellow like that who could put dynamite in the gas works, and now he's sitting here, tooting a funeral march. "Take her off my hands," stuttered Reinhold. Franz thumped on the table from sheer joy. "And what'll I do with her?" "Well, you can give her the slip." Franz was overjoyed. "I'll do you this favor, you can depend on me, Reinhold, but—they'll put you in diapers one of these days." "First take a good look at her and then let me know."

Next day Fränze came tripping up to Franz's place at noon sharp. When he heard her name was Fränze, he was happy right away; that's fine, they certainly did fit together, his name was Franz, as it happened. She was supposed to bring Biberkopf a pair of heavy boots from Reinhold, that's his Judas blood-money, laughed Biberkopf to himself, ten pieces of silver. Fancy her bringing it to me herself! Reinhold certainly is a nervy skunk. One good deed deserves another, he thought, and he went with her to look for Reinhold in the evening, but, according to plan, he wasn't to be found anywhere, whereupon there followed an outbreak of fury on Fränze's part, and a duet of pacification in his room. Next morning the truck-loader's wife turned up at Reinhold's place, he didn't stutter a word:

No, sir, he needn't bother, she didn't need him, she'd get another fellow. But who it is, she won't tell him that, no, sir. And she has hardly left when Franz comes to see Reinhold with his new boots on; they aren't too big now, for he has put on two pairs of woolen socks, the two fall into each other's arms slapping each other's backs. "Sure, I'm glad to do you a favor," says Franz and he refuses all awards of merit.

The truck-loader's wife fell head over heels in love with Franz; she had, in reality, an elastic heart, a fact she hadn't known up to that time. He was happy that she should feel possessed of this new strength, for he was a friend of all men and knew the human heart. He observed with delight how quickly she felt at home with him. That was just the department he really knew best, at first women are interested in underwear and socks to be mended. But that she always shined his boots in the morning, and Reinhold's boots at that, roused him daily to a regular laughing concert. When she asked why he laughed, he said: "Because they're too big, why, they're too big for any one man. We could both get into them." Once, they even tried to get into one of the boots together, but that was exaggeration, it didn't work.

Now Reinhold, the stutterer, Franz's true friend, had a new girl. Cilly was her name, at least that's what she said. Franz Biberkopf didn't care whether it was or not, and occasionally he saw Cilly in Prenzlauer Strasse. But he became darkly suspicious when Reinhold asked him four weeks later about Fränze, and if he had gotten rid of her. Franz was of the opinion that she was a spicy jane and he didn't understand at first. Then Reinhold averred: Hadn't Franz promised him to get rid of her soon? Which Franz denied. However, it was a bit early yet for that, wasn't it? He hadn't intended to get a new girl till spring. He had seen that Fränze didn't have any summer clothes, and he couldn't buy her any either, so she'd have to get out in summer. Reinhold opined disparagingly that Fränze was beginning to look rather shabby, she wasn't wearing real winter clothes anyway, more between seasons, not at all the thing for the weather just now. Whereupon there followed a long conversation about temperature and the barometer and weather prospects, they looked it all up in the papers. Franz insisted you could never know ahead of time about the weather, but Reinhold foresaw a sharp frost. Only then did Franz realize that Reinhold now wanted to get rid of Cilly, too, who was wearing an imitation rabbit coat. He kept on talking about that pretty imitation rabbit fur. What have I got to do with his rabbit stew, thought Franz, that man certainly can get you going. "Why, you must be off your nut. I certainly can't take on a double load, when I already got one hanging around, and business ain't exactly flourishin' either. Where shall I beg, borrow, or steal it from?" "Why, you don't need to have two girls. Did I say two? Would I except a man to saddle himself with two? Are you a Turk?" "That's what I told you." "All right, I didn't say you were, either. When did I ever tell you to take on the two of 'em? Why not three, then? No, why don't you chuck the one you got—or haven't you got somebody?" "What d'ye mean somebody?" What's he up to now, that lad's always got some bee in his bonnet. "Couldn't somebody else take Fränze off your hands?" Here our Franzeken was overjoyed and he prodded the other in the arm: "Boy, I hand it to you, but you've been to college, that's why, by God, I take my hat off to you. We'll do a kind of chain business, like they did during the inflation." "Well, why not, there are too many dames in the world, anyway." "Far too many. By God, Reinhold, but you're a card, I still can't get my breath." "Well, what about it then?" "All right, everything's O. K. I'll go look for somebody. I'll find somebody all right. Say, I feel like a dope beside you! I'm still gasping for air."

Reinhold looked at him. He's got a little screw loose somewhere. He sure is one big dub, this Franz Biberkopf. Did he really mean to saddle himself with two dames at the same time?

Franz was so enthusiastic about the business that he left at once to go and see Ede, the little cripple, in his den: wonder if he'd like to take a girl off his hands, he had a spare one, and he'd like to get rid of her.

That suited Ede to a T, he wanted to stop working for a while anyway, he had a little sick-pay and could afford to nurse himself a bit; she could go shopping for him and call at the office for his sick-pay. But if she wants to settle down here with me, he said right away, no, sir, nothing doing.

The very next day, at noon, before starting out on the street again, Franz started a hell of a row over nothing at all with the truck-loader's wife. She went up in the air. He kept cheerfully screaming at her. An hour later it was all fixed up; the hunchback helped her pack her things, Franz had gone off in a rage, and the truck-loader's wife took up quarters at the hunchback's place, because she didn't know where else to go. Then the hunchback hurried off to his doctor to ask to be put on the sick-list, and in the evening both of them together cursed and damned Franz Biberkopf.

But then Cilly turned up at Franz's room. Whatsa matter, babykins? Got a li'l' pain somewhere, what's hurting my baby? Lord, O Lord! "I only came to bring you a fur collar." Franz admiringly takes the fur collar in his hands. Grand all right. Wonder where the boy gets all those nice things from. The last time it was just a pair of boots. Cilly, who has no idea what it's all about, piped up innocently: "You must be a good friend of my Reinhold's, aren't you?" "God, yes," laughed Franz, "he sends me food and clothes from time to time, when he has any to spare. Last time he sent me some boots. Just a pair of boots. Wait a minute, you might give me your opinion about them." If only that fool Fränze, the fathead, hasn't dragged them along with her, where are they anyway, aha, here they be. "Y'see, Fräulein Cilly, he sends me these the last time. Whatcha say to these gunboats? Why three men could get into them. Go ahead and put your little pins in them." And there she goes, gets into them, sniggering away, she's dressed nice, a sweet little creature, that was tempting enough to eat, I'll say so, she looks terribly neat, too, in her black coat with the fur trimming, what a sap Reinhold is, to think he's giving her the air, wonder where he's always digging up such nice girls. And there she stands in the gunboats. And Franz thinks of the previous situation, why, it's just as if I had a season ticket for a change of women and wardrobe every month! Then he slips his shoe off and puts his foot into the boot from behind her. Cilly shrieks, but his leg gets in all right. Then she tries to run away, but they both go hopping about, and she has to take him along. Once beside the table, he plunges into the other boot. They're swaying now. They tip over, there's a scream, hold on to your imagination, lady, just leave those two merrily together, they're having a private reception, for ordinary members of the sick-fund the reception hour is from five to seven.

"But Reinhold is waiting for me, Franz, you won't tell him anything, please, please." "Of course, I won't, my li'l darling." And then in the evening he saw her all by himself, the little weeping-willow. At night they spend their time damning things up and down, and she turns out to be a very nice little girl with pretty clothes, that coat, for instance, is almost new, a pair of dancing slippers, too, she brings everything along with her right away, say, boy, Reinhold gave you all that, he must be buying on the installment plan.

It is with joy and admiration that Franz meets his Reinhold now. Franz's work is not easy, his dreams are already oppressed by thoughts of the end of the month, when Reinhold, who has now become quite taciturn, will start talking again. And one evening Reinhold, who is standing by him at the subway station in Alexanderplatz, in front of Landsberger Strasse, asks him what he is going to do that evening. Oho, the month isn't over yet; what's up, and, as a matter of fact, Cilly is waiting for Franz; but to be allowed to walk with Reinhold, of course, he jumps at the chance. And there they go strolling along—where do you think they're going—down Alexanderstrasse, they wander to the Prinzenstrasse. Franz keeps on asking, till he finds out where Reinhold wants to go. "Shall we go to Walterchen's and shake a foot?" He wants to stop by the Salvation Army in the Dresdener Strasse! He'd like to hear what they've got to say. What an idea! That's just like Reinhold! Funny notions he has. And that's when Franz Biberkopf has his first experience of an evening with the Salvationists. It certainly was funny, he couldn't get over it.

At half past ten, when the calls for the penitents' bench were starting, Reinhold began to act quite strange and stormed out, as if someone was after him, come on, let's beat it, what's the matter anyway. He cursed and swore on the stairs and said to Franz: "You gotta watch your step with those babies. They work on you till you get all out of breath and you say yes to everything." "Well, well, not with me, got to get up earlier than that." Reinhold was still cursing away, when they arrived at Hackepeter's in the Prenzlauer Strasse and then bang, it went off all at once and everything came out: "Franz, I want to get away from the dames, I don't want to go on with it." "Lord, and I was already looking forward to the next one!" "Do you think it's a joke for me to come and ask you again next week to take Trude off my hands, y'know the blonde? Nope, on that basis . . ." "No trouble, as far as I am concerned, Reinhold, why should there be? You can depend on me all right. You can send me ten of your dames and I'll take care of 'em all, Reinhold." "To hell with the janes. But suppose I don't want to, Franz?" Can't make head or tail out of this, he gets so excited. "Nope, if you don't want the dames, then it's quite simple, then you simply leave 'em alone. We'll get rid of them any time. I'll take the one you got now off your hands and that'll be the last of it." 2 times 2 is 4, if you can calculate, you'll understand me, there's nothing to look so goggle-eyed about, what's he goggling at me for? If you want to, you can keep the last one, too. Well, what's up now, that fellow is certainly funny, now he's getting his coffee and lemon-juice, can't stand booze, shaky on his pins, and those skirts all the time. Then Reinhold didn't say anything for a long time; only after he had drunk three cups of his slop did he start to unload again.

No one seriously contests the fact, I suppose, that milk is a highly valuable food for children, especially for little children and babies; furthermore, for sick people it is entirely to be recommended as a strength-builder, especially when served with a meal of nutritive quality. One of the sick-diets generally recommended by leading medical authorities, though unfortunately unappreciated, is, for instance, mutton. Of course, this is no argument against milk. Only this propaganda must not be pushed to crude or perverted extremes. At any rate, Franz thinks: I'll stick to beer, when it's good lager beer, there's nothing to be said against it.

And Reinhold turns his lamps towards Franz—the boy looks all in, if he only don't start blubbering away now. "I've been twice to the Salvation Army, Franz, I've already talked to one of them, I tell him 'yes,' I'm goin' to stick to the straight and narrow, and then I topple off." "Well, what's up now?" "Y'know I get tired of the dames very quick. You can see that, can't you? Four weeks, and that's all. I don't know why. Don't like 'em any more. And up to that time I was crazy about 'em, you ought to see me, completely gone, enough to put in a padded cell, that's how crazy I get. And afterwards—nothin', out they go, can't see 'em. I'd throw money after 'em if only I didn't have to see 'em." And Franz is astonished: "Well, old boy, maybe you really are crazy. Wait a minute . . ." "Didn't I go to the Salvation Army, told 'em about it and then I prayed with a fellow . . ." Franz grew more and more astonished: "Y'mean, prayed?" "Boy, suppose, that's the way you feel and you don't know where to turn to for advice." Well, I'll be damned. What a man, never saw the likes of him. "Helped a bit, too, for six or eight weeks, a fellow thinks of other things, you get a hold of yourself, it gets you going all right, all right." "Well, Reinhold, maybe you'd better go to the Charité Hospital. Or maybe you oughtn't to've rushed away like that up there at the hall. You might of sat down quietly on the bench in front. Needn't be ashamed before me." "Nope, don't want to any more, and it don't help me, any more, anyway and it's all a lot of bunk. Why should I be crawling around up there in front and praying, when I don't believe anyway?" "Yes, I can understand that. If y'don't believe, it won't help anything." Franz looked at his friend, who was staring glumly into his empty cup. "Whether I can help you, Reinhold, me?—well, I don't know about that. I'll have to study over that a little, first. They ought to try and give you a real disgust for the dames, or something like that." "I could puke already at the sight of that yellow-haired Trude. But tomorrow or day after tomorrow you just ought to see me when Nelly or Gusta or whatever her name may be, comes along, boy, you ought to see little Reinhold. His ears bright red. All I want is her, and if I gotta spend all my money, I gotta have her." "What is it you like especially about the dames?" "You mean how they get me? Well now, what shall I say? With nothing at all. That's it, really. One of 'em has— how do I know?—maybe she has bobbed hair, or she cracks a joke. Well, I like her, Franz, I never know why. The dames, ask 'em, they wonder about it, too, when all at once I begin to goggle at them like a bull and keep sticking around. Ask Cilly. But I can't help it, I just can't help it."

Franz is still watching Reinhold.

There is a mower death yclept. Hath power which the Lord hath kept. When he 'gins his scythe to whet, keener it grows and keener yet, soon will he slash, man must endure the gash.

A funny chap. Franz smiles. Reinhold doesn't smile at all.

There is a mower death yclept. Hath power which the Lord hath kept. Soon will he slash.

Franz thinks to himself: you need a good shaking up, m'boy. We'll push your hat a few inches farther down on your neck. "All right, that's what I'll do, Reinhold, I'm going to ask Cilly about it."

Franz meditates on White Slavery and suddenly he is off of it, he wants Something Else

"Cilly, not on my lap now. And don't start beating me right away. You're my li'l darling. Now guess who I was with today?" "Don't want to know." "Babykins, my little snookums, who do you think? With—Reinhold." The little girl grows spiteful, I wonder why: "Reinhold—is that so, what did he have to tell you?" "Well, a lot of things." "That's so. And you let him tell you all that, and you even believe him, don't you?" "Why, no Cilly, li'l girl." "Well, I might as well get out then. First I wait up for you exactly three hours and then you come with all this bunk and try to tell me all about it." "Why no, I don't, little girl" (she's nutty) "it's you who ought to tell me all about it. Not him, of course not." "Whatsa matter? I don't understand nothing." And then it started. Cilly, the little black-haired thing, got into a rage so that at times she was unable to tell her story, what with all the steam she got up, and Franz squeezed her while she was talking, because she looked so pretty, such a shining cherry-red li'l bird, and then she started crying as it all came back to her. "So that man Reinhold, he's no lover and no mack either, why he's not even a man, just a scoundrel. He goes around the streets like a sparrow, says peck, peck, and snaps up the girls. There's dozens of us could sing a song about that fellow. You don't suppose I was his first or his eighth, either, do you? Maybe the hundredth. If you ask him, he never knows how many he's had before. But how's he had 'em? Now, listen, Franz Biberkopf, if you squeal on that criminal, you'll get something from me, no, I got nothing, but you can go to police headquarters and get yourself a reward. He doesn't look it, when he sits around like that and broods and drinks his chicory, which is nothing but slop. And then a girl comes along and he bites." "He told me all that." "And you think to yourself first, what does the guy want, he ought to try some flop-house, so he can take a good long nap. Then back he comes again, a snappy lad, a fine buck, I tell you, Franz, you hold your head, what's happened to him, has he got himself some monkey-glands since yesterday? That's a fact and he starts talking and the way he can dance . . ." "What, Reinhold can dance?" "I guess, maybe. Where'd I get to know him? On the dance floor. Chausseestrasse." "He certainly must shake a mean hoof." "He picks 'em out, Franz, wherever they are. And if it's a married woman, he won't let go, he gets her." "Fine buck, all right." Franz laughed and laughed. Don't swear you'll be true, For oaths I don't care, It's always the new that makes me dare. Never peace in a warm heart dwells, There's ever a fresh inspiration that wells, Don't swear you'll be true, I like to change, too, Just like you.

"Now you're laughing, huh? Maybe you're one of those fellows, too?" "Why no, Cilly, old girl, only the guy's really too funny and he's always bellyaching to me that he can't keep off of women." Can't keep off, can't keep off, I just can't keep off of you. Franz took off his coat. "Now he's got that little blonde, Trude, and perhaps, what d'ye say, shall I take her off his hands?" How that tart does screech! She certainly can screech, that tart! She roars, Cilly does, like a wild tigress! Tears Franz's coat off and throws it on the floor, maybe she thinks I bought it on the installment plan, she'll tear it to pieces in a minute, she certainly could do it. "Franz, say, they must have been handing you lollipops. What was that, what's that about Trude, say that again." She screams like a tigress run amuck. If she goes on screaming like that, they'll call the cops who'll think I'm turning her gas off. Keep calm, Franz! "Cilly, now don't throw my clothes around like that. Them's objects of value and nowadays difficult to procure. That's it, let's have 'em. Did I bite you?" "No, but you sure are a soft one, Franz." "Fine, suppose I am. But if he's my friend, Reinhold, and is in trouble, and even trots out to Dresdener Strasse to the Salvation Army and wanted to say his prayers, imagine it, why, a fellow has to put up with him, when he's his friend, or don't he. Shouldn't I take Trude off his hands?" "And how about me?" With you, I'd like to go fishing with you. "Well, we'll have to talk it over some time, might have a drink or two and decide how to do it. Where the deuce are those boots, those big boots? Take a peep at 'em." "Leave me alone, won't you?" "I just want to show you the boots, Cilly. I got those, why, I got 'em from him, too. You remember, you brought me a fur collar that time. All right then. And before that, one of the girls brought me these boots." Tell her quietly, why not, don't keep anything back, everything comes out right if you're only frank.

The girl sits down on the footstool, and looks at him. Then she bursts out crying, doesn't say anything. "So that's the way it is. That's his scheme. I helped him. He's my friend. And I won't lie to you." The way that gal can stare. And what a rage she gets in: "Dirty common dog, low common skunk that you are! Y'know, if Reinhold is a scoundrel, then you are worse—worse than the worst pimp." "No, I'm not that kind." "If I were a man . . ." "All right, good thing you're not a man. But you needn't work yourself up, Cilly, old girl, I told you what happened. I've thought it all over while I was looking at you. I won't take Trude off his hands, you can stay here with me." Franz gets up, takes his boots, throws them on top of the wardrobe. This thing won't do, he's ruining human beings, I won't go along with him in that. Something has got to be done about it. "Cilly, you stay here today, then early tomorrow morning, after Reinhold is gone, you go to Trude and talk to her. I'll help her, she can depend on me. Tell her, wait a minute, tell her to come up here, we'll talk things over between us."

And when the little blonde, Trude, comes to see Franz and Cilly at noon, she looks very pale and sad, and Cilly tells her right off the bat that Reinhold gets on her nerves and he doesn't care about her, either. All that's true. Trude keeps on crying, but doesn't know what they want with her, so Franz explains: "The lad's not a scoundrel. He's my friend. I won't let anything be said against him. But it's downright torture, like hurting an animal, the things he does. It's cruelty." She shouldn't let him force her out, and moreover, he, Franz, well, he's going to see about it.

That night Reinhold calls on Franz at his stand, it's cold as hell. Franz lets himself be invited for a hot grog. He listens calmly to Reinhold's preface and then Reinhold pounces directly on the situation about Trude, how he's sick and tired of her and he wants to get rid of her today.

"Reinhold, I suppose you've gone and got another girl." Sure enough he has, and he says so. Whereupon Franz says, he won't get rid of Cilly, she has got used to him now and besides she's a decent sort of a jane;

Reinhold oughta really put on the brakes a bit, like any decent fellow would, things can't go on that way. Reinhold doesn't understand, wants to know if it's on account of the collar, that fur collar. Maybe Trude would bring him, well, what, a watch maybe, a silver watch, or a fur cap with ear-muffs. Franz might need them, now. Nope, nothing doing, only cut that stuff out. I'll buy all that myself. And now Franz would certainly like to talk to Reinhold as friend to friend. So he tells him what he has been thinking today and yesterday. Reinhold should keep Trude now, no matter if everything goes to hell. He should get used to her, then it'll go all right. A human being is a human being, a skirt is, too, otherwise he might just as well buy a whore for three marks, who is perfectly happy if she can trot off the moment it's over. But to begin by coddling a girl with love and a lot of soft stuff, and then push her off like that, and one girl after another, no sirree.

Reinhold listens to all this in his own way. He slowly drinks his coffee, staring dully in front of him. Then he says calmly, if Franz won't take Trude off his hands, it's all right with him. He got along without him before. Then he dashes off, got no time.

That night Franz wakes up and does not fall asleep till morning. It's ice-cold in his room. Cilly is asleep and snoring beside him. Why don't I fall asleep? Now the vegetable wagons are driving to the market-hall. I wouldn't like to be a horse, running around at night in this cold. In the stable, yes: there it's warm. Funny how that woman can sleep. She certainly can sleep. Not me. My toes are frozen, how they tickle and itch. There's something inside him, is it his heart, his lungs, his respiration, or his innermost feeling, anyway, the thing inside there is being shoved and pushed on, but by whom? By whom, it doesn't know. It can only say it's sleepless.

A bird sits on a tree, a snake has just glided past it in its sleep, the bird wakes up at the rustling sound and sits there with ruffled feathers, it hadn't sensed the snake. Well, just go on breathing quietly taking in the air. Franz tosses about. Hatred of Reinhold weighs on him, wrangles with him. It penetrates the wooden door and wakes him up. Reinhold, too, is lying in bed, lying beside Trude. He sleeps soundly. In his dream he commits murder, in his dream he frees himself.

Local News

It was the second week in April, when the weather in Berlin is sometimes spring-like, and, as the press unanimously stated, this splendid Easter weather lured people out-of-doors. In Berlin, at that time, Alex Fränkel, a Russian student, shot and killed Vera Kaminskaya, aged twenty-two, arts-and-crafts worker, in their boarding-house. Tatiana Sanftleben, same age, a governess, who had agreed to join in the suicide pact, became afraid of this decision at the last moment and ran away when she saw her girl-friend lying on the floor. She met a squad of police to whom she told the story of her terrible experience of the last few months, and led the officers to the place where Vera and Alex were lying mortally wounded. The criminal police were called in and the homicide commission dispatched its officers to the spot. Alex and Vera had planned to get married, but economic conditions did not permit their conjugal union.

Furthermore, the investigation into the question of responsibility for the street-car disaster in Heerstrasse is not yet completed. The examination of the victims and of Redlich, the conductor, is still proceeding. The opinions of the technical experts have not yet been received. Only after their receipt will it be possible to enter upon an examination of the question whether there is any culpability on the part of the conductor, because he applied the brakes too late, or whether it was a concatenation of unfortunate circumstances that caused the disaster.

Quiet conditions prevailed in the stock market; open stock prices were steadier in view of the Reichsbank statement about to be published, which is said to show a very favorable state of affairs with a reduction in the bank-note circulation of 400 millions and a reduction in the exchange situation of 350 millions. Quotations on April 18 around 11 o'clock were: I. G. Dye Stuffs 260½ to 267, Siemens & Halske 297½ to 299, Dessauer Gas 202 to 203, Waldhof Cellulose 295. Bids for German Oil at 134½.

To return once more to the street-car disaster in Heerstrasse, all those seriously injured in the accident are improving.

On April 11, Herr Braun, editor, was liberated from Moabit prison by an armed party. It was a regular Wild West scene. A search is being made for them. The Acting President of the Criminal Court immediately made a report on the matter to the superior authorities. Meanwhile, the examination of eye-witnesses and the officials involved continues.

The Berlin public at this time is not much interested in the desire of one of the most important American automobile factories to obtain offers from financially strong German firms to act as sole representatives for six- and eight-cylinder cars on a monopoly basis for Northern Germany.

A word to the wise. To the residents of the Steinplatz telephone area in particular: In the Renaissance Theater, Hardenbergstrasse, the 100th performance of "Cœur-Bube," that charming comedy in which agreeable humor is united with a deeper meaning, was given with appropriate honors. The residents of Berlin are urged by means of bill-posters to help this play to reach a still higher commemorable record. We have to consider here, of course, several different things: Collectively, Berliners may be asked to do this, but it may also happen that, through various circumstances, they will be prevented from obeying the call. In the first place, they may be away on a trip and so not know anything about the existence of the play. Or, they may be in Berlin, but have no occasion to see the announcement of the play on the poster column, perhaps because they are ill in bed. In a city of four millions, that must apply to a considerable number of people. At any rate, it may be that they are notified through the advertising news of the radio, at 6 p.m., that "Cœur-Bube," that charming Parisian comedy, in which agreeable humor is united with a deeper meaning, is now being played at the Renaissance Theater for the 100th time. The announcement, however, may have no effect other than to make them regret not being able to travel to Hardenbergstrasse, for the journey is out of the question, supposing they are really sick abed. According to reliable information, no arrangements have been made in the Renaissance Theater for the reception of sick-beds, which perhaps might be temporarily transported there by ambulances.

Nor can we ignore another possibility: there may be people in Berlin (and there doubtless are such) who read the poster of the Renaissance Theater, but doubt its truth, not the truth of the existence of the poster, but the truth and also the importance of its contents, as reproduced by the printed type. They may read with a feeling of discomfort, disgust, and reluctance, even with anger, the statement that the play "Cœur-Bube" is a charming comedy. Whom does it charm, what does it charm, with what does it charm, how do they contrive to charm me, I needn't let myself be charmed. It might cause them to make a wry face when they think that in this comedy agreeable humor is united with a deeper meaning. They do not want agreeable humor, their attitude toward life is serious, their emotional state is sad, but lofty, there having occurred a recent bereavement in their family. Nor will they let themselves be bamboozled by the information that a deeper meaning is connected with this regrettably agreeable humor. For in their opinion agreeable humor can in no case be made innocuous or neutralized. Deeper meaning must always stand alone. Agreeable humor is to be eliminated, as Carthage was eliminated by the Romans, or as the same thing befell other cities, in other ways which they can no longer remember. Some people don't believe at all in the deeper meaning that lies in the play "Cœur-Bube," praised by the poster columns. A deeper meaning: why a deeper and not a deep one? Does deeper mean more deeply than deep? Thus they argue.

It is obvious that in a big city like Berlin, many people doubt a lot of things and carp and cavil considerably. And so it happens that they may also criticize the wording of that poster which has been placed there at such great expense by the producer. As a matter of fact, they are not interested in the theater. And even if they don't carp at it, and even if they love it, especially the Renaissance Theater in Hardenbergstrasse, and even if they admit that in this play there is a union of agreeable humor with a deeper meaning, they do not want to participate in it, simply because they have other plans for tonight. Thus the number of people who will stream towards Hardenbergstrasse, and might perhaps force simultaneous performances of the play "Cœur-Bube" in adjacent theaters, would be considerably diminished.

After this instructive excursion into public and private events in Berlin we will now return, in April 1928, to Franz Biberkopf and Reinhold with his plague of girls. It may be assumed that for this news, too, there exists only a small circle of people who are interested. We prefer not to explain the reasons for this. But this shall not prevent me from following the traces of my little man in Berlin, Center and East; each of us does what to him seems necessary.

Franz has made a devasting Resolution. He does not notice that he is sitting on Nettles

Things did not go well with Reinhold after his conversation with Franz Biberkopf. Reinhold hadn't it in him, at least not up till now, to be rough with women, the way Franz was. He always needed somebody to help him, and now he was in trouble. The girls were after him, Trude, who was still with him, Cilly, the last, as well as the penultimate one, whose name he had already forgotten. All of them were spying round him, either worried and anxious (the last specimen), or seeking revenge (the penultimate specimen), or greedy for more love (the antepenultimate specimen). The very latest to appear on his horizon, a certain Nelly, from the Central Market, a widow, had fallen in love with him, but had fallen out again at once, when, one after the other, Trude and Cilly and finally even, as chief witness, a man, a certain Franz Biberkopf, himself a friend of Reinhold's, had appeared at her place and warned her. Yes, that's what Franz Biberkopf did. "Frau Labschinsky—that was, of course, Nelly's real name—I'm not doing this in order to blacken my friend or whoever he is. Not on your life. No, I don't never mix up in other people's dirty linen. No, but what's right must stay right. To push one woman after the other into the street, that's not my idea of things. And it's not true love, either."

Frau Labschinsky permitted her bosom to heave contemptuously: Reinhold, well, he mustn't put on airs on account of her. She ain't a beginner with men either. Franz continued: "I'm glad to hear it, that's enough for me. So now you know all there's to know. For you're doing a good deed, and that's exactly what I'd like to do. A fellow feels sorry for women—they're human beings like us, and then for Reinhold himself. He'll go to the dogs, you'll see. That's why he don't drink no beer now and no liquor, only weak coffee, he can't stand a drop. He'd better take care of himself. There's good stuff in him." "That's right, there certainly is." Frau Labschinsky was crying. Franz nodded gravely: "And that's what I'd like to do, he's been through a lot, but it can't go on this way, and that's where we gotta protect him."

Frau Labschinsky gave Herr Biberkopf her vigorous paw when he left: "I depend on you, Herr Biberkopf." She certainly could. Reinhold didn't make a move. He was a sedentary man, but he didn't let anyone look into his cards. He had now been living with Trude three weeks beyond his term; she gave Franz a daily report about it. Franz was exultant. The next one is going to be due soon. That means: watch out! And sure enough: Trude, trembling, reports to him one noon that Reinhold has been out for two nights in his best bib and tucker. The following noon she knew who it was: a certain Rosa, buttonhole-maker, in her early thirties, she hadn't yet found out the last name, but the address. Well, then, everything's O. K., laughed Franz.

But with destiny's mighty power there's no union that can flower. And fate moves with giant strides. If you have difficulty in walking, wear Leiser's shoes, Leiser's is the biggest shoe-store on the square. And if you don't want to walk you might ride: N.S.U. invites you to a trial ride in a six-cylinder car. That Thursday Franz Biberkopf happened to be walking alone through Prenzlauer Strasse, having remembered that he wanted to look up his friend Meck, whom he hadn't seen for a long time, just for general reasons; and then, too, he wanted to tell him about Reinhold and the janes, and Meck ought to just watch and admire him, how he, Franz, can bring a fellow like that to his senses, and how he makes him turn about face and he has gotta get used to law and order, and we'll swing it, all right.

And sure enough, as Franz ambles into the café with his newspapers, whom do the apples of my eyes behold? Meck. There he is sitting with two others, jabbering away. So Franz sits down beside them right away and starts to jabber too, and, after the others are gone, they allow themselves to be treated, at Franz's invitation, to a couple of big tankards, and Franz, gurgling and gulping away, tells him a lot of things, and Meck, gurgling and gulping too, hears from his lips, hears with amazement and satisfaction, what kind of people there are in the world. Meck is going to keep it all to himself, sure, but it's really a crazy story. Franz beams as he tells of his own achievements in the matter, how he got Nelly, who was a Frau Labschinsky, away from Reinhold, and how he had to stay with Trude three weeks after the term, and that now there is a certain Rosa, a buttonhole-maker, but we'll sew that buttonhole together again for him. And so Franz sits there with his tankard, feeling his oats, he's sitting pretty. Rejoice, all ye young choiring throats, round our table rings a roundelay, hey-dey-dey-hey-dey-dey, round our table rings a roundelay. Three times three is ni-i-ine, we swig our drinks like swi-i-ine, three times three and one is ten, let's swig another one like men—two, three, four, six, seven.

Who is that standing at the milling-bar, the swilling-bar, the rilling-bar, who is that smiling into the smoky stink-hole? The biggest of all big swine, Herr von und zu Pums. He smiles, what he calls smiling, y'know, but his little pig's eyes are looking for something or somebody. He'll have to get a broom and crack a hole in this reeking fume, if he wants to see anything. Three of them are climbing towards him now. That's so, those are the boys who are always doing partnership business with him, queer birds they are, too. Birds of a feather flock together. Better end young on the gallows, than have to go grubbing for cigar-butts in your old age. The four of them scratch their heads, clack and drone together, they're looking for something or other. They'll need a broom, if they want to see anything here, or perhaps a ventilator would help. Meck nudges Franz: "Still someone missing. They need more people to handle their stuff, Fat there can't never get enough people."

"He tried to sound me, too. But I won't join in. What would I do with fruit anyway? Must have a lot of stuff, hasn't he?" "How do I know what kind of goods he carries? Fruit—that's what he says. Better not ask too many questions, Franz. But it won't hurt to stick to him, there's always something might fall your way. He's a clever bird, the old duck, and so are the others."

At twenty-three minutes, seventeen seconds after eight, another man steps up to the bar, the milling-bar, the swilling-bar, a fellow—one, two, three, four, five, six, seven, all good children go to heaven—who might it be? You say it's the King of England? No, it's not the King of England, driving in grand style, to the opening of Parliament, as a symbol of the English nation's sense of independence. It's not he. Then who is it? Is it a delegate of the nations who signed the Kellogg Pact in Paris, surrounded by 50 photographers, the proper ink-well could not be brought in because of its enormous size, they had to content themselves with a Sèvres set? No. It's only—in comes slouching, gray woolen socks a-dangle—our Reinhold, that quite insignificant figure, a mouse-gray lad in mouse-gray. The five of them scratch their heads, look around the place. Have to get a broom, that's certain, to see anything here; or a ventilator would do. Franz and Meck, from their table, watch these five fellows intently, what're they up to, the way they sit down at the table.

A quarter of an hour later Reinhold will fetch himself a cup of coffee and some mineral water, glancing keenly round the room at the same time. And who is going to smile at him from the wall or nod at him? Dr. Luppe, Burgomaster of Nürnberg? Not on your life, for that morning he had to deliver the address of welcome at the Dürer Festival; after him spoke Dr. Keudell, Minister of the Interior, and Dr. Goldenberger, the Bavarian Minister of Education; this circumstance prevented them from being present on this occasion. Wrigley's Chewing Gum for good teeth, pure breath, better digestion. It's only Franz Biberkopf grinning all over his face, he's mighty glad, when Reinhold arrives. Why, he's his educational object, he's his pupil, he might serve him up to his friend Meck now. Just watch him as he comes along. We've got a check on him. Reinhold marches up with his coffee and water, sits down beside them, shrivels into himself and begins to stutter a bit. Franz, his curiosity aroused, would like to draw him out affectionately, so that Meck can hear it: "Well, how's everything at home, Reinhold, everything all right?"

"Well, yes, Trude's still there, a person gets used to it." He says this very slowly, letting it trickle out like a plugged-up water-pipe. Well, Franz is certainly happy. He almost jumps up, he's that glad. He fixed it, all right. Who else did it but me? He beams on his friend Meck, who doesn't withhold his admiration. "What do you say, Meck, we'll create law and order in this world, we'll smash this thing, let 'em come, if they want anything out of us." Franz pummels Reinhold's shoulder, it twitches. "Y'see, old boy, you've gotta get ahold of yourself, then everything'll go all right in this world of ours. That's what I always say: a fellow has gotta get ahold of himself and stick it out, then let 'em come on." And Franz can't get over being happy about Reinhold. A penitent sinner is better than 999 just men.

"And what does Trude say, ain't she astonished that everything's going so peacefully now? And you, m'boy, ain't you glad you're rid of all this worry about the janes? Women are all right, Reinhold, and can give us lots of pleasure. But y'see, if you ask me what I think of 'em, then I say: not too few of 'em, and not too many. If it's too many, it gets dangerous, hands off. I can tell you a thing or two about that." That story about Ida, Paradiesgarten. Treptow, canvas shoes, and then Tegel. Victory. All that's dead and gone, sunk in the deepest ocean, let's take a drink. "I'll help you all right, Reinhold, so there won't be any trouble about them women. You needn't go to the Salvation Army, we'll do all that a lot better. Well, Reinhold, here's how, you can take one glass at least, can't you?" Reinhold quietly clinked with his coffee cup: "What can you do about it, Franz, why, how can you do anything?"

Hell, that's where I almost spilled the beans. "I just mean you can depend on me, oughta get used to liquor, how about a light Kümmel?" The other quietly: "Maybe you'd like to play doctor with me?" "Why not? That's where I'm at home. Y'know, Reinhold, didn't I help you with Cilly, and the time before? Don't you think I'll be able to help you now? Franz is still a friend of men. He knows which way the road goes."

Reinhold looks up, staring at him with his sad eyes: "So you know all that?" Franz quietly endures his look, won't allow his happiness to be ruffled by it, let 'im notice something if he wants to, it'll do him a lot of good if he notices that others don't let people flatten 'em out. "Yes, Meck here can confirm it, we've got experience behind us and we're building on that. And then that thing about the booze; Reinhold, if you can stand it, we'll celebrate right here at my expense. I'll pay the whole shebang." Reinhold continues to look first at Franz, who is sticking out his chest, and then at little Meck who is gazing at him with curiosity. Reinhold lowers his eyes and searches around in his cup: "Maybe you'd like to fix me up as an old family man, who maybe can't do nothing for his wife?" "Hurray for Reinhold, the old family man, three times three is ni-i-ine, we swig our drinks like swi-i-ine, come on, Reinhold, now sing, the first ten years are the hardest, friend, but without 'em there never would be any end."

Company, halt! Form fours! By the right, march! Reinhold leaves his coffee cup. Pums, of the fat red face, is standing beside him, whispering something to him. Reinhold shrugs his shoulders. Then Pums blows through the thick smoke and starts to croak merrily: "I've asked you once before, Biberkopf, how things are going with you, do you want to go on forever running around with that paper junk of yours? What profit do you get out of it, two pfennigs a copy, five pfennigs an hour, don't you?" And then there's a lot of pushing back and forth. Franz ought to take over a fruit and vegetable wagon. Pums furnishes the merchandise, the profits are splendid, Franz wants to, and then again he doesn't want to, all those birds around Pums don't quite suit him, they're liable to give me the dirty end of the stick. Reinhold, the stutterer, remains silent in the background. When Franz asks him what he thinks about it, he notices that Reinhold has been looking at him all the time and only now looks back into his cup. "Well, what do you think about it, Reinhold?" The latter stutters: "Yes, I'm going to join up, too." Meck says, why not, Franz, but Franz wants to think about it; he doesn't want to say yes or no, he'll come back tomorrow or day after tomorrow and talk the situation over and see how the merchandise is handled and about fetching it, billing it, and which section of the town is the best for him.

All of them are gone, the place is almost empty. Pums is gone, Meck and Biberkopf gone, alone at the bar stands a street-car employee, discussing with the proprietor wage-reductions, which he finds exorbitant. Reinhold, the stutterer, is still in his seat. Three empty soda bottles stand in front of him, one of them half filled, and a coffee cup. He doesn't want to go home. At home Trude is sleeping. He thinks about it and wonders. He gets up, drags his feet across the room, his woolen socks hanging overboard. He looks a pitiable sight, pale yellow, gaping lines round his mouth, terrible wrinkles across his forehead. He takes another cup of coffee and lemonade.

Cursed be the man, says Jeremiah, that trusteth in man, and maketh flesh his arm, and whose heart departeth from the Lord. For he shall be like the heath in the desert, and shall not see when good cometh; but shall inhabit the parched places in the wilderness, in a salt land and not inhabited. Blessed, blessed, blessed, is the man that trusteth in the Lord, and whose hope the Lord is. For he shall be as a tree planted by the waters, and that spreadeth out her roots by the river, and shall not see when heat cometh, but her leaf shall be green; and shall not be careful in the year of drought, neither shall cease from yielding fruit. The heart is deceitful above all things and desperately wicked: who can know it?

Water in the dense black forest, black and terrible waters, you lie so dumb. In terrible repose you lie. Your surface does not move, when there is a storm in the forest and the firs begin to bend, and the spider-webs are torn between the branches and there is a sound of splitting. Then you, black waters, lie there below in the hollow place; and the branches fall.

The wind tears at the forest, to you the storm does not come. You have no dragons in your domain, the age of mammoths is gone, nothing is there to frighten anyone; the plants decay in you; in you move fish and snails. Nothing more. Yet, though this is so, although you are but water, awesome you are, black waters, and terrible in your repose.

Sunday, April 8, 1928

"Are we going to have snow? Perhaps we will see white again in April." Franz Biberkopf sat at the window of his little place, his left arm on the window-sill and his head in his hand. It was in the afternoon, Sunday, warm and comfy in the room. Cilly had lighted the stove at noon, now she was sleeping back there in bed with her little cat. "Are we going to have snow? The air's so gray. It would be nice."

And as Franz closed his eyes, he heard bells ringing. For several minutes he sat in silence, listened to them ringing: Boom, bim, bum, boom, bim, bam, bum, bum, bim. Then he raised his head from his hand and listened: Two deep bells and one shrill one. Then they stopped.

Why are they ringing? he asked himself. Then all at once they started again, very loud, eager, roaring. A frightening crash. Then they stopped. Everything was suddenly quiet.

Franz lifted his arm from the window-sill, stepped into the room. Cilly was sitting on the bed, a little mirror in her hand, her curl-pins between her lips, humming a friendly little tune, when Franz came up. "What's on today, Cilly? Holiday?" She was busy with her hair. "Why, yes, Sunday."

"Not a holiday?" "Maybe a Catholic holiday, don't know." "Because the bells are ringing like mad." "Where?" "Just now." "Didn't hear anything. Did you hear anything, Franz?" "Why yes. It was crashing and banging around here like anything!" "You musta been dreaming." I'm scared. "No, I wasn't dreaming, I was sitting over there." "Maybe you were dozing." "Nope." He stuck to it, felt all numb, moved slowly, sat down at his place at the table. "Funny the way a man dreams. But I heard it, all right." He poured down a swallow of beer. The scared feeling didn't leave him.

He glanced towards Cilly, who was beginning to look tearful. "Who knows, Cilly, m'darlin', if something didn't happen to somebody just now." Then he asked for the paper. She was able to laugh. "It didn't come, never on Sundays, didn't you know that?"

He picked up the morning edition, looked at the head-lines. "Only small stuff. Nope, that's all nothing. Nothing has happened." "If you hear ringing, Franz, that means you'll be going to church." "Oh, leave me alone with them sky-pilots. Not for me. Only it's funny: a fellow hears something and when you look around afterwards, there's nothing." He meditates on this, she stood beside him now, caressing him. "I'll go down and get some air, Cilly. Just for an hour or so. Want to hear what's happened. In the evening there's the *Welt* or *Montag Morgen*. I'll have to look into that." "Oh, Franz, always speculating. It probably says in the papers: a garbage truck had a breakdown at the Prenzlauer Tor and all the garbage spilled out. Or, wait a minute: a paper-seller had to change some money and gave the right amount by mistake."

Franz laughed: "Well, I'm off. Bye-bye, Cilly."

"Bye-bye, Franzeken."

Then Franz went slowly down the four flights of stairs, and he never saw Cilly again.

She waited in the room till five. When he didn't come, she went out in the street and asked for him in the cafés as far as the Prenzlauer corner. He hadn't been seen anywhere. But hadn't he wanted to read in the paper about his silly story, she thought, that thing he had dreamed? He must have gone somewhere. At the Prenzlauer corner the proprietress said: "Nope, he hasn't been here. But Herr Pums asked for him. So I told him where Herr Biberkopf lived, that's probably where he went." "Nope, nobody's been to our home." "Maybe he didn't find the place." "Perhaps." "Or maybe he met him in front of the door."

Cilly sat there till late in the evening. The café began to fill up. She kept looking towards the door. Once she went home and came back again.

Meck was the only one who came, he consoled her and entertained her with jokes for a quarter of an hour. He said: "He'll come back, that boy is used to his three squares. Don't you worry, Cilly." But while he was saying this, he remembered how Lina had once come and sat beside him, and she had been looking for Franz, too, that time, when he had the trouble with Lüders and the shoe-laces. And he almost went along with Cilly when she went out into the dark muddy street again, but he really didn't want to make her afraid, it was probably a lot of bunk anyway.

Cilly suddenly got furious and went to look for Reinhold; maybe he had talked Franz into getting another jane and simply giving her the go-by. Reinhold's place was locked, not a soul there, not even Trude.

She went slowly back to the café, Prenzlauer corner, back again into the café. It was snowing, but the snow had begun to melt. On the Alex the newsboys were calling *Montag Morgen* and *Welt am Mittag*. She bought a paper from a strange boy, even looked at it. Wonder if anything has happened, if he was right this afternoon.

Oh well, a railroad accident in the United States, in Ohio; a clash between communists and swastika-men, nope, that's not Franz's idea of a fight, big damage by fire in Wilmersdorf. What do I care. She sauntered past Tietz's bright store-front, crossed towards the gloomy Prenzlauer Strasse. She had no umbrella and got soaked to the skin. In Prenzlauer Strasse in front of the little confectionery shop, a group of street-girls stood under umbrellas, barring the passage. Right behind them a fat man with no hat approached her, as he stepped out of the hallway of a house. She walked quickly past him. I'll take on the next one, what's that boy thinking about anyway. That was the meanest trick anybody had ever played on her.

It was a quarter past nine. A terrible Sunday. At that hour Franz was already lying on the ground in another section of the city, his head in the gutter, his legs on the pavement.

Franz goes down the stairs. One step, another step, another step, step, step, step, four flights, always down, down, down, and still down. A fellow gets dizzy, all dopy in the head. Y'cook soup, Fräulein Stein, got a spoon Fräulein Stein—got a spoon, Fräulein Stein cook soup, Fräulein Stein. . . . Nope, nothing doing in that line; how I sweated with that tart. Gotta get some air. Banisters, no decent lighting arrangements here, could hurt yourself on a nail.

A door opens on the second floor and a man waddles heavily along behind him. He must have *some* belly, to puff like that, and walking down-stairs, too. Franz Biberkopf stands in front of the door, the air is soft and gray, it'll soon be snowing. The man from the staircase puffs beside him, a flabby little man with a bloated white face wearing a green felt hat. "A bit out of breath, neighbour?" "Yes, it's because I'm so fat, and then walking up and down the steps like that." They walk down the street together. The man with the short breath is puffing away. "Been up and down four flights of stairs five times today. Just figure out for yourself: twenty flights, with an average of thirty steps each, winding stairs are shorter, but it's harder to walk up, so we'll count thirty steps, five flights make a hundred and fifty steps. Up. And down." "As a matter of fact, it's three hundred. Because I see you use up a lot of strength walking down, too." "You're right, going down as well." "If I was you, I'd look for another job."

Heavy flakes of snow are now falling. They turn around, it's a pretty sight. "Yes, I follow the ads, and I've got to keep at it. There's no weekday and Sunday about it. Sunday even more than weekdays. Most people advertise on Sundays, they expect better results that way." "Yes, because people have time to read the paper. I understand that blindfolded. That's in my line." "You in advertising, too?" "Nope, I only sell papers. Now I'm goin' to read one myself." "Well, I've read 'em all. What weather! Did ye ever see anything like it?" "April, yesterday it was still nice. I tell you tomorrow it'll be all white again. What you bet?" He begins to puff again, the street-lamps are lighted already, under a lamp he takes out a little notebook without a cover, holds it far away from him, reads. Franz surmises: "You'll get your book wet." The other does not hear him and puts the book back, the conversation is finished, Franz thinks, I'll be off. At that moment the little man looks at him from under his green hat: "Listen, neighbor, what do you live on?" "Why do you ask, I'm a news-vender, a free-lance newsvender." "That so. And that's how you earn your money?" "Well, I manage it somehow." What's he want anyway, funny bird. "Yep. Look here, I've always wanted to do something like that, earn my money on my own. Must really be nice, a man does what he wants and if you're good at it, you earn enough." "Sometimes you don't. But you run around just about enough already, neighbor. Today being Sunday, and in such weather, there ain't many running around like that." "Right you are, right you are. I've been dashing around half the day. And there ain't nothin' comin' in, nothin' comin' in. People are hard up these days." "Whatcha trading in, neighbor, if I may ask?" "I got a little pension. Y'see I wanted to be a free man; work and earn my money. Well, I've had my pension for three years now, was in the postal service before, and now I do nothing but hoof it all the time. Y'see it's like this: I read the paper and then I go there and take a look at what people advertise." "Furniture, perhaps?" "Anything, second-hand office fixtures, Bechstein grands, old Persian rugs, pianolas, stamp collections, coins, clothes left by dead people." "Lot's of people die?" "By the truck-loads. Well, then I go up and look at the stuff, and sometimes I buy something." "And then you sell it again, I getcha."

Whereupon the asthmatic man grew silent and hunched himself into his coat, as they sauntered along through the soft snow. At the next street-lamp he took a package of post-cards out of his pocket, looked sadly at Franz and pressed two into his hands. "Read this, neighbor." On the card was written: "Sir (or Madam), Dated as per post-mark. I regret to state that I am obliged to cancel the agreement made with you yesterday on account of untoward circumstances. Respectfully yours, Bernard Kauer." "So Kauer's your name?" "Yep, that's me. That's done with a copying-machine which I once bought. It's the only thing I ever did buy. I do my own copying with it. Can do up to fifty an hour." "Ye don't say so? Well, what's it all about?" The fellow's not right in his upper story and then he cocks his eyes so funny, too. "Why don'tcha read it: cancel . . . on account of untoward circumstances. I buy something and then maybe I can't pay for it. People won't let you have it without payment. Can't blame 'em, can ye? So I keep rushing up all the time and buy the stuff and make an agreement and I'm glad, and the others are glad, too, because the business went off so smoothly, and I think to myself, I'm a lucky fool I am, there are so many nice things in this world, magnificent coin collections, I could tell you a thing or two about it, people who suddenly got no money: so then I come up, take a look at everything, and they tell me right away what's up. What misery people do have, if they could only get hold of a few pennies. Bought something in your house, too, they need it *that* badly, I tell you, a washing machine and a little ice-box, they're glad to get rid of 'em. And then I go downstairs, I'd really like to buy everything, but downstairs I get to worrying a lot: no money and still no money." "But then you get somebody to take the stuff off your hands, don't you?" "Never mind that. That's why I bought that copying-machine, I pull off the post-cards with it. Each post-card costs me five pfennigs; that goes on the expense account, and that's all there is to it."

Franz opened his eyes wide. "Well, I'll be doggoned, neighbor. You don't mean it." "The expenses, well, I manage to reduce them sometimes,

I save five pfennigs by throwing my card in the people's letter-box just as I go out." "And you run your legs off and get all out of breath, but what for?"

They had reached Alexanderplatz.

There they saw a crowd gathered, they went near it. The small man looked furiously up at Franz. "Suppose you try to live on eighty-five marks a month and can't make both ends meet?" "But listen, man, you gotta look out for your sales. If you want me to, I'll inquire among my acquaintances." "Rot, did I ask you to do this, I do my business alone, I won't go into partnership." They were right in the midst of the crowd, it was a common brawl. Franz looked around for the little man, he was gone, vanished. To think of his running around like that! Franz wondered at it, amazed, you could knock me down with a feather. Now where did that trouble of mine really happen? He stepped into a little café, took a Kümmel, thumbed the pages of the *Vorwärts* and the *Lokalanzeiger*. Not much more in 'em than in the *Mottenpost*, there's a big horse-race on in England, Paris, too; they probably had to shell out a lot of dough for that. May mean a big stroke of luck, when your ears ring like that.

He is about to go home and make a right-about-face. But he can't help crossing the street to see what's happening in the crowd. Try our big bock sausage with salad! Here you are, young man, the great and only bock sausage! *Montag Morgen, Die Welt, Die Welt am Montag.*

Look at those two guys; they've been at each other for half an hour now, beating the stuffing out of each other, and for no reason at all. Say, I'm goin' to stick around here till tomorrow. Heh, you, maybe you think you've subscribed to a standing-room ticket—you need a lot of room, don't you? Nope, when you're a flea, you don't need so much. Ouch, what a whack, look at 'im, he's knockin' 'im for a goal.

And when Franz has pushed his way through the crowd, till he gets up in front, who do you think is fighting there with whom? Two lads, why, he knows 'em, they're Pums's boys. Now what do ye think o' that! Bang, the tall fellow's got the other in a stranglehold; bing, he's got him eating dirt. Boy, you let that fellow kick you around like that; why, you're no good. What's this pushin' here, heh there! Oh baby, the cops, the bulls. Cheese it, the cops, the cops, beat it. Two coppers in their rain-capes are making their way through the crowd. Wow! one of the pugilists is on his feet, in the crowd, off he flies. The other one, the tall chap, he can't get up right away, he's got a punch in the ribs, and a good one, too. At that moment Franz pushes himself through, right to the front. Why, we can't leave that man lying around here, what a bunch of boobs, nobody touches 'im! So Franz takes him under his arms, and walks right into the crowd. The cops are looking around. "What's the matter here?" "Two guys've been fighting." "Get a move on, now, beat it!" They're always bawling and just the same they're always a day too late. Move on, we're going all right, sergeant, only don't get yourself all worked up.

Franz is sitting with the tall lad in a badly lighted hallway in Prenzlauer Strasse; only two numbers farther down is the house from which some four hours later a fat man without a hat will step out and try to pick up Cilly; she walks on, she'll certainly take on the next man, he's a scoundrel Franz is, that was a mean trick.

Franz sits in the hallway trying to rouse the lazy Emil. "Well now, my lad, get a hold of yourself, we gotta get along to the café. Don't carry on so, can't you stand a little punch, brush yourself up, why, you're carrying half the pavement along with you!" They cross the street. "Now I'm going to leave you in the first good café we go into, Emil. I gotta go home, my girl's waiting for me." Franz shakes hands, then the other fellow turns towards him again. "You might do me a favor, Franz, I'm supposed to go fetch some goods with Pums today. Go ahead and stop at his house, it's just a few steps from here, on the same street. Go ahead now." "How can I, man, I ain't got no time." "Just tell him, I can't today, he'll wait. He won't be able to do anything today."

At which Franz curses, goes off, what weather, go along, old boy, I wanta get home. I can't let Cilly sit around and wait, can I. He's a reg'lar monkey, I guess I didn't steal my time. He starts running. Beside a street lamp there stands a little man, reading in a notebook. Who is that anyway, why, I know him. At that moment the other man looks up, walks towards Franz. "Heh, neighbor. You're the one from the house where the washing machine and the ice-box were, aren't you. Yes. Here, you might leave this card there later, when you go home, it'll save me postage." He presses the post-card into his hand, cancel on account of untoward circumstances. Whereupon Franz Biberkopf wanders quietly on, he'll show the card to Cilly, no hurry about it. He is happy about that crazy fellow, the little mail hound, who's always running around buying things and has no money, but he's got a dickey bird in his belfry, and no common ordinary birdie either, that's a big grown chicken that a whole family could live off of.

"Evenin', Herr Pums, even'. Maybe you're wondering what I've come for. Wait a minute—what's that I'm supposed to tell you? I was walkin' across the Alex. There's a fight goin' on on Landsberger Strasse. Thinks I to myself, well, let's go see. And who's fightin' there? Guess. Your Emil, the tall fellow, with a little chap, got a name like me, Franz, you know who I mean." Pums answers: he'd been thinking about Franz Biberkopf anyway, he'd already noticed at noon that there was something up between those two. "So big old Emil isn't coming. You'll help me out, won't you, Biberkopf." "What d'you want me to do?" "It's around six now. We've gotta fetch that stuff at nine, today's Sunday, Biberkopf, you've got nothing to do, anyway, I'll pay your expenses and then some more—well, let's say, five marks an hour." Franz hesitates: "Five marks?" "Well, I'm up against it, those two left me ditched." "The little fellow's goin' to show up." "All right, shake, five marks and your expenses, all right, make it five-fifty, what do I care!"

Franz has a good laugh to himself as he walks downstairs behind Pums. This is certainly a lucky Sunday, a thing like this don't come your way every day, so it's really true, the bells did mean something. I'm goin' to clean up on this, well, fifteen or twenty marks on Sunday and I ain't got any expenses, anyway. He is happy, the mail-grifter's card crackles in his pocket, he starts to say good-bye to Pums in front of the street-door. But the latter looks astonished: "What's this? I thought we'd fixed that up, Biberkopf?" "Sure we did, it's all right, y'can depend on me. But I just gotta run over home, y'know, heehee, I got a girl, Cilly, maybe y'know her through Reinhold, he had 'er before me. Why, I can't leave the gal up in that place alone all day Sunday." "Now listen, Biberkopf, I can't let you go now, afterwards everything'll be all messed up, and I'll be left in the lurch. No, for the sake of a dame, imagine it, Biberkopf, that won't do, we're not going to let business go to pot on account of that. She won't run away from you." "I know that all right, that's where you said one true word, that gal, I can rely on her all right. But that's just it. Can I let her sit around there all by herself, and she don't hear nothing or see nothing or know nothing? What'll I do?" "Now just come along, it'll be all right."

"What'll I do?" thought Franz. They went off. Once more on the corner of Prenzlauer Strasse. Here and there the street-girls were already standing about, the same girls Cilly is going to see a few hours later, when she runs around looking for Franz. Time progresses, all kinds of things are collecting around Franz; soon he will be standing on a car, they will take hold of him. Now he wonders how he might quickly deliver the crazy man's post-card and perhaps make a dash up to Cilly for a minute or so, the gal's waiting.

He walks with Pums along the Alte Schönhauser Strasse up to the side wing; that's his office, says Pums. There's a light up there, the room really does look like an office, with a telephone and typewriters. An elderly woman with a severe face comes frequently into the room where Franz is sitting with Pums. "That's my wife, Herr Franz Biberkopf, he's going to help us out a bit today." She goes out as if she hadn't heard anything. While Pums is busying himself at his desk, just wants to look up something, Franz reads a copy of the *B.Z.* which is lying on the chair: 3000 nautical miles in a canoe, by Günther Plüschow, vacation cruises, Lania Sale, Piscator Stage in the Lessing Theater. Piscator himself directing. What's Piscator, what's Lania? What's envelope and what's contents, in other words, drama? No more child-marriages in India, a cemetery for prize cattle. News in brief: Bruno Walter will conduct his last concert this season, Sunday, April 15, at the Municipal Opera. The program will include the Symphony in E-flat major by Mozart, the net profits will go to the fund for the Gustave Mahler Monument in Vienna. Chauffeur, 32, mar., Driver's License 2a, 3b, wants place, private business or truck.

Herr Pums is hunting for matches on the table to light his cigar. At that moment the elderly woman opens a wallpaper door, and three men walk slowly in. Pums does not look up. So those are all Pums's men. Franz shakes hands with them. The woman is about to go out again, when Pums nods to Franz: "Hey, Biberkopf, didn't you want to get a letter delivered? Clara, you take care of it." "Say, that certainly is nice of you, Frau Pums, to do me that favor. Well, it ain't a letter, only a card, and to my girl." And he tells her exactly where he lives, writes it down on one of Pums's business envelopes, they are to tell Cilly not to worry, and he'll be home around ten o'clock, and then the post-card.

Well, now everything's straightened out, he feels as if a load had been taken off his shoulders. Once in the kitchen the thin, evil-looking hussy reads the address on the envelope, and puts it in the fire: she crumples the card up and throws it in the dustbin. Then she moves up close to the stove and goes on drinking her coffee, doesn't think of anything: just sits and drinks, it's good and warm. Biberkopf's joy is tremendous, when who should come shuffling in, wearing a béret and a heavy green soldier's outfit, but—well, who do you think? Who is it slouches along as if he were dragging first one leg and then the other out of the thick mud? Why, it's Reinhold. Franz feels at home now. Well, that's fine. "With a man like you, Reinhold, I'm Johnny on the spot, no matter what happens." "What, you're going to be in on this?" Reinhold sniffles and snoops around.

"That's some decision you made." And then Franz starts to tell him about the brawl on the Alex and how he helped Emil along. They listen avidly, all four of them, Pums is still writing; they nudge each other, then they start to whisper, two by two. One of them sticks close to Franz the whole time.

At eight o'clock the ride begins. All of them are well wrapped up, and Franz, too, gets an overcoat. He says, beaming, he'd like to keep it, and that lambskin cap as well. Oh Baby. "Why not?" they say. "But you'll have to earn it."

Off they go, outside it's pitch-dark, a lot of mud. "What are we going to do anyway?" asks Franz, when they reach the street. They reply: "First we'll go get a taxi or two. And then we'll fetch the stuff, apples, and whatever there is." They let a lot of taxis pass by; there are two standing in Metzer Strasse which they take, hop in, and they're off.

For about half an hour the two taxis ride along one behind the other, can't make out the district very well in this darkness, probably Weissensee or Friedrichsfelde. The boys say: The old man will most likely have to attend to something first. And then they stop in front of a house, it's a wide street bordered with trees, Tempelhof probably, the others say they don't know it either, they're all smoking a lot.

Reinhold is sitting next to Biberkopf. Strange how different this Reinhold's voice is now! He no longer stutters, but talks quite loudly, and sits straight as a captain; the boy even laughs, the others in the car listen to him. Franz takes him by the arm. "Well, Reinhold, old boy" (he whispers it to him in the nape of his neck under his hat) "well, whatcha got to say, now? Wasn't I right about the dames? Heh?" "Well, maybe, everything's O. K., everything's O. K." Reinhold slaps him on the knee, the lad has a punch, gee whiz, that boy's got some fist. Franz blusters: "Are we goin' to get excited on account of a gal? That jane isn't born yet, is she?"

Life in the desert is often very difficult.

The camels search and search and find nothing, and one day we come upon their bleached bones.

The two taxis drive through the town without stopping, after Pums had gotten back in with a suitcase. It's just about nine when they step on the Bülowplatz. And from now on they go on foot, separately, two by two. They cross under the arch of the city railway. Franz says: "Why, we'll soon be at the market." "Yes, here we are. But we gotta fetch the stuff first and then take it across."

Suddenly the men in front have become invisible, they're on Kaiser-Wilhelm Strasse, right next to the city railway, and then Franz, too, disappears in a black hallway with his companion. "Here we are," says the one next to Franz. "You can throw your cigar away now." "What for?" The other presses his arm, jerks the cigar out of his mouth. "Because I'm tellin' you, see." He is off across the dark courtyard, before Franz can do anything. Didja see that? I'll be damned, leave a fellow standing here in the dark, where's the rest of 'em anyway? And as Franz stumbles across the courtyard, there's a gleam from a pocket flashlight in front of him, he's blinded, it's Pums. "Heh there, whatcha doing? You're not supposed to be here, Biberkopf, you stand in front, you're to watch out. Better go back." "Gosh, I thought I was supposed to get something here." "Back, go back, didn't anybody tell you anything?"

The light goes out, Franz stumbles back. Something is trembling in him, he gulps: "What's all this about anyhow, where are those guys?" He is back in front of the big door when two of them come from the rear—murder, thief, they're pinching things, they're breaking into this place, I want to get away, away from here, oh, for an ice pond, a sliding-board, and away we go on the shoot the chutes, over the water and back to Alexanderplatz—but they hold him back, Reinhold among them, he's got an iron claw: "Didn't they tell you nothin'? You stand here and keep an eye out if there's any trouble." "Who? Who says that?" "Listen now, no nonsense, we're up against it. Ain't you got any backbone? Don't try to put on airs. You stand here and whistle if anything is up." "Me . . ." "Hold yer trap, you hear me." A blow crashes down on Franz's right arm with such force that he shrinks back.

Franz is standing alone in the dark hallway. He is trembling all over. What am I standing here for anyway? They've put one over on me, all right. That dirty dog beat me. They're swiping something back there, who knows what they're swiping, why, they're no fruit dealers, they're just plain burglars. The long road of black trees, the iron gate, after closing-time all the prisoners shall go to bed, in summer they are permitted to stay up till dark. That's a gang of burglars with Pums as their leader. Shall I go away, or shall I not? Shall I, what'll I do anyway? They lured me here, the crooks. They put me here as a lookout.

Franz stood there, trembling and nursing his bruised arm. Prisoners are not to conceal diseases, nor shall they malinger; both offenses are punishable. Deathly silence in the house; from the Bülowplatz comes a tooting of automobile horns. Back in the courtyard there is a sound of cracking and bustling, occasionally the gleam of a flashlight, sh . . . sh . . . One of them has gone down in the cellar with a bull's-eye lantern. They've locked me up in here, I'd rather have dry bread and boiled potatoes than stand here for such crooks. Several pocket-lamps flashed in the courtyard, Franz remembered the man with the post-card, a funny chap, really a funny chap. And he couldn't move from the spot, felt glued to the ground; since Reinhold had hit him, that's when it started, he's been stuck here ever since. He wants to, would have liked to, but it didn't work, it wouldn't let him go. The world is made of iron, you can't do anything about it, it comes rushing up at you like a steamroller, nothing to be done about it, there it comes, it rushes on, there they sit on the inside, that's a tank, inside a devil with horns and flaming eyes, they tear your flesh to pieces. And it rushes on and nobody can escape. Now it twitches in the dark; when light comes, we'll be able to see it all, how it lies there, what it was like.

I'd like to get away from here, I'd like to get away, those crooks, the dirty hounds, I don't want anything like that. He tugged at his legs, now wouldn't that be a joke, if I couldn't get away. He tried to move. Just as if somebody'd thrown me into a lot o' dough and I couldn't get out of the stuff. But it began to work, it was working. It was working with difficulty, but working nevertheless. I'll get out o' here, somehow, let 'em go ahead and swipe that stuff. I'm goin' to make myself scarce. He took off his overcoat and went back to the courtyard, slowly and anxiously. He would have liked to throw the overcoat into their faces, instead of which, he threw it into the darkness behind the house. The light flashed again, two men ran past him laden with overcoats, whole bundles of them. Meanwhile the two autos had stopped in front of the gateway; in passing him one of the men struck Franz on the arm, it was an iron blow. "Everything all right there?" It was Reinhold. Now two more men came rushing past him with baskets, and then two back and forth without a light, past Franz, who could do nothing but gnash his teeth and clench his fists. They toiled and labored away like savages in the courtyard and across the hallway, back and forth, in the darkness; otherwise they might well have been frightened by Franz. For it was no longer Franz who was standing there. Without his overcoat and cap, his eyes bulging out, his hands in his pockets, lying in wait to see if he could recognize a face, who's that, who's that, anyway, no knife at hand, just you wait, maybe in my coat, well, m'laddies, y'don't know Franz Biberkopf, you'll find out a thing or two when you grab that boy. Then all four started to run out laden with bundles, one after the other, and a small tubby fellow took Franz by the arm. "Come on, Biberkopf, we're off, everything's O. K."

And so Franz is stowed away between the others in a big car. Reinhold sits next to him, pressing Franz closely beside him, that's the other Reinhold. They travel without any lights on the inside. "Whatcha pushing me for?" whispers Franz; there ain't any knife around here.

"Hold yer trap, feller; not a peep out of anybody!" The first automobile is racing along; the chauffeur of the second looks back to the right, steps on the gas, and shouts back through the open window: "Somebody's after us."

Reinhold sticks his head out of the window: "Cheese it, get around the corner!" The other car is still after them. Reinhold sees Franz's face in the light of a street-lamp; Franz is beaming, his face is happy. "Watcha laughin' at, you monkey, what's the matter, you crazy or somethin'?" "Can't I laugh; none of your business." "If you laugh?" The lazy hound, the good-for-nothing bum! Suddenly something flashes over Reinhold, something he hadn't thought of during the whole ride: that's that fellow Biberkopf, who left him in the lurch, who gets his janes to leave him, he's got the goods on him, the fresh, fat sucker and I told him something about myself once, yep. And by this time Reinhold has forgotten about the ride.

Water in the black forest, you lie so mute. In terrible repose you lie. Your surface does not move, when there is a storm in the forest, and the firs begin to bend, and the spider-webs are torn between the branches, and there is a sound of splitting. The storm does not penetrate you.

This chap, thinks Reinhold, is sitting in clover, maybe he thinks that car back there is going to catch up with us, and here I sit, and him lecturing me, the jackass, about women, and how I should control myself.

Franz keeps laughing to himself, he looks backward through the little window to the street, yep, the car's after them all right, the jig's up, wait, that's your punishment, and even if I do get it in the neck along with the rest of you, they mustn't make a fool of me, those crooks, those scoundrels, that gang of criminals.

Cursed be the man, saith Jeremiah, that trusteth in man; he shall inherit the parched places in the wilderness, in a salt land, and not inhabited. The heart is deceitful above all things and desperately wicked: who can know it?

At that moment Reinhold gives a secret signal to the man opposite him, darkness and light alternate in the car, there's a hunt on. Unperceived, Reinhold has slipped his hand to the latch on the door, just beside Franz.

They are racing into a wide thoroughfare. Franz is still looking back. All of a sudden someone grabs him by the chest and wrenches him forward. He tries to get up, strikes Reinhold in the face; but the latter is terribly strong. The wind roars into the car, snow comes flying in. Franz is thrust right across the bundles, against the open door; with a yell, he grabs Reinhold around the neck. At that moment someone at his side strikes his arm with a stick. The second man in the car gives him a jerk and a whack on his left thigh, and, as he rolls down off the bundles of clothing, Franz is poked through the open door; he tries to catch hold with his legs wherever he can. His arms cling to the running-board.

Then a stick comes crashing down on the back of his head. Crouching over him, Reinhold throws his body out into the street. The door slams to. The pursuing car races over the man. Hunters and hunted vanish into the blizzard.

Let us be happy when the sun rises and its beautiful light is here. Gas light may go out, electric light, too. People get up when the alarm clock rattles, a new day has begun. If it was April 8th yesterday, it is the 9th today, if it was Sunday, it is now Monday. The year has not changed, nor the month, but a change has occurred nevertheless. The world has rolled ahead. The sun has risen. It is not certain what this sun is. Astronomers concern themselves a great deal with this body. According to them, it is the central body of our planetary system; for our earth is only a small planet, and what, indeed, are we? When the sun rises like that and we are glad, we should really be sad, for what are we, anyway; the sun is 300,000 times greater than the earth; and what a host of numbers and zeros there still are, and all they have to say is this: We are but a zero, nothing at all, just nothing. Simply ridiculous, isn't it, to be happy over that.

And yet, we are glad when the beautiful light is here, white and strong, and when it comes into the streets; and in the rooms all the colors awaken, and faces are there, human features. It is agreeable to touch shapes with one's hands, but it is a joy to see, to see, to see, to see colors and lines. And we are glad, now we can show what we are, we act, we live. We are also glad in April for that bit of warmth, how glad the flowers are that they can grow! Surely that must be an error, a mistake, those terrible numbers with all the zeros!

Just rise, sun, you don't frighten us. We don't care about your many miles, your diameter, your volume. Warm sun, just rise, bright light, arise. You are not big, you are not small, you are just happiness.

*

At this moment she has just stepped, beaming, out of the Paris-Nord Express, that insignificant-looking little person in the fur-trimmed coat with her huge eyes, and her little Pekingese dogs, Black and China, in her arms. Photographers, noise of a cranking film. Softly smiling, Raquel endures it all, patiently, pleased most of all by a bouquet of yellow roses sent by the Spanish colony; for ivory is her favorite color. With the words: "I am crazy to see Berlin," the famous woman gets into her car and glides away from the fluttering handkerchiefs of Berlin's morning crowd.

SIXTH BOOK

Now you see Franz Biberkopf neither boozing nor hiding away. You see him laughing now: we must make the best of things each day. He's in a rage because they had coerced him, they'll never coerce him again, not even the strongest of men. He clenches his fist in the face of this sinister power of woe, something's against him without a doubt, tho' he can't quite make it out, but it's bound to come about, he must suffer the hammer's blow.

There is no reason to despair. As I continue telling this story on to its hard, cruel and bitter end, I shall quite often use these words: there is no reason to despair; for the man whose life I am reporting is, to be sure, no ordinary man; he is an ordinary man only in the sense that we can clearly understand him and sometimes say: step by step, we might have gone the same way, experienced the very things he experienced. I have promised, unusual though it be, not to keep quiet about this story.

It is the ghastly truth, this thing I have reported, how Franz Biberkopf left his home suspecting nothing, participated against his will in a burglary, and was thrown in front of an auto. He is lying beneath the wheels: he had doubtless made the most honest efforts to go his orderly, decent, and legitimate way. But isn't this enough to justify despair, what sense can we find in this impudent, loathsome, miserable nonsense, what lying sense can be injected into it so as to construct therewith perhaps some sort of destiny for Franz Biberkopf?

I say: there is no reason to despair. I know something, perhaps many others who read this already discern something. A slow revelation is here in progress, you will experience it as Franz experienced it, and then everything will become clear.

Ill-gotten Gain thrives

Since Reinhold was in such fine form, he just went on with it. He didn't come home till Monday noon. Let us, dear brothers and sisters, cast a veil of brotherly love, ten yards square, over the intervening time. Over the preceding time we could not do it, much to our regret. Suffice it to establish the fact that after the sun had punctually risen on Monday morning and after there had gradually started the well-known rumble-bumble of Berlin—at exactly one hour after noon, in other words at 1 p. m. sharp, Reinhold kicked Trude, who was overdue, sedentary, and did not want to leave, out of his room. Oh, how I love the week-end, darling, truly, rooly, roo, when the he-goat's after the nanny-goat, darling, truly, rooly, roo. Another story-teller would probably have thought now of inflicting some punishment on Reinhold, but I can't help it, it didn't happen. Reinhold was in a gay mood, and, to magnify his gayety, for the purpose of his increasing gayety, he kicked Trude, who was of a sedentary nature and did not want to leave, out of his room. As a matter of fact, he himself did not want to do it; but the deed occurred somewhat automatically, principally with the participation of his middle-brain; for he was strongly alcoholized. Thus even fate helped our man. The alcoholic saturation is one of the things we have left to the night before; we need only, in order to get along with the story, quickly collect a few loose ends. Reinhold, the weakling, who seemed ridiculous to Franz, and who could never say a hard or energetic word to a woman, managed, at 1 p. m., to give Trude a frightful beating, to tear her hair out and break a mirror over her head, he could do everything; and what's more, when she yelled, he beat up her mouth into such a bleeding pulp that it was hugely swollen when she went to show it to the doctor in the evening. The girl lost all her beauty within a few hours, and all this as a consequence of these energetic measures on the part of Reinhold, whom she wished, therefore, to have arrested. For the moment, however, she had to put some salve on her lips and close her trap. All this, as I said, Reinhold was able to do because a couple of glasses of booze had narcotized his forebrain, whereupon his middle-brain got a free hand—it was on the whole more efficient, anyway.

When, late that afternoon, he was, to be sure, all in, though still himself, he discovered perplexedly a few welcome changes in his home. Trude, apparently, was gone. That is, completely gone. For her bag also was gone. Furthermore, the mirror was smashed, and somebody had vulgarly been spitting on the floor—and it was blood, at that. Reinhold inspected the wreckage around him. His own mouth was intact, so it must have been Trude who had spat and he had smashed up her beezer. This put him in such high spirits and self-esteem that he laughed aloud. He picked up what remained of the mirror and looked at himself: Well,

Reinhold, so it's you who did this. I never would have thought it possible. Reinhold, m'boy, Reinhold, m'boy! He certainly was glad. He patted his cheeks.

He reflected: Maybe somebody else had kicked her out? Maybe it was Franz? The events of last evening and the night weren't entirely clear to him as yet. Suspiciously he fetched his landlady, the old procuress, and tried to sound her out: "There was a big row in my place today, wasn't there?" It got that woman started off. He had done the right thing by Trude, she was a lazy pig, that one, she didn't even wanta iron her own petticoat. What, she wears petticoats; well, he never could stand for that, no, sir. So it had been he, himself. How happy Reinhold was now! And then he remembered everything about the evening and the night. Pulled a fine job, lots of dough, got fat Franz Biberkopf into trouble, and let's hope they ran over him and killed him, and now Trude's gone. Boy, we certainly got a lotta credit coming to us!

What am I going to do now? First I'll doll myself up for the evening. Let 'em come and talk about booze now. I didn't want to go at it, and didn't want to start and all that gab. It saves a man's strength all right, just look what I accomplished.

While he is changing his suit, a man arrives, sent by Pums. He whispers and talks in undertones and puts on big airs, hopping from one leg to the other; Reinhold is to come over to the café right away. But it's a good hour before Reinhold goes marching down. Today he's hotfooting it after the dames. Pums can beat his drums alone today. Over there in the café they're all scared stiff, Reinhold's got them in a nice mess about Biberkopf. If he isn't dead, he'll squeal on all of us. And if he's dead, man, oh man, then what, that'll settle our hash. They make inquiries about him at his house and hear this and that and the other thing.

But Reinhold is happy and fortune is with him. They can't do a thing with him. This is his happiest day since he can remember. He now has booze and can get as many janes as he wants, and chase them when he's through. He can lose them all, that's the latest and greatest stunt of all. He would like to start off on a bust right away, but the fellows with Pums don't let him go till he has promised to stay with them in Weissensee two or three days and keep under cover. They have got to see what's happened to Franz and what might come out of it. And so Reinhold makes a promise.

The same night he forgot all about it and scooted off. But nothing happened to him. The others hang around Weissensee in the camp and are terribly afraid. The next day they secretly come back to get him, but he's got to go to see a certain Karla whom he discovered yesterday.

And Reinhold is right. Nobody hears anything about Biberkopf. They don't see or hear anything about him. The man has completely vanished from the earth. All right with us. So they all trot back in high spirits and take up their old quarters again.

But that certain Karla is smoking in Reinhold's room, a straw blonde, she is, and she has brought three big bottles of booze along. He sips at it now and then, but she takes much more, sometimes in big gulps. He thinks to himself: Go ahead and drink. I'll drink first, when my time comes, and then it's good-bye for you.

Some of my readers are worried about Cilly. What's to become of the poor girl now Franz isn't there, when Franz isn't alive, is dead, and simply isn't there? Oh, she'll manage somehow, don't you worry, needn't get yourself worked up about her, that kind always falls on her feet. Cilly, you see, still has enough money for two days, and on Tuesday, just as I thought, she gets hold of Reinhold, who is tripping along on lover's feet, the finest dude in Berlin Center, with a real silk shirt. And Cilly is perplexed and doesn't understand, when she sees him, whether she's falling in love with the fellow all over again, or whether she wants to have it out with him, once and for all.

She carries, as Schiller might have said, a dagger in her garment. It is, to be sure, only a kitchen knife, but she wants to hand Reinhold one for his low tricks and doesn't care where the blow lands. She is standing with him in front of the house-door, while he chatters on in a friendly mood, two red, red roses and an ice-cold kiss. And she thinks: Go ahead and bray as long as you want to, afterwards I'll slash away. But where? That gets her all mixed up now. Why, you can't cut through fine stuff like that, the man's got such a nice get-up, and it fits him great, too. She says, as she trots along beside him in the street, that he must have got her Franz away from her. Why's that? Franz doesn't come home, he hasn't been home up to today, and nothing ever happens to him, and anyway, Trude has left Reinhold. That's it, sure as she's alive, and he can't say anything. Franz is gone away with Trude, Reinhold talked him into taking her off his hands, and now that's the last straw.

Reinhold is astonished how she got to know all that so quickly. Well, she's just been upstairs, and his landlady told her about that row with Trude. You crook, bawls Cilly, and here she would like to get herself courage for the kitchen knife, you've already got yourself a new one, anybody can see that all right.

Reinhold notices, at a distance of ten yards that: 1, she has no money; 2, she is furious with Franz; and 3, she's in love with yours truly, the handsome Reinhold. In this get-up all the dames love him, especially if it's a repetition, a *reprise*, as they say. Whereupon as regards point 1, he gives her ten marks. Point 2, he calls Franz Biberkopf all kinds of names. Wonder where that bozo's hanging out, as a matter of fact, he'd like to know himself. (Remorse, where is remorse now, Orestes and Clytemnestra, Reinhold doesn't know any of these fine folk, not even by name, but he simply, heartily, and sincerely would like to. Franz is dead as a doornail, and not to be found.) But neither does Cilly know where Franz is, and that is proof, argues Reinhold, deeply moved, that the man is a goner. And then, says Reinhold, to point 3, in a friendly way, regarding love, in case of a come-back: Just now I'm busy, yep, but you might call in again around May. You must be batty, she curses him, and doesn't want to believe it, for sheer joy. Everything's possible with me, he beams, says good-bye, and walks off. Reinhold, oh my Reinhold, you're my cavalier so true, Reinhold, oh my Reinhold, I love only you.

In front of every café he thanks his Creator that booze exists. Suppose now all the saloons should close up or that Germany should go dry, what would I do? Well, a fellow'd have to lay in a stock in time at home. We'll do that right away. I'm a clever lad, he thinks, as he stands in the store and buys various brands, he knows he has his forebrain and, when necessary, his middle-brain.

Thus ended, anyhow, for the time being, Reinhold's Sunday-to-Monday night. And if you ask again whether there is any justice in the world, you'll have to be satisfied with the reply: Not for the time being; at any rate, not till next Friday.

Sunday Night, Monday, April 9th

The big private car into which Franz Biberkopf is put—he's unconscious and has been given camphor and scopolamine—has been racing ahead for two hours. Now we are in Magdeburg. He is unloaded near a church; the two men ring the alarm-bell at the hospital. That night Franz is operated on. His right arm is sawn off at the shoulder joint, parts of the shoulder bones are reassembled, the bruises on his chest and right upper thigh are unimportant, as far as one can say for the present. Internal injuries are not impossible, perhaps a small rupture of the liver, but it can't be very serious. We have to wait. Did he lose much blood? Where did you find him? On the x-y road, that's where his motorcycle was, they must have collided with him from behind. You didn't see the auto? No. When we found him, he was lying there, we separated at z, he drove to the left. Get you, it was quite dark. Yes, that's how it happened. Are the gentlemen going to stay here? Yes, for a few days; he's my brother-in-law, his wife will arrive today or tomorrow. We have taken rooms across the street if you need us. In front of the door of the operating-room one of the two gentlemen talks again with the people at the hospital: It's a terrible thing, but we shall greatly appreciate, on your part, at any rate, if there would be no report about the affair. Well, wait till he comes to, we'll see what he himself thinks about it. He's no friend of court-proceedings. He himself once ran into someone, his nerves. As you like. First we'll have to see him through.

At eleven there is a change of bandages. It is Monday morning—the authors of the accident are fighting and bawling at this hour, including Reinhold, merrily tight and dead drunk, in the company of their fence in Weissensee—Franz is quite awake, lying in a fine bed, in a fine room, his chest seems tight and he feels terribly packed in, he asks the nurse where he is. She repeats what she had heard from the night-service and picked up during the previous conversation. He is awake. Understands everything, touches his right shoulder. The nurse takes his hand away: he must lie quiet. Blood had run down his sleeve into the street mud, he had felt it. Then there had been people around him and then something had happened inside him. What had happened at that moment inside Franz? He had made a decision. He had trembled before Reinhold's iron blows on his arm in the hall of the Bülowplatz, the ground had trembled under him, Franz understood nothing.

When the auto took him away, the ground was still trembling; Franz did not want to notice it, but that's how it was all the same.

Then, while he was lying in the mud, a difference of five minutes, something moved in him. Something tore its way out, broke through him, and rang, rang, Franz is turned to stone, he feels, I am being run over, he is cool and collected. Franz observes: I am going to the dogs—and he starts to give commands. Maybe I'll go to smash, what's the odds, I won't go to smash. Forward, march! They bind up his arm with his suspenders. Then they want to drive him to Pankow Hospital. But he watches every move like a hawk: not to the hospital, and calls out an address. What address? Elsasser Strasse, Herbert Wischow, his chum of former days, before Tegel. The address comes to him at once. Something moves in him, as he lies in the mud, tears its way out, breaks through, then rings and rings. He feels this jerk at once; and now, no more uncertainty.

They shan't catch me. He is safe, Herbert is still living there, and is at home. The people hurry all through the café in the Elsasser Strasse, inquiring for a certain Herbert Wischow. A slender young man beside a beautiful dark woman gets up, what's the matter, what's up, out there in the car, then runs out with them to the car, the girl behind them, half the café with them. Franz knows who is coming now. He commands time.

Franz and Herbert recognize each other, Franz whispers ten words to him, the people outside make room, Franz is laid on a bed in the café, a doctor is called. Eva, the beautiful dark girl, brings some money. Then they change his clothes. An hour after the accident they take him in a private auto from Berlin to Magdeburg.

Herbert comes to the private hospital at noon, to talk things over with Franz. Franz is not going to stay there a day more than necessary. Wischow will come back in a week, Eva, meanwhile, takes lodgings in Magdeburg.

Franz is lying still as a stone. He has complete control over himself. He does not think backward one inch. Only when, at two o'clock, after inspection, a lady is announced, and Eva arrives with tulips, he weeps unrestrainedly, weeps and sobs, and Eva has to wipe his face with her handkerchief. He bites his lips, blinks his eyes and grits his teeth, but his jaw trembles, he can't help sobbing, and the nurse hears it outside, knocks and begs Eva to go for today, the meeting upsets the sick man's nerves too much.

Next day he is quite calm and smiles at Eva. A fortnight later they take him away. He is back in Berlin. He breathes Berlin again. When he sees the houses on Elsasser Strasse again, something stirs within him, but he doesn't break out in sobbing. He thinks of that Sunday afternoon with Cilly, of the ringing of the bells, the ringing of the bells, and here I am at home, and something awaits me, and I have something to accomplish, something will happen. Franz Biberkopf knows this positively, and he does not stir, but lets them carry him quietly out of the car.

I have something to do, something will happen, I won't stir from here, I am Franz Biberkopf. So they carry him into the house, into the home of his friend, Herbert Wischow, who calls himself a business agent. It is the same heedless sense of security which had surged up in him after the fall from the auto.

Supply at the slaughter-house: Hogs 11,543, Beef 2016, Calves 920, Mutton 14,450. A blow, bang down they go.

Hogs, oxen, calves—they are slaughtered. There is no reason why we should concern ourselves with them. Where are we? We?

Eva is sitting by Franz's bed, Wischow comes back to it again and again: Who was it, man alive, how did it happen? Franz isn't spilling anything. He has built an iron coffer around himself and there he sits and he'll let nobody in.

Eva, Herbert, and the latter's friend, Emil, are sitting together. Since Franz was run over in the night, the man is a mystery to them. He certainly didn't just happen to be run over by the auto, there's something behind it, why should he be hanging around in the North End at 10 p.m., he wouldn't be selling papers at ten o'clock, when there's nobody about up there. Herbert doesn't budge from his opinion, Franz was up to something, then this thing happened, and now he's ashamed because business didn't go well with his old newspaper junk, and then there are surely a few others behind it, whom he doesn't want to give away. Eva shares his opinion; he must have been up to something or other, but how did it happen, now he's a cripple. We'll get that out of him all right.

They get it out of him, when Franz gives Eva his last address and asks that his bag be brought along; but she's not to say where. Herbert and Eva know all about that, the landlady doesn't want to let the bag go either, but she does it for five marks, and then she starts to shoot her mouth off: they've been asking here for Franz every day; why, who; well, Pums and Reinhold and so on. So it's Pums, is it? Now they know. Pums's gang. Eva is beside herself, Wischow, too, is furious: if he has to go back to it, why with Pums? But, of course, afterwards, we're good enough for him; going with that guy, well, now he's a cripple, half a corpse, otherwise I'd talk to him differently.

Eva had to use compulsion in order to be present when Herbert Wischow settles things with Franz. Emil is also there, the affair has cost them a cool thousand.

"Well, Franz," starts Herbert, "well, I guess you're about fixed now. Now y'can get up, and then—whatcha goin' to do? Been thinkin' about that?" Franz turns his stubbly face towards him. "Say, lemme get on my pins first." "Oh well, we won't hurry you, don't think that. With me you're still in good hands. Why didn'cha come to see us any more? You been out of Tegel a year now." "Not that long." "Well, then half a year. Don't want to see us, maybe?"

The house, the sliding roofs, a high, dark courtyard, there comes a call like thunder's peal, tra-la-la-la-la-la-la, that's how it all started.

Franz lies down on his back and looks at the ceiling: "Been peddlin' papers. What you drivin' at?"

Emil joins in, shouting: "Listen, y'weren't peddlin' papers." What a liar. Eva keeps trying to calm him. Franz notices there's something in the wind, they know something, just what do they know? "I been peddlin' papers. Ask Meck." Wischow: "What Meck'll say, I can imagine that right now. You peddled papers. Pums's people peddle fruit, too, a little bit. They also deal in flounders; you know that yourself, doncha?" "But not me. I was peddlin' papers. I earned my money. Ask Cilly who was with me the whole day, what I did." "Two or three marks a day, go on!" "Oh, it's more than that; it was enough for me anyway, Herbert."

The others are uncertain. Eva sits down next to Franz. "Say, Franz, you knew Pums, didn't you?" "Yes." Franz no longer thinks, they're questioning me, Franz remembers, he's alive. "Well, and?" Eva strokes him: "Go ahead and tell us what you were doing with Pums." Herbert, beside her, bursts out: "Go ahead and let's hear it, ole boy. I know, anyway, what you were doin' with Pums. Where you were that night. You think I don't know it. Well, all right, you went along. It's none of my business. It's your affair. You go to see them folks, that's the kind y'want to know, that ole sap, that ole fool, and us—you never come near us." Emil shouts: "Y'see we're only all right when—" Herbert gives him a signal. Franz is crying. It's not as bad as in the hospital, but it's terrible, too. He sobs and weeps and rocks his head to and fro. He got a blow on the head, they gave him a kick on the chest; then they threw him through the door in front of an auto that ran over him. His arm is gone. He's a cripple. The two men leave. He keeps on sobbing. Eva wipes his face time and again with the towel. She watches him; he's sleeping, she thinks. Then he opens his eyes, wide awake, and says: "Tell Herbert and Emil to come on in."

They come in with abashed faces. Franz asks: "What d'ye know about Pums? Know anything about him?" The three others exchange glances and don't understand. Eva taps his arm: "Why, Franz, you know him, too." "Well, I want to know, what you know about him." Emil: "That he is a real crook and he's got only five years hard behind him in Sonnenburg, he should have had life or fifteen, anyhow. Him and his fruit wagons." Franz: "Why, he don't live off of fruit wagons." "Nope, he eats meat, too, so he does, and a-plenty." Herbert: "But my God, Franz, you're not as dumb as all that, y'know that yourself, can't you spot that in looking at the man?" Franz: "I thought he made his living offa the fruit-trade." "Well, and what didja want to do then Sunday, when y'went with him?" "We went to fetch fruit for the market." Franz lies quite still. Herbert bends over him to see his features: "And you believed that?"

Franz is crying again, very quietly now, with his mouth shut. He went down the stairs, a man was looking for addresses in his notebook, then he was at Pums's house and Frau Pums was to send a note to Cilly. "Of course, I believed 'em. But then I noticed, they got me to stand watch, and then—"

The three look at each other. What Franz says is true, but that's incredible. Eva touches his arm: "And then?" Franz has his mouth open, say it now, it's going to come out now, it'll be over soon. And he says: "Then I didn't want to, and then they kicked me out of the auto, because another car was coming right in back of us."

Hush, don't say any more, and I was run over, I might have been dead, too, they wanted to finish me. He doesn't sob, but holds onto himself steadily, his teeth clenched and his legs stretched out.

The three hear it. Now he's told it. It's the naked truth. At this moment all three know it. There is a mower death yclept, has power which the Lord has kept.

Herbert asks: "But tell me, Franz, we'll be going soon; y'didn't come to see us because y'wanted to sell newspapers?"

He cannot speak but thinks to himself: Yes, I wanted to stay decent. I did stay decent till the end. So you mustn't get offended that I didn't come around. You remained my friends, I didn't betray any of you. He lies mute; they go out.

Then, after Franz has taken another dose of his soporific, they sit downstairs in the café, speechless. They don't look at each other. Eva is trembling like a leaf. The girlie would have liked to have Franz, while he was still going with Ida, but he didn't leave Ida, despite the fact that she was already keen on the Breslau fellow. She gets on fine with her Herbert, and has everything she wants from him—but she's still in love with Franz.

Wischow orders hot grogs in a hurry, all three of them pour it down at once. Then Wischow orders another round. Their throats are still tight.

Eva has icy hands and feet, every minute a cold shiver runs down the back of her head and neck, even her thighs have grown cold, and she crosses her legs. Emil leans his head heavily on his arms, chews, sucks at his tongue and swallows his saliva, but then he can't help sniffing up his nose and spitting on the floor. Young Herbert Wischow sits erect on his chair, as if on horseback; he looks like a lieutenant in front of his platoon, his face motionless. None of them is sitting here in this place, they are not in their skins, Eva's name is not Eva, Wischow's not Wischow, Emil's not Emil. A wall around them has tumbled, different air, darkness comes pouring in. They are still sitting beside Franz's bed. A shudder goes from them to Franz's bed.

There is a mower death yclept. Has power which the Lord hath kept. When he 'gins his scythe to whet, keener it grows and keener yet.

Herbert turns around to the table and asks hoarsely: "Who was it, anyway?" Emil: "Whaddya mean?" Herbert: "Who threw him out?" Eva: "Promise me one thing, Herbert, if you get that man." "Don't you worry! Imagine, a thing like that running around loose. But just wait." Emil: "Say, my God, Herbert, can you imagine anything like that, now!"

Mustn't hear anything about it, not think about it at all. Eva's knees are trembling, she begs: "Herbert, go ahead and do something, or you, Emil." Let's get some fresh air! There is a mower, death yclept. Herbert concludes: "What kin a guy do if he don't know what's up. First, we'll find out what it's all about. If worst comes to the worst, we'll let Pums's whole gang of crooks get theirs." Eva: "And Franz along with them?" "If worst comes to the worst, I said, we'll do that. Franz wasn't with 'em, not really, a blind man kin see that, any judge would believe him. It can be proved, too; they threw him in front of the auto. Otherwise they wouldn'ta done it." He starts back. The dirty dogs! Think of it. Eva: "Maybe he'll tell me who it is."

But he lies there like a log, Franz does, and they can't get anything out of him. Let him rest, let him rest! His arm is gone, it won't grow again. They kicked me out of that car, they did leave me my head, however. We gotta start going, we gotta see it through and get the wagon out of the mud. Gotta learn to crawl first.

With surprising speed, he comes to life again on these warm days. He is not supposed to get up yet, but he gets up, and it's all right. Herbert and Eva, who are always flush, supply him with whatever he wants and what the doctor thinks is necessary for him. Franz wants to get on his feet, he eats and drinks everything they bring him, and doesn't ask where they get the money from.

In the meantime, there are conversations between him and the others, but nothing of importance, they don't touch the Pums affair. They talk about Tegel and a great deal about Ida. They speak of her with esteem and regret that things should have gone the way they did with her, she was still so young, but Eva adds: The girl was on the down-grade. Things between them are now just as they were before Tegel, and nobody knows or mentions the fact that in the meantime the houses have wobbled and the roofs have nearly slid down, and Franz has sung in the courtyard and has sworn, as sure as his name is Franz Biberkopf, that he meant to stay decent, and that the old days were finished and over with.

Franz lies or sits quietly with them. A lot of old acquaintances come also, bringing their girls and wives along. They don't mention anything, they talk with Franz as if he had just been discharged from Tegel and had had an accident. Where or how, the lads don't ask. They know what an industrial accident is, can well imagine what it is. A fellow gets in a jam, and first thing he knows he's got a grape in his arm or has his legs broken. Well, it's better anyhow than the watery soup at Sonnenburg, or croaking from consumption. That's clear enough.

Meantime Pums's gang has smelled out where Franz is. Who fetched Franz's bag? They quickly found that out, and don't they know that guy! And before Wischow notices anything, they learn that Franz Biberkopf is staying with him; why, isn't he his friend from the old days, he only lost an arm in the affair, damned lucky he was, too, there's no two ways about it, so the fellow is on his feet again, and, who knows, he might squeal on them? In fact, they all but fell out with Reinhold, for being such a sap and bringing a fellow like Franz Biberkopf into the gang. But as for really doing anything to Reinhold, they didn't before and surely won't now, even old Pums won't get at that one. That lad has a way of looking at you, it's enough to frighten you, with his yellow face and the wrinkles across his forehead. He's not healthy, he won't live to be fifty, but the fellows who have got something wrong with them, they're the most dangerous of all. Some day he'd just as lief stick his hand in his pocket, smiling coldly the while, and pepper away at somebody.

That business about Franz, his not getting killed, however, remains dangerous. Only Reinhold shakes his head and says: Don't get excited. Biberkopf'll take good care not to show up here. It'll only be if he can't get along with his one arm, then he'll turn up. Well, what do we care? Maybe he's got a head to lose, too.

They needn't be afraid of Franz. Once, to be sure, Eva and Emil together give Franz a talking-to, he has to say where it was and who it was, and, if he can't act alone, there'll be a few to help. A lot of people in Berlin would help in a case like that. Franz, however, grows tongue-tied when they come to him with that stuff, says No, just let it drop. Then he turns pale, breathes heavily, if only he doesn't start to cry again, if I could, I'd like to go clean away from Berlin, but what can a cripple do? Eva: "It's not on account of that, Franz, you're not a cripple; but we can't let that pass, the way they fixed you up, throwin' you out of the car." "That won't make my arm grow, either." "Well, then they oughta cough up." "What?"

Emil starts explaining: "Either we bash that certain fellow's skull in, or the fellows in his club, if he's got one, have all got to pay you. We'll fix that up with the club. Either others jump in for him, or Pums and the club can kick him out, and then let's see where they can join up again and how they'll get it in the neck. That arm's gotta be paid for. It's the right one, too. They gotta pay you a pension for it." Franz shakes his head. "Whaddya mean shakin' your head? We'll knock the fellow's brains out who did this; it's a crime and if we can't go to court with it, it's up to us to settle it." Eva: "Franz didn't belong to any club, Emil. Did'ncha hear he didn't want to go along at all, and that's why they did it." "That was his privilege, he didn't have to go. Since when can people force a fellow to do anything? Are we civilized people or not? They'd better go live with the Indians."

Franz shakes his head: "What you've paid out for me, you'll get back, every pfennig of it." "Oh, we don't want it, don't need it, we can get along without it. This thing's got to be fixed up, what the devil! No, sir, we can't let it go at that."

Eva, too, is resolute: "No, Franz, we gotta do something about it, those fellows knocked your nerves to pieces, that's why you don't say anything. But you can depend on us: Pums didn't knock *our* nerves to pieces. You oughta hear what Herbert says: There's gonna be a carving up in Berlin some day that'll make people sit up and take notice." Emil nods: "Bet your life on that."

Franz Biberkopf looks straight ahead and thinks to himself: None of my business what they say. And if they do something, it isn't my business either. That won't make my arm grow again, and that's true all right: my arm sure is gone. It had to come off, no use bellyaching. But that's not the last of it.

And he reflects, and reflects, how everything happened: Reinhold had a spite against him, because he didn't take that jane off his hands, and that's why he kicked him out of the car. So there he lies in the clinic at Magdeburg. And he wanted to stay respectable, and that's how it turned out. And he stretches out in his bed and clenches his fist on the covers: that's how it came about, just so. Well, we'll see about it. We certainly will.

And Franz doesn't betray who it was threw him in front of the car. His friends are quiet. They think he'll tell it yet some day.

Franz is not K.O. and they can't get him K.O.

Pums's gang, flush with money, have vanished from Berlin. Two of them are away on a jaunt in the Oranienburg district, at their summer quarters, while Pums is taking the cure at Altheide on account of his asthma, getting his machine oiled up. Reinhold tipples a bit, every day a few little nips of brandy, in fact, the man is enjoying things and getting used to it, a fellow has to get something out of life sometimes and he discovers he was quite silly to have lived so long without it, only on coffee and lemonade, that's not living at all! Reinhold has a few thousand marks lying around, but nobody knows that. He would like to do something with the money, but at first he can't decide what. Certainly not go to that summer dump like the others. He's just picked up a fine dame who once saw better days, and he rents a swell house in Nürnberger Strasse for her, so he can dig himself in there when he wants to play the grand mogul or perhaps when things get hot. Everything's in fine shape, he has his regal place in the West End and, of course, on the side, the old joint, too, with a jane in it, every few weeks another one. The boy can't get along without his little game.

Then it so happens, at the end of May, that a couple of men from Pums's gang meet again in Berlin and start chattering about Franz Biberkopf. They've heard there's been some talk in the club about him. Herbert Wischow is getting people all het up against them, we're a pack of swine, they say. Biberkopf didn't want to help us in that affair at all, they say, and then we tried to use force, and afterwards we kicked him out of the car. So we let them know: he wanted to squeal on us, there was no question about using force, nobody grabbed him, but afterwards we couldn't do anything else. There they sit, shaking their heads, none of them wants to have a row with the club. A fellow's hands would be tied that way and then he'd be left out in the cold. And then they suggest this, we ought to show our good will and take up a collection for Franz, since he showed in the end that he was a decent fellow all right, we ought to help him get a good rest, and put up the money it cost him in the hospital; we oughtn't to act shabby about it.

Reinhold is adamant: We gotta kill that fellow dead. The others are not against the idea, really not at all, but there isn't any one of them ready to do a thing like that, moreover it won't hurt to let the poor boob go around with his one arm. You can't tell how it will end once you start anything with a fellow like that, the man's got the luck of the devil himself. Well, they collect the money, a couple of hundred marks, only Reinhold doesn't give a pfennig, and one of them is to go to see Biberkopf, but not when Herbert Wischow is around.

Franz is quietly reading first the *Mottenpost* and then the *Grüne Post*, he likes it best because there's no politics in it. He studies the number for November 27, 1927, it's an old number, dating from before Christmas, that was the time of Polish Lina, wonder what she's doing? It tells here in the paper about the ex-Kaiser's new brother-in-law getting married, the princess is 61, the bridegroom 27, that'll cost her a heap of gold, for he won't become a prince. Bullet-proof armored vests for police officers, I'll never believe that.

All of a sudden, there's Eva squabbling outside with somebody, somebody, well, well, don't I know that voice. She doesn't want to let him in, better peep out and see. Franz opens the door, his *Grüne Post* in his hand. It's Schreiber, one of Pums's men.

Well, well, what's the matter? Eva shouts into the room: "Franz, he's only come here because he knows Herbert isn't around." "What do you want, Schreiber, something out of me, what do you want?" "Told Eva and she won't let me in. Why not, are you a prisoner here?" "No, I'm not." Eva: "You're afraid he'll squeal on you. Don't let him in, Franz." Franz: "Now what do you want, Schreiber? Come on in with him, Eva, let him in."

They are sitting in Franz's room. The *Grüne Post* is lying on the table, the new brother-in-law of the ex-Kaiser is getting married, two men behind him are holding the crown over his head. Lion-hunting, rabbit-hunting, to truth all honor. "Why do you want to give me any money? I wasn't in with you on that job." "Why, good Lord, you stood watch, didn't you?" "Nope, Schreiber, I didn't, I didn't know a thing, you just stuck me there; I didn't know what I was supposed to do there." Ain't I glad to be out of that, no need to stand in that dark courtyard any longer. I'd pay him something not to have to stand there any more. "Nope, that's all bunk, and you needn't be afraid of me, I never squealed on anybody in my life." Eva shakes her fist at Schreiber: There are others watching, I tell you, you're taking a risk to come up here. Herbert'll show you a thing or two.

Suddenly something terrible happens. Eva saw Schreiber put his hand in his pocket. He wants to take out the money and coax Franz with the bills. But Eva has misunderstood the movement. She thinks he wants to get out a revolver and shoot Franz down, so he won't say anything, he's sent here to put Franz on the spot. And she jumps up from her chair, white as the wall, her face terribly distorted, screaming piercingly, then all at once she falls over her own legs, and gets up again. Franz rises with a start, Schreiber rises with a start, whatsa matter, whatsa matter wit' her, oh boy, oh boy! She runs around the table to Franz, quickly, what am I to do, he's going to shoot, it's death, the end, it's all over, murder, the world's coming to an end, I don't wanta die, don't wanta get my block knocked off, it's all over.

She stands, runs, falls, stands in front of Franz, white, yelling, quivering throughout her whole body: "Beat it behind the mirror! Murder! Help! Help!" Her eyes are big as fists, as she screams: "Help!" An icy chill goes through the bones of the two men. Franz doesn't know what's the matter, he only sees the movement, what's going to happen next? Then he understands: Schreiber has his right hand in the pocket of his trousers. Franz goes all a-tremble. It's like that time when he was standing watch in the courtyard, they want to start up again. But he doesn't want to, I tell you, he doesn't want to, he doesn't want to let himself be thrown under a car. He groans and tears himself free from Eva; the *Grüne Post* is lying on the floor, the Bulgarian is married to a Princess. Gotta see, first gotta get the chair in my hands. He groans aloud. As he has eyes for Schreiber alone and not for the chair, he kicks the chair over. We gotta get that chair and pounce on him. Gotta—auto on the Magdeburg road—they are ringing the alarm-bell of the hospital, Eva is still yelling, well, let's save ourselves. Forward the air is thick, but we'll push through! He bends to take hold of the chair. Schreiber, aghast, rushes out by the door, why they're all crazy here! The doors begin to open along the corridor.

Downstairs in the café they heard the screams and the tumult. Two men rush up at once and meet Schreiber on the stairs as he runs past them. But he keeps his head, and calls out as he waves towards them: Get a doctor quick, an apoplectic fit. And he's off, clever dog, that he is.

Upstairs in the room Franz is lying unconscious beside the chair. Eva crouches to one side between the window and the mirror, and screams as she crouches, as if she had seen a ghost. They lay Franz cautiously on his bed. The landlady knows all about Eva's condition. She pours water over her head. Then Eva says softly: "Gimme a roll." The men laugh: "She wants a roll." The landlady lifts her by the shoulders, they put her on a chair. "She always says that, when she has an attack. But that's not an apoplectic fit. It's only nerves and her troubles with that sick man. He probably fell down. Well, why does he get up, anyway? He's always getting up, that makes her nervous." "Then why was that fellow shouting about an apoplectic fit?" "Who?" "The one we passed on the stairs just now." "Why, because he's a damned ass. Don't I know my Eva, five years now! Her mother is the same. When she screams, water's the only thing that helps."

When Herbert gets home that evening, he gives Eva a revolver, it may come in handy, she must not wait till the other fellow shoots, then it's too late. He himself starts off right away, looks for Schreiber, of course he can't be found. All of Pums's people are on a vacation, none of them wants to get mixed up in the affair, Schreiber, of course, has faded into space. He has pocketed Franz's money and is off to Oranienburg, to the summer quarters. But not before he's humbugged Reinhold; Biberkopf didn't take the money, but Eva listened to reason, he slipped it to her, and she'll fix it up. Well, that's that.

In spite of everything, the month of June has come to Berlin. The weather is still warm, but it looks like rain. Many things are happening in the world. The airship "Italia," with General Nobile, has crashed, and sends a wireless to say where it is lying: viz., northeast of Spitzbergen, it is a difficult place to get to. Another airship has better luck, in one swoop it has raced from San Francisco to Australia, in 77 hours, and made a smooth landing. Then the King of Spain is at odds with Primo, his dictator, well, let's hope things will be straightened out again. A pleasant impression, which one receives from the very first, is afforded by a certain betrothal between two young people from Baden and Sweden: A princess from matchbox land has made a safety-match with a prince of Baden. If you consider how far apart Baden and Sweden are, you are astonished that things can go pit-a-pat across such a distance. Yes, my son, I'm weak about women, they touch the spot where it's too much for me! I kiss the first and think of the second, and steal a sly look at number three. I'm weak about women, yes, it's no joke. What shall I do, I don't try any more, and if some day for the women I go quite broke, then I'll write "sold out" on my heart's front-door.

To which Charlie Amberg adds: I'll pull out an eyelash and stab you dead with it. Then I'll take a lipstick and make you all red with it. And if you're still angry, there's one more thing I'll do: a poached egg I'll order and splash spinach over you. You, you, you, you. Then I'll order a poached egg and splash spinach over you.

So the weather is still warm and it looks like rain; at noon it touches 72° Fahrenheit. Under these climatic conditions the girl-murderer Rutowski appears before the Criminal Court of Berlin and is called on to exonerate himself. In this connection the question crops up: Is the victim Else Arndt the run-away wife of a certain school-board member? He has written to say he considers it a possibility, perhaps a desirability, that the murdered woman, Else Arndt, should be his spouse. In the case of an affirmative answer, he wishes to give important testimony before the court. There is objectivity in the air, in the air there is objectivity, there it is in the air and it's in the air, in the air. In the air there is something idiotic, in the air there is something hypnotic, it's in the air, it's in the air, and it won't get out of the air.

But next morning the municipal electric railway is opened. The National Railroad Board takes this as a pretext to stress once more the danger, attention, look out, don't get on, wait your turn, you render yourself liable to punishment.

Arise, weak Spirit, and get on your Feet

There are states of swoon which amount to death in the living body. Franz Biberkopf, still unconscious, is put back into bed, he keeps on lying there on into the warm days and reaches this conclusion: I'm at death's door, I feel it, I'm going to croak. If you don't do something now, Franz, something real, final, comprehensive, if you don't take a club in your hand, a saber, and beat around you, if you don't run loose, no matter how, Franz, my li'l Franz, li'l Biberkopf, old horse, then it's all over with you for sure, then you can have your measure taken for a coffin.

Groaning: I don't want to, and I don't want to, and I won't croak, he looks at the room, the wall-clock ticks, I'm still here, still am I here, they want to close in on me, Schreiber almost shot me down, but that shall not happen. Franz lifts his remaining arm: it shall not happen.

A real fear pursues him now. He will not stay in bed. And even if he croaks in the street, he just must get out of bed, he has got to get out. Herbert Wischow has gone to Zoppot with dark-eyed Eva; she has a rich beau well on in years, a stock-exchange man whom she exploits. Herbert Wischow goes along with them incognito, the girl works well, they see each other every day, united they march, but sleep separately. In this beautiful summertime Franz Biberkopf goes marching back to the street again, alone again, our one and only Franz Biberkopf, tottering, but on his feet. Look at the cobra now, it creeps along, it moves, it has been injured. But it's still the same old cobra, even if it has black circles under its eyes, and the fat reptile is now thin and wasted.

Something has become clearer to the old boy, who drags himself through the streets now, in order not to croak in his room, something has become clearer than it was before to this old boy who is now running away, away from death. Life has been worth something to him, anyway. Now he sniffs the air, he noses the streets as if they belonged to him and wanted to take him in. He gapes at the poster columns, as if they were an event in his life. Yes, my boy, you can't go far now on your two legs, now you've got to clutch and cling tight to something firm, now you must set as many teeth and fingers as you have left together and hold on fast, just so as not to be knocked off.

Life is a hellish thing, isn't it? You knew it once before, that time in Henschke's saloon when they wanted to kick you out with your arm-band, and that fellow attacked you, and you hadn't done anything to him. And I thought that the world was peaceful, that there was law and order, but there's something out of order, there they are and how terrible they seem now! That was in a moment of clairvoyance.

And now come thou, come hither and I will show thee something. The great whore, the whore of Babylon, that sitteth upon many waters. And I saw a woman sit upon a scarlet colored beast, full of names of blasphemy, having seven heads and ten horns. And the woman was arrayed in purple and scarlet color, and decked with gold and precious stones and pearls, having a golden cup in her hand. And upon her fore-head was a name written, MYSTERY, BABYLON THE GREAT, THE MOTHER OF HARLOTS

AND ABOMINATIONS OF THE EARTH. And I saw the woman drunken with the blood of the saints, and with the blood of the martyrs.

But Franz Biberkopf goes through the streets, jogging along in his own little way. He does not give in, and asks for nothing more than to get really well again and strong in his muscles. The weather is warm and summery; Franz wanders from café to café.

He dodges the heat. In the café the big schooners of beer come sliding up.

The first schooner says: I come from the cellar, from hops and malt. Now I am cool, what do I taste like?

Franz says: Bitter, fine, cool.

Yes, I cool you off, I cool all men off, then I make them warm and then I dispel their idle thoughts.

Idle thoughts?

Yes, the majority of all thoughts are idle. Aren't they?—Maybe so. I leave you the last word.

A small brandy stands before Franz with its bright yellow lights. Where did they pick you up?—They burnt me, man.—You certainly do bite, old fellow, you got claws.—Goshalmighty, that's why I'm a brandy. Maybe you haven't seen any of me for a long time?—Nope, I was almost dead, my little brandy-sprite, I was almost dead; I rode away without a return ticket.—You look it.—What d'y' mean, look it, don't talk rot! Let's try you again, come here! Ah you're good, you've got fire, you certainly have, young fellow.—The liquor ripples down his throat: and what fire!

The smoke from the fire rises in Franz and makes his throat so dry that he has to take another schooner: you're schooner number Two. I've had one already, what have you got to tell me?—Say, Fat, taste me first, then you can talk.—All right.

The schooner says: Listen, if you have two more schooners and another kümmel and then a grog, you'll bubble up just like peas.—Is that so?—Yes, then you'll get fat again, gee, you're looking bad, feller! You really can't go around with people like that. Take another swallow.

Franz takes up the third: I'm swallowin' all right. One after the other. Keep everything in order.

He questions number Four: Watcha know, darling?—It only yawps delightedly. Franz pours it down his throat. I believe it. Everything, darling, everything you say, I believe, you're me lambkin, we'll go into the green pastures together.

Third Conquest of Berlin

And so Biberkopf has come to Berlin for the third time. The first time the roofs were about to slide off, then the Jews came and he was saved. The second time Lüders cheated him, but he swigged his way through. Now, the third time, his arm is gone, but he ventures courageously into the city. The man's got courage, two- and threefold courage.

Herbert and Eva had left him a nice wad of money which the bartender downstairs keeps for him. But Franz only takes a few pfennigs, resolving at the same time: I won't take any of their money, I've got to make myself independent. He goes to the "Charity Association" and asks for help. "We'll have to make inquiries first." "And what'll I do in the meantime?" "You may come back in a few days." "A fellow might starve to death in a few days." "People don't starve as fast as that in Berlin, that's what they all say. And then we don't hand out money, only tickets, and we pay your room-rent from here, and that's your address all right, isn't it?"

And Franz leaves the "Charity Association," and when he gets downstairs, the scales fall from his eyes: inquiries, say, they're going to make inquiries, maybe they'll inquire about my arm and how it all came about. He is standing in front of a cigar-store ruminating: they'll try to find out what's the matter with my arm, who paid the bill and what hospital I was in. That's what they might ask. And then, what I was living on those last few months. You just wait.

He broods as he strolls along: what can a fellow do then? Who shall I ask, what am I going to do now, and I don't want to live offa their money, either.

So for two days he walks around looking for Meck, between the Alex and the Rosenthaler Platz, he might talk to him about it, and he finds him all right, the second evening, on the Rosenthaler Platz. They look at each other. Franz wants to shake hands with him—how they had greeted each other that time after that affair with Lüders, with what joy, and now—Meck hesitantly gives him his hand, does not press it. Franz wants to start shaking again with his left hand, but Meck suddenly makes such a serious face; what's the matter with him, what's up now? And they walk up Münzstrasse and walk and walk, and back through Rosenthaler Strasse again, and Franz still waits to hear whether Meck is not going to ask about his arm. But he doesn't even do that, he keeps on looking sideways. Maybe I look too dirty for him. Whereupon Franz gets gay and asks about Cilly, what she's doing.

Oh, she's fine, why shouldn't she be, and Meck talks at great length about her. Franz forces himself to laugh. But the other still doesn't ask about his arm, and suddenly Franz sees everything clearly, and he asks: "You still hang around the café in the Prenzlauer?" Meck says disparagingly: "Yes, sometimes." Then Franz catches on, and he walks slowly, keeping always a step behind Meck: Pums has told him something about me, or Reinhold or Schreiber, and now he thinks I'm a burglar. And if I should start talking now, I'd have to tell him everything, but he can wait a long time till I open my mouth.

And Franz gives a jerk and stands in front of Meck: "Well, Gottlieb, then let's say good-bye, gotta go home, a cripple's got to hit the hay early." Meck looks him full in the face for the first time, takes his pipe out of his mouth, and wants to ask him something, but Franz waves him aside, no use asking questions, he has already given him his hand, and is gone. Meck scratches his head and thinks to himself, I gotta give that one the once-over one of these days, and is dissatisfied with himself.

Franz Biberkopf marches across the Rosenthaler Platz, he feels happy and says to himself: What's the use of all this yapping, I gotta earn money, what's Meck to me, I gotta get some money.

You should have seen the way our Franz Biberkopf went hunting for money. Something new raged inside him. Eva and Herbert put their room at his disposal, but Franz would like to have a place of his own, otherwise he can't get started right. Then comes the cursed moment, when Franz has found a place and his landlady puts the police registration papers in front of him. There he sits, our Franz, and he starts brooding again: if I write my name's Biberkopf, they'll look me up in their files right away, they'll phone headquarters, and they'll say, this way, old boy, and why don't you show up once in a while, and what's the matter with that arm, what hospital did you stay in, who paid for it, and it's none of it true.

And he rages across the table: Charity, do I need charity? I don't want that, that's no good for a free man; and still brooding and raging away, he writes a name on the registration blank, first Franz, and before him he sees the police station and the charity association in Grunerstrasse and the auto out of which they had thrown him. He strokes the stump of his arm through his coat, they're going to ask him about his arm, let 'em go ahead, damn it all, I don't care, I'll do it.

And as if writing with a stick he chisels thick letters into the paper: I've never been a coward, and my name, I won't let any of 'em steal it from me, that's my name, that's what I was born, and that's what I'll remain: Franz Biberkopf. One thick letter after the other, Tegel Prison, the street bordered with black trees, the convicts sitting there, at their gluing, carpentry, repairing. Dip it in again, I'll put a dot over the I. I'm not afraid of the coppers, nor of the bulls with their brass badges. Either I'm a free man or I'm not.

There is a mower death yclept.

Franz hands the registration blank to his landlady, well, that's settled. All settled. And now let's hitch up our breeches, straighten our legs out, and march right into Berlin.

Clothes make the Man and another Man sees Things with other Eyes

On Brunnenstrasse, where they are excavating for the subway, a horse has fallen into the hole. People have been standing around watching for half an hour when the firemen come with a wagon. They put a strap around the belly of the horse. It is standing on a lot of conduits and gas pipes, who knows if it hasn't broken a leg, it trembles and neighs, from above only its head can be seen. They draw it up with a pulley, the animal strikes out with force.

Franz Biberkopf and Meck are in the crowd. Franz jumps into the hole with the firemen and helps pull the horse up. Meck, and everybody else, is astonished at what Franz can do with his one arm. They tap on the sweaty animal and find that nothing has happened to it.

"Franz, you certainly got courage; where'd you get so much strength in that one arm of yours?" "Because I got muscles; if I want to do a thing, I can do it all right." They ankle down Brunnenstrasse, they have just met again for the first time a little while ago. Meck had thrown himself at Franz. "Yes, Gottlieb, that comes from eating and drinking well. And shall I tell you what else I do?" I'll let him have it, Meck's not going to give me any more of his lip. I'd rather not have friends like that. "Well, listen now; I gotta nice job. I stand in a circus on the Fair Grounds in Elbingerstrasse and bark for the merry-go-round, fifty pfennigs, ladies and gentlemen, for one time around, and back there in Romintenerstrasse I'm the strongest one-armed man, but that's only since yesterday; why don't you come and box with me once?" "You don't say you box with one arm!" "Come and take a look for yourself. If I can't cover up above, I use footwork." Franz kids him good. Meck is amazed.

They wander down to the Alex in their same old jogtrot, then a short way through Gipsstrasse, where Franz takes him to the Alte Ballhaus. "It's all done over, you kin watch me dance here or else take a look at me at the bar." Meck is agog. "What's happened to you all of a sudden, say?" "Righto. I'm starting over again, like in the old days. Well, why not? Any objections? Come in and look at me dance with one arm." "No, no, no, I'd rather go to Münzhof, then." " 'S all right with me; they won't let us in, anyway, like this. But come around some Thursday or Saturday. I guess you think I'm playing the eunuch because they shot off my arm." "Who shot it off?" "Oh, I had a shooting party with a bunch of bulls. 'Twasn't really nothin' at all, it happened back there on the Bülowplatz, a few lads wanted to pull off a job, a decent lot they were too, but they didn't have anything and where could they get it? Well, I walk up and down outside, and look around to see what's up, when what should I see right on the corner but two suspicious-looking characters standing back there with shaving brushes in their hats. Well, I'll tell ye: me for the house, and I whisper the alarm to the boy who's the lookout, but they don't want to go yet, just on account of two bulls, not on your life. Boy, they was some fellows, and they gotta get the stuff away first. Then up comes the bulls and starts sniffing around the house. I suppose one of the guys musta noticed something in the house, furs, something for the womenfolks, when coal is scarce. So we lie in ambush, and when the bulls try to get in, y'see they can't get the house-door open. The others, of course, beat it out the rear. And when the bulls call in a locksmith to try and get in, I shoot through the key hole. What d'you think o' that, Meck?" "Where'd it happen?" He can't believe his ears. "In Berlin, just around the corner, on the Kaiserallee." "Aw, go on with that stuff." "Well, so I took a blind shot. Some shot it was, too, right through the door. But they didn't catch me. By the time they got the door open, I was gone. Except for my arm. You see." Meck bleats: "Well, what about it?" Then Franz gives him his hand with a magnificent gesture: "Well, so long, Meck. And if you ever need anything, I live— I'll tell you that later. And good luck to your business."

Off he goes through Weinmeisterstrasse. Meck is dumfounded. Either the boy's pulling my leg, or I'll have to ask Pums about it. They told me an entirely different story.

And Franz wanders through the streets back to the Alex.

I cannot accurately describe to you how the shield of Achilles looked, nor what arms and decorations he wore when he went forth to battle, I can only dimly recall armlets and greaves.

But how Franz looks as he now goes forth into a new battle, that I must tell you. Well, Franz Biberkopf has on his old dusty things all covered with horse-dirt, a sailor's cap with a crooked anchor on it, and a worn-out brown coat and pants that were cheap to start with.

He has been into the Münzhof and, after drinking down a mugful, left it again ten minutes later with a rather fresh little thing who had been stood up by somebody else. He walks along with her through Weinmeisterstrasse and Rosenthaler Strasse, because inside it's kind of muggy and outside it's nice, although a bit misty.

And Franz's heart opens up, he sees so much cheating and fraud wherever he looks! Another man, other eyes. As if he had just gotten his eyes. He and the girl laugh themselves sick at all the things they see! It is six o'clock, a bit past six, it is raining, it's pouring, thank God, the little tart has got an umbrella.

The shops, they look in all the windows.

"Here's a shopkeeper selling beer. Just watch how he serves it. Didja see that, Emmi, didja see that: foam down to here." "Well, what of it?" "Foam down to here? It's cheating! Cheating! Cheating! But he's right, too, the lad's smart. That does me good."

"Oh dear! Then he must be a crook." "That fellow's smart."

A toy-shop:

"I'll be blowed, Emmi, y'know when I stand here and look at all them little things, just take a peep at 'em, well, I can't say it does me good any more. What a lot o' trash, and all those painted eggs. Say, when we were kids, my mother set us to gluing pictures on 'em. I won't tell ye what they paid for 'em." "So you see!" "They're a lot o'hogs! We better smash the window in! Rubbish! Exploiting poor folks is a dirty trick."

Ladies' cloaks. He wants to go on, but she puts on the brakes. "For if you really want to know, I can tell you a thing or two about that subject. Making ladies' cloaks. Say! For the swell ladies. Whatcha think they pay for a thing like that?" "Come on, kid, I don't want to know. If you let 'em give it to you." "Well, well, hold on now, what do ye want to do?"

"Wouldn't I be a jackass if I let 'em pay me just a few pfennigs. I'll wear a silk coat myself and nothing less, that's what I say." "Well, say it then!" "And I'll see to it so's I can wear a silk coat. Otherwise I'd be a fool, wouldn't I, and he'd be right to hand me his eight groschen." "That's the bunk." "Because I've got on dirty pants I s'pose? Y'know, Emmi, that comes from a horse that fell into the subway shaft. Nope, nothing doing with eight groschen as far as I'm concerned, a thousand marks, that's what I want." "Think you'll get 'em?"

The girl rivets her eyes on his. "Haven't got 'em now. I'm just saying it, but I'll get 'em, and not eight lousy groschen." She clings to him heavily in wonder and delight.

American Quick Pressing, an open window, two steaming ironing-boards, in the background several men, not much American about them, sitting smoking, in the front a swarthy young tailor in his shirt-sleeves. Franz looks the place over. He chuckles: "Emmi, cute li'l Emmi, it was nice I found ye today, wasn't it?" She doesn't yet understand the man, but is mightily flattered, he can go to hell, that other guy who had stood her up, let 'im get mad, if he wants to. "Emmi, sweet Emmi, just take a peep at this shop." "Well, he certainly don't make much with his pressing." "Who?" "That little black fellow." "Nope, not him, but the others." "Those fellows back there? How do you know? I don't know 'em." Franz chuckles: "Neither do I, never seen 'em before, but I know 'em just the same. Just look at 'em. And the boss: he presses in front, but in the back— well, he does something else." "Rooming house?" "Maybe so, nope, oh, they're all a lotta crooks. Who do all those suits hanging there belong to? I'd just like to be a bull with a brass badge and ask that guy—you'd see 'em beat it, all right." "What is it?" "It's all stuff they've hooked, and just deposited here! Quick-pressing place, my eye! Swell guys, eh? Look at 'em puffing away! They take it easy all right."

They continue walking. "You oughta do like 'em, Emmi. That's the only real thing. Only don't work. Get that out of your head, that stuff about working! Working gives you blisters on your hands, but no money, or at best, a hole in your head! Work never made a man rich. I'm tellin' you. Only cheating. You bet!"

"And what do you do, anyhow?" She is full of hope. "Come along, Emmi, I'll tell you." They are back again in the Rosenthaler Strasse crowd, then they go through Sophienstrasse into Münzstrasse. Franz goes his way. Trumpets are blaring a marching song beside him. A battle was fought upon the open wold, ratatata, ratatata, ratatata. We have sacked the town and taken all their heavy gold. Sacked it—racked it, ratatata!

They both laugh. This girl he fished up has class. To be sure, her name's only Emmi, but she has the reformatory and divorce behind her. They are both in high spirits. Emmi asks: "Where's your other arm?" "It's at home with my girl, she didn't want to let me go, so I had to leave my arm in hock." "Well let's hope that arm's as gay as you are." "You said it. Say, haven't you heard: I've started up a business with that arm o'mine. It stands on a table and says the whole day long: Only he who works shall eat. He who doesn't work must go hungry. That's what my arm says all day: Admittance one groschen, and the proletarians gather and enjoy it." She holds her belly, and he laughs, too. "Listen, dearie, you're going to tear my other arm off."

Another Man gets another Head as well

A funny little wagon passes through the town, on its chassis a paralyzed man, trundling himself forward with his arms. The little cart is decorated with a lot of colored streamers; and he rides along Schönhauser Allee and stops at all the corners, people gather around him, while his assistant sells penny post-cards:

"Johann Kirbach, globe-trotter, born February 20, 1874, in München-Gladbach, healthy and active till the outbreak of the World War. My industrious efforts were brought to a close by a paralytic stroke on my right side. But I recovered enough to be able to walk for hours on end, which permitted me to carry on my calling. Thus my family was protected from distress. In November 1924, the entire population of the Rhineland rejoiced when the state railroad was liberated from the oppressive Belgian occupation. Many German brothers drank their fill with glee; but for me it was disastrous. That day, on my way home, not 400 yards from my house, I was struck down by a troop of men coming out of a saloon. Such was my bad luck, that as a result I am a cripple for life and can never walk again. I have no pension nor other means of support. Johann Kirbach."

In the café where Franz Biberkopf passes these lovely days reconnoitering, looking out for any opportunity, a brand-new, reliable one which will help a fellow get on, there's a young smart aleck who has seen the wagon with the paralyzed man in front of the Danziger Strasse station. And he fills the café with his yapping on the subject, as well as all about what they did to his father, who had been shot in the chest and can hardly breathe now, and then all at once they decide it's only a nervous disease and reduce his pension, and soon he won't get any at all!

Another young fellow with a big jockey-cap listens to all this gibble-gabble; he is sitting on the same bench, but has no beer. This boy has a lower jaw like a boxer's. "Pooh" says he, "them cripples—they ought'n to give 'em a pfennig." "You would say that. First let 'em shove ye into the war and then not pay ye nothing." "That's the way it should be, pard. If you make a fool o' yourself anywhere else, nobody's goin' to hand you any dough, either. If a little boy steals a ride on a wagon and then falls down and breaks a leg, he don't get a single pfennig. Why not? He was a fool all right." "Listen here, you weren't even alive during the war, you were still in diapers." "Tommyrot, the trouble with Germany is they pay out doles. There's thousands of 'em running around, not doin' nothing, and gettin' money for it."

Others at the table get in on the conversation: "Well, now, just hold your horses, Willy, m' boy. What you working at, anyway?" "Nothin'. I don't do nothin', either. And if they go on paying me, then I'll go on doin' nothin'. Jest the same, it's a lot o' rot for 'em to give me somethin'." The others laugh: "Well, he's a bunk-artist all right."

Franz Biberkopf is sitting at the same table. The youngster over there with the jockey-cap and his hands thrust cheekily in his pockets, looks at him as he sits there with his one arm. A girl embraces Franz: "Say, why, you've only got one arm. What pension you gettin'?" "Who wants to know?" The girl makes eyes at the lad opposite. "Him, over there. He's interested in it." "Nope, I don't really take no interest in it. I only say this: any fellow who was damn-fool enough to go to war—well, that's all there is to it." The girl turns to Franz: "Y' see, he's scared." "Not o' me. He needn't be afraid o' me. Don't I say the same thing, I don't say nothin' else. Y' know where my arm is, the one that's off here, I put it in alcohol and now it's settin' on the press at home, and it says all day long: Howdy, Franz, hey, you old blockhead."

Haha. Great guy that one, he's a hot one. An elderly man has taken a few thick sandwiches from out of a newspaper wrapping, he cuts them up with his pocket-knife and stuffs the pieces into his mouth. "I wasn't in the war, they kept me locked up in Siberia all the time. Well, and now I'm at home with my folks and got the rheumatism. Now suppose they should come and want to take my dole money away—hell, are you all daft?" The youngster: "How didja get the rheumatism? Peddling on the streets, didncha, eh? Well, if you got sick bones, you better not go around peddling on the streets." "I might be a pimp, then." The youngster bangs on the table right in front of the sandwich-paper. "Righto! That'll be fine. And it's not to be laughed at. You ought to see my brother's wife, my sister-in-law, they're decent people, hold their own with anybody, d'you think they felt embarrassed about it, letting themselves be paid that junk, dole money? Why, he went running around looking for work, and she didn't know what to do with them few pfennigs, and two little brats at home. A woman, of course, can't go out to work. Then she got to know a fellow, and then maybe she got to know another one, get me? Till he noticed something, my brother did. Then he comes to me and says he wants me to come and hear what he's got to tell his wife. Well, he came to the right party that time. Say, you shoulda heard that show! He flew off like a wet hen. She gave him and his couple of dirty simoleons such a good talking to that he simply shook on his pins, he did, my brother, her honored husband. He won't never show up again." "Ain't he never showed up again?" "He'd like to all right. But nope, she don't want to have nothing to do with a damn fool, a fellow who lives on the dole and then shoots off his mouth when somebody else earns some money."

They're all of about the same opinion. Franz Biberkopf is sitting next to the youngster, Willy, they call him, and drinks to his health: "Y' know, you're only ten or twelve years younger than us, but you're a hundred years cleverer. Boys, would I 'a' dared talk like that when I was twenty? For the love o' mike! As the Prussians used to say: hands on the seam of your trousers!" "And so say we, only not on our own!" Laughter.

The room is full; the waiter opens a door, a narrow room in back is empty. So the whole table troops in under the gas light. It's very hot, the room is full of flies, a straw mattress is lying on the floor, they lift it up onto the window-sill to air it. The talk goes on. Willy sits between them, doesn't give in.

Just here, the young smart aleck they had snubbed before notices a wrist-watch on Willy's arm and can't get over it's being gold. "Bet you bought that cheap." "Three marks." "Somebody hooked it." "None of my business. Want one, too?" "Nope. Thanks. So somebody can catch me and say: Where didja get that watch?" Willy grins at the company: "He's afraid of theft!" "That's enough from you." Willy stretches his arm across the table: "He's got something against my watch. To me, it's just a plain watch that runs and is made outa gold." "For three marks." "Then I'll show you somethin' else. Lemme have your mug a minute. Tell me, what's that?" "A mug." "Right. A mug to drink out of." "Can't deny that." "And this here?" "That's a watch. Say, are you trying to kid me?" "That's a watch. It's neither a shoe nor a canary bird, but if you want to, you can call it a shoe, too; you can do that, it's just as you want, that's your business." "Don't get that. What you after, anyway?" Willy seems to know what he's after. He takes his arm away, grabs a girl and says: "Say you, walk for us a bit." "What for? What do you mean?" "Aw, go ahead and walk along the wall." She doesn't want to. The others call out to her, "Go ahead and walk for him. Don't put on airs."

Finally she gets up, looks at Willy and walks along the wall. "Hop to it, little filly!" "Walk," cries Willy. She sticks her tongue out at him and starts forward, shaking her buttocks. They laugh. "Now you can come back. Well, what did she do?" "She stuck her tongue out at you!" "What else?" "She walked." "O.K. Walked." The girl puts in a word: "Not on your life, that was dancing." The elderly man with the sandwiches: "That wasn't dancing. Since when is it dancing when a person sticks out her behind." The girl: "When you stick yours out, it ain't." Two fellows shout: "She walked." Willy hears them and laughs triumphantly. "Well, all right, then, and I say she marched." The smart aleck gets peevish: "Well, what's it all about, anyway?"

"Nothing at all. Don't you see; walked, danced, marched, whatever you want. You don't understand that yet. Then I'll chew it for you first. This here is a mug o' beer, but you could call it spit just as well, then maybe we'd all have to call it spit, but we'd drink it up all the same. And so, when she marched, then she either marched or walked or danced, but what it was, you saw for yourself. With your own eyes, too. It was what you saw. And if anybody takes my watch from me, then it's not stolen, by a long run. Do you get me now? It's taken away, out o' your pocket or out of a display-window, or a shop. But stolen? Who says so?" Willy leans back, his hands in his pockets again. "Not me." "Well, what do you say then?" "Listen, I say, taken away. Changed owners." Tableau. Willy sticks out his boxer's chin and says nothing. The others reflect. Something queer hovers about the table.

Willy, in his penetrating voice, suddenly attacks one-armed Franz: "You had to join up with the Prussians, you've been in the war. Now I call that theft of liberty. But they had their own courts and police, and because they had them, they put a muzzle on you, and so now it's not a theft of liberty, according to a poor bum like you, but military service. And you've got to put up with it, like taxes, which go for something you don't understand any better."

The girl pouts: "Now don't talk politics. That's no way to spend an evening." The youngster hawhaws himself out of a tight hole: "It's all a lot of hooey! The weather's too nice for that bunk." Willy challenges him: "Then suppose you go out in the street. I guess you think, you poor nut, you, that politics only exists here in this room and that I'm just makin' it up for your benefit. It don't need me for that. It pukes on your head, m'boy, wherever you go. If you let it, that is." A man yells: "Oh, forget it, shut your traps."

Two new customers arrive. The girl sways daintily, then serpentines along the wall, and, dandling her buttocks, slithers sweetly across to Willy. He jumps up, grabs her for a brazen rollicking dance, after which they clinch in a ten-minute burner. Deep immured beneath the earth stands the mold of dry-burnt clay. Nobody looks at them. One-armed Franz starts tilting his third beaker and strokes his shoulder stump. The stump burns and burns. A clever hound, that Willy, a damned clever hound. The boys drag the table out and throw the straw mattress through the window. One of them has come along with an accordion, he's sitting on the footstool by the door, wheezing away at it. My Johnnie, he's the one who can, my Johnnie's the essence of a man.

They carouse merrily, their coats off, swigging, brawling, sweating. If anyone can, it's Johnnie, my man. Then Franz Biberkopf gets up, pays, and says to himself: I'm not a youngster any more, to go around raising hell, and then I ain't crazy about it either, gotta get some money. Where I get it from, don't matter.

Cap on and off he goes.

Two men are sitting in Rosenthaler Strasse at noon, ladling out pea soup; one has the *Berliner Zeitung* beside him. He laughs: "Fearful domestic tragedy in Western Germany." "What do you mean, what's that to laugh at?" "Listen to this: 'A father throws his three children into the water.' Three at one stroke. A rambunctious fellow, all right." "Where'd it happen?" "Hamm, in Westphalia. That's some mess. Boy, he musta had it full up to here. But you can depend on a fellow like him, all right. Wait a minute, let's see what he did with the wife. Musta given her—nope, she did it on her own, did it beforehand. Whatcha say to that? A gay li'l family that, Max, they know how to live. Letter from wife: Deceiver! With an exclamation point, he ought to hear that! As I am tired of leading this life, I have decided to jump into the canal. Get yourself a rope and hang yourself. Julia. Full stop." He doubles up with laughter. "There's not much harmony in that family: the canal for her and the rope for him. The wife says: hang yourself, and he throws the children into the water. The man didn't listen to her. Nothing could come from a marriage like that."

They are two elderly men, construction-workers from Rosenthaler Strasse. One disapproves of what the other is saying. "That's a sad case, if you was to see a thing like that in the theater or read it in a book, it'd make you blubber!" "You maybe. But, Max, tell me, is anybody going to cry over such things as that, what for?" "The wife, three children, say, stop." "The way I'm made, I get fun out of that, I like that man; of course, you might feel sorry for the children, but to get rid of the whole family at one stroke like that, I got a sort of respect for that, and then—" He explodes again: "And then I think like this, you can say what you want, but I think it's all so terribly funny, the way they squabble up to the last. The wife says, he's to get a rope, and he says: Not on your life, Julia, and chucks the children into the water."

The other puts on steel-rimmed glasses and reads the story again: "The man is still alive. They got him. Well, I wouldn't like to be in his skin, you bet." "Who knows? You don't know nothin'." "Well, I know that, all right." "You know, I kin imagine it. He's sitting in his cell, smoking his tobacco, if he can get any, and says: 'You can all—' " "So you think you know something. Pangs of conscience, me boy. Either he's bawling in his cell or not saying anything. He can't get to sleep. Say, man, why you're talkin' yourself into a sin." "I say no to that. I bet he can sleep fine. If he's that rambunctious, he can sleep well and probably eat and drink better than he did outside. I guarantee you that." The other looks at him curiously. "Then he must be a rotten dog. If they cut his head off, sure, I'll give 'em my blessing." "You're right, too! He'd say the same thing. You're absolutely right." "Well, now, let's cut out all that rubbish. I'm goin' to order some pickle." "It certainly is interesting though, a paper like that. A dirty dog, but maybe he's sorry about it now, there's many a man goes further than he meant to." "I'm gonna take pig's head with pickle." "Me too."

Another Man needs another Calling, too, or maybe None at all

When you notice the first hole in your sleeve, then you know it's high time to get busy about a new suit. Be sure to go at once to the right house where you will find a comprehensive choice, displayed in nice bright rooms, upon wide tables, of all the clothing you may need.

"I can't do nothin', you can say whatever you please, Frau Wegner: a man with one arm, and when it's the right one at that, is a goner." "That certainly is true, it's hard, Herr Biberkopf, but then a man needn't go around yapping and making such a face. Why, a body gets really scared o' you." "Well, what am I going to do with one arm?" "Take the dole, or maybe you might open up a little stand o' some sort." "What kind of a stand?" "Oh, papers or dry-goods or garters or neckties in front of Tietz's or some such place." "Newsstand?" "Or fruit, a fruit business." "I'm too old for that, a man's got to be younger for that."

That's too much like the old days, I won't fool with that any more. I don't want to, and so that's that.

"You ought to have a sweetheart, Herr Biberkopf, she'd tell you all about it and help you when you needed it. She could help to pull the wagon or take charge of the stand when you have to go away somewhere."

Cap on and downstairs, it's all rot, the next thing I'll be strapping a hurdy-gurdy on my shoulder and go tooting around town. Where's Willy?

"Howdy, Willy." Presently Willy says: "Nope, you can't do much. But if you're clever, you can do something, anyway. If I let you have something every day, for instance, to sell or get rid of quietly, and you've got good friends and can keep mum, you can sell the stuff and earn pretty well with it."

And so Franz agrees. He'll do it, absolutely. He wants to stand on his own feet. Something that'll get him some money quick—that's what he wants. Work, a lot o' rot. As for newspapers, to hell with 'em, and he gets in a rage when he sees those nincompoops, the paper-peddlers, and sometimes wonders how anybody can be so pig-headed as to work his head off when others go riding by in motor-cars. Not for me. That was once upon a time, old boy. Tegel prison, the avenue of black trees, houses that totter, roofs threatening to fall on your head, and I've got to be decent! Funny, Franz Biberkopf simply has to be respectable—what do you say to that, eh, it's killing, ain't it? Too funny, I musta got soft in the head from prison. Completely gone off my noodle. Gotta have money, gotta earn money, a man needs money.

So now you see Franz Biberkopf in the rôle of a fence, a criminal, the other man has another calling, and the worst is yet to come.

The woman is arrayed in purple and scarlet color and decked with gold and precious stones and pearls, having a golden cup in her hand. She laughs. And upon her forehead is a name written, MYSTERY, BABYLON THE GREAT, THE MOTHER OF HARLOTS AND ABOMINATIONS OF THE EARTH. And I saw the woman drunken with the blood of the saints, and with the blood of the martyrs. The whore of Babylon sitteth upon many waters, drunken with the blood of the saints.

What kind of togs did Franz Biberkopf wear when he lived in Herbert Wischow's house?

What does he wear now? An immaculate summer suit bought on a bargain counter for 20 marks cash down. For special occasions an iron cross on his left breast, which he wears as a justification of his missing arm. He enjoys the respect of passers-by and the anger of proletarians.

He looks like a well-fed, good-natured saloon-keeper or butcher, with creases in his trousers, glove and a derby hat. Just in case he should need them, he has papers with him, false papers, the papers of a certain Franz Räcker, who died in 1922 during the riots, and whose papers have already helped a lot of others before. Franz knows everything that's written on that paper by heart, where the parents live, when they were born, how many sisters have you, what work have you, when did you last work, everything a bull might ask, the rest will be plain sailing.

That happened in June. In the wonderful month of June, the butterfly emerged after its pupal stage was over. And Franz is by way of flourishing nicely, when Herbert Wischow and Eva arrive from Zoppot. A number of things had happened at the spa, it's a long story, and Franz hears it all with pleasure. Eva's stock-broker had bad luck. Things went well at gambling, but just the day when he drew 10,000 marks from the bank, somebody stole the money from his hotel room while he was dining with Eva. Funny, a thing like that happening! The room neatly opened with a false key, his gold watch gone, as well as 5000 marks which he had left lying in the drawer of the bedside table. Shockingly careless, no doubt, but who would imagine a thing like that? That thieves should be able to get into a first-class hotel! Where does the watchman keep his eyes? I shall bring a suit against you, is there no protection here? We are not responsible for valuables left in the rooms. The fellow bullies Eva, because she had rushed him down to dinner in such a hurry, and why? Just to see that baron, next time you'll be kissing his hands out of respect, you'll send him a box of candy out of my pocket! You forget yourself, my dear Ernst. And the 5000 marks? Can I help it? Oh, let's go home. The banker grumbles: Not a bad idea, anything to get away from here.

Herbert continues to live in Elsasser Strasse, while Eva has to occupy a smart room in the West End, that's nothing new to her; she says to herself, it'll only last a short time, then he'll have enough of me, and I'll move back to Elsasser Strasse.

Even now, on the train, as she sits in a first-class compartment with her banker, suffering his caresses with boredom and feigned enjoyment, she begins to dream: Wonder what Franz is doing. And when her banker gets out before Berlin and she is alone in the compartment, she shudders with anxiety; Franz is gone again! What joy and surprise, what a dropping of jaws then, for Herbert and Eva and Emil, when, on July 4th (Wednesday) there enters—well, you can imagine it, can't you? Clean, spick-and-span, the I. C. clamped to his heroic chest, his dog-like brown eyes as devoted as ever, his warm manly fist and strong handclasp; that's Franz Biberkopf. Keep steady now, or you'll lose your balance. Emil knows about the transformation already, he feasts his eyes on Herbert and Eva. Franz is a real dude. "Boy, so you're washing your feet in champagne these days!" That's how pleased Herbert is. Eva sits there and does not understand. Franz carries his empty right sleeve in his pocket, at any rate the arm hasn't grown again. She falls on his neck and kisses him. "Lord, Franz, darling, there we were sitting and racking our brains trying to guess what Franz was doing, we were so afraid, you can't imagine it!" Franz makes the rounds, kisses Eva, kisses Herbert and Emil, too. "What a lotta bunk, to be afraid about me!" He winks slyly: "And how do you like me as a war hero with my swell coat?" Eva chuckles: "But what's happened, what's happened? Why, I'm ever so happy about the way you look!" "And me, too." "And who are you going with now, Franz?" "Going with? Oh, yes. Nope, nope. Nothin' doin'. I ain't got no girl." He starts off telling his story and promises Herbert he'll pay back all his money, to the last pfennig, to the very last pfennig, yes, in a few months it'll all be paid off. Herbert and Eva laugh. Herbert flashes a brown thousand-mark bill in front of Franz's eyes. "Want it, Franz?" Eva begs: "Take it, Franz." "Nothin' doin'. Don't need it, no, sir! Tell you what, we'll have a drink on that thousand downstairs, eh, that's the stuff!"

A Girl bobs up. Franz is in Clover again

They give their blessing to everything Franz does. Eva is still in love with Franz, and would gladly get him a girl. He resists, I know that girl, no, you don't, neither does Herbert, where did you get to know her, she hasn't been in Berlin long, she's from Bernau, she used to turn up every evening at the Stettin station, and I got to know her there and told her: You'll get into trouble, child, if you don't quit that and keep on running into town, nobody here in Berlin can keep going like that. Then she laughed and said she just wanted to have some fun. Well, y'see, Franz—Herbert knows the story already, Emil too—one day at twelve she sits there in the café. I walk up to her and ask her: well, what kind o' face is that you're making there, girlie, mustn't start any nonsense here! Then she starts crying about how she had to go to the police-station, had no papers, a minor, too, and don't dare go home. They kicked her out where she was working, because the police asked about her, and her mother kicked her out, too. So she says: Just because I try to have a little fun? What's a body to do in Bernau at night?

Emil listens, as usual, with his arms propped up, and says: "The girl's quite right. I know Bernau myself. Nothin' doing there at night."

Eva speaks: "Well, I'm lookin' after the kid a bit, but I won't let her go to Stettin station any more."

Herbert is smoking an imported cigar: "If you're a man who knows what's what, Franz, then maybe you kin make something out of the gal. I've seen her. She's got class."

Emil observes: "A bit young, but she's got class all right. Solid bones." They go on tippling.

Next day at noon sharp the girl knocks at his door, and Franz is enraptured at first sight. Eva had made his mouth water, and he'd like to please Eva, too. But this one's really a knockout, first-class, a wow, he's never found anything like this in his cook-book. She's a small person, in her little thin white dress with her bare arms she looks like a school-girl, she has soft slow movements and in a flash is right beside him. She's been there hardly half an hour, and now he can't imagine his room minus the little minx. Her real name is Emilie Parsunke, but she'd rather be called Sonia, that's how Eva always addressed her, because she has such Russian cheekbones. "And Eva," the girl cajoles him, "why Eva's name's not really Eva, her name's Emilie like mine. Didn't she tell me that herself?"

Franz rocks her on his lap, struck by the trim, taut wonder of her, and is flabbergasted by this bit of sunshine the good Lord's sent to his home. Wonderful how things go up and down in life. He knows who the man was who baptized Eva, wasn't it he himself? She was his girl before Ida, if only he'd stayed with Eva! Well, he's got this girl now . . .

But it's only for a day that he lets her name be Sonia, then he starts pleading—he can't abide such foreign names. If she's from Bernau, she must have another name, surely. He has had a lot of girls before, he says, as she can guess, but never one called Marie. He'd like to have a Marie. And so he calls her "his Miezeken."

It isn't long—about the beginning of July—before he has a nice experience with her. It's not a child on the way, nor is she sick. It's something else, something that hits Franz right in the solar plexus, but it doesn't turn out badly. That's the time Stresemann goes to Paris, or perhaps he doesn't, at Weimar a ceiling crashes down in the telegraph office, and maybe a man out of work traipses along after his sweetheart, who's gone to Graz with another fellow, and then shoots them both dead and lodges a bullet in his own head, as well. Such things will happen in any weather, and the wholesale dying of the fish in the Weissen Elster fits in with the picture. When one reads things like that, it's striking; but if one is on the spot it doesn't seem so impressive, as a matter of fact, something is always happening in every household.

Franz often stands in front of the pawnshop on Alte Schönhauser Strasse, inside in the loan parlor he palavers with first one and then the other, they all know each other, Franz studies the newspaper column of purchases and sales; at noon he meets Mieze. Then, all at once, it strikes him as queer that Mieze should be so hurried and excited when she comes to Aschinger's on the Alex, which is where they eat. She says she overslept—but there's something odd about the girl's manner. He forgets that right away, the lassie is so tender, unbelievably so, and in their room everything's so spick and span with flowers and doilies and ribbons everywhere, just like a little girl's room. And it's always so well aired, and sprayed with lavender water that he is right pleased when they come home together at night. And in bed, she's as soft as a feather, and still just as quiet and gentle and happy as she was at first. But she's always a bit grave, and he can't quite make her out. Wonder if she's thinking about something when she sits there doing nothing, and what's she thinking about. If he asks her, she always laughs and says: she isn't thinking about anything at all. A person can't be thinking about something all day long. And so it seems to him, too.

But there's a letter-box on the door with Franz's name on it, his alias, that is: Franz Räcker, which he always gives for advertisements and for the mail. One day Mieze tells him she had distinctly heard the postman put something in the box before noon and when she went to fetch it, there was nothing. Franz wonders about it and asks what that could mean. Mieze thinks someone must have fished it out; it must be the people across the way, they're always looking through the peephole, and they probably saw the postman come and then they took it out. Franz gets red in the face with rage, and thinks to himself: gosh, maybe somebody's after me. So in the evening he knocks on the door across the way; a woman appears and says right away she'll call her husband. An old man steps up—his wife is younger, the man's probably 60, the woman 30; Franz asks him if a letter has been left there for him by mistake. The man looks at his wife. "Has a letter been left here? I just got home." "No, nobody left a letter here." "When could it have happened, Mieze?" "Around eleven, he always comes around eleven." The woman says: "Yes, he always comes around eleven. But the young lady always gets the mail herself, if any comes: he always rings the bell." "How come you're so sure about that? I once met him on the stairs and he gave me a letter and I put it in the box, too." "I don't know whether you put it in the box or not. Only I saw him give you the letter. But what's all that got to do with me?" Franz: "So then there's no letter here for me, Räcker's my name, and no letters have been left here for me?" "Lord sake's alive, would I accept letters for strangers? You can see for yourself, we don't have no letter-box, 'tain't often the man comes for us." Franz is annoyed and walks off with Mieze, he lifts his cap: " 'Scuse me, g'd evening!" "G'd evening, g'd evening!"

Then Franz and Mieze talk the matter over from every angle. Franz wonders if those people aren't perhaps spying on him. He's going to tell Herbert and Eva about it. He impresses on Mieze to tell the postman to ring the bell. "I'll do it, darling, but sometimes it's another one that comes, an extra."

When he comes home unawares at noon a few days later, Mieze has already gone to Aschinger's. Franz finds out the answer, something quite extraordinary it is, too, that gives him a nasty jar, but doesn't hurt a great deal, at that. He goes into the room, which is of course empty, clean, too, but there's a box of fine cigars waiting for him on which Mieze has put a slip of paper: "For my Franz," and two bottles of Allasch. Franz is happy, and thinks, that gal sure knows how to take care of money, a man ought to marry a girl like that! He's simply delighted, and say, how about that, she's bought me a little dicky-bird too, why it's just as if it was my birthday, well, just you wait, little kitten, I'll get something for you, too. And he feels around in his pockets for money, there's the bell, yes, that's the postman, he's damned late today, it's twelve already, I'll tell him so, myself.

*

Franz walks to the hallway, opens the door and listens. No postman there. He waits, the man doesn't come, probably talking in somebody's room. Franz takes the letter out of the box and goes into the room. In the open envelope he finds a sealed letter with a slip on it, written crosswise in a disguised handwriting: "Wrongly Delivered," and an undecipherable name. It did come from across the hall, then, who are they spying on, anyway? The sealed letter is addressed to "Sonia Parsunke, care of Herr Franz Räcker." Now that's funny, who does she get letters from, Berlin too, it's a man. He reads—and an icy feeling goes through Franz: "Dearest little sweet-heart, how long are you going to keep a fellow hankering for an answer—?" He can't read any further, he sits down—and before him are the cigars and the canary cage.

Then Franz goes out, not to Aschinger's, but to see Herbert, and he grows very white as he shows him the letter. Herbert confers in whispers with Eva in the next room. Then Eva suddenly appears, gives Herbert a kiss, and pushes him out, after which she falls on Franz's neck: "Well, Franz darling, do I get a kiss?" He looks at her flabbergasted. "Let go o' me." "Franz darling, just a little kiss. Aren't we old pals?" "Say, woman, what's it all about, behave yourself, what'll Herbert think?" "I've just kicked him out; come in here, you can look for him if you want to." She leads Franz through the room, Herbert is gone. All right, let him be. Eva closes the door: "So you see you can give me a kiss, can't you?" She winds herself around him, and in a moment she's all on fire.

"Listen, girlie," pants Franz, "you're crazy, ain't you, what you want with me anyway?" But she's beside herself, and he is powerless to resist her. Dumfounded, he pushes her off. Then something runs wild in him. He doesn't know what's come over Eva, it's nothing but blind passion and savagery in both of them. Afterwards they lie together, biting each other on the arms and neck, and she lies with her back across Franz's chest.

Franz grunts: "You're sure Herbert's really not here?" "Doncha believe me?" "Still, it's a swinish trick for me to pull on my friend." "You're such a sweet man, Franz, I'm terribly in love with you." "Say, baby, but you're gonna have a lot o' marks there on your neck." "I could eat you up, that's how much I love you. And when you came in just now with that letter, why, boy, I almost jumped around your neck, right in front of Herbert." "Eva, what's Herbert going to say when he sees those tooth-marks after-wards? They'll turn all green and blue." "Oh, he won't know about it. I'm going to my banker presently, and I'll say I got 'em from him." "That's all very nice, Eva, sure, and you're my sweet little Eva. But I can't stand such a filthy mess. And what's the banker going to say when he sees you?" "And what's auntie and granny going to say? Gee, what a 'fraidcat you are!"

Eva then pulls herself together, grabs Franz's head, gives him a good squeeze and presses her hot cheeks against his shoulder stump. Then she takes the letter, gets dressed, and puts on her hat: "Now I'm goin', y'know what I'm gonna do, I'm goin' to Aschinger's right now and talk to Mieze." "No, Eva, what for?" "Because I wanta. You stay here. I'll be back soon. Lemme do what I want, will you. Can't I look after a young chicken like that if I wanta, with no experience and just come to Berlin? Well, then, Franz—" She kisses him once more, and almost gets in heat again, but then she pulls herself up and runs off. Franz understands nothing.

That's at 1:30 p. m. At two-thirty she is back, grave, quiet, but contented, and she helps Franz, who has fallen asleep, into his things, swabbing his sweaty face with her perfume. Then she starts off, as she sits on the bureau, smoking cigarettes. "That Mieze, well, how she did laugh, Franz! I won't have anything said against her." Franz is astonished. "No, Franz, I wouldn't bother about that letter. She was still sitting at Aschinger's waiting for you. I showed her the letter. And she asked me how you liked the booze and the canary." "All right, then." "Now, listen. Let me tell you, she didn't bat an eye. I thought she was great. She's a good girl. I didn't hand you a dud." But Franz is gloomy and impatient, what's it all about anyway? Eva jumps down, taps him on the knee: "You're a dear, Franz. Can't you understand? A gal likes to do something for her man, too. What does she get out of it when you go running around all day long, tending to your business and so on, and all she does is to make your coffee and clean up the room? She wants to give you something, she wants to do something for you that'll give you pleasure. And that's why she does it." "That's why! You let her hand you that! So that's why she cheats on me?" Eva grows serious: "Who said anything about cheating? That's what she said right away: that don't enter into the question. Suppose somebody does write to her—there's nothing to it, Franz, suppose a fellow does happen to get stuck on her once in a while, and he writes to her, that's no news to you, is it?"

Slowly, slowly, something begins to dawn on Franz. So that's the way things are. She notices that he's beginning to understand. "Well, of course. And what of it? She wants to earn money. And isn't she right? I earn my money, too. And it don't suit her to let you support her, all the more since you can't quite do it with your arm." "That's so." "She told me right away. Didn't bat an eye. You bet, that's a fine girl, you can depend on her all right. You must take care of yourself, she says, after all the trouble you had this year. And before that too, dearie, things didn't go any too well for you, out there in Tegel, y'know what I mean. She'd be ashamed to let you sweat and drudge like that. So she works for you. Only she don't dare say anything to you about it."

"Well, well," Franz nods and lets his head sink on his chest. "You don't believe me?" Eva is beside him, stroking his back. "How that girl clings to you. Me, you don't want me, anyway. Or—do you, Franz?"

He seizes her by the waist, she seats herself carefully on his knees, he can only hold her with one arm. He presses his head against her breast and says softly: "You're a good girl, Eva, stay with Herbert, he may need you, he's a good guy." She had been his friend before Ida's time, let sleeping dogs lie, better not start all over again. Eva understands. "You better go see Mieze now, Franz. She's still sitting waiting at Aschinger's or in front of the door. She don't want to come home if you don't want her."

Very silently, very gently, Franz has taken leave of Eva. In front of Aschinger's, on the side facing a photographer's place, he sees little Mieze standing there on the Alex. Franz takes his stand on the other side, in front of the fence around the construction work, and watches her a long while from behind. She walks to the corner, Franz follows her with his eyes. It's a decisive moment, it's a turning-point. His feet start to move. He sees her in profile, at the corner. How small she is! She is wearing saucy brown shoes. Watch out, now somebody's going to pick her up soon. That little blunt nose o' hers! She's looking around. Yes, I came from over there, from Tietz's, but she didn't see me. One of Aschinger's bread-wagons is standing in the way. Franz walks along the fence as far as the corner, where the sand-heaps are; they're mixing cement. Now she'll be able to see him, but she doesn't look his way. An elderly gentleman keeps on ogling her, she looks past him and wanders towards Loeser & Wolff's. Franz crosses over to the other side. He keeps ten steps behind her, lingering in the offing. It is a sunny July day, a woman offers him a nosegay for sale, he gives her 20 pfennigs and holds the flowers in his hand, but still doesn't come any nearer. Not yet. But the flowers have a nice smell; she put some in the room today, and a canary cage, and some drinks, as well.

Then she turns around. She sees him at once, he has some flowers in his hand, he did come after all. She flies up to him, her face aglow, it glows a moment, flares up, when she sees the flowers in his left hand. Then it turns pale, only a few red splotches remain.

His heart beats a tattoo. She grasps him by the arm, and they walk along the pavement to Landsberger Strasse, not saying a word. From time to time she glances furtively at the wildflowers he holds in his hand, but Franz looks straight ahead as he walks beside her. The No. 19 autobus thunders past, yellow, two-storied, full from top to bottom. An old poster clings to the construction fence to the right. The National Business and Tradesmen's party, impossible to cross the street, those cars from Police Headquarters have the right of way. When they come to the poster column with "Persil" on it, across the way, Franz remembers that he is still holding the nosegay, and wants to give it her. And as his eyes look down at his hand, he asks himself again, sighing, he can't make up his mind—shall I give her the flowers, or shall I not? Ida, but what's that got to do with Ida, Tegel, how I love that kid.

And when they reach the little island where the "Persil" poster is, he can't help but press the flowers into her hand. She has looked up at him several times beseechingly, but he did not speak; now she clasps his left forearm and, lifting his hand, presses it to her face, which flares up again. The warmth from her face streams through him. Then she stands there alone, as she lets his arm fall loosely, and her head seems to droop of its own accord onto her left shoulder. She whispers to Franz, who holds her anxiously by the waist: "It's nothing, Franz, don't bother." They walk diagonally across the square, where Hahn's department store is being pulled down, and then on farther. Mieze is walking quite upright again. "Whatcha standing up so straight for, Mieze?" She presses Franz's arm: "I was so afraid a while ago." She turns her head away, tears fill her eyes, but she soon manages to laugh again before he notices anything; those were terrible hours!

They're upstairs in his room, the girl, in her white dress, sits in front of him, on a footstool; they have opened the windows as it has become burning hot, heavy and sultry. He sits on the sofa in his shirt-sleeves, and keeps looking at the girl. He certainly is in love with her! Gee, I'm glad she's here! What pretty little hands you have, baby! I'll buy you a pair of kid gloves, just you wait; and then you'll get a nice blouse, too, do whatever you want, it's nice to have you here. I'm so glad you're back again, damn it all. He nestles his head on her lap. He pulls her over to him, can't have his fill of looking at her, hugging her, caressing her. Now I'm a human being again, now I'm a man again, no, I won't letcha go, I won't, never again, no matter what happens. He opens his mouth: "Miezeken, baby, you can do whatever you want, I won't letcha go."

How happy they are! Their arms around each other's shoulders, they watch the canary. Mieze looks for her hand-bag, and shows Franz the letter that had come at noon. "And you got so upset about the rot that fellow wrote!" She crumples it up and throws it on the floor behind her: "Say, kid, I could show you a whole package of stuff like that."

Defensive War against Bourgeois Society

The following days Franz Biberkopf walks abroad again in great tranquillity. No longer is he so taken up with this shady business of acting the go-between from one fence to another, or from the fence to the purchasers. He just doesn't give a damn if a job doesn't come off. Franz has time, patience, and calm. If the weather were better, he would do what Mieze and Eva suggested to him: go to Swinemünde and give himself a little treat, but there's nothing doing on account of the weather, it's raining and pouring and drizzling every day; it's cold, too. In Hoppegarten whole trees have been uprooted, what must it be like out there! Franz is on great terms with Mieze and goes around with her all the time, running in and out at Herbert and Eva's. Of course, Mieze also has a gentleman friend in good circumstances, whom Franz knows. Franz is supposed to be her husband, and he occasionally likes to get together with one or the other of her men friends, when the three of them eat and drink amiably at the same table.

To what heights has our Franz Biberkopf now attained! How well off he is, how things have changed for him! He was on the point of death, and what a resurrection now! What a satiated creature he has become, one who lacks nothing, neither in the line of food, drink, nor clothing. He's got a girl who makes him happy, he's got money, more than he needs, all the debt to Herbert has been paid off, Herbert, Eva, and Emil are his friends, and they wish him well. For days on end he sits around at Herbert and Eva's, waits for Mieze or rides out to Müggel Lake, where he goes canoeing with two other men: for each day Franz is getting more active and stronger in his left arm. From time to time, he also listens in around Münzstrasse, or around the pawnshop.

You swore, Franz Biberkopf, you would stay straight. You led a rotten life, you got under the wheels, in the end you killed Ida and did time for it, that was terrible. And now? You're sitting on the same old spot. Ida's name is Mieze, and one of your arms is gone, but look out, you'll take to boozing, too, and everything will start all over again, only much worse this time, and that'll be the end of you.

—Hot air, can I help it, did I force myself to become a pimp? A lotta bunk, I say. I did what I could, that's me. I did everything a man kin do. I let 'em drive over my arm—I'll tell the world! I just got about enough of it! Didn't I go out peddling, didn't I ankle around from morning till night? Now I got my dander up! No, I ain't respectable. I'm a pimp. I don't feel ashamed about that, either. And what are you living off of, off of something different from other people, I suppose? Do I put the screws on anybody, say?

—You'll end in prison, Franz, somebody's gonna stick a knife in your guts, yet.

—Let 'em just start with a knife. First, they'll have to try mine!

The German Reich is a Republic, and whoever doesn't believe it gets one in the neck. In Köpenicker Strasse at Michaelkirchstrasse there is a meeting, the hall is long and narrow; workers, young men with Schiller collars and green collars sit in rows one behind the other, girls and women and pamphlet-sellers circulate through the hall. On the stage behind the table, between two other men, is a stout, half-bald man; he agitates, baits, laughs, and solicits successively.

"And when you get down to it, we're not here to talk into thin air. Let's leave that to the fellows in the Reichstag! Somebody once asked one of our comrades if he wouldn't like to get into the Reichstag. Into the Reichstag with its golden cupola overhead and club-chairs below. Says he: Y'know, comrade, if I was to do that and go into the Reichstag, it'd be just one more scoundrel. We got no time to talk through our hats, comrades, no phoney stuff for us. The communists say in all sincerity: We're out to pursue a policy of exposure. We've seen what comes out of that; the communists got corrupted themselves, and we need waste no words on their policy of exposure. It's all a big swindle, even a blind man can see all there is to expose in Germany, and for that we don't have to go to the Reichstag, but a man who can't see that, why there's nothing to be done for him, with or without the Reichstag. That hot-air shop is good for nothing except to soft-soap the people, and all the parties know it, except the so-called representatives of the working classes.

"Our pious socialists. Well, we already see religious socialists in the party, and that's the last straw: they've all got to get religion, so let them run after the priests! For it don't matter whether the man they all run to is a priest or a bonze, the only thing is: obey. (A voice in the audience: And believe.) Why, that's understood. The socialists want nothing, know nothing, can do nothing. They always have a majority in the Reichstag, but they don't know what to do with it, beg pardon, yes, they do: they give them club-chairs to sit on, cigars to smoke, and ministerial jobs. For that the workers gave them their votes, for that they've given the pennies from their pockets every pay-day: just another fifty or hundred men who're going to line their purses at the expense of the workers. The socialists don't conquer political power, it's political power that conquers the socialists. We get old as a jackass every day, and are always learning, so they say, but such a jackass as the German worker is yet to be born. Again and again German workers take their ballots in their hands, go to the polls, and vote and think to themselves: well, that's done. They say: we want to make our voices resound in the Reichstag; well, they'd do better to found a singing-club!

"Comrades, men and women, we're not going to touch a ballot, we're not going to take part in the election. A Sunday picnic is better for our health, is what I say. And why? Because the voter is hidebound by legality. But legality is the brute force, the violence of the ruling class. Those tub-thumpers want to mislead us into putting a good face on it, they want to humbug us, to prevent our realizing what legality means. But we won't vote, because we know well what legality means and what the state is, and there are no holes and doors by which we can penetrate into it. At best, as official donkeys or beasts of burden. And that's what the electioneers are out for. They want to decoy us and train us as their official donkeys. They attained their aim long ago with the majority of workers. We in Germany are trained in the spirit of legality. But, comrades, you cannot marry fire and water, the worker must understand that.

"The bourgeois parties and the socialists and communists shout in a joyful chorus: All blessings come from above. From the State, from Law, from Order in the highest. But look at the way it works. Certain liberties have been set down in the constitution for everybody who lives in the state. They've been set down, all right. But the liberty we need, no one will give us, we must take it ourselves. This constitution is out to batter down the constitution of reasonable people, for what can you do, comrades, with rights which are only on paper, with coded liberty? If you look for liberty anywhere, up comes a cop and knocks you over the bean; if you yell: what's the matter, the code says so and so, then he replies: None o' your lip, citizen, and he's right, he doesn't recognize any constitution, only his own regulations, and he's got a club for that, and you've got to keep your damned mouth shut.

"Soon there won't be any possibility for strikes in the principal industries. You've got the guillotine of the arbitration committees on your necks, and it's only under that you can move freely.

"Comrades, men and women, you vote again and again, and you say, this time it'll be better, just watch us, a little effort, spread your propaganda at home, in the factory, only five more votes, ten more, twelve more, just wait, then you'll see, then we'll get things going. Yep. You'll get 'em going. Just an eternal blind circle, everything going round the same old way. Parliamentarism prolongs the misery of the workers. They may talk of a crisis of justice, and indeed justice ought to be reformed, reformed lock, stock, and barrel, the juridical body should be renewed, it should be made republican, constitutional, just. But we don't want new judges. We want, instead of this justice, no justice at all. We must overthrow all state institutions by direct action. We have the weapon: Refusal of labor. All wheels at a standstill. But that's not a song to be sung out loud. As for us, comrades, we must refuse to be lulled to sleep by parliamentarism, social service, and all such social-political buncombe. We have only one enemy, the government, and our watchwords are: anarchy and self-help."

Franz walks around the room accompanied by the clever boy Willy, listens in here and there, and buys a few pamphlets which he stuffs into his pocket. He is not made for politics, but Willy hammers away at him and Franz listens curiously. He touches it with his fingers, it touches him, then again it does not touch him. But he does not leave Willy.

—The existing social order is based upon the economic, political, and social enslavement of the working class. It is expressed in the rights of property, monopoly of possession, and in the state monopoly of power. Not the satisfaction of natural human needs, but the expectation of profit is at the basis of modern production. Every technical advance multiplies the wealth of the possessing classes to an infinite degree, in shameless contrast to the misery of vast sections of the community. The state works for the protection of the privileges of the possessing class, and for the oppression of the teeming masses, it acts with weapons of cunning and force for the preservation of monopoly and class distinction. With the genesis of the state begins an age of artificial organization from above down. The individual thus becomes an automaton, a dead wheel in a vast mechanism. We must rouse ourselves! We do not, like all other parties, strive for the conquest of political power, but for its radical elimination. Do not work with the so-called legislative bodies: the slave is invited there only in order that he may impress the seal of law upon his own slavery. We reject all arbitrarily established political and national frontiers. Nationalism is the religion of the modern state. We reject every national unity: behind that lurks the rule of the owning classes, comrades, wake up!—

Franz Biberkopf swallows what Willy gives him to swallow. There follows a debate after the meeting, and they stay on and join in a discussion with an older worker. Willy knows him; the worker thinks that Willy is a comrade from the same trade as his own, and urges him to agitate more effectively. Cocky Willy just laughs and laughs: "Say, since when are we co-workers? I'm not employed by the coal barons." "Well, then, do something, wherever you are, wherever you work." "I don't have to do nothin'. Where I work, they all learnt long ago what they got to do." Willy leans over the table, he laughs so hard. That's a lot of bunk, he pinches Franz's leg, one of these days a fellow'll come running around here with a pastepot, sticking up posters for 'em. He laughs at the workman, who has long iron-gray hair and wears his shirt open at his chest: "You sell those papers, eh, the *Priests' Mirror*, the *Black Flag*, and the *Atheist?* But did you ever look to see what's in 'em?" "Now, listen here, comrade, you needn't open your trap half that wide. Me, I'm gonna show you what I wrote myself." "Aw, cut it out. Wanta show off, don't you? But one of these days maybe you'll read what you wrote yourself and stick to it. F'r instance; it says here: Civilization and Technology. Listen: 'Egyptian slaves spent many decades working without machines to build a royal grave; European workers toil at machines for decades to build a private fortune. Progress? Perhaps. But for whom?' Well, I'll be going to work myself one of these days so that Krupp in Essen or Borsig may have a thousand marks more a month, like a sort of Berlin king. Say, old man, if I look straight atcha, what do I see anyway? You're out to be a man of direct action. Where do you keep it, eh? I don't see nothing. D'you see anything, Franz?" "Aw, leave him go, Willy." "Now, tell me, Franz, if you can see

219

what's the difference between this comrade here and a fellow from the Socialist Party."

The worker settles himself solidly in his chair. Willy: "For myself, I don't see no difference, comrade, and that's a fact. The only difference is on paper, in the newspapers. All right, as far as I am concerned, have it your way. But watcha gonna do with it, that's what I'd like to know. And if you want to ask me what you do, why, then I'll answer right off the bat: exactly the same thing as a man from the S. P. Exactly, precisely the same thing: you stand in front of a turning-lathe, you carry your coupla pfennigs home with you, and your corporation pays out dividends on your work. European workers toil at machines for decades to build a private fortune. I guess you wrote that by yourself."

The gray-haired worker lets his eyes rove from Franz to Willy, he looks around again and sees a few men standing at the bar behind him. The worker moves closer to the table and whispers: "Well, what do you do?" Willy flashes across to Franz: "You tell him." Franz doesn't want to at first, he says political conversations do not interest him. But the gray-haired worker keeps hammering away at him: "This here is no political conversation. We are just talking about ourselves. What kind of work do you do?"

Franz draws himself up in his chair and grabs his beer-mug and looks steadily at the anarchist. There is a mower, death yclept. In the mountains will I take up a weeping and a wailing, and for the habitation of the wilderness a lamentation, because they are burned up so that none can pass through them, both the fowl of the heavens and the beast are fled, they are gone.

"What I work at, I can tell you that, my friend, for I'm not a comrade. I go about, do a bit here and there, but I don't do any work, I let other people work for me."

He's giving me a lot of bunk, they're poking fun at me. "Then you must be an employer, with people working under you, how many have you got? And what do you want here, anyway, if you're a capitalist?" I will make Jerusalem heaps, and a den of dragons, and I will lay the cities of Judah desolate, without an inhabitant.

"Say, don't you see I only got one arm. The other one's gone. That's what I paid for working. That's why I don't want to listen to any more talk about respectable work, get me?" Get that, get that, open your lamps, shall I buy you a pair of specs, eh, go ahead and make goggle-eyes all you want. "Nope, can't say I understand yet, pardner, what kind of work you're in. If it ain't respectable, why, I guess it must be a disreputable sort o' job."

Franz bangs his fist on the table, points his finger at the anarchist and thrusts his head towards him: "Y'see, he's tumbled to it now! That's it, all right! Disreputable. All your decent work is slavery, didn't you say so yourself, that's what decent work is. Yep, and that's what I found out." Spotted that without you, too, didn't need your help for that, you soft-soaper, you ink-splasher, you bunk-artist.

The anarchist, who is a skilled mechanic, has lean white hands. He looks at his finger-tips and muses: It's a good thing to show up such crooks, they compromise a fellow. I'm gonna call somebody to listen to him. He gets up, but Willy holds him back: "Where you going, old man? Are we through already? You better settle things up with my pal here first. Trying to slip off, eh?" "I'm just going to get a fellow to listen to this, you're two against one." "What's that, you say you're gonna get somebody? But I don't want anybody. Here, what were ye saying to my friend here?" The anarchist sits down again, we'll have it out alone, then. "So he's not a comrade, and he's not a fellow-worker. For he don't work. And he don't seem to be getting the dole, either."

Franz's face grows hard, his eyes are glaring: "Nope, he don't do that." "Then he's no comrade of mine and no fellow-worker, and he's not one of the unemployed, either. Well, I only ask one thing and all the rest don't matter a damn: what's he after here?" Franz looks at him with grim decision: "I just been waiting for you to ask that: Whatcha want here? You people here sell all kinds o' papers and pamphlets, and when I start asking you what it's all about, what's in 'em, you say: How's it come you ask me that? What do you want here? Didn't you write yourself all about that damned wage slavery and how we are just outcasts who don't dare to move!" Awake, you pariahs of the earth, doomed by all to starve! "Well then, you didn't listen to the rest. When I spoke about refusal to work. First of all a fellow has got to work." "I refuse to." "That's no use to us. You might just as well go to bed. I was talking about strikes, mass strikes, general strikes."

Franz raises his arm and laughs, he's furious now. "And what you're doing now, you call that direct action? Running around pasting up posters and making speeches? And in the meantime you go and make the capitalists all the stronger. Say, comrade, you bonehead, you're turning out the shells they'll shoot you down with and that's what you want to preach to me? Willy, whatcha say to that? You could knock me down with a feather." "I ask you again, what are you working at?" "Then I will tell you again, nothin'! Crap! Nothin', I tell you. Why should I? I can't, anyway. According to your own theories, I can't. I ain't goin' to make the capitalists stronger! As a matter of fact, I don't give a hoot for the whole racket, your strikes and them little goofers that are supposed to come after. A man's got only himself, just himself. I look after myself. I'm a self-provider, I am!"

The worker gulps down his seltzer-water and nods: "Well, then, try it out alone." Franz laughs and laughs. The worker: "And I've told you that three dozen times already: you can't do anything alone. We need a fighting organization. We've got to bring enlightenment to the masses, to cope with the despotic rule of the state and the economic monopoly." Franz laughs and laughs. No higher being will save mankind, no Kaiser, people's tribune, God, can rescue us from misery's grind, alone we have to bear the rod.

They sit opposite each other, silent now. The old worker in the green collar stares at Franz, who looks him hard in the eyes, whatcha looking at, boy, y'can't get me, eh? The worker opens his mouth: "I tell you, I can see, comrade, I'm wasting my breath on you. You're thick-skulled. You'll butt your head against the wall. You don't know what the main thing for the proletariat is: solidarity. That you don't know." "Well, pardner, you know what, we're going to get our hats right away and get along, heh, Willy? That's enough. You're only saying the same old things over and over again." "So I do. You can go down to the cellar and bury yourself if you want to. But you shouldn't go to public meetings." "Excuse me, boss. We just had a little free half-hour. And now, many thanks to you. Waiter, how much is it? Here: I'm paying for this: three beers, two brandies, one mark ten, there you are, I'm paying for this, that's direct action!"

"What are you, anyway, mate?" The fellow won't let go. Franz pockets the change. "Me? Pimp. Don't I look it?" "Well, you're not far from it." "Me, I'm a pimp, get me? Did I say it or not? Well, Willy, tell him what you are." "None of his business." Hell, they're crooks, sure enough. Probably true. That's what I thought. Those crooks have humbugged me, the rotters, they wanted to pull my leg. "You're the dregs of the capitalistic morass. Go ahead and beat it. You're not even proletarians, you're what we call bums." Franz is already standing. "But we're not going to the poor-house. Good day, Herr Direct-Action. Just go on fattening the capitalists. Get in line at seven o'clock in the morning at the bone mill and get your coupla pfennigs from the wage-bag for the missus." "Don't let me see you here, any more!" "No, Herr Direct-Bunkaction, we don't have any dealings with the slaves of capitalists."

Quiet exit. On the dusty street, the two walk arm-in-arm. Willy breathes deeply: "You certainly gave him an earful, Franz." He is astonished to hear Franz talking in monosyllables. Franz is furious, it's even funny how full of hate and rage Franz left the hall, it's fermenting inside him, but he doesn't know why.

They meet Mieze at the Mocca-Fix Café in Münzstrasse, where there's a lot of noise. Franz decides to go home with Mieze, he wants to talk to her, sit by her. He tells her about the conversation with the gray-haired workman. Mieze is very gentle with him, but he wants to know if he had said the right things. She smiles, uncomprehending, and strokes his hands, the bird has waked up, Franz sighs, she can't calm him down.

A Ladies' Conspiracy, our dear Ladies have the Floor, Europe's Heart does not age

But Franz can't get away from politics. (Why? What's torturing you? What are you defending yourself against?) He sees something there, he sees something, he wants to bash them all in the face, they are always baiting him, he takes to reading the *Red Flag* and the *Unemployed*. He often turns up with Willy at Herbert and Eva's. But they don't care for the fellow. Franz is not crazy about him either, but you can talk to the chap and he has them all beat when it comes to politics. When Eva begs Franz to leave that fellow, this Willy, who only takes his money, and is nothing better than a pickpocket, Franz is entirely of her opinion; in reality Franz has no use for politics, it's made him sore as long as he can remember. So today he promises to give Willy his walking papers, but the next day he is around again with the lout, and he takes him along canoeing.

Eva says to Herbert: "If it wasn't Franz and he hadn't had this rotten business about his arm, I'd know how to cure him." "Yeah?" "I can promise you in two weeks time he won't be going around with that young big-mouth any more, who's only wheedling money out of him. Who goes with that fellow, anyway? First of all, if I were in Mieze's place, I'd get the cops after him." "Who? Willy?" "Willy, or Franz, one or the other. I wouldn't care. But they oughta know it. When he's sitting in the bull-pen, he'll realize who was right." "Gee, Eva, but you're really mad at Franz." "Yeah, that was why I threw Mieze his way, and her working and slaving for the two fellows she's got, so Franz can do tricks like that? No, Franz has got to listen to reason a bit, too. Now he's got only one arm, where is it all gonna end? Wanting to play at politics and making the girl mad!" "Yes, she's mighty mad. Told me that yesterday, too. Sits there, waiting for him to come home. What does a girl like that get out of life, anyway?" Eva kisses him: "Yes, I feel the same way. Suppose you were to stay away like that and start that kind of bunk, running around to meetings, eh, Herbert!" "Well, what would happen then, honey?"

"First I'd scratch your eyes out, and then you could look for me in the moonshine." "I'd like to do that, honey." She gives Herbert a tap on the mouth, laughs, then gives him a good shaking: "I'll tell you, I won't let that kid, Sonia, get ruined, she's too good for that. As if the man hadn't burnt his fingers enough already, and at that it don't bring him in five pfennigs." "Well, try to do something with our Franzeken. As long as I've known the boy, he's been a good enough sort, but you might as well talk to the wall, for all he listens to what you say." Eva remembers how she had wooed him, that was when Ida came, and later how she had warned him, all she had suffered through that man, and even now she's not happy.

"I just don't understand," she says, standing in the middle of the room, "there he went and had all that trouble with Pums and that gang of criminals, but he doesn't lift a finger. He's nicely fixed now, sure enough, but an arm is an arm, after all." "That's what I think." "He don't like to talk about it, that's as sure as you're alive. Now I'm going to tell you something, Herbert. Of course, Mieze knows the story about his arm. Only where it happened and who did it, that she don't know. I've asked her already. She don't know nothing and wouldn't like to rake it up. She's a bit soft, that Mieze. Well, maybe she worries about it now, when she sits there all alone waiting, wondering where our Franz is, and, of course, he might easily come to grief again. Mieze cries quite enough as it is; of course, not when he's around. That man just looks for trouble. He ought to look after his own affairs better. Mieze should make him get a move on in this Pums business." "Wow!" "That's better. That's what I say. That's what Franz ought to do. And if he took a knife or a pistol, wouldn't he be doin' right?" "As far as I'm concerned; I've always thought so. I certainly asked around enough myself. Those Pums people keep mum, all right; there's not one of 'em seems to know anything." "Certainly somebody knows all about it." "Well, what can you do?" "That's what Franz ought to be thinking about, and not about Willy and those anarchists and communists and the whole bunch of lousy bums that don't get him any money." "Say, Eva, mind out your fingers don't get burnt with that."

Eva's gentleman friend has gone to Brussels, and so she can invite Mieze to her place and show her all about how smart folks live. That's out of Mieze's line, so far. The man is so crazy about Eva that he's even fixed up a little nursery for her, where two monkeys are kept. "You think all that's for my little monkeys, don't you, Sonia? Yes, well, not on your life. I only put 'em there because it's such a pretty little room, ain't it, and those monkeys, well, Herbert just dotes on 'em, and he always has such a lot of fun when he comes here." "What? You bring him here?" "What of it? The old boy knows him, of course, he's mighty jealous, but I guess it's just as well. D'you think if he wasn't jealous he wouldn'ta canned me long ago? He wants a child by me, imagine it, and that's what the little room is for!" They laugh, it's a cozy, gayly painted, beribboned little room with a low baby's cot. The little monkeys climb up and down the bars of the bed, Eva clasps one to her breast and stares mistily into space: "I mighta done him that little favor all right, about the child, but I don't want one from him. No, not from him." "Yes, and Herbert don't want a baby." "No, but I'd like one by Herbert. Or by Franz. Are you angry, Sonia?"

But Sonia does something quite different from what Eva expects. She gives a little scream, her features seem to crumple up, as she pushes the little monkey away from Eva's breast and embraces Eva violently, happily, beatifically, tenderly. Eva can't understand and turns her face away, when Sonia tries to kiss her again and again. "Look here, Eva, why, of course I'm not angry, I'm only happy you like him. Tell me how much you like him? You'd like to have a child by him, why not tell him that?" Eva frees herself from the girl's embrace. "Are you crazy, kid? But just tell me, Sonia, what's wrong with you? Tell me truly, now: do you really want to hand him over to me?" "No, why should I, I want to keep him, of course, he's my Franz. But you're my Eva." "What am I?" "My Eva, my Eva."

Eva can't prevent Sonia from kissing her on the mouth, the nose, the ears, the nape of her neck; Eva keeps quite still, but then when Sonia nestles her face on Eva's breast, she abruptly lifts Sonia's head: "Listen, girl, are you queer?" "Not a bit," she stammers, and frees her head from Eva's hands, resting against Eva's face. "I love you and I never knew it before! Until a minute ago when you said you'd like to have a child by him—" "What's that? Did you suddenly go crazy?" "No Eva, I really don't know." Sonia's face is as red as fire as she looks up at Eva. "You'd really like to have a child by him?" "No, I only said it." "Yes, you would like one, you only said it; but you really do want one, you really do." And again Sonia nestles on Eva's breast, and pressing Eva to her, murmurs happily: "That's lovely, that you should want a child by him, oh, it's just lovely! I'm happy, ever so happy."

Eva leads Sonia into the next room and lays her on the sofa. "Sure, you're queer, Sonia." "No, I'm not queer, I never touched a girl before in all my life." "But you'd like to touch me." "Yes, it's because I love you so and you want a child by him. And you shall have one, too." "You're crazy, kid." She has been carried off her feet, and when Eva tries to get up, she clasps her hands tightly: "Don't say no, please, you do want one by him, you must promise me that. Promise me you'll have a child by him." Eva has to use force to tear herself from Sonia, who lies there limply, eyes shut, moist lips a-quiver.

Sonia gets up and sits beside Eva at the table, on which the maid has set a luncheon with wine. She brings coffee and cigarettes for Sonia, who is still dreaming, enchanted, with swimming eyes. As usual, she has on a simple white dress. Eva is in a black silk kimono. "Well, Sonia, kid, can I talk reason to you now?" "There's no law against it." "How do you like it at my house?" "Swell." "You do? And how about Franz, you like him, don't you?" "Yes." "Well, what I mean is, if you love Franz, you better look after the boy. He's running around where no good can come and always with that lousy bum, Willy." "Yes, he likes him." "And how about you?" "Me? Oh, I like him, too. If Franz likes him, then I like him too." "That's the way you are, girlie, you simply haven't got any eyes, you're too young yet. That's no company for Franz, I tell you, Herbert says so too. He's a louse. He'll lead Franz into trouble. Hasn't he got enough already with that one arm of his?"

Sonia grows pale instantly, lets her cigarette hang from the corner of her mouth, puts it down, and asks softly: "What's the matter? For God's sake, tell me." "Who kin tell what's the matter. I don't run after Franz, nor you either. Well, I know, you ain't got any time. But get him to tell you sometime where he goes. What does he tell you, anyway?" "Oh, only politics, and I don't understand that." "So y'see that's what he's doin', politics, and nothing but politics, with those communists and anarchists and such low people who ain't got a decent pair of pants to their behinds. That's what Franz is running around with. And you like that, Sonia, is that what you're working for?" "But I can't say to Franz he must come here and go there, Eva, a girl can't do that." "If you weren't so little and not yet twenty, I'd box your ears for you. All of a sudden you can't say anything. You want him to get caught under the wheels again?" "He won't get caught under the wheels again, Eva. I'll watch out for him." Strange, little Sonia has tears in her eyes and her head droops. Eva looks at the girl but can't make her out, does she really love him as much as that? "Here, take some red wine, Sonia, my old man's always swilling red wine, come on!"

She measures out half a glass for the girl, but the tears continue trickling down the child's cheeks, and her face remains as sad as ever. "Another little sip, Sonia." Eva puts down the glass, strokes Sonia's cheeks and says to herself, she's going to get worked up again. But the girl continues staring in front of her. Then she gets up, stands before the window and looks out. Eva now stands beside Sonia, can't make her out for the life of me, damn it. "You mustn't take that business with Franz so much to heart, little Sonia, what I just said, you know I didn't mean it that way. But you shouldn't let him run around with that slob of a Willy. Franz is such a good-natured fool, y'see, he'd do better to go after this Pums feller, or whoever it was ran over his arm and do something about it." "I'll watch out," says little Sonia softly, and without raising her head she puts an arm around Eva, and thus they stand for almost five minutes. Eva thinks: I don't begrudge this one Franz, but I would any other.

Afterward they tear through the room with the little monkeys; Eva shows her everything. Sonia is amazed by it all: Eva's wardrobe, the furniture, the beds, the rugs. Do you dream of that lovely hour when you will be crowned the Pixavon Queen? Kin a guy smoke here? Sure. I don't understand how, year after year, you are able to carry this high quality cigarette at such a low price; I am happy to confess to you. Say, but that smells nice! The wonderful scent of the white rose, as delicate as the cultivated German woman demands, and yet strong enough to develop the entire personality. Ah, the life of the American film star, in reality, differs essentially from what the legends surrounding her would lead us to assume. The coffee arrives; Sonia sings a song:

Once there roved at Abrudpanta Brigands wild and daring, too. But their chief whose name was Guito Had a noble heart and true. Once he met in darkling forests Count von Marschan's little lass. Soon there echoed through the branches: I am yours till death shall pass!

But they are discovered later, Hunters come with loud halloo. They're awakened from their rapture, Ask themselves, what shall we do. And her father damns the maiden, Curses loud the chieftain grim, Oh, have pity, father, darling, I shall go to death with him.

Soon there lies in darkness Guito, Fearful is his woe and pain! Isabella seeks to shatter Her own sweetheart's heavy chain. And she does succeed—oh wonder, He is once more safe and free, Hardly rid from ghastly shackles, He can stop a murderer's glee.

To the castle then he hastens With the woman he released, But already she is kneeling, Ready for the wedding feast, Forced to say "yes" to the union Which she loathes with all her might, But the crime's revealed by Guito, And his lips are pale and tight.

Swoon of death grips Isabella, And she lies so sweet and pale, Ah, there is no kiss can wake her, Nobly then he tells his tale. To her father he has spoken: Yours the guilt that she be dead, You, alone, her heart have broken. You made pale those cheeks once red.

When the chief again beholds her Lying on the silent bier, He bends down, her face descrying, She still lives, Death is not near. Off he bears her, gently crooning, Struck with fear the people stand, And she wakes up from her swooning, He's her mate and helping hand.

And they flee by love's wind carried, Peace and quiet have left them now, By the courts pursued and harried, Solemnly they take this vow: Freely let us both surrender, When the poison cup we've drained, God his judgement then will render, Up in heaven our love we've gained.

Sonia and Eva know it's only a common little song from the street fair; the kind they toot as an accompaniment to illustrative posters; but both have to weep when it's finished, and they're unable to relight their cigarettes right away.

Enough of Politics, but this eternal Far-Niente is still more dangerous

Franz Biberkopf muddles around in politics a bit longer. The smart boy Willy has not much cash; but he has a sharp bright mind, even though he is only a beginner in the pickpocket business, and that's why he exploits Franz. He was once an inmate in a house of correction where somebody had told him all about communism, to the effect that it's nothing at all; and that a reasonable man believes only in Nietzsche and Stirner, and does what he pleases; all the rest is bunk. So the sharp, ironical lad gets a lot of fun out of going to political meetings, and heckling the speakers. At the meetings he fishes up people with whom he wants to do business, or whose legs he simply wants to pull.

Franz goes about with him for a while only. Then it's all over, finished with politics, even without Mieze's and Eva's intervention.

Late one evening, he is sitting at table with an elderly carpenter whom they got to know at a meeting; Willy, in the meantime, is standing at the bar talking with another man. Franz has his arm propped up on the table, his head in his left hand, as he listens to what the carpenter says. "Y'know, mate, I only went to the meeting because my wife is sick, and she don't need me at home at night. She needs her rest; at eight o'clock sharp she takes her sleeping tablets and tea, and then I've got to put out the lights. What can I do upstairs? That's what drives a man to the saloons, when a man's got a sick woman."

"Put her in a hospital, why doncha? It's no good at home."

"She's already been in a hospital. I took her out again. She didn't like the meals there, and besides she didn't get any better, either."

"Is she very sick, your wife?"

"Her womb has grown onto the rectum or something like that. They've operated on her once, but it don't help any. Something internal. And now the doctor says she's only nervous and there's nothing the matter with her. But she's got pains all right, she groans all day long."

"The hell she does."

"He'll write her down as cured, just you watch. She was supposed to go twice to see a specialist, get me, but nothing doing. He'll write her down as healthy, sure enough. If a person's got sick nerves, then he's healthy."

Franz listens, he's been sick, too, his arm was run over, and he was in the Magdeburg Hospital. He can get along without that, it happened in another world. "Another beer?" "Sure." "One beer." The carpenter looks at Franz: "You don't belong to the party, do you?"

"Used to, in the old days. Not any more now. It's no use."

The proprietor comes and sits at their table, greets the carpenter with a "g'd evening, Ede," and asks about the children, then he whispers: "Gee whiz, are you talking politics again?"

"We just been talking about that. Don't pay no attention to it now." "Well, that's the stuff. I tell you, Ede, and my boy says the same thing as me, you don't earn a penny with politics, politics don't help us to get ahead any, only the others."

The carpenter looks at him with narrowed eyes: "Is that so? Little August already has that idea, too?"

"The boy's good, I'm telling you, you can't fool 'im. I'd like to see anybody try it. We want to make money. And—things are goin' pretty well. Only no grumbling."

"Well, here's how, Fritze. I don't begrudge you nothin'."

"Me, I don't give a damn for all that Marxism or Lenin and Stalin and those guys. Whether somebody'll give me credit or not, the dough, I mean, and how much and how long—get me, that's what makes the world turn round."

"Well, you've got somewhere." Whereupon Franz and the carpenter grow silent. The proprietor goes on chattering, but the carpenter gets himself all worked up:

"Me, I don't understand nothing about Marxism. But watch out, Fritze, it's not as simple as you paint it here in your skull. What do I want with Marxism or what those fellows say, those Russians, or Willy with his Stirner. Maybe it's all bunk. What I need, I can figure that out on my fingers every day. Sure, I can understand when a fellow beats hell out of me, what that means. Or when I'm up at my place and tomorrow I'm kicked out, because there ain't no orders comin' in, the boss stays, and the big foreman stays too, of course, only me I've got to go out into the street and look for the dole. But—I've got three kids and they go to the public school, the eldest girl has got crooked legs from the rickets. I can't send her away, but maybe the school will do it some day. Maybe my wife can go to the Children's Aid or something like that, the wife's got to work, but now she's sick, otherwise she's a good worker. She peddles fish, but as far as learning somethin' is concerned, the kids don't learn a lot, you can imagine that. So y'see how it is. And I can't understand either, how other folks learn their children them foreign languages, and in summer they go to the seaside, and we ain't even got the cash to pay our fare out to Tegel. And the swell children, they don't get crooked legs so easy, either. But when I've got to go to the doctor, with my rheumatism, there's thirty of us sittin' in the waiting-room and afterwards he asks me: that pain in your legs, well, you had it before most likely, and how long have you held this job, and have you got your papers: he don't believe me, not on your life, and the next thing, off I go to the specialist, and if I want to be sent on a trip by the state insurance people, they're always docking your pay for that, well I tell ye, you gotta carry your head under your arm before they'll do that. I tell ye, Fritze, ye don't need no glasses to see that. A fellow sure has to be a jackass from the Zoo if he don't get it. We don't need no Karl Marx to tell us that. But, Fritze, but—yea, that's the gospel truth, s'help me God."

The carpenter raises his gray head and stares, wide-eyed, at the proprietor. He puts his pipe back into his mouth, then puffs and waits for someone to answer. The barkeeper grumbles, purses his lips, and looks fed up. "Yep, you're right. My youngest girl's got crooked legs, too. I ain't got any money for the country. But there's always been rich and poor, and that's all there is to it. And us two won't change it, either."

The carpenter calmly puffs away: "Only the ones that likes it ought to be poor. Let the others have a try at it first. I ain't got no liking for it. A fellow gets tired of it after a while."

They are talking quite calmly, slowly sipping their beer. Franz listens. Willy comes over from the bar. Franz decides to get up, he takes his hat and goes out: "No, Willy, I want to hit the hay early. You know how it was yesterday."

Franz tramps alone along the hot dusty street, marching along, bumbledly, bumbledy, bumbledy, bee, tumbledy, rumbledy, tumbledy, bee. Wait awhile, my little beaver, soon will Haarmann come to you, with his little chopping cleaver, he'll make sausage out of you, wait a while, my little beaver, soon will Haarmann come to you. Damn it, damn it, where am I walking to? He pauses, can't get across the street; he turns around, marches back along the hot street, past the café, where they are still sitting, where the carpenter sits with his beer. I won't go in. The carpenter told the truth. That's the truth. What do I want with politics, it's a lot of tripe! It don't help me any. Don't get me anywhere.

So Franz marches again through the hot, dusty, restless streets. August. In Rosenthaler Platz the crowd is thicker, a man is there selling news-papers, *Berlin Workers' Journal, Marxist Fehmic Court*, Czech Jew as Sadist, seduced 20 boys, but no arrests made, I used to peddle here, too. Terribly hot today. Franz stops and buys a paper from the man who has a green swastika on his cap, the one-eyed war veteran of the *Neue Welt*. Drink, drink, brother, let's drink, Leave all your worries at home, Shun all trouble and shun all pain, Then life's a happy refrain, Shun all trouble and shun all pain, Then life's a happy refrain.

He drifts round the square into Elsasser Strasse, shoelaces, Lüders, Shun all trouble, and shun all pain, Then life's a happy refrain. It's some time ago now, Christmas last year, boy, that's a long time, I stood here in front of Fabisch's, what a lotta trash that was, things for neckties, tie-holders, and Lina; Lina, the fat Polish girl who used to come fetch me here.

Franz keeps on tramping along, he doesn't know what he wants, back to Rosenthaler Platz, and finally he stands in front of Fabisch's at the car-stop, opposite Aschinger's. And there he waits. Yes, that's what he wants! He stands there and waits and feels like a magnetic needle— towards the North! To Tegel, to prison, to prison-walls! That's where he wants to go! That's where he must go.

Then it so happens that car No. 41 comes by, stops, and Franz gets on. He feels that's as it should be. Off he rides, as the car speeds on to Tegel. He pays 20 pfennigs, he has his ticket, it goes like greased lightning, that's the stuff! He feels fine. So it's true that he's riding out there. Brunnenstrasse, Uferstrasse, tree-bordered streets, Reinickendorf, it's real, every bit of it, that's where he's going, it's written there. And now all is well. As he sits there, it grows truer, more intense, more potent. The satisfaction he feels is so deep, so strong, and so overpowering is his sense of well-being that Franz, as he sits there, shuts his eyes and is engulfed in a profound sleep.

The car has passed the city hall in the dark. Berliner Strasse, Reinickendorf West, Tegel, end of the line. The conductor wakes him up, helps him to his feet. "We don't go any farther. Where did you want to go, anyway?" Franz stumbles out: "Tegel." "Well, here you are!" He's got a good load on, that's how those cripples booze their pensions away.

A tremendous need for sleep has so overcome Franz that he sets out full sail across the square into which he has drifted, up to the first bench he finds, behind a streetlamp. A police-squad wakes him up, it's three o'clock, they don't do anything to him, the man looks like a decent fellow, he's got a good load on, but somebody might rob him. "You mustn't sleep here, where do you live?"

Franz has had enough. He yawns. He wants to go sleepy-bye. Yes, that's Tegel, what did I want here, anyway, did I want anything here? His thoughts run into each other. I've got to hit the hay, there's nothing else to be done. He broods gloomily: Yes, yes, that's Tegel, he doesn't know what it's all about, he did time here once. An automobile. What was it, what did I want in Tegel? Say, wake me up, if I go to sleep.

And a profound sleep seizes him again, unsealing his eyes. Franz knows everything.

Now in that place there is a mountain and the old man arises and says to his son: Come with me. Come, says the old man to his son, and he goes forth and his son goes with him, goes behind him, up into the mountains, up, up, mountains, valleys. How far is it, father? I do not know. Are you tired, my child, will you not come with me? No, I am not tired; if you wish me to come, I will do it. Yes, come with me. Uphill, downhill, valleys, a long way, noon, here we are. Look around you, my son, yonder is an altar. I am afraid, father. Why are you afraid, my child? You woke me up early, we walked forth, we have forgotten the ram we wanted to slaughter. Yes, we have forgotten it. Uphill, downhill, long valleys, we have forgotten all that, the ram did not come with us, yonder is the altar, I am afraid. I must take off my cloak, are you afraid, my son. Yes I am afraid, father. I am also afraid, my son, come nigh, and fear not. We must accomplish it. What must we accomplish? Uphill, downhill, long valleys, I arose so early. Do not be afraid, O my son, do it with joy, come nigh unto me, I have already taken off my cloak, for I must not defile my sleeves with blood. I am afraid, because you hold the knife. Yes, I hold the knife, I must slaughter you, I must offer you for a burnt offering, the Lord commands, do it with joy, O my son.

No, I cannot do it, I will cry out, touch me not, I will not be slaughtered. Bend down now on your knees, do not cry out, my son. Yes I shall cry. Do not cry; if you do not suffer it, I cannot accomplish it, but you must endure it, my son. Uphill, downhill; why may I not return home again? What do you want to do at home, the Lord is more than home. I cannot, yes, I can, no, I cannot. Come nearer and see. I have the knife ready, here, look at it, it is sharp, it is ready for your throat. To cleave my throat? Yes. The blood will spurt? Yes. The Lord commands it. Will you endure it? I cannot, not yet, my father. But come soon, I cannot murder you, if I do this deed, it must be as if you yourself did it. Myself? Ah. Yes, and without fear. Ah. Not to live out your life, for you offer your life to the Lord. Come nearer. Is it the Lord God's will? Uphill, downhill, I have risen so early. You will not play the coward? I know, I know, I know! What do you know, my son? Take the knife to me, wait; I will turn my collar back so that my neck may be quite free. You seem to know something. You must will it and I must will it, and thus we will both accomplish it, and then the Lord will call and we will hear him call: Cease!! Yes, come, offer your neck. There! I am not afraid, I do it with joy. Uphill, downhill, long valleys, there, take the knife to me and begin to cut! I shall not cry out.

The son lays bare his throat, the father steps behind him, presses against his forehead and with his right hand wields the butcher knife. The son has willed it. The Lord calls out. The twain fall on their faces.

Hear the voice of the Lord calling; Hallelujah. Through the mountains, through the valleys. Ye have obeyed me, hallelujah! Ye shall live. Hallelujah! Cease! Fling the knife into the abyss. Hallelujah! I am the Lord whom ye shall serve and ye shall serve none other. Hallelujah, Hallelujah, Hallelujah, Hallelujah, Hallelujah, Hallelujah, Hallelujah, Hallelujah, lujah, lujah, lujah, Hallelujah, lujah, hallelujah.

"Mieze, baby, little Miezeken, why don't you wade into me good and proper?" Franz tries to pull Mieze to his knees. "Do say something. What of it, if I came home late last night?" "Say, Franz, you'll get in trouble yet, the people you go around with." "How so?" "The chauffeur had to help you up them stairs. And I said something to you, too, but didn't get no answer, there you lay, dead to the world." "I tell you I went out to Tegel, yeah, alone, all by myself." "Now tell me Franz, is that true?" "By myself, yep, I had to do a few years there, once." "Well, is there some time left over?" "No, I did my time right up to the last day. I just wanted to have a look at it, and you don't need to get mad about that, Miezeken."

She sits down beside him and looks at him tenderly, as usual: "Listen, Franz, don't play politics." "I ain't playin' politics." "Don't go to meetings, either." "I ain't thinkin' o' going." "You'll tell me if you do?" "Yes."

Mieze puts her arm around Franz's shoulder, rests her head on his, they are silent.

And so once more it would be hard to find anything more contented than our Franz Biberkopf, who has sent politics to the devil. He's not going to beat his skull against that thing. So he sits in cafés, singing and playing cards, and now Mieze has got to know a gentleman almost as rich as Eva's fellow, but he's married, which is better still, and sets up a swell little joint for her, out of two unfurnished rooms.

And Franz can't help doing what Mieze wants. One day Eva makes a surprise attack on him at his place; why not, if Mieze wants it herself, but say, Eva, supposing now you really do have a little one, say, if I was to get that way, my old man'd build me ten castles, he'd be that glad!

The Fly crawls upward, the Sand falls from it, it will soon start humming again

There really isn't much to tell about Franz Biberkopf, we know the lad already. You can guess what a sow will do when she gets into the trough.

Only a sow is better off than a man, because she's just a lump of flesh and fat, and what can befall her later, doesn't matter much, if only the swill lasts: at most she might litter again, and at the end of her life there is the cleaver, but that's not really so horrid or exciting after all: before she's noticed anything—and what does an animal like that notice? —she's gone, finished. But a human being, he's got eyes, you bet, there's a lot in him, and everything's all topsy-turvy; he can think a hell of a lot and has to think (he's got that terrible head of his) about what may happen to him.

Thus lives our dear, fat, one-armed Franz Biberkopf; our big baby Biberkopf goes his little jog-trot way on into the month of August, when it's still tolerably warm. And our little Franz has already learnt to row pretty nicely with his left arm, and, as far as the police are concerned, he hears nothing at all, though he doesn't register any more. At the police-station they're enjoying their summer vacation, too; good Lord, after all, even an officer has only got two pins, and for the few measly shekels they earn, they ain't going to wear their legs out, and why should a guy run around trying to find out what's happened to Franz Biberkopf, what Biberkopf, that man Biberkopf, why's he got only one arm now, when he certainly had two before? Just leave him molder in the official records, a fellow has other things to worry about, damn it all!

But the streets are still there, and on them one hears and sees all sorts of things, something comes back from the old days, something quite unwanted, and then life slips by so fast, day after day, and today something comes our way, and we miss it, then tomorrow something else comes, and we forget it again, something's always happening to us. Life will surely work out all right, he dreams in a kind of trance. One warm day we might catch a fly on the window and put it in a flower-pot and blow sand over it. If it's a real healthy fly, it'll clamber out again, and all that blowing over it didn't hurt it. That's what Franz sometimes thinks when he sees one thing or the other, I am all right, what do I care for this or that, politics don't interest me, and, if people are so silly as to let themselves be exploited, it ain't my fault. Why should I worry myself sick for other people?

Mieze has trouble keeping him off the booze, that's Franz's sore spot. He's got a sort of innate need for boozing, that's inside him, and keeps coming out again. He says: a fellow gets fat on it, and don't think too much. But Herbert advises Franz: "Old boy, don't swig so much. You're really a lucky devil. What were you before, anyway? A paper-peddler. Now you got one arm missing, but you got your Mieze and your income, so don't go to boozin' again like you did that time with Ida." "No question of that, Herbert. When I booze, it's only in my spare time. A fellow sits there, and what's he gonna do? You drink; and then you take another drink, and another. And then, look at me, can I stand it or can't I?" "Man, you say you can stand it. All right, you got good and stout again, but look at yourself in the mirror, and see what your lamps look like." "What's wrong with 'em?" "Well, just grab a hold of 'em once, you got regular bags like an old man. Say, how old are you, anyway? You're gettin' old with all this drinking, drinking makes a man old."

"Aw, cut it out. What's the news? What you doing anyway, Herbert?" "Things'll soon start up again, we've got two new fellows, fine fellows. Y'know Knopp, the fire-eater? Well, he got the lads together. He says to 'em: what's that, you want to work with me? First of all, you gotta show me what you can do. Eighteen, nineteen years old. Well, Knopp stands across the street, on the Danziger corner, to see what they can do. They've got their eye on an old dame they saw get some money from the bank. Keep right on her track. Knopp thinks to himself they'll just give her a little push, grab the stuff and off with it. Well, they stick around after her in no hurry, till they come to the place where she lives, and there they are when the ole girl comes rolling along, and they look her right in the face. Say, are you Frau Müller? That's her name all right; so they palaver a bit with her, till the street-car heaves in sight; then they throw pepper in her face, snatch her bag, slam the door to, and across the street in a jiffy. Knopp swears up and down and says they were fools to jump on the damned street-car; before she'd a got the house-door open, or anybody'd known who it was, they coulda been sitting quietly in the café. They made themselves suspicious running like that." "Hope they jumped off soon, anyway." "Yes, and then them two did something else, when Knopp started to grumble and fuss, they just took Knopp along and then simply picked up a brick-bat, it was around nine in the evening, and plugged it right through the window of a watch-shop in Romintener Strasse, shoved a hand inside and off they went. They didn't get caught, either. Them lads is fresh as paint, why, they just mingled in the crowd afterwards. Yes, sir, we kin use them two." Franz's head droops. "Smart guys, all right." "Well, you don't need it." "Nope—I don't need it, now. And I ain't gonna worry my head about later on." "Just cut out the booze, Franz."

Franz's features quiver: "Why not booze, Herbert? What do you folks want outa me? Why I can't, I just can't, I'm a hundred-per-cent cripple."

He looks into Herbert's eyes, the corners of his mouth droop. "Y'see they're all after me all the time; one of 'em says I shouldn't booze, another, don't go around with Willy, and another says, just leave politics alone!" "Politics, I ain't got nothing against politics, believe me."

Franz leans back in his chair and keeps looking at his friend Herbert who thinks to himself: His face sure looks like it's fallin' to pieces, he's a dangerous fellow, good-hearted as our Franz is in other ways. Franz whispers as he grasps him with his outstretched arm: "They've gone and made a cripple out of me, Herbert, just look at me, I ain't good for nothin'." "Now just stop that. Just tell that to Eva or Mieze." "Good for lying in bed, yes. I know that. But you, you're at least somebody, you do something, and those lads, too." "Well, and you, if you really want to, you kin do business with that one arm o' yours, why not?" "They didn't let me, did they? And Mieze didn't want me to, either. She got around me again." "Why not go ahead then and try again?" "Yes, that's the tune now—try again. Stop and try again. Just as if I was a little dog: on the table, Fido, down again, on the table."

Herbert pours out two cognacs: I must give Mieze a tip one o' these days, the boy's not kosher, she ought to look out, he'll get furious again and then it'll be like that time with Ida. Franz tosses off his drink. "I'm a cripple, Herbert, look at that there sleeve, nothin' in it. You don't know how that shoulder hurts at night, I can't sleep with it." "Better go see a doctor." "Don't want to, don't want to, don't want to hear nothin' about doctors, I got enough o' that at Magdeburg." "Then I'm gonna tell Mieze, she ought to take you away from Berlin for a change of air." "Just let me booze, Herbert." Herbert whispers in his ear: "One of these days you'll do to Mieze what you did to Ida." Franz listens: "What's that?" "Yeah. Now I guess you're looking at me, better take a good look at me, too, y' didn't have enough with your four years!" Franz clenches his fist in front of Herbert's nose: "Say, are you . . . ?" "No, not me, you!"

Eva, who is ready to go out, has been listening at the door. She comes in dressed in a smart tan suit, and gives Herbert a tap. "Why not let him booze, are you crazy?" "Aw, you don't understand. Want him to get like he was before?" "You're nuts, hold your trap."

Franz gapes stupidly at Eva.

And half an hour later, in Mieze's place, he asks her: "How about it, can I booze or not?" "Yes, but not too much. Not too much." "Maybe you'd like to get boozed up, too?" "Sure I would, with you." Franz is exultant: "Mieze, old kid, you want to get drunk, but you never was drunk before?" "Sure I was. Come on, let's get drunk together. Right away."

A moment before he had been sad, but now Franz sees how she flares up; it's like the other day when she started with Eva about that child. And Franz stands there beside her, what a darling girl, what a sweet little girl she is, she seems so small beside him, he could put her into his coat-pocket. She flings her arms around him, and he holds her around the waist with his left arm and then—and then—

Then Franz passes out, but only for a second. His arm, which has grown quite stiff, is entwined around her waist. But in fancy Franz couldn't help making a movement with his arm. His face is set like stone. In fancy, he held in his hand—a little wooden instrument—with which he dealt a downward blow at Mieze, in the chest, once, twice. He's broken her ribs. Hospital, cemetery, that man from Breslau.

Franz releases Mieze, she doesn't know what is the matter, as she lies beside him on the floor and he grumbles and bawls and kisses her and weeps; she weeps, too, without knowing why. And then she fetches two bottles of brandy, and he says again and again: "No, no," but it makes them so jolly, so jolly, oh Lord, what fun they have, and how they do laugh! Mieze should have gone to her gentleman-friend long ago, but what's the girl to do, she stays with her Franz, she can't stand up, much less walk. She sucks the brandy from out of Franz's mouth, and he wants to have it back again; but it runs out of her nose. And then they giggle, and soon he's snoring away loudly into the bright daylight.

Why does that shoulder hurt me so, they've hacked my arm off.

Why does that shoulder hurt me so, my shoulder hurts me so. Where is Mieze gone? She's left me lying here alone.

They hacked my arm off, off with it, my shoulder hurts, my shoulder. The dirty dogs, my arm's gone, they did it, the dogs, they did it, the dogs, arm off, and they left me lying there. My shoulder, my shoulder, it hurts, they left it on, but if they coulda done it, they woulda torn my shoulder off, too. They woulda torn my shoulder off, too. They woulda torn my shoulder off too, then it wouldn't hurt so much, damn it. They didn't take me for a ride, the dogs, they didn't manage to do that, they didn't have much luck with me, the lousy skunks, but now it's no good either, now I can lie around forever and nobody's here and who's going to listen to me bawling away? My arm hurts so, my shoulder, them dirty dogs sure woulda liked to run over me and give me the whole works. Now I'm only half a man. My shoulder, my shoulder, I can't stand it any more. The damned skunks, the skunks, they smashed hell out of me and what'll I do now? Where is Mieze, anyway, leaving me lie here like that. Ow, ouch, ow, ow, oooooooh.

The fly crawls and crawls, it's now in the flower-pot, the sand trickles off it, but it doesn't care, it shakes off the sand, it pushes its black head forward and creeps out.

There sitteth upon the many waters Babylon the great, the mother of harlots and abominations of the earth. She sitteth upon a scarlet colored beast, having seven heads and ten horns, for all to behold, that all may see. Each step thou makest delighteth her. She is drunken with the blood of the saints whom she hath rent asunder. Behold the horns wherewith she doth gore, she ascendeth from the bottomless pit and goeth into perdition. Behold her, the pearls, the scarlet, the purple, and the fangs of her, and how she clencheth her thick, close lips, wherein blood hath flowed, and wherewith she hath drunken! Whore of Babylon! Golden yellow thy venomous eyes and bloated thy throat! And she laughs you to scorn!

Forward, in Step, Roll of Drums and Battalions

Look out, old man, when the shells fall, there'll be dirt flying around, forward, step high, straight on through, I gotta get out, forward, all they can do is smash my bones, drumdumm, druummmmmmmmmmm. In step, one two, one two, left right, left right, left right.

Franz Biberkopf marches through the streets with a firm step, left right, left right, don't pretend to be tired, no saloons, no boozing now, we'll see about it, one ball wing'd by death came flying, that's what we'd like to see, if it's sent for me, I'm down, left right, left right. Roll of drums and battalions. At last he breathes easy.

Marching through Berlin. When the soldiers go marching along through the town, oh why, just why, that's why, that's why, just because of tararara, tararara, tararara, just because of tararara taraboomdeeay.

The houses stand still, the wind blows where it will. Oh why, just why, that's why, that's why, just because of tararara taraboomdeeay.

*

In his dirty dreary room—dirty room, oh why, just why—that's why, that's why, just because of tararara taraboomdeeay—sits Reinhold, the guy from Pums's gang, when the soldiers go marching along through the town, from the doors and the windows the maidens look down, reading the newspapers, left right, left right, is it meant for me or thee, he reads about the Olympic Games, one, two, and that pumpkin seeds are a remedy for tapeworm. He reads this very slowly, in a loud voice, to cure his stuttering. When he is alone, it goes smoothly enough. He cuts out the bit about the pumpkins, when the soldiers go marching along through the town, for he once had a tapeworm, probably has it still, maybe it's the same, maybe it's a new one, the old one has spawned a youngster, must try those pumpkin seeds, gotta eat the skin as well, not peel it. The houses stand still, the wind blows where it will. Skat Convention in Altenburg, I don't play. A world tour, all expenses only 30 pfennigs a week, that's another swindle. When the soldiers go marching along through the town, from the doors and the windows the maidens look down. Oh why, just why—that's why, that's why, just because of tararara taraboomdeeay. A knock at the door, come in.

Attention! March, march! Reinhold's hand flies to the gun in his pocket. One ball wing'd by death came flying, is it sent for me or thee? Torn away from life and dying, As at my feet he's lying, He seems a part of me. He seems a part of me. There he stands, Franz Biberkopf, his arm's gone, a war-cripple, the fellow's drunk, or maybe not? If he makes a move, I'll bump him off.

"Who let you in?" "Your landlady." Take the offensive, the offensive. "That bitch! Is she crazy?" Reinhold goes to the door: "Frau Tietsch! Frau Tietsch. What d'yuh mean? Am I at home or ain't I? When I say I ain't at home, I ain't." " 'Scuse me, Herr Reinhold, nobody told me nothin'." "Then I'm not at home, damn it! Why, you might be lettin' God knows who in here." "Maybe you said it to my daughter, she runs downstairs and don't say nothin'."

He slams the door to, holds on to his gun. The soldiers. "Whatcha want here? Wha—whatta we got to say to each other?" He stutters. Which Franz is this? You'll find out soon. The man's arm was run over some time ago; he was a decent fellow once, y'can take an oath on it, now he's turned into a pimp, we'll discuss later on, through whose fault. Boom of drums, battalions, there he stands. "Gee, Reinhold, you got a revolver!" "Well, what of it?" "Whatcha want to do with it? Whatcha after?" "Me? Nothin'." "Well, then you can put it away, cantcha?" Reinhold lays the gun on the table in front of him. "What're you comin' up here for?" There he stands, there he is, he socked me one in the hallway, he kicked me outa the car, before that nothing was wrong, Cilly was still around, I went down the stairs. It all comes back. The moon above the water, a glaring, blinding evening moon, the ringing of bells. This time he has a gun.

"Sit down Franz, say, you musta taken a few drops, heh?" The fellow has got such a vacant stare, he must be tight, he can't leave boozing alone. That's probably it, he's tight; but I've got the gun, all right. It's just because of tararara, taraboomdeeay. Franz sits down. And is seated. That glaring moon, all the water gleams. He sits beside Reinhold. That's the man he had helped with the girls, one skirt after another he took off his hands, then he wanted to get me to stand watch, but he didn't say a word, and now I'm a pimp, and who knows how it will go with Mieze, and that's the situation. But that's all in his thoughts. Just one thing is happening really: Reinhold, it's Reinhold sitting there.

"I just wanted to see ye, Reinhold." That's what I wanted; to look at him, look at him, that's enough, and here we sit. "You probably wanta put the screws on me, blackmail, on account of that time, heh?" Hold on, not a move, m'boy, forward march, that's only a coupla shells. "Blackmail, eh? How much do yuh want? We're armed. And we also know you're a pimp." "So I am. What kin a guy do with one arm?" "Well, whatcha want then?" "Oh, nothin' at all, nothin' at all." Just sit tight, hold on firm, that's Reinhold, that's the way he noses around, only watch out he don't knock you down.

But Franz is beginning to tremble already. There were once three Kings, who came from the East, laden with incense, which they swung to and fro, and they kept on swinging it to and fro. They envelop us in smoke. Reinhold reflects: either the fellow's tight, then he'll go soon and that'll be an end of it, or maybe he wants somethin'. Nope, he wants somethin', but what? He's not after blackmail, but what then? Reinhold gets some liquor and thinks to himself, I'll worm it out of my Franz this way. If only Herbert hasn't sent him here to spy on us and then get us in Dutch. As he puts down the two little blue glasses, he notices that Franz is trembling. The moon, the glaring white moon, has risen over the water, and nobody kin look up, I'm gone blind, whatsa matter with me anyway? Look, he's all in. He's tryin' to keep a stiff upper lip, but he's all in. Reinhold certainly is relieved, slowly he takes the gun from the table and puts it in his pocket, then he pours out a drink and looks again: why, his paw is all trembling, he's got the shivers, he's just plain yellow, the big noise, he's either afraid of the gun or of me, well, I won't hurt him. And Reinhold is very calm and friendly, you bet. It's great to see him shaking like that, no, he's not tight, Franz ain't, he's afraid, he's going to smash, he'll be doing it in his pants—and he wanted to try out his big mouth on me!

And Reinhold starts talking about Cilly, as if we had just seen each other yesterday; she stayed with me again for a couple weeks, yes, such things do happen, if I haven't seen one of 'em for a couple months, I didn't mind havin' her again, it was a kind of a revival, it's a funny thing. Then he gets some cigarettes and a pack of smutty pictures and some photographs, Cilly also is in the lot, along with Reinhold.

Franz can't say anything, he keeps on looking at Reinhold's hands, he's got two hands, two arms, and I've only got one; with those hands Reinhold pushed me under the car, oh why, that's why, I oughta bump him off maybe, just because of tararara. Herbert thinks, but all that don't interest me, what do I think, anyway? I can't do nothin' I can't do nothin' at all. But I've gotta, didn't I wanta do somethin', oh just because of tararara taraboomdeeay. I'm not a man at all, I'm just a lily-livered fool. He sinks down into himself, and then, still shaking, he emerges, back to life again. He sips a cognac, and then another, what's the use, and then Reinhold says softly, very softly: "Say, Franz one o' these days, I'd like to see your wound." It's just because of tararara taraboomdeeay. Then Franz—that's it—opens his coat, and points to the stump in his shirt-sleeve. Reinhold scowls: it looks disgusting, Franz closes the coat. "It was worse before." Then Reinhold looks again at his Franz, who says nothing, and can do nothing; he's as fat as a hog, and he can't open his mouth, so Reinhold keeps on grinning at him and can't seem to stop.

"Say, d'you always wear your sleeve in your pocket like that? D'you always stick it in, or is it sewed on?" "Nope, I always stick it in." "With the other hand? Nope, probably before you start dressing, dontcha?" "Well, sometimes one way, sometimes the other; once I've put my coat on, it don't go in so good." Reinhold stands beside Franz and tugs at his sleeve. "But you oughta always look out you don't put it into your right pocket. They might easily pick your pocket that way." "Not with me." Reinhold is still thinking about it: "Say, how do you manage with your overcoat, must be very uncomfortable. Two empty sleeves." "Why, it's summer now. That don't start till winter." "You'll see, it won't be so easy. Why couldn't you get yourself an artificial arm, when a fellow loses his leg, he gets himself a false leg, don't he?" "Because he can't walk without it." "You could have a false arm hooked on, it looks better." "No, no, it only presses on you."

"I'd either buy myself one, or I'd stuff the sleeve out. Say, let's do it."
"What for? No, I don't want to." "Then you wouldn't be runnin' around
with your sleeve flappin' like that, why it'd look very nice, nobody'd
notice nothin'." "What would I do with it? I don't want to." "Come along,
wood's no good. Look here, a coupla socks or shirts in it, look."

And Reinhold sets about it. He pulls the empty sleeve out, shoves his fist
up into it, and, going to his chest of drawers, he starts stuffing it with socks
and handkerchiefs. Franz tries to stop him. "What's the use, it ain't got no
hold, it'll get like a sausage, aw, leave it go." "No. Look here, you oughta
get a tailor to do that for you, it's gotta be braced up, why, it'd look twice
as well, and you wouldn't have to go around lookin' like a cripple, you'd
just have your hand in your pocket, that's all." The socks fall out again.
"Yep, that's a tailor's job. I can't stand cripples, to me a cripple's a fellow
who's good for nothin'. When I see a cripple, I say, better get rid of him
altogether."

Franz listens and nods, he nods a lot. He begins to tremble, he can't help
it. He's somewhere out on the Alex, with the burglars, everything's been
taken from him, probably connected with the accident, it's his nerves, got
to see about that. But something's tearing at him, making him shudder.
Let's get away, downstairs, bye-bye, Reinhold, got to blow, in step now,
right left, right left, taraboomdeeay.

So stout Franz Biberkopf comes home after he's been to Reinhold's, his
hand and arm shake, and he is still shivering, the cigarette falls out of
his mouth, as he reaches home. Mieze is sitting upstairs with her gentleman-friend, waiting for Franz, to tell him she's going away for a couple of
days with her beau.

He draws her aside. "You certainly act nice to me." "But Franz, what am
I to do? Oh Lord, Franz, what's the matter?" "Nothin', beat it." "I'll be
back tonight." "Beat it!" He almost yells it. She looks at her gent, gives
Franz a hasty kiss on the nape of his neck and is gone. Downstairs she
phones Eva. "If you got time, do go see Franz, what's the matter with
him? I don't know. Please do come." But Eva can't manage it, Herbert is
damning and cursing her all day long, she can't get off.

Meantime Franz Biberkopf, the cobra, the iron warrior, sits alone, all
alone, he sits at his window, clawing his hand around the window-sill
and wondering if it isn't a lot of tripe, a damned lot of bunk, going to
Reinhold's place, and the hell with it, and that's all bunk, when the
soldiers go marching along through the town, bunk, and a dumb trick,
I've gotta get out of it, gotta do something else. And in the meanwhile he

thinks, I'll do it anyhow, I've gotta go there, no use goin' on like this, he's made a fool of me, he's stuffed my coat out, I can't tell nobody about it, did anything like this ever happen before?

Franz leans his head heavily against the sill, and digs himself in, he is ashamed, bitterly ashamed: that's what I'll do, to think I let 'im get away with it, what a damn fool I am, shaking in my boots before him. Huge is his shame, and strong. How Franz gnashes his teeth, he could tear himself to bits, I didn't want to do it, I ain't yellow, am I, even if I have got only one arm?

I've gotta go to him. And he spreads himself. Evening has come when Franz makes up his mind, and gets up from his chair. He looks around the room, there's some brandy over there, Mieze put it there, I won't drink. I won't feel ashamed. They've got to look Franz in the eye now. Yep. I'll go over to him. Bim-bam-boom, the cannon, trumpets. Forward, downstairs, coat on—and him wanting to stuff it out. I'll sit down in front of him, and this time I won't bat an eye, no, sir.

Berlin! Berlin! Berlin! Deep Sea Tragedy, U-boat Sinks. Crew suffocates. If they're suffocated, then they're dead, and nobody will give a tinker's damn for it, then it's all over, then it's finished, let's forget it, march, march. Two military aeroplanes fall. Then they're down, then they're dead, nobody's to give a tinker's damn for 'em, if they're dead, they're dead.

"G'd evenin', Reinhold, yessir, y'see, I'm back again." Reinhold looks at Franz: "Who letcha in?" "Me? Nobody. The door was open, so I simply walked in." "Is that so, and you can't ring the bell, can ye?" "Why should I ring a bell when I come to see you, I ain't tight, am I?"

They sit facing each other, smoking, and Franz Biberkopf doesn't tremble, but holds himself stiffly erect and is happy that he is alive; that's the best day he's had since he fell under the car, and this is the best thing he has done since that night: sitting here, damn it, that's fine. And it sure is better than public meetings, and almost better—better than Mieze. Yes, and that's the nicest part of it all: he won't bite me.

It's eight o'clock at night, when Reinhold looks Franz in the face: "Franz, I s'pose you know what we got to settle together. Say, if you want anything from me, let's have it out." "What d'you think I have to settle with you?" "About that car." "What's the use, that won't make my arm grow again. And then—" Franz bangs his fist on the table. "And then, it was all right. Things couldn't go on with me that way. It had to happen."

Haha, so that's what we've come to, it's been on the way a long time. Reinhold tries to sound him out: "Ye mean about that street peddling." "Yes, sir, that, too. I wasn't right in my upper story. Well, now, it's all over." "And the arm's gone." "I still got one arm and I got my head and a pair of legs." "Whatcha doing now? Pullin' jobs on your own, or with Herbert?" "With one arm? I can't do nothin' with that." "But say, just being a pimp, that sure must get tiresome after a while."

Reinhold muses, noticing how stout and stalwart he looks, sitting there. I'd like to have a little fun with that goof. He's kickin' back. I'd better crack his bones for 'im. One arm ain't enough for that fellow.

They start talking about the janes, and Franz tells him about Mieze whose name was Sonia before; she earns good money and is a nice kid. And Reinhold thinks to himself: That's fine, I'll take her away from him, and then I'll kick him all the way to kingdom come.

For even if the worms eat earth, and pass it out again behind, they always eat it anew. And for this the beasts can show no mercy, even though you cram their stomachs full today, tomorrow they have to go to it and start gobbling all over again. With a human being it's the same as with fire: while it burns, it must eat, and if it can't eat, it goes out, it must go out.

Franz Biberkopf is pleased with himself, at being able to sit there without trembling, quite calm and festively happy, like a new-born babe. And, as he walks downstairs with Reinhold, he encounters it again: when the soldiers go marching along through the town, right left, it's nice to be alive, these people are all my friends. Nobody here is gonna give me a kick, just let anyone try it! Oh, why, that's why, from every window and door the girls look down.

"I'm goin' dancin'," he says to Reinhold, who asks: "Is your Mieze comin' along?" "Nope, she's gone off with her gentleman-friend for a coupla days." "When she comes back, I'll trot along with ye." "Attaboy, she'll be delighted." "Think so?" "I'm tellin' you, she won't bite ye."

Franz is mighty gay; happy, and like one new-born, he dances his way through the evening, first in the old Ballhaus, then in the café with Herbert, and they're all pleased with him, but most of all he's pleased with himself. As he dances with Eva, he loves best of all two beings: one is Mieze whom he'd like to have with him, and the other is—Reinhold. But he doesn't dare say it. All through that wonderful night, dancing with first this one and the other, he loves those two who are not there, and is happy with them.

The Fist lies on the Table

Now all who have read thus far can see the turn things have taken: it's a turn backward, and for Franz it is finished. That strong man, Franz Biberkopf, the cobra, has actually bobbed up on the scene again. It was not easy, but he has come back.

He seemed to be there already, when he became Mieze's pimp, and went around quite free with a gold cigarette case and an oarsman's cap. Now he is really there, and how happy he is, now that all fear has left him. The roofs no longer totter, and his arm, well, that's what he got for it. That screw which was loose in his head has been successfully operated on and taken out. He is a pimp now, and will become a criminal again, but all this does not hurt him, quite the contrary.

Everything is as it was in the beginning. But, as we may clearly see, it is not the old cobra we knew. It's our old Franz Biberkopf, you can see that all right, but no more than that. First he was betrayed by his friend Lüders and bumped out of gear. The second time he was to be a lookout against his will, so Reinhold kicked him out of the car, and he was run over. Franz has had enough of it all; it would be enough for any plain man. He does not go into a monastery, nor does he work his head off, he goes on the war-path. He becomes not only a pimp and a criminal, but now he feels: just for spite. Now you will see Franz, not dancing alone, nor gluttonously enjoying his life, but in the dance itself, in a rattling dance with something else, something which will have to show not only how strong it is, but which is the stronger of the two, Franz or this other thing.

Franz Biberkopf had taken an oath out loud, when he got out of Tegel, and walked on solid earth again: I will lead a decent life. They did not let him keep that oath. Now he will see what he has left to say. He will ask if and why his arm was run over and cut off. Perhaps, who knows how things look in such a fellow's head, perhaps Franz will get his arm back from Reinhold.

Seventh Book

Now the hammer crashes down, it crashes against Franz Biberkopf.

Pussi Uhl, Height of American Invasion, is Wilma spelt with a W or a V?

On the Alexanderplatz they go on fussing and bustling around. On the Königstrasse, at the corner of Neue Friedrichstrasse, they want to pull down the house over the Salamander shoe-store. They are already pulling down the one next to it. Traffic beneath the Alex arch of the municipal railway becomes enormously difficult: they are building new pillars for the railway bridge; here you can look down into a nicely walled shaft where the pillars put their feet.

In order to get to the municipal railway station you have to walk up and down a little wooden staircase. The weather in Berlin is cooler. It often pours buckets. Autos and motor-cycles suffer a great deal from that, every day some of them start skidding and careening about, then they are sued for damages, and so on: frequently people break something or other, that's the weather's fault. Have you heard of the tragic case of Beese-Arnim, the aviator? He was questioned today by the criminal police; he is the leading figure in the shooting affray at the home of that old washed-out whore, Pussi Uhl, peace to her ashes! Beese (Edgar) started shooting wild in the Uhl woman's home; but he's always had queer things happen to him, according to the police. Once during the war they shot him down from a height of 1700 meters, hence the tragic case of aviator Beese-Arnim, shot down at 1700 meters, cheated out of his inheritance, in prison under an assumed name; the last act is still to come. After being shot down, he goes home and an insurance agent bilks him out of his money. But he was a sharper, and so the money wandered in the simplest way possible from flyer to sharper, and the flyer had no money left. From that moment on Beese changes his name to Auclaire. He is ashamed to face his family, because he is down and out. The dicks have ferreted all this out this morning at police headquarters and have written it down. It is also recorded there that he now found himself on the path of crime. Once he was sentenced to two years and a half in prison, and, because at that time he called himself Krachtowil, he was later on deported to Poland. It seems that it was then this peculiarly nasty and obscure affair with Pussi Uhl developed in Berlin. This Pussi Uhl baptized him "von Arnim" with special ceremonies which we would rather not talk about here, and all he subsequently did in the way of mischief was done under the name of "von Arnim." Thus it was that on Tuesday, August 14, 1928, von Arnim planted a bullet in Pussi Uhl's body, as to the why and the how, the underworld keeps mum about it, they don't tattle out of school, even if they're about to have their heads chopped off, why should they say anything to the bulls, their natural enemies? All that is known, is that the boxer Hein plays a rôle in the affair, and anyone who pretends to know human nature goes wrong in assuming it was a case of jealousy. Personally, I'd put my hand in the fire that there was no jealousy involved. Or if there was jealousy, then jealousy arising from some money matter, but money being the main motive. Beese, according to the police, has completely collapsed; believe it or not, as you want. You can take my word for it, the boy collapsed (if it's true, at all) simply because the bulls are going to make inquiries now, and especially because he is angry with himself for shooting down that old Uhl woman. For what is he going to live on now? If only that broad don't die on me now, he thinks. So we know quite enough about the tragic case of the flyer, Beese-Arnim, shot down at 1700 meters, cheated out of his inheritance, in prison under an assumed name.

The flood-tide of Americans visiting Berlin continues. Among the many thousands visiting the German metropolis, there are numerous prominent persons who have come to Berlin for professional or private reasons. Thus we have here (Hotel Esplanade) the chief secretary of the American Delegation to the Interparliamentary Union, Dr. Call, of Washington, who will be followed in a week by a number of American senators. Furthermore, in the next few days the chief of the New York fire department, John Kenlon, will arrive in Berlin; like Davis, the former Secretary of Labor, he will stop at the Hotel Adlon.

Claude G. Montefiore president of the World Union for religious and liberal Zionism has arrived from London; these conferences will take place in Berlin from August 18th to 21st: he is staying with Lady Lily H. Montague, his co-worker, who accompanies him, at the Hotel Esplanade.

Since the weather is so very bad, it might be better if we were to go inside, in the Central Market Hall, but there is a lot of noise there, we are almost knocked down by the handcars and these guys don't even warn you. So we prefer to ride out to the Labor Court in Zimmerstrasse and take breakfast there. If you have had much to do with petty lives—and in the last analysis, Franz Biberkopf is far from being a famous man—you like to ride out occasionally to the West End and see what is happening there.

Room No. 60, Labor Court, refreshment room, a rather small room with a bar, quick coffee boiler, the bill-of-fare reads: Lunch: rice soup, roulade of beef (roll that r) 1 mark. A stout young gentleman wearing horn-rimmed glasses is sitting in a chair, eating his lunch. You look at him and you establish the fact that he has a steaming plate of roulade of beef, gravy, and potatoes standing in front of him, and is about to gulp them all down, one after the other. His eyes roam back and forth across the plate, though nobody is trying to take anything away from him, there's nobody near him, he's sitting all alone at his table, and he's worried, he cuts up and mashes his fodder, and quickly shoves it into his mouth, bit by bit, bit by bit, by bit, and as he works one bit in, one out, one in, one out, as he cuts, bolts, and gulps, smacks, sniffs, and stodges, his eyes examine, his eyes observe, the ever-diminishing remnant upon the plate, watching it on all sides like two snappish dogs, and estimating its quantity. Another bit in, another out. Period. Now it is finished, now he gets up, flabby and stout, the fellow has put everything away, now he'd better pay. He fumbles in his vest pocket and smacks his lips: "How much is it, miss?" Then the fat baby goes out, puffing and blowing, and he loosens his trouser-buckle behind a bit, to give his belly enough room. He has got a good three pounds stowed away in his stomach, all victuals. Now things are going to get started in his belly, some labor, now his belly has got to be busy with what that goof has thrown into it. His bowels shake and wobble, winding, twisting like earthworms, the glands do what they can, they squirt their juice into all that stuff, squirt away like firemen, saliva flows down from above, the fellow swallows, it flows down into his bowels, there is an attack on the kidneys, just like in department stores when the white-goods sales are on, and gently, gently, lo and behold, little drops begin to fall into the bladder, one little drop after the other.

Just wait, my boy, wait, soon you will walk back, retrace your steps to the door marked "Gentlemen," and that's the way the world wags.

They are negotiating behind the doors. Wilma, domestic servant, how do you spell your name? I thought you spelt it with a V, here it is, well, let's make it W. She became very fresh. She behaved improperly, get your bags packed, clear out of this house, we have witnesses for it. She doesn't do it, too much sense of pride. Till the sixth, three days' difference included, I am ready to pay ten marks, my wife is at the hospital. You may make a claim, Fräulein, 22.75 marks is the sum in dispute, but I wish to state that I absolutely refuse to stand for things like that. "You common, low-down dog," I suppose my wife will be called to court when she is up again, but the plaintiff herself behaved insolently. The parties contract the following agreement.

Chauffeur Papke and Wilhelm Trotzke, film distributor, what kind of a case is this, it has just come up. Well, then please write: Wilhelm Trotzke, film distributor, appears in person, no, I have only his power of attorney, all right: So you have been employed as a chauffeur, that is to say, a relatively short time, I bumped into him with my car, bring me the keys, so you got in dutch with the car, what have you to say? On the 28th, it was a Friday, he was supposed to fetch the boss's lady from Admiralsbad, it was in the Viktoriastrasse, they can testify that he was completely drunk. He is known as a drunkard in the whole neighborhood. See here, I never drink bad beer, anyhow. It was a German car, the repairs cost 387.20 marks. What kind of a collision was it anyway? I start slidin' in a jiffy, it hasn't any four-wheel brakes—and my front wheel hit his rear wheel. How much did you drink that day, you must have drunk something at breakfast, went to the boss's house; that's where I get my meals, the boss looks out for his help all right, because he's a good man. Why, we don't hold the man responsible for the damage, but the dismissal without giving notice, he forgot himself because of drunkenness. Get your things; they're in the Viktoriastrasse, all dirtied up. And then the boss said over the telephone: he's a damn fool, he smashed up the car. But you couldn't hear that, yes, your telephone talks that loud, if he hasn't any better manners than that; he also telephoned that I stole the extra wheel, I would like to ask that the witnesses be examined, I wouldn't do anything of the kind, you're both at fault, the boss said ass or fool, giving also the surname, do you want to settle it with 35 marks, it's a quarter to twelve, there's still time, you can call him up, if it's all right, let him come here around quarter to one.

*

A girl is standing in front of the door downstairs in Zimmerstrasse; she has just passed by here, she raises her umbrella and puts a letter into the box. The letter says: Dear Ferdinand, your two letters received with thanks. I've been really disappointed by you a lot, never thought things would take such a turn with you. Well, you must admit yourself, we are both still awfully young to unite ourselves for good. I think that in the end you must see that. Maybe you thought I'm just a girl like all the others, but that's where you got burnt, my boy. Or maybe you think I am a rich match? But that's where you're also on the wrong track. I'm only a working girl. I tell you this so you can act according. If I had known what was to come of it, I wouldn't of started writing them letters. Well now you know my opinion, act according, you must know what you feel about it. Sincerely, Anna.

In the same house, a girl is sitting in the back building in the kitchen. Her mother has gone out shopping, the girl is secretly writing in her diary. She is 26 years old, out of work. The last entry on July 10th was as follows: Since yesterday afternoon I feel better again, but the good days are now so few and far between, I cannot speak freely to anybody, as I would like to. So I have decided now to write everything down. When my periods come, I am no good for anything; the least trifle causes me great distress. Everything I see at that time keeps calling forth new thoughts in me, I can't get rid of them, and I get so nervous that I can hardly force myself to do anything at all. A great unrest within me drives me from one thing to another, and yet I cannot finish anything. For instance: Early in the morning, when I wake up, I would prefer not to get up; but I nevertheless force myself to do it, and talk myself into courage. But even dressing makes me very tired, and it takes a long time, because so many fancies are going round and round in my head. I am constantly tortured by the thought of doing something the wrong way, and causing some disaster. Often when I put a piece of coal into the stove, and a spark flies up, I get so frightened and feel I must examine everything about me to see that nothing has caught fire, and I might spoil something and start a fire without knowing it. All day long it's the same thing: everything I have to do seems so difficult and if I force myself to do it, it takes a long time, in spite of all the pains I take to do it quickly. Thus the day passes and I haven't done anything, because I have to think for such a long time before I make a move. When, in spite of all my efforts, I cannot get along in life, it makes me desperate, and then I cry a lot. This is the way my periods always show. They began when I was

12 years old. My parents took all this for deceit. At the age of 24 I tried to end my life on account of these periods, but I was saved. At that time I had had no sexual intercourse as yet, and so I put my hopes in this, but, alas, in vain. I have only had very moderate intercourse, and of late I don't want to hear about it any more, because I also feel so weak, physically.

August 14th. For the last week I am again in a very bad state. I don't know what will become of me if this goes on. I think that if I had nobody in the world, I would turn on the gas without further thought, but I cannot do this for mother's sake. But I really wish very much I could develop some serious illness from which I would die. I have written everything down the way things really look inside me.

The Duel starts! It is rainy Weather

But for what reason (I kiss your little hand, madame, I kiss) for what reason, let's think it over, think it over, Herbert, his felt slippers on, muses in his room, and it is raining, it drizzles and drizzles, can't go downstairs at all, no more cigars left, no cigar-store in the house, for what reason, I wonder, is it raining like that in August, the whole month simply swimming away from a fellow, it splashes off like nothin' on earth, for what reason does Franz go to see Reinhold of late and jaw and jaw about him? (I kiss your little hand, madame, and no less a person than Sigrid Onegin made people happy with her song, till he gave the whole thing up, risked his life and thus won his life.) He surely knows why, for what reason, he probably knows it all right, and then it's always raining, he might as well come here.

"Gee, why brood about it? You oughta be glad, Herbert, that he gave up politics—if that fellow's his friend—maybe." "Well, Eva, his friend, just put a period there, young lady, I know better, betcha. He wants to get somethin' outa him, he wants somethin'." (For what reason, I'd like to know, the sale is agreed upon by the General Administration and so the price may be regarded as adequate.) "He wants somethin', and why he wants it, and why he's always goin' around there and always jawin' about it, well: he wants to give him the works; he wants to be in his good graces, you'll see, Eva, and if he can get near 'im, he'll just bang away, and nobody'll ever find out what happened." "You think so?" "Well, maybe not!" That's clear, I kiss your little hand, madame, but what rain! "Clear as mud!" "Think so, Herbert? I thought right away, too, it was a bit queer, that a man should let a fellow run over his arm and then go up and see him." "Clear as mud. I getcha!" I kiss. "Herbert, d'you mean it, that we shouldn't tell him nothin' about it, pretend we hadn't noticed nothin', and are quite blind?" "We're jackasses, people can do anything with us they want." "Yes, Herbert, that's what we got to do about him, we'll do it, got to. He's such a funny guy." The sale agreed upon by the General Administration so that the price obtained, but why, for what reason, must think it over, must think it over, the rain.

"You'll see, Eva, we can keep mum all right, but we gotta look out. Watcha think, suppose those Pums fellows smell a rat? Eh?" "That's what I say. I thought that right away. Oh Lord, why does he go there with his one arm?" " 'Cause it suits him. Only we gotta keep a sharp lookout, and Mieze, too." "I'll tell 'er. What can we do, then?" "Gotta keep our eyes on Franz." "If her old man would only leave her time for it." "She might give him his walkin' papers." "Why, he's talkin' about marriage!" "Ha, ha, ha! That's certainly rich. What's he after? And Franz?" "Oh, that's nothin'. She just lets the old guy babble away, why not?" "She'd better watch out for Franz. He's tryin' to get his man in that gang, and just wait, one of these days somebody'll be brought up here in a coffin." "For Lord's sake, Herbert, now stop that!" "Eva, old girl, it needn't be Franz, y'know. So Mieze'd better watch out." "I'll keep an eye on him, too. Y'know, that's much worse than politics." "Ye don't understan' that, Eva. A dame wouldn't get that! I'm tellin' you, Eva, it's just beginning with Franz. He's just gettin' started."

I kiss your little hand, madame, he mastered life, won his life by risking it outright, a funny August we're having this year, just look, it's raining cats and dogs.

"What's he want with us? I said he was crazy, he's batty all right, clean gone off his nut, and I told him, if a fellow's got only one arm and comes and wants to play around with us. And him." Pums: "Well, what does he say?" "What does he say? He just laughs and grins, why, he's dumb as hell; he must have a screw loose from what happened that time. First I says to myself, I ain't hearin' right. Whatsat, says I, about that arm of yours? Well, well, why not, the feller grins, he's got strength enough in the other one, I should see him liftin' weights with it, shootin', even climbin' if necessary." "Is that true?" "None o' my business. Don't like that guy. Do we want a bozo like that? Look here, Pums—we can't use him in our work. Anyhow, when I see that guy with that bull's face of his, aw, it gives me a pain." "All right, if that's what you think. Got no objection. Gotta go now, Reinhold, to get a ladder." "But get somethin' solid, steel or somethin' like that. Extending or folding. But not in Berlin." "I getcha." "And the bottle. Hamburg or Leipzig." "I'll find it all right." "And how'll we get it here?" "Oh, leave that to me. Hamburg or Leipzig." "I'll get the info." "And how we gonna move it here?" "Leave that to me." "So I won't take Franz then, heh?" "Reinhold, about Franz, he'll only be a burden to us, I think, but we won't bother about that. You better fix it up with him alone." "Wait a minute, old boy, you really like that guy's face? Listen. I kick him out of the car and he comes right up to me, I thinks to myself I'm seein' things, by gosh, and there he stands, the boob, imagine it, what a jackass, dodderin' away, and why did the jackass come up here, any-way? And then he grins at me and posolutely wants to come along." "Well, just fix it up with him, and lemme go." "Maybe he's goin' to snitch on us, heh?" "Maybe so, maybe so. Y'know, you'd better keep that feller outa your way, that's the best thing, g'bye." "He'll squeal on us, sure. Or, when it's dark, he'll put one of us on the spot." "So long, Reinhold, gotta beat it. The ladder."

He's some bonehead, that Biberkopf. But he wants somethin' from me. Tries to play the hypocrite. Wants to start somethin' with me, heh? That's where you got the wrong number, if you think I won't do nothin'. I'll let you stumble over my toes. Gimme rum, by gum! Rum's good for what ails you, all right. Auntie Paula eats tomatoes in her bed. On the urgent advice of a woman-friend who said . . . If that guy thinks I'm gonna worry about him, I ain't an old age insurance company. If he's only got one arm, let him go and get in on the dole. Reinhold ambles around the room, and takes a look at the flowers. When a fellow's got flower-pots and that tart gets two marks extra every first of the month, she might water them pots, look at 'em now, nothin' but sand. She sure is a dumbdora, a lazy wench, good for nothin' but gulping down the money. But I've gotta knock the cobwebs off her. Another rum. I learned that from him. Maybe I'll take that louse along with me, wait a minute, you'll get it yet, if you're so bent on havin' it. Maybe he thinks I'm afraid of him. That's how much you know, Jack. Let him come, let him come! He don't need any money, the mack, he mustn't try to put that over on me, he's got Mieze, and then he's also got that dirty louse, that loafer of a Herbert, that old bum, sittin' there right in the pig-sty. Where are them boots? I'll step on his toes for him. Come to my bosom, sweet-heart, come on, come straight up, m'boy, to the sinners' bench. I've got a sinners' bench where you can repent your sins.

He ambles around his room, and dabs at the flowerpots with his fingers, I pay two marks, and that tart don't water 'em. Up to the sinners' bench, me boy, that's the stuff, glad you're comin'. To the Salvation Army, I'll get you there, too, he'll have to go to the Dresdener Strasse, he's gotta go to the sinners' bench, that pimp, that swine, with his big slimy goggle-eyes, that mack, that brute, sure he's a brute, there he sits in front, that brute, prayin' while I look on, I could die laughin'.

And why shouldn't he go up to the sinners' bench, Franz Biberkopf? Isn't the sinners' bench the place where he belongs? Who says that?

What can be said against the Salvation Army, and how does Reinhold, this Reinhold of all people, get that way, poking fun at the Salvation Army, when the guy went there himself once, what do I mean, once, often, five times at least, he went to Dresdener Strasse, and what a state he was in, and they helped him, too. Why, his tongue was hanging out, and they fixed him up; but, of course, not in order that he should get to be such a scoundrel.

Hallelujah, hallelujah! Franz knows what it is, all that singing and shouting. The knife touched his throat, Franz, hallelujah! He offers his neck, he wants to seek his life, his blood. My blood, my innermost being, at last it all comes forth, it was a long voyage before it came, O Lord, how hard it was, but there it is, I gotcha now. Why didn't I want to go up to the sinners' bench, if only I'da come sooner, oh, but here I am, I've come.

Why shouldn't Franz go up to the sinners' bench, when will that blessed moment come, when he will flop himself down before his terrible death and open his mouth and be allowed to sing with many others behind him:

Come, sinner, to Jesus, do not hesitate so, oh bondsman awake, come up to the light, come to the light's bright glow, you may find complete salvation here on this happy day, oh, believe in Him, and light and joy will live in you alway. Chorus: For the all-conquering Saviour, He can break every chain, the all-conquering Saviour, He can break every chain, and lead you forth to victory down the happy lane, and lead you forth to victory down the happy lane. Music! Blow horns and trumpets, taraboomdeeay: He can break every chain, and lead you forth to victory down the happy lane. Tara, tara, tara, boom! Taraboomdeeay!

Franz does not give in, it haunts him all the time, he does not ask about God and the world, it is as if the fellow were drunk. Along with the other Pums gangsters, who don't want him, he slips into Reinhold's room. But Franz lashes about, showing them the one fist he's got left and yells: "If you won't believe me and wanta take me for a swindler and think I want to squeal on you, why, let it go. Do I need you if I want to do something? I can go to Herbert or anywhere I like." "Then go ahead and do it." "'Go ahead and do it!' You numskull, do you have to tell me 'Go ahead and do it!' Look at my arm, you, that fellow over there, Reinhold, pushed me out of the automobile, and with a bang too. I'll tell you. I stood that all right, and now I'm here and you needn't tell me 'Go ahead and do it'! If I come to you and say, I'm with you, then you oughta know who Franz Biberkopf is. He ain't never swindled anybody, you can ask anywhere you want. I don't give a hoot in hell for what happened, my arm's gone. I know you all, I'm here, and that's the reason why, so maybe you know now." The little tinner still can't understand. "Then I'd like to know why you want to come here all of a sudden, after you used to run around the Alex with newspapers, and you said let anybody try to tell ye that ye oughta join up with us."

Franz straightens himself up in his chair and says nothing for a long time; the others are also silent. He has taken an oath to be respectable and you have seen how he stayed respectable for many a week, but that was only a respite, so to speak. He is dragged into a criminal case, he does not want this, he defends himself, but the issue he must face. For a long time they sit and say nothing.

Then Franz suggests: "If you want to find out who Franz Biberkopf is, just go to the Landsberger Allee, to the cemetery, there's a dame lyin' there. I did four years for that. It was still my good arm that did it. Then I peddled papers. I thought I'd be a respectable man."

Franz groans softly and gulps: "You can see what I caught. Once you've lost that, you gotta stop paper-peddlin' and lots of other things, too. That's why I'm here." "I suppose we ought to give you a new arm, because we smashed it up." "You can't do that, Maxe, I'm satisfied with sittin' here and not runnin' around on the Alex. I don't blame Reinhold, just ask him if I ever said a single word about it. When I sit in the car and there's a suspicious character with us, don't I know what to do? Now let's stop talkin' about my damn-foolishness. Max, if you do a damn-fool trick one of these days yourself, well, I hope it'll learn you a lesson." Then Franz takes his hat and walks out of the room. So that's the way things are.

In the room Reinhold pours a nip of brandy from his little pocket flask and says: "As far as I'm concerned I'm through with all this stuff. I fixed him up the first time and I'll do it again. You may say it's risky startin' somethin' with him. But first of all, he's already in deep, he's a pimp, he admits it himself; as for going straight, that's all over. The only question now is, why does he come to us and not to Herbert, who's his friend. Don't know. But I'm thinkin' a lot. Anyway we'd be fools if we couldn't hold our own with certain Herr Franz Biberkopf. Let him join us. If he pulls somethin', he'll get one on the beezer. I say let him come on." Whereupon Franz comes.

Burglar-Franz, Franz is not under the Auto, he sits Inside now, on Top, he's fixed it

In the early part of August these gentlemen, the so-called criminals, are still in rest-billets behind the lines, recuperating and attending to small jobs. As long as the weather's fairly nice, a man who's an expert or a professional doesn't burgle or exert himself. He saves himself up for the winter, when he's got to go at it like hell. Franz Kirsch, for instance, the well-known yegg, escaped eight weeks ago, in the early part of July, with another man from Sonnenburg prison; Sonnenburg, though the name be ever so charming, is, as a matter of fact, little suited for vacation purposes, and now he has had a pretty good recovery in Berlin, has about eight quiet weeks back of him, and is perhaps going to think of doing some work. But there's a hitch, such is life. The man happens to take a street-car. Along come the bulls, it's the end of August, and take him out of the street-car in Reinickendorf West, good-bye to rest, nothing doing any more. But there are still many outside, they are slowly going to start action.

Before starting I should like to give you hastily the weather conditions according to the reports of the public meteorological service for Berlin. General weather conditions: The region of high pressure in the west has extended its influence as far as Central Germany, and generally brought better weather. The southern area of the high-pressure region is already diminishing. We may, therefore, expect that this improvement in the weather will not last very long. On Saturday the high-pressure area will still determine our weather and it will be fairly fine. But the depression which is now developing over Spain will affect the climatic conditions on Sunday.

Berlin and vicinity: Partly cloudy, partly sunshine, weak air currents, gradually rising temperature. In Germany: cloudy in the west and south, in the rest of Germany cloudy to fair, in the northeast somewhat windy, gradually warmer again.

In this very temperate weather, the Pums gang, our Franz among them, set themselves slowly in motion; the ladies belonging to the mob are of the opinion that the swains should step out a bit, for otherwise they'd have to go out on the streets, and none of the girls likes to do that, unless she's obliged to. Well, first of all, they've got to study the market, find purchasers, and if men's and ladies' wear don't go, they had better tackle furs, the ladies think: they'll do that in a jiffy, they're always doing exactly the same job, and it's easy to learn a trade like that. But they ain't got the slightest mind for switching jobs when business conditions are bad. Anyway, the girls got nothing to say about it.

Pums has got in with a tinner who knows something about oxygen blow-pipes, so we got him with us; then they have a business man who has gone to the wall, he looks classy; of course, that louse doesn't work, that's why his mother kicked him out, but he is a light-fingered gent, and knows his business, so they can send him everywhere to look round and fix up an expedition. Pums says to the veterans of his gang: "Of course, we don't really need to worry about competition, naturally we have it in our business like everyone else, but we don't interfere with each other. However, if we don't try to get good people who know their business and understand their tools, then we'll get it in the neck. Might as well take to plain hooking, and we don't need six or eight men for that, anybody can do that on his own."

Since they're out for ladies' and men's wear and furs now, everybody who can walk has got to start trotting and finding shops where one easily gets rid of things without too many questions being asked, and where the police aren't likely to pay an early visit. The stuff can be faked up or sewn in a different way, or, as a last resort, stowed away for a while. Got to find it first, however.

For one thing his fence in Weissensee gives Pums endless trouble. When a fellow works like he does, you can't do any business with him. Live and let live. All right. But just because he claims to have suffered some losses last winter—that's what he says—and to have had no profits and incurred debts, while we had a good time in the summer, he comes now and asks for money and bellyaches a lot about having made a bad speculation. That's it, he's simply made a bad speculation, for he's a jackass, a rotten business man, simply knows nothin' about business, the fool, then he ain't for us. Gotta look for somebody else. It's, of course, easier said than done, but it can't be helped, and as for things like that, it's good old Pums who, alone of the whole gang, can attend to them. Anyhow, it's queer, they hear everywhere that the other boys are also worrying about that; they want to know what becomes of the stock, for no one ever got fat just by cribbing things, it has got to be turned into money, but as I said: with Pums around, they stretch their legs and say: "As long as Pums is there, he'll fix it up all right." He'll do it, he'll do it all right. But suppose Pums ain't able to do it? Ha! Hah! Pums can't always do it. Couldn't somethin' happen to Pums, too? He's only human, after all. Then how're ye goin' to get rid of the stuff, that's what you gotta think about, and all your burglary won't help you any. . . . Nowadays it's not crowbars and blow-pipes alone that get a fellow ahead in the world, today he's got to be a business man.

That's why, as September rolls along, Pums worries not only about oxygen blow-pipes, but who's going to take that stuff off my hands? He started all that in August already. And if you want to know who Pums is: he's the silent partner in five good little fur-shops—never mind where— and then he's put a little money into a couple of quick-pressing places, American plan, with ironing-boards in the window, a tailor stands around in his shirt-sleeves, he's always lifting the board up and down, it's steaming, but in the rear they've got a lot of suits hanging up, well, they're what matters, it's the suits that matter, and where we got 'em from, well, you simply say, from customers, they brought 'em in here yesterday to be pressed and altered, here are the addresses, and when a dick comes in to look around, everything's jake. So good old Fatty Pums has made his preparations for the winter, and now we can say, let 'er go. If anything happens, a man can't prepare everything in advance, can he now? It won't go without a bit of luck, but we should worry about that.

Now let's get on with our story. It's early in September, and our classy loafer, the go-between, who is also an imitator of animal-cries—but that's another story—Waldemar Heller is the baby's name, and he's really bright as hell, now, that lad has been snooping around the big clothing stores in Kronenstrasse and Neue Wallstrasse to get the lay of the land. He knows all about entrances and exits, front-doors, back-doors, who lives upstairs, who lives downstairs, who shuts up the place, where the time-clocks are, etc. Pums pays his expenses. Sometimes Heller pretends to represent a Posen firm which has recently started in business; well, people would first like to make some inquiries about that Posen firm; all right, why not, I just wanted to see how high your ceiling is, next time we'll come down from upstairs.

The job is to come off during the night from Saturday to Sunday. It is the first time Franz goes along. He fixed it. Franz Biberkopf is sitting in the automobile, they all know what to do, he has an assignment like the others. It all goes in a very business-like way. Another fellow has to be the lookout, that is, he's not a lookout in the real sense of the word, three of the boys simply sneaked their way into the printers' shop on the floor above during the previous night, they carried the ladder and blowpipe upstairs in boxes and hid them behind the reams of paper, one of them drove the car away; at eleven they open the door for the others, not a damned soul in the house notices anything, there are nothing but office rooms and stores in the building. They sit peacefully working, one of them at the window keeps looking out while another watches the courtyard. Then they start blasting the floor, more than half a yard square, the tinner with the horn-rimmed glasses does that. Next they cut through the wood of the ceiling, there is a rattling noise downstairs, but that's nothing, that's just the débris of heavy stucco falling down, the ceiling bursts with the heat, through the first opening they thrust a fine silk umbrella into which the lumps fall, that is, most of them, of course it is impossible to catch them all. But nothing happens, downstairs everything is black and dead quiet.

At ten they climb in, classy Waldemar first, because he knows the place. He walks down the rope-ladder like a cat, the boy's doing that for the first time, he's not the least bit afraid, people like that are regular greyhounds, they have all the luck, that is, of course, till things go wrong. Then it's another's turn to come down, the steel ladder is only 8 feet high, it doesn't reach to the ceiling, so downstairs they drag up some tables, then slowly lower the ladder till it rests on the upper table, and here we are. Franz remains upstairs, lying across the hole on his belly. He gathers up the bundles of cloth handed up to him, like a fisherman, then puts them behind him, where another man is standing. Franz is strong. Reinhold himself, who is downstairs with the tinner, is astonished at the things Franz can do. A funny thing to be pulling off a job with a one-armed man. His arm grabs things like a crane, he sure has got a mighty punch, he's some bloke. Afterwards they drag the baskets down. Although one of them is on the watch downstairs at the exit of the courtyard, Reinhold is also patrolling the place. Two hours, now we're sitting pretty, the watch-man walks through the house, better leave that man alone, he won't notice anything, never mind, he'd be a fool to let himself be shot dead for the few pennies he gets, well, there you are, he's gone, he's a good fellow, we might leave a blue-back beside the time-clock for him. By that time it's two o'clock, at half-past two the car arrives. Meantime the men upstairs have a nice supper, but not too much liquor, otherwise they'd make a lotta noise, and then it's half-past two, anyway. Two men pull off their first job with the gang today. Franz and the classy Waldemar. They quickly toss a coin, Waldemar wins, he has to put the seal on today's trip, he's got to go down the ladder again, into the dark devastated stockroom; and there he crouches down, pulls off his trousers and presses on the floor what he has in his belly.

At half-past three, after they have unloaded, they quickly pull another job, for we won't get together so young again, and who knows when we'll see each other again upon the Spree's green bank? Everything goes according to schedule. Only on the trip back they run over a dog, fancy a thing like this happening to them, of course it gets Pums excited beyond all reason, because he likes dogs, and he bawls out the tinner who acts as chauffeur, can't he blow his horn, they chased that kiyoodle into the street, because they can't pay their taxes, and here you come and run over him and kill him. Reinhold and Franz roar with laughter at the way the old fellow has a crazy fit over a mutt like that, he's really a bit weak in the head. That dog was hard of hearing, I blew my horn, sure I did, once, and when did you ever hear of a dog being hard of hearing, well, maybe we'll turn back and take him to the hospital, cut it out, you'd better watch out, I can't stand that, a thing like this brings you bad luck. Whereupon Franz nudges the tinner: he means cats. Everybody roars with laughter.

For two days Franz Biberkopf says nothing at home about what has happened. Only after Pums has sent him two hundred, and if he doesn't need it, he's to give it back, Franz laughs, he can always find use for it; supposing now I gave it to Herbert for Magdeburg. And to whom is he going, whom does he look straight in the eyes at home, well, whom, which tiny whom, well, whom do you think? For whom, for whom, have I kept my heart pure? For whom, for whom, sure, for you alone, tonight will happiness come near, boldly I call to you, my dear, for you, I swear, I'll always pine, tonight I'm yours and you are mine. Miezeken, my darling Miezeken, you look like a little bride made of marchpane, with little golden shoes, there you stand and wait, wondering about all the fuss your Franz is making with his pocket-book. He squeezes it between his knees, and then he pulls out a couple of flimsies, holds them out and puts them on the table, beams at her and is as gentle with her as only he can be; he's her big boy, he holds her fingers tight, what sweet slender little fingers she's got!

"Well, Mieze, Miezeken?" "What is it, Franz?" "Well, nothin'; I'm just glad aboutcha." "Franz." How that one can look atcha, how she can say a fellow's name! "I'm just happy, that's all. Look here, Mieze, that's so funny about life. With me things ain't like they are with other people. They got no trouble, they flop around and run and earn somethin' and doll themselves up. And me—I can't do like them others. I got to look at my outfit, my coat, the sleeve, the arm's missin'." "Franzeken, you're my dear old Franzeken." "Well, look here, Miezeken, that's the way things are, and I can't change it, nobody can, but if you carried this around with you, and it's like an open wound!" "Why, Franzeken, whatsa matter, ain't I still here, and everything's all right, so don't let's start talkin' about all that again." "I ain't. That's just it. I ain't doin' it." He smiles up into her face, that smooth, taut, pretty little face of hers, what bright lively eyes that kid has: "Take a look, pipe what's on the table, them bills, I earned 'em, so I did, Mieze—they're yours." Well, what about it? Whatcha makin' such a face for, heh, looking at that money like that? It won't bite you, it's nice money. "Ye earned that?" "Yep, you see, girlie, I did that myself. I've gotta work, otherwise I'm no good. Otherwise I go blooey. Don't tell nobody, it was with Pums and Reinhold, on Saturday night Don't tell Herbert nothin' and Eva neither. Baby, if they hear anything, it'll be my finish with 'em." "Where didja get it?" "Pulled a job, sweetie, I told you, with Pums, now what's the matter, Mieze? I'm givin' you this. Do I get a kiss, well, how about it?"

Her head droops on her breast, then she lays her cheek against his and kisses him, holding him tight. She says nothing. She will not look at him: "You're giving me that?" "Yes, baby, who else do you think?" Funny girl! What a lot of fuss she's making. "Why—why do you want to give me any money?" "Well, don't you want none?" Her lips tremble, she frees herself from him, and Franz understands now: she looks like she did that time on the Alex when they came from Aschinger's, she's turned pale as a sheet, she's getting unsteady on her pins. She sits down, staring at the blue table-cover. What's wrong now; can a man ever understand them janes? "Honey, dontcha want it? I been lookin' forward to it like anything, say, we can go on a trip with this, you bet we can." "That's so, Franzeken."

She leans her head on the edge of the table; the girl is crying, really crying, what's the matter with her? Franz strokes the nape of her neck, and is ever so gentle and kind to her, so gentle from the bottom of his heart, for whom, for whom have I kept my heart pure, for whom, for whom alone? "Honey, my Mieze, when we can start on a trip, then dontcha want to, say, dontcha want to come along with me?" "Sure." She raises her head, that sweet, smooth little face of hers, the powder's all mixed up with tears like a mayonnaise, and puts an arm around Franz's neck and presses her little face to his, and then quickly she lets it go, as if something were tickling her, and starts bawling again, over the edge of the table, but you can't see anything, the girl's quite still, she doesn't give herself away. What have I done wrong again, don't she want me to work? "Come on, hold up that li'l head of yours, come on, baby-face, whatcha cryin' for?" "You want to, you want to," she slips away from him, "you want to get rid of me, Franz?" "Honey, for the luva . . ." "You don't want to, Franzeken?" "No, why, for the luva . . ." "Why d'you wanta do anything, don't I earn enough for you? I earn enough." "Mieze, I just wanted to give you a present or somethin'." "No, I don't want it." She leans her head again on the hard edge of the table. "Well, Mieze, dontcha want me to do nothin' at all? I can't live that way." "I don't say that, but you needn't just on account of the money, I don't wantcha to."

And Mieze sits up, grabs her Franz around the waist and looks him beatifically in the face, babbling a lot of sweet nothings, and begging and coaxing: "Don't wantcha to, don't wantcha to." And why doesn't he ask when he wants something, but, darling, I've got somethin', I don't need nothin'. "And so I shouldn't do nothin'?" "Ain't I here for that, Franzeken?" "But me—me . . ." She falls around his neck. "Oh, don't gimme the slip." She prattles away, kisses him, coaxes him. "Get rid of it, hand it over to Herbert, Franz." Franz is so happy with the girl. That skin of hers! He can't say it was a lotta boloney that stuff he said about Pums, but, of course, she don't understand nothin' about that. "Promise me, Franz, you won't do that any more." "But I'm not doin' it for the money, Mieze." Only then does she remember what Eva told her, how she should watch Franz.

It dawns on her now, he doesn't really do it for the sake of the money, that thing he said about his arm just now, he can't stop thinking about his arm, and it's true what he says about the money, he doesn't care about that, he can get as much as he wants from her. She thinks and thinks, holding him in her arms.

Love's Pain and Joy

After Franz has hugged and kissed her, she goes out into the street again, on her way to Eva's. "Franz has brought me 200 marks. Y'know where he got it? From them fellows, y'know, dontcha?" "Pums?" "Yeah, he told me so himself. What'll I do?"

Eva calls in Herbert. "Franz was out with Pums on Saturday." "Did he say where?" "No, but what'll I do now?" Herbert is astonished: "Imagine it, so he's in cahoots with that crowd!" Eva: "Can you understand it, Herbert?" "No, that's some mess." "What'll we do now?" "Leave him go. Y'think he cares about the money? I told ye that. He's goin' at it with a bang, we'll hear more about him one of these days." Eva stands opposite Mieze, the pale little whore she had picked up in Invalidenstrasse; both of them suddenly remember where they met for the first time; the saloon next to the Baltikum Hotel. Eva's sitting there with a man from the sticks; she doesn't need it, but she loves stepping out on the side, a lot of girls are there and three or four boys. And at ten a police raiding party comes trotting along, and all of them are carted off to the Stettin Depot Police Station, marching in goose-step, cigarettes in their mouths, cocky as hell. The bulls march in front and behind, with drunken Wanda Hubrich, the old war-horse, in front, of course, and then all the squawking at the station, and Mieze, Sonia, who bawls and clings to Eva, because everything will be known in Bernau. One of the cops knocks the cigarette out of boozey Wanda's hand, after which she walks off alone to the cell and starts kicking and cursing inside.

Eva and Mieze look at each other, Eva eggs her on: "You've got to watch out now, Mieze." Mieze implores her: "What can I do, anyway?" "It's up to you. A person ought to know herself what to do." "But I don't know nothin'." "Well, don't start bawling again, kid." Herbert beams on them. "I tell you, the boy's all right, and I'm glad he's hittin' out now, he's got a plan, he's a clever lad." "My God, Eva." "Don't start blubberin', don't blubber, kid, I'll watch out." You really don't deserve Franz, no she don't, making all that fuss! What's the damn fool sniveling about now, the bitch? I'll box her ears for her.

*

Trumpets! The battle is on, the regiments are marching, tarara, tarari, tarara, Artillery and Cavalry, Cavalry and Infantry, the Infantry and the flying corps, tarari, tarara, tarara, we're pushing into the enemy's land. Whereupon Napoleon said: Forward, forward, without respite, go, it's dry above and wet below. But if it gets dry below we'll conquer Milan, and a medal be given every man, tarari, tarara, tarari, tarara, we're going strong, we won't be long, oh, what joy to be a soldier boy!

Mieze does not have to blubber for long and think what to do. It comes to her like a flash. There's Reinhold sitting in his room with his swell girl-friend, or visiting the shops which Pums has fixed up for getting rid of the stuff. He still has time to think about things. That bozo is always bored and it doesn't agree with him. When he's got money it doesn't agree with him, nor does boozing agree with him, but he's getting along better, he sloshes around the café, listens in here and there, works, and drinks his coffee.

And now, whenever he goes to Pums's place or anywhere else, it's always this fellow Franz who is sitting there, right in front of his nose, that boob, that cocky fool with his one arm, who plays the grand Mogul, and still hasn't got enough of it, and plays the hypocrite, too, as if that jackass couldn't harm a fly, and sure as two times two is four he wants somethin' outa me. The louse is always in a good humor and wherever I am, wherever I work, he's there, too. Well, we've gotta get some air. Let's get some air.

But what is Franz doing? He? Well, what do you think he's doing? He goes flopping around, the picture of the most complete tranquillity and peacefulness. You can do anything you want with that fellow, he always falls on his feet. There are such people, not many, of course, but they do exist.

In Potsdam, there once was in Potsdam a man whom they afterwards called the living corpse. He was some card. The fellow, a certain Bornemann by name, pulled it off, after his business had gone to smash and he was staring fifteen years' prison in the face, he blows, the fellow blows; as a matter of fact it wasn't Potsdam at all, it was near Anklam, Gorke was the name of the burg. So our Bornemann, while walking one day near Neugard, finds a dead man floating on the water, in the Spree, and Neugard, no, Bornemann from Neugard, says: "Why, I'm really a dead man, now," puts the stiff's papers in his pocket and is now a stiff himself. Frau Bornemann wonders: "What'll I do? There is nothin' to be done about it, he's dead, and if it's my husband, well, thank God it's him, not much loss with a man like that! What did I get from him anyway, a fellow like that does time half his life, to hell with the fool." But my little Otto, live and let live is his motto, is far from dead. He gets to Anklam, and as he happened to notice that water is a nice thing, and he has a fancy for water, he becomes a fishmonger. He deals in fish at Anklam under the name of Finke. There ain't no Bornemann any more. But they caught him nevertheless, and in what way and how, say, just hold your horses, now.

Of all things to happen in the world, one day his stepdaughter chances to come to Anklam to get a job, fancy it, when the world is so big, she just happens to move to Anklam; and discovers this resurrected fish, who is by now 100 years old and hails from Neugard, and meanwhile, of course, a girl like that has grown up and flown the coop, so, of course, he doesn't recognize her, but she spots him. "Say, ain't you our father?" Says he: "Nope, you must be batty." And as she won't believe him, he calls his wife and his—count 'em!—five children, they can testify sure enough: "He's Finke, the fishmonger." Otto Finke, everybody in the village knows it. Everybody knows it, Herr Finke is the man's name, the fellow who died was named Bornemann.

As for her, it has had no effect, and she's not convinced. Off she goes, that's the way with the female soul, a bee firmly lodged in her bonnet. She writes a letter to Berlin, to the police, Div. 4a: "I have bought things from Herr Finke several times; I am his stepdaughter, but he does not consider himself as my father, and he is deceiving my mother, for he has five children by another woman." Finally the children are allowed to keep their front names, but behind they're given the dirty end of the deal. Their name now is Hundt, with a dt, their mother's name, so they became all at once illegitimate children, concerning whom the Criminal Code says: An illegitimate child and his father are not held to be related.

Like this man Finke, Franz Biberkopf is the picture of complete tranquillity and peacefulness. Once he was mauled by a wild beast that bit his arm off, but then he stopped it with a blow that made it reel, now it mews and ramps along at his heel. Only one of Franz's companions saw how he stopped the beast, and made it reel, so that it mews and ramps along at his heel. Franz walks with a very firm step, and carries his thick skull very straight. Although he can do nothing like other people, his eyes are ever so bright. But the man to whom he hasn't done anything so far wonders: "What's he after? He wants somethin' outa me." He sees things others don't see, and understands everything. That muscular neck of Franz's shouldn't really affect him, nor should his taut legs and his excellent step, but they, nevertheless, do something to him, and he can't keep quiet about it. He's got to get back at him. And how?

Just as when a door opens before a gust of wind, and a herd of animals rushes out of the pen. Just as when a fly excites a lion that taps at it with his paws, uttering a turrible roar.

Just as when a guard takes his little key, gives a little push to a bolt, and out come a bunch of criminals, and then begin murder, manslaughter, burglary, theft, murder for robbery, etc.

Reinhold walks up and down in his room, or in the saloon at Prenzlauer Gate, thinking up and down and round about it all. One day, when he knows Franz is with the tinner, working on a new idea, wonder what'll come of it, anyway, he goes to see Mieze.

So she gets to see the man for the first time. There is nothing much to be seen about the fellow, Mieze you're right, he doesn't look bad, that chap, a bit sad, flabby, a trifle sick, too, he's so sallow. But he doesn't look bad.

But take a good peep at him, give him your little paw and study, yes, study his face well. That's a face, Miezeken, that's more important for you than all the other faces on earth, more important than Eva's, yeah, more important even than your beloved Franzeken's face. He is walking up the stairs now, today is just like any other day, Thursday, September 3rd, just look, you feel nothing, know nothing, suspect nothing of your fate.

Now, what will it be, Mieze, little Mieze from Bernau, this fate of yours? You're healthy, you earn money, you love Franz, and that's why it comes walking up the stairs and stands before you, fondling your hand, Franz's fate, and—there it is—yours, too. You needn't stare at his face very closely, only at his hand, his two hands, those two insignificant-looking hands in gray leather.

Reinhold is in his best bib and tucker, and Mieze at first does not know how to behave towards him. Franz has sent him up perhaps, or maybe it's a trap laid by Franz, but no, that can't be true. Now he says Franz mustn't know he's been there, he is so sensitive. It's about this, he just wanted to have a talk with her, things are going pretty difficult with Franz now, he's got that trouble with his arm, and if he really needs to work, well, they are all interested in that. But Mieze is too clever for that, and she knows what Herbert said, what Franz wants, and says: No, as far as earning money goes, he doesn't really need it, there are always people ready to help him. But maybe that's not enough for him, a man wants to work, too. Reinhold suggests: Very true, yep, he ought to. But what they do is hard work, it ain't ordinary work, even people who got two healthy arms can't always do it. The conversation goes back and forth. Mieze doesn't quite know what he's after, then Reinhold starts asking her to let him have a cognac: he just wanted to find out about his financial condition, well, if it's like that, they'll all be careful about their friend's interests, of course. Then he drinks another cognac, and asks: "D'you know me, Fräulein? Hasn't he told you anything about me yet?" "No," says she, wonder what that man's after anyhow, if only Eva were here, she understands that kind of conversation much better than I do. "We've known each other a long time, Franz and I, before he had you, there were others around then, Cilly." Maybe that's what he's after, he wants to give Franz a black eye with me, he's one of those fellows who tell all they know. "Well, why shouldn't he have had others? I've had another one, too, but he's still my man, all right."

They sit opposite each other very quietly, Mieze on the chair, Reinhold on the sofa, both taking it easy. "Well, certainly, he's yours; say, Fräulein, I hope you don't think I'm tryin' to cut him out, wouldn't think of it. Only some mighty funny things happened between him and me, hasn't he talked to you about 'em?" "What kinda funny things?" "They were really funny, Fräulein, I'll tell you something frankly: if Franz is with our gang now, it's only on account o' me, just for me, and because of them stories. We two always stuck together as much as we could. That's where I could tell you a lotta funny things." "Is that so? Say, ain't you got no work that you got time to sit here telling stories?" "Even the Lord sometimes takes a holiday, Fräulein, shouldn't we plain mortals take two at least?" "Well, I should say you're takin' three." They both laugh. "Maybe you're not far wrong there; I save up my strength, laziness prolongs life, as otherwise you spend too much energy." She smiles at him. "A person's gotta be saving, then." "You know all about it, Fräulein. One man's like this, another's like that. Well, I'll tell ye, Fräulein, Franz and me, we've always exchanged women, what do you say to that?" He turns his head to one side, sips his drink and waits to see what the little girl is going to say. She's a pretty little thing all right, we'll soon make her, you bet, and how I'm gonna pinch her legs.

"Better tell that to your grandmother about exchanging women. That's what somebody told me once, they do it in Russia. Maybe you're from there, that don't happen here." "But I'm tellin' ye." "Then it's just a lot of apple-sauce." "Franz can tell ye about it." "Those musta been nice janes, for 50 pfennigs, yes, from the flop-houses, eh?" "Now you're gettin' smart, Fräulein, that ain't our line." "Tell me, why on earth are you handin' me that bunk, anyway? What's your game, heh?" Just look at the little devil. But she's nice all right, she's crazy about him, that's fine. "Nothin', Fräulein, what do you mean, game? I just wanta get the low-down (a sweet little devil, she knocks you flat, come, come, Caroline, come), Pums himself gave me them orders, well, I'm goin' to hop off, won't you come to our club one of these days?" "So you can tell some more stories like that!" "No harm intended, Fräulein, I thought you knew it all. Well, I also got some business I'd like to talk over. Pums said I'd better come to see you and ask about the money, and so on, seeing as Franz is so sensitive about his arm, but you mustn't blab it to him. Franz needn't know about it. I mighta inquired about it in the house, too, then I thought to myself: why all this secrecy? But you were in, and so I'd rather come up to you openly and directly to ask you about it." "I'm not to tell him nothin'?" "No, better not. But if you really insist on it, I can't do nothin' to stop you. Just as you wish. Well, so long." "No, the door's on the right." A fine baby, we'll swing it, m'boy, sure.

Little Miezeken hasn't seen or noticed anything on the table, in the room, she just thinks, as she sees the liquor glass standing there, yes, what does she think? She's thinking something now, as she puts her glass away, she knows nothing. I am so excited, that fellow's got me all excited, everything is jumping around in me. What a story he told me. Did he just want, what did he want, anyway? She looks at the glass, which is in the closet, the last one on the right. Everything is dithering inside me, I must sit down, no, not on the sofa, that's where that fellow was layin' around. On the chair. So she sits on the chair and looks at the sofa where the man had been sitting. I'm terribly excited, what can it be? My arms and my breast, everything's dithering inside me. Franz certainly ain't that kind of a dirty dog to exchange women, I could believe it about that scoundrel Reinhold, but Franz, no—they simply got him to act the fool all round, if that's really true.

She chews her nails. If it's true; but Franz, why he's a bit stupid, he let's 'em do anything with him. That's why they threw him out of the car. That's the kind of fellows they are. That's the kind of society he goes with.

She chews and chews her nails. Tell Eva about it? I don't know. Tell Franz about it? I don't know. I won't tell nobody. Nobody was here.

She is ashamed, puts her hand on the table, bites her index finger. It doesn't help any, something is burning her throat. Maybe they'll do that with me too, they'll sell me, too.

A hurdy-gurdy grinds away in the courtyard: In Heidelberg Town, I lost my heart. That's for me, I've lost my heart, and now it's gone blooey, and she moons into her lap; it's gone, so I ain't got any left; and what'll I do about it, and if they drag me through the sewer, I can't do nothin' about it. But my Franz don't do that, he ain't no Russian, to go about exchanging women, that's all a lotta hooey.

She stands at the open window in her blue-checked dressing-gown and sings with the organ-grinder: In Heidelberg Town I lost my heart (that's a deceitful gang, he's right to smoke 'em out); on a sweet and luscious summer night (when is he coming home anyway, I'll go meet him on the stairs), I had been hit by love's old dart. (I won't tell him a word, I won't come to him with such mean stories, not a word, not a word, I love him so. Well, I guess I'll put on my waist.) Her mouth laughed like a red rose bright. And as before the gates we had to part, the last kiss made me see it clear (and it's true, what Herbert and Eva say, they smell a rat, and they just want to find out from me if it's true; they can listen a long time, they must think I'm a dumbbell, if they want to catch me nappin'!) In Heidelberg Town I lost my heart, it beats on the Neckar's banks, not here.

Brilliant Harvest Prospects, but there's many a Slip . . .!

He goes around and around everywhere, the very picture of tranquillity and peacefulness. You can do whatever you please with that boy, he always falls on his feet. There are such people. In Potsdam there was a fellow, at Gorke near Anklam, Bornemann by name, well, he makes a get-away from prison and comes to the Spree. There's somebody floating on the water.

"Well, Franz, what about it? What's her name anyhow, your sweetheart?" "Mieze, you know that, Reinhold, her name was Sonia before." "Is that so? Afraid to show her, I guess she's too swell for us." "Go on, d'ye think I got a menagerie and I got to exhibit her? Why, she goes around the streets, has her gentleman-friend and earns good money." "Only you don't show her to anybody." "What do you mean, show her? The girl's busy." "Might bring her along sometime, I hear she's pretty." "Maybe so." "I'd like to see her sometime, maybe you don't want me to." "Well, you know, Reinhold, we were in business together once, you remember, with boots and fur-collars." "Nothin' doin' in that line any more." "No, that's all over. You can't get me any more for filthy tricks like that." "All right, m'boy, I only asked about it." (Dirty goof with his filthy tricks, always talking about them tricks, just you wait, old horse.)

When Bornemann to the water hied, a fresh corpse floating he espied, a bright idea that boy descried. Out of his pocket he pulled all his papers, gave 'em to him and gave 'em to her. Certainly we heard that all before, but it can't harm to hear the tale once more. Then to the tree the corpse he tied, it might have floated away, and got lost upon the tide. He straightway took the local to Stettin, bought a ticket, and when he arrived in Berlin, called up mother Bornemann from a saloon, she was to come at once, there was somebody there. Money and clothes she brings him here, he whispers something in her ear, then, alas, he must leave his lady dear. She promised to identify the corpse, he'll send her money, if he gets any, but try to find some yourself. Then quickly, quickly he had to leave her behind, or somebody else the corpse might find.

"That's just what I wanted to know, Franz, so you like her a lot, eh?" "Ah, stop talkin' about the janes and all that stuff." "Just wanted to know. Don't hurt to tell me, does it?" "No, don't hurt me none, Reinhold, but y'know, you're such a scoundrel." Franz laughs, so does the other. "What about your sweetie, Franz, cantcha really show her to me just once?" (My, what a little wag you are, Reinhold, ye kicked me out of the car, but now you're runnin' after me.) "Well, what d'you want, Reinhold?" "I don't want nothin' at all. Just wanta see her." "You wanta see if she cares for me? I tell ye she is all heart, from head to foot, a heart for yours truly, that kid. All she knows about is lovin' and cooin' and nothin' else. Ye know, Reinhold, you'd never imagine how crazy she is. You know Eva, dontcha?" "Do I?" "Well, y'see, Mieze would like me to . . . with her. No, I won't tell you nothin'." "Well, what is it? Go ahead!" "Nope, you wouldn't believe it, but that's the way she is, ye never heard the likes of it, Reinhold. I ain't never struck anything like it in all my born days." "Say, what's it all about anyway? With Eva?" "Yep, but keep it mum, well, she wants, that gal Mieze wants Eva to have a kid by me."

Bang! Both of them sit still and look at each other. Franz slaps his legs and explodes. Reinhold smiles, starts to laugh, but gets stuck.

And so the fellow's name is Finke, he goes to Gorke, where he becomes a fishmonger. One fine day who should come along but his stepdaughter. She has a job in Anklam and wants to buy a little feesh; she goes to Finke with a net in her hand, and says.

Reinhold smiles, starts to laugh and gets stuck. "Maybe she's a dike." Franz goes on smacking his legs and snickers. "Nope, she's got a case on me." "I can't imagine it." (Unbelievable that things like that should happen, but it's happened to this boob, and he's grinning about it at that!) "What does Eva say about it?" "Why, they're friends, those two, she knows her all right. In fact, I got to know Mieze through Eva." "Say, Franz, you certainly make my mouth water. Look here, can't I see Mieze some day, at twenty yards' distance, through bars, as far as I am concerned, if you're afraid?" "Gee, I ain't at all afraid; she's as true as gold and that sweet, you'd never imgine it. Ye remember I told you that time you should stop that business with so many girls, it ruins your health, why the best nerves can't stand that. A man can get a brain-storm from that, that's where you ought to watch out, it would do you a lotta good. Well, you gotta see how right I am, Reinhold, I'll show her to you." "But she mustn't see me." "Why not?" "Nope, I don't want to. Can't you just show her to me like that?" "Certainly, old horse, glad to do it. That'll do you good."

And then it gets to be three o'clock in the afternoon, Franz and Reinhold are walking along the streets. Enamel signs of every kind, enamel ware, German and genuine Persian rugs, payable in 12 monthly installments, hall runners, table- and sofa-covers, quilts, curtains, awnings, Leisner & Co., do you read *Fashions for All*, if not, ask to receive it free by return post, look out, danger of death, high-tension wires. They go to Franz's house. You are now going into my home: all's well with me, nothing can touch me, you'll see how things stand with me, my name's Franz Biberkopf.

"And now, we've gotta walk quiet. I'll open the door first to see if she's here. Nope. Wait, here's where I live. But she oughta be here soon. Now let's see, how we're gonna do it. It's just a lotta playactin', but mind you, not a peep outa you." "Dontcha worry." "Best thing is, you lie down here in bed, Reinhold, it's not used during the day anyway, and I'll watch out so she don't come in here, and then you can look through the lace-cover from up above. Go ahead, lie down, can you see anything?" "Yep, sure. But I gotta take my boots off." "Might be better, at that, I'll put 'em out in the hallway and afterwards when you go, you can take 'em yourself." "Gee, Franz, if only that don't go wrong." "You afraid? Ye know I ain't afraid, even if she spots something, you ought to know her." "Nope, it's better if she don't see me." "Now lie down. She might come in any minute."

Enamel signs, enamel ware of all kinds, German and absolutely genuine Persian Persian rugs, Persians and Persian rugs, ask for free mail delivery.

In Stettin Chief Detective Blum says: "How did you come to know that man? How did you recognize him, by what, you must have recognized him by something?" "He is my stepfather." "Well, then, we might as well go to Gorke. And if it's true, we'll bring him along right away."

Somebody puts the key into the lock of the door downstairs. Franz calls out in the hallway. "Well, are you frightened, Mieze? Well, honey, here I be. Come on in! Don't you put nothin' on that bed. I got a surprise for you there." "I'm gonna see what it is right away." "Stop, first you gotta swear! Mieze, hands up, swear, everybody stand up, now, repeat after me: I swear." "I swear." "That I won't go near the bed." "That I won't go near the bed." "Till I tell you." "Till I go over there." "You're to stay here. Swear again! I swear." "I swear I won't go near the bed." "Till I put you in it myself."

She is serious now, she clings tight to his neck, and stays a long time like that. He notices there is something wrong with her, and he tries to push her towards the door out to the hallway, the thing can't be done today. But she stands still: "I won't go near the bed, lemme go." "What's the matter with my Miezeken, my little pussy cat, my li'l kitten?"

She pushes him to the sofa, where they sit together, clasped tight, and she says nothing. She begins to mumble something, starts pulling his necktie, and then it comes out: "Franzeken, can I tell you something?" "Why, of course, Miezeken." "It's about my old man, somethin' has happened." "Well, kitten." "There." "Well, what is it, kitten?" She fumbles with his necktie, what's the matter with the girl, too bad that guy should be there just today.

The Chief Detective says: "What do you mean your name is Finke? Have you got any papers?" "Well, all you need to do is go over to the City Hall." "What's in the City Hall doesn't concern us." "Papers, yes, I got 'em all right." "Fine, we'll take them along first of all. There is an officer from Neugard outside, who had a man named Bornemann from Neugard in his section, we'll ask him to come in."

"Franzeken, the last few times the old man has always had his nephew with him, that is, he didn't really invite him, he just came along." Franz mutters something and grows cold. "I see." She keeps her face close to his. "Ye know him, Franze?" "Why should I know him?" "I was just wondering. Well, he's always been around, and then one day he came along with us." Franz is shaking, things are growing black before his eyes. "Why didn'tcha tell me nothin', heh?" "I thought I could get rid of him. And why should I, if he just comes along." "Well, and so . . ." The twitching of her lips against his neck grows more violent, then he feels a certain moisture there, she clasps Franz tightly, the kid's sure holding me close, that's how she is, stubborn as a mule, she don't say nothin'. Ye can't get the hang of it, when she starts like that, and what's she blubbering about anyway, and now that guy's laying there, I'd like to take a stick and beat on that bed till he couldn't get up any more, damn ass, to make a fool out of me like that. But he's shaking. "What's wrong now?" "Nothin', Franzeken, you mustn't worry, only don't hurt me, there wasn't anything at all. Well, he came along again, was watchin' all morning till I came away from the old man's, and there he was, and I hadda go out driving with him, just couldn't help it, I just hadda." "Of course you hadda, didn'tcha?" "Yes, I hadda, what could I do? Franz, when a man acts that crazy. And he's such a young man, too. And then . . ." "Where did you go?" "Before this we always went across Berlin, Grunewald, I don't know myself, then we walked, and I kept askin' him to go away. And he cries and begs like a child and gets down on his knees before me. He's such a young fellow, a locksmith." "Well, he'd better be workin', the lazy hound, instead of runnin' around like that." "Don't know. Please, don't get mad, Franz." "I still don't know nothin' about what happened. Whatcha cryin' for, anyway?" She says nothing again, just cuddles up to him and fondles his necktie. "Don't get mad, Franz." "Got a case on the guy, Mieze?" She says nothing. How afraid he is, he goes ice-cold, from head to foot. He whispers through her hair, he has forgotten all about Reinhold: "Got a case on him, eh?" She has clasped his body tight to hers so that he can feel every line of her body, and now comes her whispered word: "Yes." Ow, he's heard it, yes, heard it. He wants to release her, shall I hit her, Ida, that man from Breslau, now it's coming, his arm goes numb, he is paralyzed, but she holds him tight, like an animal, what does she want, she says nothing, holds him tight, her face pressed to his neck, he looks stonily beyond her toward the window.

Franz shakes her, bellowing: "Whatcha want anyway? Lemme go now!" What'm I gonna do with the bitch. "But I'm here, Franzeken. I ain't run away from you. I'm still here." "Beat it, I don't wantcha around." "Don't holler at me, my God, what have I done?" "Go ahead and stay with him, if you love him, you bitch." "I ain't a bitch, be nice, Franzeken, I told him already nothing doing and I belong to you." "I don't want to have anything to do with ye. I don't want a bitch like you." "But I belong to you, that's what I told him, and then I beat it, and now you oughta console me." "Say, you must be crazy! Let go of me! You're crazy! Because you're in love with that fellow, you expect me to console you!" "Yes, you oughta, Franzeken, ain't I your Mieze, and you love me, so you can console me; oh, that young feller's probably around now, looking . . ." "Say, stop that now, Mieze! You gotta go back to that fellow." Mieze shrieks, he can't get rid of her. "Yes, you're gonna go there and you're gonna let go o' me." "No, I won't, either. Then you don't love me, then you don't want me, what have I done?"

Franz succeeds in getting his arm free, and he breaks loose. She runs after him, Franz turns around at once and strikes her in the face, so that she reels back, he pummels her shoulder and she falls, he's over her now, hitting her with his one hand wherever he can. She whimpers, writhes, oh, oh, he's beating me, he's beating me, she tosses about, first on her belly, then on her face. He stops to take a breathing-spell, the room is whirling around him, now she turns around, pulls herself up. "Don't take a stick, Franzeken, that's enough, don't take a stick."

She sits there, her blouse all torn, one eye shut, with blood streaming from her nose, smearing her left cheek and chin.

But Franz Biberkopf—Peeperkopf, Sleeperkopf, he's got no name—the room's turning round, the beds are over there, now he clings to one of the beds. And there's Reinhold, the big bozo, there he lies, with his boots on, dirtyin' up a fellow's bed. What's he want here? Hasn't he got his own room? I'll git 'im out, I'll kick 'im out, that's what I'll do, d. o. do, o as in shoe. So Franz Biberkopf, Heebiekopf, Jeebiekopf, Sleepykopf, hops on the bed, grabs the fellow under the cover by the head, he makes a move, the cover flies high, and Reinhold sits up.

"Well, Reinhold, git out now, git out, take a look at her and then git out."

Mieze's mouth is wide open. Earthquakes, lightning, thunder, the tracks are rent asunder, twisted, the station, signal cabin, in ruins; there's a roaring, rolling, fuming, smoking, clouds, nothing to be seen, everything gone, gone, blown away, vertically, horizontally.

"What's the matter, what's hit this place?"

She's screaming, screams keep coming from her mouth, agonizing screams against the thing behind the smoke on the bed, a scream-wall, scream-lances hurled against that thing, higher and higher, scream-stones.

"Hold your trap, what's hit her, stop, the house is comin' down."

Screams welling up, scream-masses, against that thing, no time, no hour, no year, everything's gone.

And already Franz is being swept by the scream-wave into raving, ravening, raging madness. He stands by the bed and swings a chair in the air, it falls and crashes out of his hand. Then he bends over Mieze, who is still sitting up, yelling away, yelling and shrieking and shrieking; he puts his hands over her mouth from behind, flings her on her back, kneels over her, then lies chest-down against her face. I'll—kill—her.

The screams stop, she tries to struggle up with her legs. Reinhold wrenches Franz aside: "Heh, you'll choke her." "Get away, you!" "Get up now, get up." He succeeds in dragging Franz off her, the girl is lying on the floor on her belly, she turns her head, whimpering, gasping, and lashes about with her arms. Franz stammers: "Take a look at the bitch, the bitch! Who do you want to hit, you bitch, you?" "Now you beat it, Franz, put your coat on and come back when you're cooled down again." Mieze lies whimpering on the floor, she opens her eyes, her right lid is red and swollen. "Beat it, feller, you'll kill her yet. Put your coat on. There."

Franz pants and puffs; he lets Reinhold help him on with his coat.

Then Mieze gets up, spits out phlegm and tries to talk; she straightens herself a bit, then sits down and mutters with a rattle in her throat: "Franz." He has his coat on. "Here's your hat."

"Franz . . ." she is not screaming now, her voice has gone queer, she spits. "I . . . I . . . I'll—I'll go along with you." "No, just stay here, Fräulein, I'll help you afterwards." "Franzeken, wait, I—I'll go with you."

He stands there, fools with his hat, sucks his gums, pants, spits, and goes towards the door. Bang. Shut.

Mieze moans, gets up, and, pushing Reinhold aside, feels her way towards the door. At the door into the hallway, she can't go any farther, Franz is gone, downstairs already. Reinhold carries her back into the room. After he has laid her panting on the bed, she sits up without help, clambers out, spits blood, and pushes her way towards the door. "Lemme get out, lemme get out!" She keeps on saying: "Lemme out, lemme out!" One glassy eye on him all the time. Her legs are limp. What a lotta slobber! It makes him sick the way she slobbers, I won't stay here any longer, people might come along, and then it's me who fixed her up like that. What the hell do I care about it. Good-bye, Fräulein, lid on, exit center.

Downstairs he wipes the blood off his left hand, a lotta drool, he laughs out loud. So this is what he took me upstairs for, some show the boob gave me. So he put me in his bed with my boots on for this. The boob's mad enough to pop. He got a good wallop on the chin, wonder where he's at, now.

He ambles off. Enamel signs, enamel ware of all kinds. It was very nice up there, very nice! What a boob he is, did a fine job, my son, much obliged, just keep on that way! I have to laugh myself sick!

And so Bornemann was in jail again in Stettin. They fetched his wife, the real one. Chief, you might leave my wife alone, what she swore is true, if I get another two years, I don't care.

And it's a great evening in Franz's room. They laugh. They lie in each other's arms, they kiss each other, silly as lovebirds. "Why, I almost killed ye, Mieze, I certainly fixed you up, sweetie." "That don't matter s'long as you came back." "Did Reinhold go right away?" "Yes." "Ain't you gonna ask me, Mieze, why he was here?" "No." "Dontcha wanta know?" "No." "But, Mieze." "No. It ain't true, anyhow." "What ain't true?" "You wanted to palm me off on him." "What?" "That ain't true?" "Say, Miezeken." "I know all about it, and it's all right." "He's my friend, Mieze, but he's certainly filthy-minded with the girls. I just wanted to show him what a respectable girl's like. That's what I wanted him to see." "Well, all right." "Ye still love me? Or only that other feller?" "I'm all yourn, Franz."

Wednesday, August 29th

And she keeps her gentleman-friend waiting two whole days, which she spends entirely with her beloved Franz, riding out with him to Erkner and Potsdam, and being generally nice to him. She now has her secret with him, now more than ever in fact, the little devil, and she is not a bit afraid as to what her beloved is up to with that Pums gang; she's going to start something herself. She's going to look around on her own and see who's there in the dance-hall or the bowling-alley. Anyhow, Franz doesn't take her along with him, Herbert takes his Eva along, but Franz says: that's no place for you, I don't want you to go with such hell-cats.

But little Sonia, Miezeken, wants to do something for Franz, our little kitten wants to do something for him that's nicer than earning money. She's going to ferret everything out and protect him.

And when the next ball comes off, and the Pums mob and their friends go out to Rahnsdorf, it's a private party, there's a girl with them nobody knows, the tinner brought her along as his girl, she wears a mask, and once she even dances with Franz, but only once, afterwards he'd smell her perfume. That's in Müggelhort, at night they hang paper lanterns in the garden, an excursion steamer leaves for home, full to the gunwale, the band sounds a flourish of farewell as it leaves, but they're still dancing and drinking inside till after three.

Thus Miezeken floats around with her tinner, who brags and shows off what a fine gal he has. She sees Pums and her Grace, his lady, and Reinhold looking very gloomy—he's always in the dumps—and the classy go-between. Around two she decamps in an automobile with the tinner; she lets him kiss her wildly in the car, why not? She knows more now than she did before, it won't do her any harm. What does Miezeken know? How all the Pums boys look, that's why he can love her up, she'll always be Franz's girl anyway, they ride on into the night, on just such a night these blokes had thrown her Franz out of the car, and now he's after this fellow, and he certainly knows who he is, and they're all afraid of him, else why did Reinhold come up to Franz's place, that's certainly a fresh feller, my Franz, he's a darling boy, I could die kissing this tinner, that's how much I love my Franz. Yes, go ahead and love me up, I'll bite your tongue off, baby, the way that fellow drives he'll get us into a ditch yet, hurray, it sure was heavenly with you boys tonight, shall I turn to the right or the left now, drive any way you want, you're one sweet little duck, Mieze, well, do I taste right to you, Karl, you'll take me out again, wontcha, wow, the dumbbell's tight, he'll drive us into the Spree yet.

No, that's not possible, then I'd have to drown, and I have lots to do yet, I've got to follow my dear Franz, I don't know what he wants to do, he doesn't know what I want, it must be kept between us as long as he wants to and I want to, we both want the same thing, the same thing do we both want, oh, but it's hot, kiss me some more, there, hold me tight now, Karl, I'm melting away, baby, I'm melting away.

Li'l Karl, my dear li'l Karl, my joy, you're my best and dearest boy, along the road the black oak trees whizz by, I'll give you 128 days out of the year, each one with its morning, noon, and night.

There came two cops all dressed in blue along to the graveyard, hallee, halloo. They sat down on a tombstone fine and inquired of the people who came by, after a certain Kasimir Brodowicz, had they seen him? He did something thirty years ago, they don't know quite what, and as likely something'll happen again, you never can tell with those lads, so now we want to take his fingerprints, and measure his length, and best of all, to catch him first, bring him along, tralee, trala.

Reinhold pulls up his trousers and strides back and forth in his room, this tranquil life and so much money don't agree with him. He's sent his last girl away now, he's tired of the classy jane anyhow.

A fellow has got to do something else occasionally. He'd like to start something with Franz. That jackass is going around again now, beaming and bragging about his girl. As if it amounted to anything. I might take her away from him, yet. She gave me the creeps the other day with her slobbering.

The tinner, whose name is Matter, but he's known to the police under the name of Oskar Fischer, looks astonished when Reinhold asks him about Sonia. Just like that he asks about Sonia, and Matter confesses without further ado, well, if you know it, then you know it, that's all. So Reinhold puts his arm around Matter's waist, and asks if Matter could let him have her for a little party. Then it develops that Sonia belongs to Franz and not to Matter. Well, then, Matter might get the girl to join him in an automobile ride out to Freienwalde, some time.

"Then you gotta ask Franz and not me." "I can't ask Franz, he's got something against me, dating from the old days, and besides I don't think she falls for me, I noticed that." "I won't have nothin' to do with that. Suppose I want her for myself." "Ah, go ahead. Just for a ride." "As far as I'm concerned, you can have all the dames you want, Reinhold, her, too, but how can I get hold of her?" "Well, don't she run around with you? Listen, Karl, suppose I letcha have a coupla brownbacks." "Hand 'em over!"

Two cops in blue sat on a stone, questioned everybody who passed by, and held up all the automobiles, had they seen a fellow with a yellowish face and black hair? They're looking for him. They don't know what he's done or will do, that's in the police records. But nobody has seen him, or rather nobody wants to admit having seen him. So the two cops have to go farther along the road, and two dicks join up with them.

On Wednesday, August 29, 1928, after this year has already lost 248 days and hasn't many more to lose— and they are irrevocably gone, what with a ride to Magdeburg, a restoration and a recovery, Reinhold's adjustment to liquor, Mieze's emergence, and now they commit their first burglary this year, and Franz is again the picture of beaming tranquillity and complete peacefulness—the tinner shoots off with little Mieze into the landscape. She told him, Franz, that is, that she was going out with her gentleman-friend. Why she takes the ride, she doesn't know. She only wants to help Franz, but just how, she doesn't know. In the night she had dreamed that her and Franzeken's beds were under the lamp in their landlady's living-room, the curtain in front of the door moves, and something gray, a kind of ghost, emerges slowly from it and comes into the room. Help, she cried, and sat up in bed with Franz fast asleep beside her. I'll help him, nothing shall happen to him, and then she lay down again, it's funny how our beds roll forward into the living-room.

Bang, they are out in Freienwalde, it's nice in Freienwalde, a bathing resort, with its pretty Kurgarten and yellow gravel, and lots of people walking about. Whom will they meet now, just after they have eaten their lunch on a terrace next to the Kurgarten?

Earthquake, lightning, lightning, thunder, tracks torn up, the station in ruins, rolling, fuming, smoking, clouds, everything gone, clouds of vapor, nothing to be seen, clouds of vapor, screams up-welling. . . . I'm yourn, yours forever!

Let him come, let him take a seat, I'm not afraid of him, not that one, I'll look him straight in the face. "This is Fräulein Mieze, you know her, don't you, Reinhold?" "Slightly. Glad to meetcha, Fräulein."

And so they sit in the Kurgarten at Freienwalde; somebody in the place is playing the piano very nicely. I'm sitting here in Freienwalde, and he's sitting opposite me.

Earthquake, lightning, clouds of vapor, everything gone, but it's nice we met him, I'll sound him out about everything that happened with Pums, and what Franz does, I'll make him hot, that'll do the trick; keep him on tenterhooks, then he'll come around, Mieze dreams now of how fortune will favor her. The pianist sings: Answer *oui,* that's French, my baby, Answer *ja,* or in Chinese, maybe, As you wish, it doesn't matter, Love's an international chatter, Say it under the rose, Or through the nose, Say it ecstatically, Or emphatically, Answer *oui,* Say *ja,* or *yes,* And anything else you want, I guess.

A few glasses of liquor are brought and they all treat themselves to a wee little nip. Mieze betrays the fact that she was at the ball, which gives rise to a splendid conversation. The conductor at the piano plays by general request: *In Switzerland and Tyrol,* words by Fritz Roller and Otto Stransky, Music by Anton Profes.—In Switzerland and on Tyrol's height, One feels so well by day and night, In Tyrol the milk comes warm from the cow, In Switzerland there's the tall Jungfrau. But here, we'll honestly admit, Life isn't such a grand old hit; And that's why I think it's simply grand, In Tyrol and in Switzerland, Yipiaddyi.—On sale in all music stores. Yipiaddyi, Miezeken laughs, my darlin' Franz thinks I'm with my old man now, but it's with himself I am, and he don't notice it.

Then, afterwards, we'll drive around in the neighborhood with that there car. That's what Karl, Reinhold, and Mieze want, backwards it's Mieze, Reinhold, and Karl, or Reinhold, Karl, and Mieze, they want it all together. Just at that moment, the telephone has to ring and a waiter calls: Herr Matter wanted on the telephone, didn'tcha give the high sign, Reinhold, young man, well, we won't say anything, Mieze smiles, too, if neither of you got anything against it, looks as if it would develop into a pleasant afternoon. And now little Karl is back again, oh, Karl, my boy, Karl, my boy, you're my love and you're my joy, somethin' hurtin' my baby, nope, gotta rush back to Berlin, you stay, Mieze, I gotta go, you never can tell. He gives Mieze another li'l kiss, and don't say nothin', Karl, you know me, honey, for every man, if he can, everywhere, likes a little change of air, so long, Reinhold, happy Easter, merry Xmas. Hat off the hook, and he's gone.

Well, here we are. "Now whatcha say to that?" "Well, Fräulein, there wasn't any use in yellin' like that the other day, now was there?" "That was just because I was afraid." "Of me?" "A person gets used to people." "Very flatterful." How the little tart rolls her eyes, a sweet, nice little baggage! Let's bet I'll get her today; you just wait a bit, m'boy, I'm just gonna keep ye flopping around a little, and then you'll tell me everything you know. Gosh, he certainly looks funny. He musta drunk a whole bottle of vinegar.

The pianist has sung himself out and the piano is tired, it would like to go to sleep, too; Reinhold and Mieze wander up the hill together, and stroll into the wood. They talk of this and that, walking arm-in-arm, he's not such a bad sort. And when, around six, they come back to the Kurgarten again, Karl is there waiting for them, he's already back with the car. Are we going home so soon, it's full moon tonight, let's go into the woods together, it's so nice there, all right let's go. So at eight the three of them wander into the woods together, and Karl has to hurry back to the hotel to reserve rooms, and see about the car. We'll meet in the Kurgarten later on.

There are many trees in this wood, and many people walking arm-in-arm together, there are lonely paths as well. They walk dreamily side by side. Mieze would like to ask something, but she doesn't know what, it's ever so nice walking arm-in-arm with this man, oh, I'll ask him another time, it's such a nice evening. Lord, what must Franz think of me? I must soon get out of the woods, it's so nice walking here. Reinhold has taken her arm, he's got a right arm, he walks on my left side, Franz is always on my right, strange to walk like this, he has a strong, vigorous arm, what a great big fellow he is! They walk between the trees, the ground is soft, Franz has good taste. I'll get her away from him, and she'll belong to me one month, then he can do about it as he pleases. If he starts anything he'll get it in the neck on our next trip so he'll forget to get up again, she's a nice jane, a frisky jane, too, and she's true to him.

They walk and talk of this and that. It is getting darker. It's better if they talk, Mieze sighs, it's so dangerous to walk without talking, and only just feel the fellow beside you. She's always looking at the road, wants to see where it goes. I don't know what I want with him; oh, my God, what do I want with him anyway? They walk around in a circle. Without his noticing anything, Mieze leads him back to the road. Open your eyes, here we are back again!

It's eight o'clock. He pulls out his flashlight, they are on their way back to the hotel, we've left the woods behind, the little birds, the little birds, ah, how sweetly they were singing. He begins to tremble. That was a strangely silent road. He's got good eyes. He walks peacefully beside her. The tinner's waiting, all alone on the terrace. "Got the rooms?" Reinhold looks around for Mieze; she's gone. "Where's the lady?" "Gone to her room." He knocks. "The lady has given orders, she's gone to bed."

He's trembling now. How lovely that was. The dark wood, the birds. What'm I after with that girl? Franz certainly has a fine girl. I'd like to have her. Reinhold is sitting on the terrace with Karl. They are smoking thick cigars. They smile at each other. Why should we stay here, anyway? We might as well sleep at home. Reinhold is breathing deeply, slowly, slowly drawing at his fragrant weed, the dark wood, we walk around in a circle, she leads me back again. "If you wanta, Karl. I'll stay here tonight."

And then they tramp together to the edge of the wood, and sit there, watching the autos pass. There are lots of trees in this wood, the ground is soft to walk on, lots of people are wandering arm-in-arm, I certainly am a dirty bastard.

Saturday, September 1st

That was Wednesday, August 29, 1928.

Three days later everything repeats itself. The tinner comes with a car,

Mieze—didn't Mieze just say yes right away when he asked her if she wanted to go out to Freienwalde again, and Reinhold would like to come along, too. I'll be stronger this time, she thinks, as she takes her seat in the car, I won't go into the woods with him. She said yes right away, for Franz has been very sad these last few days, but he don't say why, and I must know why, I must get at the bottom of that. He has plenty of money from me, he has everything in fact, he lacks for nothing, I wonder what is worrying him.

Reinhold is sitting in the car beside her, and right away puts his arm around her waist. Everything has been well thought out. Today you're gonna ride away from your beloved Franz for the last time, today you're gonna stay with me, as long as I want you to. You're the five-hundredth or the thousandth woman I've had, everything went fine and in apple-pie order up till now, it'll all go well again. She sits there and doesn't know what's going to happen, but I know it, and that's all right.

At Freienwalde they leave the car in front of the inn, Karl Matter goes walking alone with Mieze through Freienwalde, it is Saturday, September 1st, and four o'clock. Reinhold would like to sleep another hour in the inn. After six Reinhold comes creeping out, tinkers a bit with the auto, then swills a coupla drinks and goes off.

Mieze feels happy in the woods. Karl is so nice and has heaps to talk about, he has taken out a patent, but the firm where he works pinched it from him, that's the way employees get cheated, they have to agree to that in advance, in writing; so thanks to the patent the firm became millionaires, he only works with Pums because he's inventing a new model now, which will completely cut out the one the firm stole from him. A model like that costs a lot of money. He can't give it away to Mieze, it's a huge secret, but everything in the world will be changed if it comes off, all the street-cars, fire-engines, garbage disposal, everything, it can be adapted to everything, anything at all. They tell each other stories about their auto trip to the masked ball, how the oak trees whizzed by, along the road, I give you 128 days of the year, each with its morning, noon, and night.

"Yoo-hoo, yoo-hoo," Reinhold calls across the wood. That's Reinhold. They answer: "Yoo-hoo, yoo-hoo." Karl goes and hides, but Mieze grows more serious when Reinhold comes up.

The two cops in blue got up from the stone. And they said that their investigation had been futile and without results, there's nothing to be done, only unimportant things happen here, all we can do is to give a written report to the authorities. And if something should happen, well, we'll read about it anyway, it'll be on the poster column.

But in the woods Mieze and Reinhold are walking alone, a few little birds chirp and twitter softly. Overhead the tree-tops begin to sing.

First one tree sang, and then another tree, then they sang together, then they were silent again, and then they sang above the heads of the two.

There is a mower, death yclept, has power which the Lord has kept. When he 'gins his knife to whet, keener it grows and keener yet.

"Oh, I'm glad, really glad, to be back again in Freienwalde, Reinhold. You know, day before yesterday, it was pretty wasn't it, really pretty." "Only a bit too short, Fräulein. You musta been tired, I knocked at your door, but ye didn't open it." "The air stings my skin, and then that ride and everything." "Well, wasn't it just a bit nice, though?" "Certainly, what do you mean?" "I just mean, when you go for a walk like that, and with such a pretty little young lady." "Pretty young lady, now stop your joshin'. Do I say pretty gentleman?" "Well, the fact that you go walkin' with me—" "What about it?" "Well, I imagine there ain't much in a fellow like me. That you should go walking with me, Fräulein, you can believe me, it gives me really a lotta pleasure." He's a lamb. "Haven't you got a girl-friend?" "Girl-friend, what's a girl-friend nowadays?" "Oh, well." "Yep. There's all kinds of 'em. You don't know anything about that, Fräulein. You got a friend there who's straight, and he does something for you. But a girl, she just wants to amuse herself, and as for her heart—why, she ain't got any." "You certainly must be outa luck." "You see, Fräulein, that's how all that—well, that business of exchanging dames came up. But you don't want to hear nothin' about that, do you?" "Oh, go on, what was that, anyway?" "I can tell you exactly what it was, and you'll understand it then. Can a fellow keep a dame longer than a coupla months or a coupla weeks when she ain't worth nothin'? Well, supposin' she flops around, or she ain't worth nothin', don't understand nothin', gets mixed up in everything, or boozes, maybe?" "Why, that's rotten." "Y'see, Mieze, that's what happened to me. That's the way things happen to a feller. Just a lotta trash, rubbish, filth. It all come outa the garbage-can. Would you like to be married to somethin' like that? Well, not me, not for a single hour. And so a fellow stands it for a little while, a coupla weeks, maybe, and then he simply don't go any more, she's just got to get out, and there I am again, 'taint nice. But it's nice here." "I suppose there's a little variety in it too, ain't there?" Reinhold laughs: "Whatcha mean, Mieze?" "Well, well, you probably like a change, too, once in a while, eh?" "Well, why not, we're all human beings after all, ain't we?"

Laughing, they walk along arm-in-arm, it's September 1st. The trees keep on singing. It's one long sermon.

To everything there is a season, and a time to every purpose under the heaven; to everything its hour, to everything its year, a time to be born, and a time to die, a time to plant and a time to pluck up that which is planted; to everything its season, a time to kill, and a time to heal; a time to break down and a time to build up; a time to get, and a time to lose; a time to keep and a time to cast away; a time to rend and a time to sew, a time to keep silence, and a time to speak. To everything there is a season. Therefore I say there is nothing better than to laugh and to be happy. Better than to be happy. Happy, let us be happy. There is nothing better beneath the sun than to laugh and to be happy.

Reinhold holds Mieze's hand, he is walking on her right, what a strong arm he has! "You know Mieze, as a matter of fact, I didn't have the courage to invite you, that time, y'know when I mean." And then we walk for half an hour and talk very little. It's dangerous to walk so long without saying anything. But you can feel the pressure of his right arm.

Where shall I take the sweet little minx, gosh, she certainly is a very special line, I believe I'll save that girl up for later on, a fellow's got to enjoy life, maybe I'll drag her into the hotel, and in the night, in the night, when the moon shines bright. "Why, you've got your hand all covered with scars and you're tattooed on your chest, too?" "Yep, d'ye want to see it?" "Why did you have yourself tattooed?" "It depends where, Fräulein." Mieze sways on his arm, sniggering: "I can guess it, the feller I had before Franz, the way he had himself painted up, you wouldn't believe it!" "It hurts, but it's nice. You want to see it, Fräulein?" He lets go her arm, quickly bares his chest, shows his chest, here we are. It's an anvil with a laurel-wreath around it. "Now just you button yourself up, Reinhold." "Have a good look at it." There's fire in him, blind hunger, he grabs her head and crushes her to his breast: "Kiss it, you, kiss it, you must kiss it." But she does not kiss it. Her head remains there crushed beneath his hands: "Lemme go." He releases her: "Say, don't put on like that." "I'll be goin'." The little bitch, I'll get you yet, the way that bitch talks to me. He fastens his shirt, I'll get her yet, she's putting on airs, hold your horses, old boy, quiet now: "Have I done anything to you, look, I'm buttoning myself up. There. Well, I suppose you've seen a man before, ain't you?"

Why am I hanging around with this here fellow, he's mussed up my hair, a regular rowdy, I guess I'll beat it. To everything there is a season, to everything, to everything.

"Now don't get sore, Fräulein, it just came over me, all of a sudden. Just on the spur of the moment. Y'know, there are moments like that in a man's life." "Y'needn't grab my head for that." "Don't get sore, Mieze." I'll grab ye somewhere else. That wild passion sweeps over him again. All I need is to touch her. "Mieze, let's be friends again." "All right, but you must behave." "O.K." Arm-in-arm. He smiles at her and she smiles down into the grass. "Wasn't so bad, Mieze, now was it? We only bark, we don't bite." "I'm wondering what that anvil's for, some men have a woman there, or a heart or somethin' like that, but an anvil!" "Well, what do you think it is, Mieze?" "Nothin'. How should I know?" "That's my coat of arms." "An anvil?" "Yep. It's to lay somebody on." He grins at her. "You certainly are a pig. Mighta been better if you'd had 'em put a bed on it." "Nope, an anvil's better. The anvil's better." "Are you a blacksmith?" "Kinda. A guy like me is everything. But you don't quite understand about that anvil, Mieze. Nobody can come too near me, Fräulein, without there bein' trouble right away. But you mustn't believe I bite right away, certainly I wouldn't bite you. We're takin' such a nice walk and I'd like to sit down, too, if there's a hollow around anywhere." "You're all about the same, you Pums fellers, ain't you?" "All depends, Mieze, it's not so easy to get along with us." "Well, and what are you guys up to, anyway?" How am I gonna get her to sit down in the hollow, there ain't a soul about. "Gee, Mieze, you'd better ask Franz about that, he knows just as much as I do." "But he don't say nothin'." "That's fine. He's clever. Better not say nothin'." "He could to me!" "What do you want to know?" "What you're up to." "Will I get a kiss for it?" "If you tell me."

Then he has her in his arms. That boy has a strong pair of arms. And how he can hug! To everything there is a season; a time to plant and a time to pluck up; a time to get and a time to lose. I can't breathe. He won't let go. It's hot all right. Lemme go. If he does that again a couple of times, I'm done for. Gee, he's got to tell me first, what's the matter with Franz, what Franz really wants, and everything that's happened and what those fellows think about it. "Now, lemme go, Reinhold."

"All right." He lets her go, stands there, then he falls down on the ground before her, kisses her shoes, he must be crazy, kisses her stockings, farther up, her dress, her hands, to everything a season, all the way up to her throat. She laughs, and moves her arms about excitedly: "Go away, go away, you must be crazy." He is on fire; they ought to give you a shower-bath. He pants and coughs, he tries to bite her throat, he stammers something, but she can't understand him, of his own accord he releases her throat, why, he's just like a bull. His arm lies on hers, and while they walk, the trees keep singing. "Look here, Mieze, here's a nice little hollow place, just built for us—just look. A week-end love-nest. Somebody's been cookin' here. Let's clear it up. Might get my pants dirty." Shall I sit down now? Maybe he'll talk better then. "Well, I don't care. It'd be nicer to sit on a coat." "Wait a minute, Mieze, I'll take my coat off." "That's sweet of you."

They are lying on a slope in a grassy hollow. She pushes a tin can away with her foot, then turns on to her belly and quickly slips her arm across his breast. So here we are. She smiles at him. When he pushes his vest off his chest and the anvil appears, she does not take her head away. "Now you're gonna tell me something, Reinhold." He crushes her to his breast, so here we are, fine, here's the girl, everything's jake, a fine kid, a humdinger. I'll keep her a long time, and Franz can beef as much as he likes, he won't get her back so soon as all that. Reinhold slides downwards, pulling Mieze along, presses her in his arms and kisses her mouth. He sucks himself in, not a thought in his head, only an ecstasy, a wild desire, pure savagery and that's all there is to it, every gesture is prescribed, let none come near to impede him now! A rending, a tearing which no hurricane, no avalanche of rocks can hinder, it is the shell from a cannon, a mine exploding. All that rushes against it is shattered, thrust aside and on and on it goes, on and on.

"Oh, not so tight, Reinhold!" He makes me weak; if I don't look out, he'll get me. "Mieze." He looks up blinking, but does not release her. "Well, Miezeken?" "Well, Reinhold?" "Whatcha studyin' about me?" "Say, it's really wicked what you're doing to me. How long have you known Franz?" "Your Franz?" "Yes." "Your Franz, well, is he still yours?" "Well, whose, then?" "Well, who am I?" "How d'you mean?" She wants to hide her head on his breast, but he forces it up. "Well, who am I?" She throws herself at him, presses her lips against his mouth, and he flames up again, I love him a bit too, the way he twists and burns. No flood of water, no giant firehose could extinguish that; flames are streaming out of the house, they grow from within. "So now you better let me go again." "What do you want, girlie?" "Nothin'. To be with you." "All right then, I'm yours too, ain't I? Did you break with Franz?" "No." "Did you break with him, Mieze?" "No, I'd rather you'd tell me somethin' about him. You've known him for a long time." "Can't tell you anything about him." "Aw, go on!" "I won't tell you nothin', Mieze." He seizes her and throws her down by his side, but she wrestles with him: "No, I don't want to." "Don't be such a mule, girlie." "I wanta get up, I'm gettin' all dirty here." "And suppose I was to tell you somethin' now." "That'd be fine." "What'll I get for it, Mieze?" "Whatever you want." "Everything?" "Well—we'll see." "Everything?" Their faces are close together, aflame. She doesn't say anything. I'm not sure myself what I'll do, something flashes through him, all thought gone, no thoughts, unconsciousness.

He sits up, must wipe my face off, pugh, the woods, you sure get dirty here. "I'll tell you somethin' about your Franz. I've known him a long time. You know, he's a special kind of a bozo. We met in the Prenzlauer Allee saloon. Last winter. He was peddlin' papers. And then he knew somebody there, Meck, that's right. That's where I got to know him. Then we used to meet there, and I told you somethin' about the girls before, didn't I?" "Is that true?" "And how! But he's a boob, Biberkopf, that dumbbell, he can't brag about it, it all comes from me, maybe you think it's him that got me all them women? My God, his women! No, if he'd had his way, we'da gone to the Salvation Army, so as to mend my ways." "But you ain't mendin' 'em, are you, Reinhold?" "No, you can see that. Nothin' doin' with me. You got to take me the way I am. That's as sure as you're alive, and you can't do nothin' about it. But that guy, Mieze, that pimp o' yours, that's the guy you can change. You certainly are a pretty baby. Listen, sweetie, how can you pick up a bozo like that, with one arm, a pretty kid like you; you can get ten on each finger if you want to." "Ah, cut that out." "Well, yes, love's blind in both eyes, but that's the limit. You know what that pimp o' yours wants with us now? He wants to play the big guy with us. Us, of all people! First he wanted to send me to the sinners' bench at the Salvation Army, but it didn't work. And now!" "Say, don't knock him like that, I can't listen to it." "Tickle-tickle! I know, he's your darlin' little Franz, he's still your dear little Franzeken, ain't he?" "He don't do nothin' against you, Reinhold."

To everything its season, to everything, everything. A terrible man, wish he'd let me go, I don't want to bother with him, he needn't tell me anything. "No, he don't hurt us, he'd have a hard time doin' it, Mieze. But you certainly caught a fine specimen in him, Mieze. Did he ever tell you anything about his arm? What? Ain't you his girl, or wasn't you? Come here, Miezeken, you're my sweet little darling, don't put on." What'll I do? I don't want him. To everything its season, a time to plant, to pluck up, to rend, and to sew; to weep, and to dance; to lament, and to laugh. "Come on, Mieze, whatcha want with a nut like that? You're my sweet little girl. Now don't pretend. You're not a countess yet, just because you're with that feller. You oughta be glad to be rid of him." You oughta be glad; why should I be? "Let 'im beef now, he ain't got his Mieze any more." "Just stop that, and don't push me like that, I'm not made of iron." "No of flesh, of nice flesh, say Mieze, let's have your little beak!" "What's the matter with you, you fool, I told you not to push me. You're on the wrong track. Since when am I your Mieze?"

Let's get out of here. Left my hat down there. He'll smash me up. Better run off. Already—he hasn't gotten out of the hollow yet—she begins to yell, she yells "Franz" and starts to run. He gets up, and runs like mad, he's caught her, he's in his shirt-sleeves. They fall near a tree, and lie there. She kicks, but he's over her, holding her mouth. "Are you goin' to scream, you bitch, are you screamin' again? What are you yellin' about? Am I doin' anything to you, will you keep quiet? He didn't smash any of your bones the other day, did he? Better look out, that's not my way of doin' things." He takes his hand away from her mouth. "I won't yell." "Then it's all right. And now you get up, you, and go on back there and get your hat. I never use force on a woman. I ain't never done it as long as I live. But you'd better not get me mad this way."

He walks behind her.

"Needn't brag about your Franz, even if you are his whore." "I'm goin' home now." "Whatcha mean, goin' home, got a screw loose, or somethin', maybe you don't know who you're talkin' to, you can talk that way to that poor nut o' yours, but not to me." "Oh—I don't know what to do." "Go back to the hollow like a good girl."

When a little calf is to be slaughtered, they tie a rope round its neck and lead it to the bench. Then they lift the little calf, put it on the bench, and tie it firmly.

They walk to the hollow. He says: "Lie down." "Me?" "If you yell! I like you, kid, otherwise I would'na come here, I tell you; even if you are his whore, that's no reason why you should act like a countess. Better not start any of that with me. You know that don't do no good to nobody. I don't care whether it's man, woman or child, I'm ticklish about it. You can learn a thing or two from your pimp. He can tell you somethin'. If it don't embarrass him, that is. But you can hear it from me, too. I can tell you all about who he is. And what you'll be in for, if you start somethin' with me. Y'know he once wanted to try all that stuff he's got up there in that noodle of his. I guess he wanted to squeal on us. He stood watch once where we was workin'. And he says he won't help, he's a respectable man. He ain't got no holes in his jacket, that fellow. Come along, says I to him. So then he had to come along in the car, and I didn't know what to do with the bozo, he always did have a big mouth, but wait a minute, there's a car back of us, and I thinks to myself, now watch out, m'boy, you with your highfalutin' airs, you gotta act decent to me. And out of the car he flies. Now you know where he left his arm."

Icy hands, icy feet, so it was him. "Now you just lie down, and be nice, and behave proper." He's a murderer! "You dirty dog, you crook." He beams. "Y'see. Now yell as hard as you can." Now you're goin' to behave. She screams and weeps: "You dog, you wanted to kill him, you got him into trouble and now you want to have me, you nasty thing." "Yep, that's what I want." "You nasty thing, I could spit on you." He holds her mouth closed. "Are you goin' to?" She turns blue, and tugs at his hand: "Murderer, help! Franz, Franzeken!"

Its season, its season, to everything its season! A time to strangle, a time to heal; to break down and to build up, to rend, and to sew, to everything its season. She throws herself down, trying to escape. They wrestle in the hollow. Help, Franz!

We'll pull that job all right, we'll play a little joke on your Franz, then he'll have something to think about the whole week. "I wanta go home." "Try and do it. Many a one has tried it."

He kneels on her back, his hands are around her throat, his thumbs in the nape of her neck, her body contracts, contracts. Her body contracts. There's a season, to be born, and to die, to be born and to die, to everything its season.

Murderer, you say, and you coaxed me here, and I guess you wanta fool me, you tart, but you don't know Reinhold.

Power, power, there is a mower, has power which the Lord hath kept. Lemme go. She's still writhing and kicking, she kicks from behind. We'll set the child a-rocking, and the dogs can eat what remains of you.

Her body contracts, contracts, her body, Mieze's body. Murderer, she says. She'll find out, he probably told you that, your sweet Franz.

Whereupon the animal is given a blow on the neck with a wooden club, and the arteries on both sides of the neck are opened with the knife; a tin basin receives the blood.

It is eight o'clock, and the wood is fairly dark. The trees rock and sway.

That was heavy work. Is she still talkin'? No, she's stopped her yapping. The bitch. That's what you get when you go out on an excursion with a tart like that.

Heap it with brushwood, tie a handkerchief to the next tree, so we can find it again. I'm through with her, where's Karl? Must fetch him. A full hour later he is back with Karl, that guy has no guts, look how he's trembling, his knees are wobbly, and a fellow is expected to work with such a greenhorn! It is quite dark, they search with flashlights, here's the handkerchief. They get spades from the car. The body is buried deep, sand on top, brushwood above, watch out for tracks, old boy, wipe 'em away, pull yourself together, Karl. You act as if you were already in for it yourself, by golly.

"All right then, here's my passport, it's a good passport, Karle, and here's some money and you'd better make yourself scarce as long as things are so hot. You'll get some money, don't you worry. Write to Pums's address, as usual. I'll go on back. Nobody's seen me, and they can't do anything to you, you've got your alibi. O.K. Now beat it."

The trees rock and sway. To everything, everything.

It's pitch dark. Her face is smashed, her teeth are smashed, her mouth, lips, tongue, throat, body, limbs, abdomen, all are smashed. I'm yourn, you shall console me. Stettin Depot Police Station, Aschinger's; I'm feeling bad, come on, we'll soon be home, I'm yourn.

The trees rock, and a wind rises. Whoo, hooh, hooh, oo, hoo. Night advances, her body lies there, all smashed up, her eyes, her tongue, her mouth, come on, we'll soon be home. I'm yourn. A tree creaks on the edge of the wood. Whoo, whoo, whoo, whoooo, that's the storm, it's coming with fife and drum, it's now lurking there above the wood, now it breaks loose howling and slithers down. A wailing in the brushwood. Like a scraping sound, and then it howls like a dog that's locked up and wails and whimpers, just listen to him whimper, someone must have stepped on him, and with a heavy heel, now it is silent again.

Whoo, whoo, whoo, the storm is coming up again, it is night, the woods lie quiet, tree beside tree. They have grown up in peace. They are serried like a herd. They stand so penned together that the storm does not easily assail them, only the sentinels on the edge and the weaklings get it in the neck. Let's cling together, let's hold fast, it is night, the sun is gone, hoo, hooh, hoo, there it starts again, it's here, it's below, above, around us. A yellow-red glare in the sky, and night again, a yellow-red glare, night, the whimpering and whistling grows louder. It's the sentinels, they know what's coming, and they whimper, and with them the grass, it may bend and quiver, but what of the massive trees? Then suddenly the wind has ceased blowing, has given up, abandoned the game, but leaves them squeaking still, what will it do now?

If you want to demolish a house, you can't do it with your hand, a steam-shovel is needed, or a charge of dynamite from below. All the wind does is to expand its chest a bit. Watch now how it draws in its breath and then puffs it out, whoo, whoo, whoo, it draws it in and puffs it out, whoo, whoo, whoo. Every breath is heavy as a mountain. Puffs it out, whoo, whoo, whoo. The mountain is rolled forward, rolled back, puffs it out, whoo, whoo, whoo. Back and forth. Its breath is weighty as a ball that drives and pushes against the wood. And when the wood stands serried, like a herd on the hills, the wind runs over the herd and goes roaring by.

Now it starts: boom, zoom, without fife or drum. The trees sway right and left. Boom, zoom, boom. But they cannot keep in time. Just when the trees bend towards the left, boom it goes to the left again, and they snap and crack, grate and grind, burst, crackle, and thud down. Boom, mutters the storm, bend over to the left, hoo, hoo, oo, hoo, now back, it's passed, it's gone, it's just a question of watching for the proper moment. Woom, there it is back again, look out, boom, zoom, zoom, those are bombs from airplanes, it wants to tear the wood down, to crush the whole wood.

The trees howl and rock, there is a crackle, they break, there's a rattle, boom. Life's at stake, boom, zoom, the sun is gone, tottering weights, night, boom, zoom.

I am yourn, come now, we'll soon be there, I'm yourn. Boom, zoom . . .

EIGHTH BOOK

It was no use. It was still no use. Franz Biberkopf has received the hammer blow, he knows he is lost and he does not yet know why.

Franz notices Nothing; the World goes on

September 2nd. Franz goes about as usual, rides out with the frisky business go-between to the public baths in Wannsee. On the third, a Monday, he's astonished that Miezeken hasn't come back yet, she didn't leave any word, the landlady can't remember anything, she hasn't telephoned, either. Well, perhaps she's on an excursion with her exalted friend and protector! He'll probably unload her soon. Let's wait till evening.

It's noon, Franz is sitting at home, the bell rings, a special delivery letter, from her beau, to Mieze. What's this? I thought she was with him, what does it mean? I'll open the letter: "And I am wondering, Sonia, why you don't even call me up. Yesterday and the day before I waited at the office, as agreed." What's this, where is she?

Franz gets up, where's my hat, don't get this at all. I'll go see this man. Taxi. "She hasn't been with you? When was she here the last time? Friday? Is that so." They both look at each other. "Haven't you a nephew, maybe he went along." The gentleman gets wild, what, I'll have him up here right away, you stay here a while. Slowly they drink red wine. The nephew arrives: "This is Sonia's fiancé, do you know where she is?" "I, what's the matter?" "When did you see her last?" "Oh, a long time ago, about two weeks." "That's right, she told me about that. Not since?" "No." "You've heard nothing?" "Nothing at all, but why, what's the matter?" "Our friend here will tell you himself." "She's been away since Saturday, didn't say a word, left everything lying around, not a word as to where

293

she went." The gentleman-friend: "Maybe she's found somebody else." "Don't think so." The three of them drink red wine. Franz sits there quietly: "I suppose we'd better wait a bit."

Her face smashed, her teeth smashed, her eyes smashed, her lips, tongue, neck, body, legs, abdomen smashed.

She's not back next day. She's not back. Everything's lying around just as she left it. She's not there. Wonder if Eva knows anything. "Didja have a row with her Franz?" "Nope, two weeks ago, but everything's all right now." "A pick-up?" "Nope, she told me about her friend's nephew, but he's there, I saw him." "Maybe it might be well to watch him, maybe she's with him." "Think so?" "Y'might keep an eye on him. Y'never know with Mieze. She's funny that way."

She is not there. Franz does nothing for two days, thinking, I won't run after her. Still he hears nothing, nothing at all, and then he trails the nephew for one whole day, till the next noon; as the nephew's landlady is out, Franz and the classy go-between slip quickly into the room, the door's easily opened with a hook; not a soul in the place, in his room there are lots of books, no sign of a dame. Some nice pictures on the walls, books, she's not here. I know her powder, it don't smell like that, come on, don't take anything along, leave that poor woman alone, she makes her living letting out furnished rooms.

What's the matter? Franz sits in his room. For hours. Where is Mieze? She's gone, not a word from her. What do you say to that? Everything topsy-turvy in the room, he took the bed apart, put it together again. She's let me down. It's not possible. It's not possible. Let me down. Did I do somethin'? I didn't do nothin'. She didn't hold that business about the nephew against me.

Who's that? Eva. "You're sittin' in the dark, Franz, why don't you light the gas?" "Mieze's given me the slip. Is that possible?" "Don't bother, old kid. She'll come back. She likes you, she won't run away from you, I understand people." "I know all that. You think I'm worryin' about that? She'll come all right." "You see, the girl's likely gone off somewhere, met some old friend from the old days, out on a little flyer. I knew her before, when you hadn't got to know her yet, that's the way she does, she gets ideas like that into her head." "But it's queer just the same, I can't understand it." "She loves you. Say, put your hand on my stomach, Franz." "What is it?" "Well, it's by you, don't you remember, a kid. She wanted that, Mieze, didn't she?" "What?" "Why, yes."

Franz lays his head against Eva's body. "Mieze wanted it. Lemme sit down. It's not possible." "Well, look out, Franz, when she comes back, she'll make a face." Eva starts crying herself. "Say, Eva, who's excited now? You are!" "It's driving me batty. I just can't make that girl out." "Now I have to console you." "No, just nerves, on account of the kid, maybe." "You just watch out, when she comes back she'll start a grand old rumpus about it." She goes on crying. "What'll we do about it, Franz? That isn't like her at all." "First you say: that's what she always does, she goes on a bust with somebody, and afterwards you say, that's not like her!" "I don't know, Franz!"

Eva presses Franz's head against her arm. She looks down on Franzeken's head: the hospital in Magdeburg, they ran over his arm, he killed Ida, Lord, what's the matter with the man? He is always in trouble. Maybe Mieze is dead. There's something after him. Something happened to Mieze. She collapses on a chair, and, terrified, lifts her hands to her face. Franz is startled. She sobs and sobs. She knows there is something after him, something has happened to Mieze.

He urges her to speak, but she is silent. Then she recovers herself. "I won't let nobody take this child from me. And I don't care what Herbert thinks about it." "Has he said anything?" He skips over six miles of notions. "No, he thinks it's his. But I'll keep it." "All right, Eva, and I'll be godfather." "You're in a good humor, Franz." "They can't put it over on me so easy. Now, cheer up, Eva. Don't I know my Mieze? She won't roll under a bus. I know it'll come out all right." "If you think so, Franzeken, all right; so long!" "Well, let's have a kiss." "To think that you should be so cheerful, Franz."

We got legs, we got teeth, we got eyes, we got arms, let any guy come on that wants to bite us, that wants to bite Franz, let him come. Franz has got two arms, he's got two legs, he's got muscles, he smashes everything into a cocked hat. They ought to know Franz, he's no milksop. Whatever lies behind us, whatever lies before us, let any guy come along that wants, we'll take a drink on it, we'll take two drinks on it, we'll take nine drinks on it.

We got no legs, alas, we got no teeth, we got no eyes, we got no arms, anyone can come up and bite Franz, he's a milksop, alas, he can't defend himself, he can only drink.

"I gotta do somethin', Herbert, I can't just go on lookin' at this thing." "What do you wanta do, honey?" "I can't just go on lookin' at this thing.

He don't notice nothin', he sits there and says she'll come back, and she'll come back, and I look in the papers every day, and there's nothin' in 'em. Didja hear anything?" "Nope." "Can't you go around investigatin' a bit and see if anybody has heard, heard anything from anybody?" "That's foolish, Eva, what you're sayin' now. What you find mysterious about the business, why, that's not really mysterious at all. What is it, anyway? The kid's left him. My God, we won't tear our hair out for that. He'll get another jane." "Would you talk like that about me, too?" "Now cut that stuff out, Eva, but, when a girl's like that." "She ain't, I got her for him, I've looked around in the morgue already, watch out, Herbert, somethin' has happened to her. He's always in trouble, our Franz. Something's after him. Say, haven't you heard nothin' at all?" "I don't know nothin' at all." "Well, sometimes something comes out when they get together at the club. Hasn't anybody seen her? She certainly ain't disappeared from the earth like that. Say—if she don't get back soon, I'm gonna go to Police Headquarters." "You'd do a thing like that, you would?" "Don't laugh, sure I'd do it. I've gotta find her, Herbert, somethin' has happened, she hasn't gone off by herself, she'd never go away from me like that, and from Franz neither. And he don't notice it." "I can't listen to all this. That's a lotta hot air, and now let's go to the movies, Eva."

At the movies they watch a play.

In the third act when the noble hero is apparently killed by a bandit, Eva sighs. And when Herbert looks her way, she's just about to slide off her seat, and she faints, imagine it. Afterwards they walk silently arm-in-arm through the street. Herbert is astonished: "Your old man is goin' to have lots of fun, if you act like this." "He shot him, did you see that, Herbert?" "That wasn't real, it was only a trick, didn't you spot that? Why, you're still trembling." "You gotta do somethin' about it, Herbert, it can't go on like this." "You'd better go on a trip, tell your old man you're sick." "No, what'll we do? Please do somethin', Herbert. Didn't you help Franz when he had that trouble with his arm, now go ahead and do this, too. Please, please, do." "I can't Eva, what can I do?" She cries. He has to help her into the automobile.

Franz doesn't have to go begging, for Eva slips him something and he gets something from Pums, too, they have a new project for the end of September. Towards the end of September, Matter, the tinner, comes back. He has been abroad, working at something or other. When he sees

Franz again, he says he was recuperating, lung trouble. He still looks wretched; he hasn't got much better. Franz says Mieze is gone, he knew her, didn't he? But he's not to tell anybody about it, there are some people who laugh themselves sick when a girl runs away from a fellow. "Keep mum about it to Reinhold, will ye, I've had some trouble with him about dames, he'd laugh himself sick, if he heard about that. I haven't got another one yet," Franz smiles, "and don't want any, either." He has lines on his forehead, and around his mouth. But he holds his head firmly upon his neck and presses his lips together.

There's lots of activity in the city. Tunney retains the heavyweight championship of the world, but the Americans are not really pleased about it, they don't like the man. He was down in the 7th to the count of nine. Then Dempsey got groggy. That's Dempsey's last great fight. The whole thing was over at four fifty-eight o'clock, September 23, 1928. You can hear about that and about the flying record on the Cologne—Leipzig line as well, and then they say, there's an economic war on between oranges and bananas. But we listen to it with tightly closed eyes all through a little dormer-window.

How does a plant protect itself against the cold? Many vegetables cannot resist even a slight frost. Others are able to counteract the cold by protective measures of a chemical nature in their cells. The most effective protection is the transformation of the starch content of their cells into sugar. The utility of some garden produce is, to be sure, not increased through this formation of sugar, and the best proof of this can be seen in potatoes which become sweet when frozen. But there are also cases where the sugar content of a plant or fruit produced by the influence of frost is needed to make them palatable; this is the case with wild fruit. If you leave such fruit on the tree until the light frost begins, they soon develop so much sugar that their flavor is changed and substantially improved. The same thing applies to haws.

What does it matter if two Berlin rowers are drowned in the Danube, or Nungesser falls near Ireland with his "White Bird"? What are the newsboys yelling outside, you can buy it for 10 pfennigs, then throw it away, leave it lie somewhere. They wanted to lynch the Hungarian Prime Minister, because his automobile ran over a peasant boy. If they had lynched him, the headline would have been: "Lynching of the Hungarian Premier near the City of Kaposvar," that would have added to the excitement, the highbrows would have read "lunching" instead of lynching and laughed over it, the other 80 per cent would have said: too bad, only one, or else, none of my business, as a matter of fact, we ought to do the same thing here.

They are laughing a lot in Berlin. Near Dobrin, at the corner of the Kaiser-Wilhelm Strasse, three persons are sitting around the table, a fat old boy, a cheery bird he is, and his little patootie, a nice plump little thing, if only she wouldn't scream so much when she laughs, and then another fellow, his friend, who's rather out of it, the fat boy pays for him and he just listens and has to laugh with them. Fairly well-to-do folks. The plump little broad slaps her sugar-daddy's mouth every five minutes and screams: "That man certainly has funny notions!" Then he necks her, it lasts a good two minutes. What the other chap, who just looks on, thinks about it, is none of their business. The sugar-daddy tells a story. "So she says to him: What have you done to me? Says she to him: What have you done now? And item number three's just: bing!" His companion grins: "You sure are a prize funny man." The sugar-daddy, with delight: "Not as funny as you are dumb." They drink some bouillon, and the fat boy starts telling stories again.

"An aviator walks on to a field, and there's a girl sitting there. Says he: 'Hey, Miss Lindbergh, how about some trick flying together?' Says she: 'My name ain't Lindbergh, its Fokker.' 'Oh, boy, let's go!' " All three roar with laughter. The fat man states: "As a matter of fact, we're having Scotch broth at home tonight." The little dame: "That man certainly has funny notions."

"Now, listen, ever heard this one: A girl says: 'Tell me, what does this mean: bomme de terre?' 'Bomme de terre? In from the front.' 'You see!' says she, 'I thought right away it was somethin' dirty! Sh-sh-sh!' " It's very nice and comfortable and lots of fun in here; the young lady has to step out to the toilet six times. "Said the hen to the rooster, said she: You'll let me get near it, maybe. Waiter, check, I owe for three cognacs, two ham sandwiches, three bouillons and three pieces of shoe leather." "Shoe leather? Those were biscuits." "Well, you can call them that if you want to. I call them shoe leather. Nothin' smaller? Because I got a little one at home in the cradle, and I always stick a groschen in his mouth for him to chew on. Well, sweetie, let's go. The laughing hour's over, we're off, we're on our way to Mandelay."

Some women and girls are walking across Alexanderstrasse and the square, each carrying a fetus in her belly, protected by law. It is hot, and the women and girls are sweating outside, but the fetus within sits quietly in his corner, the temperature is just right for him as he walks across the

Alexanderplatz, but many a fetus will fare badly later on: he'd better not laugh too soon.

Others are running about trying to hook whatever they can; some have their bowels full and others are wondering how to get them filled. Hahn's department store is entirely wrecked, all the other houses are full of shops, but they only look like shops, as a matter of fact, there are nothing but calls, just decoy calls, twittering bird-notes, crickle-crackle, a chirping without words.

So I returned and considered all the oppressions that are done under the sun; and behold the tears of such as were oppressed and they had no comforter; and on the side of their oppressors there was power; but they had no comforter. Wherefore I praised the dead which are already dead.

The dead I praised. To everything a season; a time to rend, and a time to sew, a time to keep, and a time to cast away. I praised the dead who lie sleeping beneath the trees.

Eva comes gliding up again. "Franz, aren't you ever goin' to do somethin'? Three weeks have passed, y'know, if you were mine and worried so little—" "I can't tell nobody, you know about it, Eva, and so does Herbert, and the tinner, and nobody else. I can't tell nobody, they'd only laugh at me. And I can't report to the police either, can I? If you don't wanta give me nothin', Eva, then don't bother. Why—I'll go back to work again." "And to think you're not showing any grief, not a tear! Gee, I could shake you. I can't do anything, anyway." "Me neither."

Things are getting Lively, the Gangsters quarrel among themselves

Early in October the dispute which Pums had feared started among the members of the gang. About money. Pums, as usual, regards the sale of their stuff as the main business of the gang, Reinhold and others, including Franz, its acquisition. It's according to the latter and not according to the sales, that the division of the spoils should be regulated; they constantly attribute too high receipts to Pums and resent his monopoly in the dealings with the fences; the reliable fences want to deal with Pums alone. The gang, although Pums makes many concessions and allows them a free hand wherever possible, insist that something has to be done about it. They are more for union methods. He says they've got them already. But they refuse to believe that.

Then the burglary in Stralauer Strasse takes place. Though Pums can no longer take an active part, he goes along with them. It is a bandage factory in Stralauer Strasse, a building with a courtyard. They got wind that there is money in the cash-box of the private office. That's supposed to be a blow against Pums: not goods, but money. There won't be any cheating, when there's money to be divided. That's why Pums himself takes a hand in it. Two of them climb up the fire-escape and quietly unscrew the lock on the front-door of the office. The tinner starts. All the office safes are cracked, but there are only a few marks lying about, and some stamps; two gasoline tanks in the corridor, we might need them. Then they wait for Karlchen, the tinner, to start operations. As bad luck would have it, he burns his hand with his blow-pipe and can't go on working at the safe. Reinhold tries but he has no practice. Pums takes the pipe out of his hand, but nothing doing. Things are getting ticklish. They have to stop, as the watchman is due soon.

Furiously they take the gasoline tanks and pour oil all over the furniture, on the damned safe too, and throw matches into it. Pums is going to score, is he? But they'll be damned if they'll let him. So they do it, but they throw the match a little too soon and it singes Pums a bit. The feller isn't supposed to be here, anyhow. His back is all burnt, they run down the stairs, signal: "Watchman." Pums just succeeds in getting into his car. That'll teach him a lesson, I'll tell the world. But how will they get any money now?

Pums has the laugh on 'em. Goods are and remain a better proposition. This is the age of the specialist. What shall we do? Pums is decried as an exploiter, a blood-sucker, a crook. But you can never be sure; if things are pushed too far, he may take advantage of his connections to form a new gang. In the Sporting Club next Thursday he's going to explain, I'll do what I can; if you want to, I can submit bills to you in writing, that's just it, you can't get anything on him, and, if you don't work with him, they'll say in the Club, it's not our fault if you don't wanta come along, the feller does what he can, and if he gets a little bit more in his pockets, don't get on your high horse, haven't you got your molls to earn for you, but he's got his old woman, and that ain't much. So they keep on working with him in the same old way, damned exploiter that he is!

The rage of the entire gang explodes on the head of the tinner who missed fire in Stralauer Strasse, and made 'em look like fools. We got no use for a bungler like that. He's burnt his hand, has to go to the doctor now, he always worked well, but all he gets now is a lot of abuse.

They gave me a dirty deal, he thinks, and goes around growling. They tripped me up in my business when I had one; I take a swig here and there, and my wife bawls me out, and on New Year's Eve when I come home, that damned tart o' mine ain't there. Doesn't get home till seven o'clock, been sleeping with another fellow, that's how she cheats on me. I've lost my business, and my wife too. And little Mieze, that dirty dog Reinhold. She was mine, she didn't wanta go with him, she rode with me out to that party along the road, she could kiss all right, and then he took her away from me, because I'm just a poor fool. The lousy bastard, then he killed her, the murderer, because she didn't want him, now he acts the big gazook, and I've burnt my hand, and I helped him to carry her, too. He sure is one big yegg, a real murderer. And to think I wanted to take the whole blame for a crook like that. That's the kinda jackass I am!

Keep your Eyes on Karl the Tinner, Something's going to happen in that Man

Karl the tinner looks around for somebody to talk to. He's sitting in the Alexander Quelle opposite Tietz's, two boys escaped from the reformatory beside him and another man, nobody knows who he is, he says he does all kinds of business, anything that turns up, otherwise he's a master wheelwright. He can draw well, they sit together at the table, eat bockwurst while the young wheelwright draws a lot of smutty pictures in his notebook, janes and men and so on. The reformatory boys are mighty pleased, Karl the tinner looks on and thinks that feller can draw very well. The three laugh all the time, the two youngsters are in high spirits, they have just been in Rückerstrasse, there was a raid and they made their escape through the back-door. Karl the tinner goes to the bar.

At that moment two men walk slowly through the place, look right and left, talk with one man who takes out his papers, they look, say a few words, and now the two men are standing at the table beside the three companions; they're frightened, but don't let out a peep, don't say a word. Just go on talking, those are dicks, of course, they have just come from the Rücker bar, they saw us there. The wheelwright goes on drawing his smutty pictures as if nothing had happened, but then one of the bulls whispers to him: "Criminal Police." He opens his coat, there's a brass badge on his vest. His companion does the same thing with the two boys. They have no papers; the wheelwright has a sick-leave ticket and a letter from a girl, all three are ordered to the Kaiser-Wilhelm Strasse police station. The boys say right away what they have been up to, but get the surprise of their lives when the bulls tell them they hadn't noticed them at Rückerstrasse. It was just an accident that they met them in the Alexander Quelle. Well, in that case, we wouldn't have told how we had beat it, and they all laugh together. The bull pats them on the back: "The director will certainly be delighted to see you back." "Oh, he's on his vacation." The wheelwright stands in the station room with the cops, he can talk himself out of the situation, his address is all right, only his hands are too soft for a wheelwright, that's what one of the bulls can't quite understand, he turns his hands around and around, but I haven't been working for a year, shall I tell ye what I think you are, a queer fellow, a fairy, well, I don't know what that is.

Half an hour later he is back in the café. Karl the tinner is loafing around the table; the wheelwright accosts him right away.

"How do you earn your living?" It's twelve o'clock when Karl questions him. "Guess. And what do you do?" "Anything that comes along." "Maybe you're afraid you'll tell me somethin'?" "Well, I bet you ain't a wheelwright, at that." "I'm as good a wheelwright as you are a tinner." "Now don't say that. Look at my hand, it's all burnt. I'm workin' even as a locksmith." "I guess you burnt your fingers at that business of yours, did'ncha?" "Business! Didn't get nothin' out of it." "Who are you workin' with, anyway?" "Are ye tryin' to kid me, askin' questions like that?" Karl asks the wheelwright: "D'you belong to a union?" "Schönhauser Quarter." "I see, the Bowling Club." "Know it?" "Sure enough, I know the Bowling Club. Just ask 'em if they don't know me, Karl the tinner; Paul the mason's there, too." "Well, I'll be damned, so you know him? Why, he's a friend of mine." "We were together in Brandenburg once." "That's right. I'll be . . . Say, how about letting me have 5 marks, I'm broke, my landlady's going to kick me out, and I won't go to the Augusta Shelter, the air's too thick there." "Five marks, here you are, if that's all you want." "Thanks a lot. Well, how about talkin' business?"

The wheelwright is a windbag. Sometimes he's interested in women and then again in boys. If he feels the ground getting hot under him, he makes a touch or hooks something. He, the tinner, and another chap from the Schönhauser Union start an independent partnership, and, whoa, up and at it, and let's pull a coupla jobs in a jiffy. Wherever anything is to be pinched, there's always somebody from the wheelwright's union around. First they hook motorcycles, which gives them freedom of movement and enables them to look around in the vicinity. In this way they're not limited to Berlin, in case they should have something up their sleeves, and chances on something outside the city crop up.

One of their jobs is really nifty. There is a clothing store in the Elsasser Strasse, and there are a couple of tailors in the union who can dispose of things. One night the three of them are standing in front of the shop, it's around three in the morning and the watchman happens to be there, too, looking at his house. The wheelwright asks what's wrong in the house, the others sorta join in the conversation and get to talking about burglaries, how these are dangerous times now and a lot of birds carry revolvers in their pockets, and if they're caught, they put a fellow on the spot. Well, say all three, they wouldn't get mixed up in a thing like that, but is there anything to hook up there? You bet, it's full of goods, men's wear, overcoats, and so on. Might go up and get a new outfit. "You must be cuckoo. Are you goin' to get the man in trouble?" "Trouble, who says anything about trouble? The old gentleman's a human being, after all, he ain't rollin' in money either, what do they pay you for watchin' here, mate?" "Them guys, you know, no use asking about 'em. When a man's 60, and has a coupla pennies as pension and can't do nothin' any more, well, they can treat him any way they like." "That's what I say, here's this old gentleman standin' about all night and catching the rheumatics, I suppose you were in the war too, weren't you?" "Territorial, in Poland, but not digging trenches. No, sir, we had to fight in the trenches." "Needn't tell me. That's the way it was with us, too. Everybody who didn't carry his head under his arm had to go right into the trenches, and that's why you're standing here, mate, watchin' to see if nobody's pinching anything from them fine gentlemen up there. What do you think, neighbor, let's do something here. How do you feel about it, neighbor?" "No, no, say, I ain't got the nerve for that, the boss lives next door and he might hear us, he's such a light sleeper." "We'll be quiet, all right, I tell ye. Come on, let's drink a cup of coffee together, you must have a coffee pot, ain't you, and we'll chew the rag. Why should you worry about that guy, that fat hog?"

Sure enough, the four of them are soon in the watchman's room, upstairs in the office, drinking coffee; the wheelwright is the cleverest of them all, and he whispers something to the watchman, in the meantime the two others sneak outside and start fetching things. The watchman wants to get up, he's got to make his rounds, he doesn't want to know anything at all about this business, so finally the wheelwright suggests: "Let those two go ahead, if you don't notice anything, there's nobody can do nothin' to you, can they?" "What do you mean—don't notice anythin'?" "Tell ye what we'll do: I'll tie you up, you've been attacked, you're an old man, you can't defend yourself now, can you, if I throw a cloth over your head before you've noticed anything, and you've got a gag between your teeth and your legs are tied." "Gee whiz!" "Yeah, now don't act dumb, are you goin' to have your head bashed in for the sake of a stuck-up guy like that, the fat hog? Come on, we'll finish up the pot and then we'll settle it day after tomorrow. Where do you live? Just write it down, we'll divide honestly, let's shake on it." "How much will I get for this?" "Depends on what they get. A hundred marks, no kiddin'." "Two hundred." "All right." Then they smoke, finish up the pot, they fix up everything together, first they need a safe automobile, the tinner telephones for one, they're in luck, in half an hour the Soren auto is at the door.

Then comes the joke; the old watchman sits down in his armchair, the wheelwright gets some copper wire and ties his legs together, but not too tight. The old chap has varicose veins, and he's sensitive down there. The wheelwright binds his arms together with telephone wire, and then the three of them start their fun with the old man, asking how much he wants to get, maybe three hundred, or three hundred and fifty. Then they fetch two pairs of boys' pants and a coarse summer topcoat. They tie the watchman to the chair with the boys' pants, and he says, that's enough now. But they go on joshing him, he defends himself, and gets a couple of whacks in the face, and, before he can yell, he's got the coat over his head. For safety's sake, they tie a towel across his chest. They drag the stuff down to the car. The wheelwright writes out two pasteboard notices: "Fragile. This side up," and hangs them on the watchman's back and front. Then they march off. We haven't picked up any money that easy for a long while.

But the watchman gets scared and he boils with rage at being tied up like that. How'm I gonna get free? They left the doors open so others can come in, too, and pinch things. He can't get his hands free, but the wire on his legs comes undone, if I could only see a bit. Then the old man wriggles and short-steps forward with the armchair stuck to his back like a snail's shell, he marches blindly across the office, his hands pressed against his body, he can't get 'em out, nor can he get the thick topcoat off his head. Thus he gropes his way towards the door, banging his head against things in the hallway, but he can't get through the door. He flies into a terrible rage now, and retreats, bashing the armchair forward and sideways against the door. The armchair won't come off, but the door splits, and the sound echoes through the silent house. The blind watchman keeps walking back and forth, crashing and bashing against the door, somebody's gotta come, I wanta see somethin', them dirty dogs will find out a thing or two, I gotta get this coat off, he calls for help, but the coat muffles his voice. This goes on for two minutes and then the boss wakes up. Others arrive from the second story. Then the old man sits back on his armchair and flops over; he has fainted. Some rumpus, burglars have broken in, they've tied the old man, what's the use of having such an old man, that's to save money, penny wise, pound foolish, as usual.

General rejoicing among the little gang.

Hell, do we need Pums and Reinhold and that whole damned crowd?

But things come to a head, and very differently from what they expect.

Things come to a Head, Karl the Tinner gets caught and spills the Beans

In the Prenzlauer café Reinhold goes up to the tinner and tells him they need him, they've been looking for a locksmith, but can't find one. Karl must join them. They walk into the back room. Reinhold says: "Why dontcha want to come? What are you doin', anyway? We've heard all about it." "Because I won't let you guys get my goat." "Well, I suppose you got somethin' else."

"That's none o' your business." "I can see you're earnin' dough, but you can't get away with that, y' know, first workin' with us, earnin' money, and then good-bye everybody." "What do you mean, get away with what? First you holler I'm no good, and then, all of a sudden, you say Karl's gotta come along." "You gotta come, we got nobody, or give back the money you got with us. We don't need no day-laborers." "Search me, that money's all gone." "Then you gotta work with us." "I won't, and I told you so before." "Karl, see here, we'll break every bone in your body, we'll make you starve to death alive." "Don't make me laugh. Are you drunk or somethin'? Maybe you think I'm one of them little broads you can do anything you want to with." "Is that so, old boy? Now you just beat it. I don't care what the hell you are. Think it over. I'll be round again." "Attaboy." There is a mower.

Reinhold discusses with the others what they are to do. They're S. O. L. without a locksmith, and just now the season's favorable, Reinhold has orders from two fences, he got them over Pums's head. They're all of the same opinion, we gotta put Karl into the sweat-box, he's nothing but a crook, and he'll get kicked out of the club one of these days.

The tinner notices that there's something in the wind. He looks up Franz and often visits him in his room, trying to pump him or to get him to help him. Franz says: "First you got us in a hole up there in Stralauer Strasse, and then you ditch us. Now that's enough." "It's because I don't wanta have nothin' to do with Reinhold. He's a damned bastard, only you don't know it." "He's a good guy." "You're a jackass, you don't know nothin' about the world, you ain't got eyes to see with." "Don't give me any of that bunk, Karl, I got enough, we go on a job and then you ditch us. Just watch out, I'm tellin' you, or things'll go bad with you." "On account of Reinhold and Company? Just watch me laugh. Couldn't open my mouth any wider, could I? My belly's shakin'. I'm as strong as he is, anyhow, I guess he thinks I'm like one of his little broads, well, I won't say no more. But just let him come and try somethin'." "Beat it, but I tell ye, watch out."

And then chance would have it that the tinner, with his two friends, pulled a job two days later in Friedenstrasse, and he got nabbed. The wheelwright got caught as well, only the third man who kept watch escaped. They soon found out at headquarters that Karl was involved in the burglary in Elsasser Strasse, there are plenty of fingerprints on the coffee cups.

Why did I get nabbed, thinks Karl. How did those bulls dig it out anyhow? Musta been that dirty louse, Reinhold, who squealed. Out of spite, because I didn't go along with 'em. The dirty bastard wants to put me out of commission, that crook, he got us into this trap, he's the prize yegg, sure, never saw the likes of him. He sends a secret note to the wheelwright to say it's Reinhold's fault, he gave 'em away, I'll say he was in on it. The wheelwright nods to him in the hallway. Karl has himself brought before the examining judge, and at headquarters he insists: "Reinhold was in it, only he got away."

They promptly arrest Reinhold in the afternoon. He denies everything, he can prove an alibi. He is pale with rage, when he faces the two men in the office of the examining judge, and hears those dirty hounds state that he was in on the burglary in the warehouse. The judge listens to all this, watches their faces, there's something fishy about it, they're furious with each other. Two days later, the thing's cleared up, Reinhold's alibi is valid, he's a pimp, but he had nothing to do with this affair.

This is early in October.

So Reinhold is discharged, but the bulls smell a rat and decide to watch him more closely. The others, the wheelwright and Karl, are reprimanded by the examining judge, they mustn't rake up a lot of nonsense, Reinhold has an alibi. Whereupon both are silent.

Karl sits in his cell, boiling with rage. His brother-in-law, the brother of his divorced wife, with whom he is on good terms, visits him. He gets a lawyer through him, he insists on having a lawyer, a good criminal lawyer. After sounding him out a bit to find out if he knows his job, he asks the lawyer what would happen if a man helped to bury a dead person. "What do you mean?" "If a man finds somebody who's dead and then buries him?" "Someone you want to conceal, perhaps, shot dead by the police, eh?" "Well, anyway, if a man didn't kill the person himself and he wouldn't like to have the body found, can anything be done to him for that?" "Well, did you know the dead person, and did you gain anything by burying him?" "No, didn't gain nothin', it was for friendship's sake; supposin' a man simply helped, the corpse is lyin' there, he's dead all right and you don't want to have him found." "Found by the police, you mean? As a matter of fact, that's merely suppression of evidence. But how did he die?" "How do I know? I wasn't there, I'm just askin' about this for somebody else. I didn't help at all. Didn't know nothin' about it either, nothin' at all. The corpse was just lyin' there. Then somebody says to me, just take a hold, we're gonna bury it." "Who told you that?" "To bury it? Well, somebody. I just wanta know how I stand. Did I commit a crime when I helped to bury a corpse?" "Look here, the way you put the thing, it's hardly a crime at all, or only a petty one. If you were not involved at all and had no interest in it. But why did you help?" "I'm tellin' you, I just gave a hand for friendship's sake, but that didn't matter, at any rate, I wasn't involved in the affair and it didn't matter to me whether the person was or wasn't found." "Was there some kind of a femic murder in your gang?" "Well—" "Look here, old man, keep out of this. But I still don't know what you're driving at." "It's all right, Mister, what I wanted to know, now I know." "Won't you tell me about it a little more in detail?" "I'd like to sleep over it a bit."

So Karl the tinner lies in his bunk all night long, trying to sleep, to sleep, but he can't, and he gets in a rage. I certainly am the biggest boob in the world, now I wanted to squeal on Reinhold, and that fellow sure tumbled to something, and now he's gone, he's beat it. I'm a boob. That crook, that gorilla, gets me into trouble, but I'll get even with him, you bet your life.

It seems to Karl that the night will never end; when's the first bell goin' to ring, it's all the same to me, just helping to bury a person don't get a man into trouble, and if I get a coupla months, it'll be life for him; he'll never get out again, unless they knock off his bean altogether. When's the examining judge coming, wonder what time it is, and meanwhile Reinhold's in the train and skiddoos. The crook. I never saw the likes of him, and what's more, Biberkopf's his friend, wonder how he'll manage with one arm, they're doin' all kinds of funny things to the war-cripples.

Then things begin to stir in the old panopticon. Karl puts out his signal flag, and at eleven he's before the judge. Well, the latter looks astonished. "You certainly have it in for him. This is the second time you have reported him. Let's hope you don't get into trouble yourself." But then Karl gives such precise information that they take an automobile at noon, the examining judge goes along himself, two sturdy detectives with him, Karl between them, handcuffed, and they go out to Freienwalde.

So they ride once more over the old roads. It's nice to ride along like this. Damn it, if only I knew how to get out of this car. The lousy fools have handcuffed me, nothing doing. They got guns, too. No use, no use. Riding, riding, the road shoots past him. 180 days I give you, Mieze, on my lap, a darling gal, he's a crook, Reinhold, he walks over corpses, well, just wait, old boy! Got to think about Mieze again, I'll bite your tongue, she knows how to hug, which way are we going to drive, right or left, don't care, what a sweet kid.

They cross the hill, and come to the wood.

There's a pretty bathing-beach in Freienwalde, a small summer resort. There is yellow gravel neatly spread over the paths of the Kurgarten, back there is the restaurant terrace, that's where we three sat. In Switzerland and on Tyrol's height, One feels so well by day and night, In Tyrol the milk comes warm from the cow, In Switzerland there's the tall Jungfrau.

And then he rushed off with her, and I made myself scarce for a few lousy bills. To think I sold that poor kid to such a crook, and now I'm in trouble on accounta him.

Here's the wood, autumnal, sunny, the tree-tops are still. "We gotta walk along here, he had a flashlight, it's not easy to find, but when I see the place, I'll know it again. There was a clearing with a fir tree standing crooked and then there was a little hollow." "There are lots of hollows here." "Wait a minute, chief, we've gone too far, it wasn't 20 or 25 minutes from the restaurant. It wasn't that far." "But you said you were running." "Only in the woods, not on the road, of course, somebody might have noticed us." Now they have found the clearing; the crooked fir tree is standing there, everything is as it was that day. I'm yourn, her heart smashed, eyes smashed, mouth smashed, how about walking a bit, don't hug me so tight. "That's the black fir, that's it."

Men came riding over the land, they sat on little brown horses, they came from far away. They kept on asking where the road was, till they came to the water, to the great lake, there they dismounted. They tied their horses to an oak tree, they said prayers beside the water, they threw themselves on the ground and then they took a boat and rowed across the water. They hailed the lake with singing, they talked with the lake. They sought no treasure in the lake, they only wished to worship the great lake wherein one of their chieftains lay. For this is the reason, the reason these men.

The detectives had brought some spades along, Karl the tinner showed them the spot. They stuck their spades into the ground, and no sooner had they stuck them in than it became loose; they dug still deeper throwing the earth high, the ground has been disturbed here, there were fir cones lying underneath. Karl the tinner stands and looks and looks and waits. It was here, it was here all right, here's where they dug the girl in. "How deep was it?" "A foot or so, no more." "Should have got there by now." "It was here all right, just go on diggin'." "Go on digging, digging, all very well, when there's nothing there." The ground is all torn up, they shovel green grass from the bottom of the hole, there's been somebody digging here, yesterday or today. She oughta come now, he goes on holding his sleeve to his nose, she must be decomposed by now, how many months is it, and it's been raining, too. One of the men digging down there asks from below: "What kind of a dress did she have on?" "A dark skirt and a pink waist." "Silk?" "Maybe silk, anyhow, light pink." "Like this?" One of the men holds up a strip of lace, all loamy and sodden, but it's pink. He shows it to the judge. "Part of the sleeve perhaps." They go on digging. It's obvious: something was buried here. Yesterday or perhaps today, someone was digging here. Karl stands there; so that's it, he smelt a rat and dug her out, maybe he has thrown her into the water. The judge takes the police commissioner aside, their conversation lasts a long time, the commissioner takes notes. Then the three return to the automobile; one of the men stays behind.

While they are walking, the judge asks Karl: "When you came, the girl was already dead, wasn't she?" "Yes." "How can you prove it?" "Why?"

"Well, suppose your Reinhold now says it was you who killed her, or you helped." "I helped carry her all right. Why should I kill the gal?" "For the same reason that he killed her, or is supposed to have killed her." "I wasn't with her in the evening at all." "But in the afternoon." "But not afterwards, she was still alive then." "That'll be a difficult alibi."

In the car the judge asks Karl: "Where were you in the evening, or the night following this business with Reinhold?" Damn it all, I'll tell you. "I was on a trip, he gave me his passport, I beat it, so that I could prove my alibi in case the thing got out." "Strange, but why should you do that, that's really odd, were you such good friends?" "Oh, I'm poor, and he gave me some money." "But now he's not your friend any more, is he? Or hasn't he any money now?" "Him, a friend of mine? No, judge. You know why I'm in jail—it's on account of that affair with the watchman and so on. He snitched on me."

The judge and commissioner look at each other, the automobile flies along, plunges into holes in the road, jumps up, the trees flash past, here's where I rode with him, 180 days I give you. "I suppose something happened between you two and your friendship went to smash, heh?" "Yeah, you know how it is (he wants to give me the works, but I won't let him get away with it, stop, I getcha). It's like this, Judge: Reinhold is a tough customer, and, as a matter of fact, he wanted to get rid of me, too." "Well, did he start anything against you?" "Nope, it was what he said." "Nothing else." "Nope." "Well, we'll see about that."

Two days later the body of Mieze is found about a half a mile away from the hollow, in the same wood. As soon as the newspapers report the case, two of the garden laborers present themselves and testify that they saw a man walking through the wood alone, near that spot, carrying a heavy trunk. They both spoke of it at the time, wondering what he was carrying, later the man took a rest and sat in the hollow. When they came back half an hour later, he was still sitting there in his shirt-sleeves, they didn't see the trunk, it probably was in the hole. They give a pretty exact description of the man; about 5 feet 8, very broad shoulders, wearing a black derby, a light-gray summer suit, a pepper-and-salt coat, he drags his legs when he walks, looks like an invalid, a very high wrinkled forehead. There are many hollows in the region indicated by the two witnesses, and the police dogs prove useless; so they have to dig up all the hollows thereabout. In one of them, after a few spadefuls of earth have been cleared, they come upon a big brown cardboard box, tied with string. When the commissioner opens it, they find a woman's clothes, a torn chemise, a pair of long light stockings, an old brown woolen dress, dirty handkerchiefs, two toothbrushes. The cardboard box is somewhat wet, but not soaked through, its general appearance suggests that it has not been lying there for long. Incomprehensible, wasn't the corpse wearing a pink blouse?

Soon afterwards they find the trunk in another hollow, and the body is inside it in a crouching position, firmly tied with curtain-cords. In the evening reports are flashed to all the stations, to the provincial police stations as well, with a description of the suspect, and so on.

Reinhold realizes, when he is questioned at headquarters, that the game is up. So now he gets Franz involved in trouble, as well. Why shouldn't it have been him? What can Karl prove? It's doubtful if anybody saw me in Freienwalde. Maybe somebody saw me at the restaurant or on the road, but it don't matter, it's worth trying, gotta get Franz to go away, so it'll look as if he was in it, too.

That afternoon, after leaving headquarters, Reinhold is upstairs with Franz, Karl the tinner is snitching on us, he says, make yourself scarce. So Franz, helped by Reinhold, gets his things packed in a quarter of an hour. They curse Karl together. Then Eva gets Toni, one of her old girl friends in Wilmersdorf to put Franz up. Reinhold rides out to Wilmersdorf in the automobile and they buy trunks together. Reinhold wants to go abroad and he needs a huge trunk; at first he chooses a wardrobe trunk, then decides on a wooden trunk, the biggest he can carry, don't trust porters, they spy on a guy, you'll get my address, Franz, remember me to Eva.

Terrible disaster in Prague, 21 dead have already been brought to the surface, 150 persons are still buried; in a few minutes a new building 7 stories high was reduced to a heap of ruins, there are still many dead and injured lying underneath. The whole structure of reinforced concrete weighing nearly 1000 tons plunged into the two underground basements. The policeman on duty in the street warned passers-by when he heard sounds of cracking in the building and had the presence of mind to jump on to a street-car coming up at that moment and apply the brakes himself. Terrible storms are raging on the Atlantic. The weather report for the Atlantic ocean is as follows: cyclonic depressions, one after another, are coming from North America in an easterly direction, while the two high-pressure areas in Central America and between Greenland and Ireland, are stationary. The newspapers are full of long articles about the Graf Zeppelin and its prospective flight. Every detail of the airship's construction, the personality of the commander and the prospects of success in the enterprise is discussed exhaustively, enthusiastic editorials extol German efficiency and the prior achievements of the Zeppelin airship. Despite all the propaganda that has been made in favor of airplanes, the airship affords, we are assured, the ideal means of air travel in the future. But the Zeppelin does not start, for Eckener will not incur needless risks.

They open the trunk in which Mieze lay. She was the daughter of a street-car conductor from Bernau. There were three children in the family, the mother deserted her husband and left the home, why, nobody knows. Mieze was alone in the house and had to do everything herself. Sometimes at night she rode in to Berlin and went to dance-halls or to Lestmann and other places nearby, occasionally she was taken by this one or the other to a hotel; then it was too late and she didn't dare come home, so she stayed on in Berlin and met Eva; that's how it started. They were at the police station near the Stettin Depot. A cheerful life began then for Mieze, who at first called herself Sonia, she had many acquaintances and friends, but later on she always lived with one man, a strong fellow with one arm whom Mieze loved at first sight and to whom she remained true till the end. A bad end, a sad end, was the last end of Mieze. And why, why, why? What crime had she committed? She came from Bernau into the whirl of Berlin, she was not an innocent girl, certainly not, but her love for him was pure and steadfast; he was her man and she took care of him like a child. She was struck down because she happened by chance to encounter this man; such is life, it's really inconceivable. She rode out to Freienwalde to protect her friend, and there she was strangled, strangled, killed, extinguished; such is life.

They take the finger-prints on her throat and face, and now she's only a case for criminal inquiry, a technical process, just as when a telephone wire is laid, that's what she has come to. They take her death-mask, paint everything in natural colors, it's an exact likeness, in a kind of celluloid. So there is Mieze, her face and throat are in a cupboard filled with legal documents, come on now, come on now, we'll soon be home, Aschinger's, you must console me, I'm yourn. She is displayed under glass now, face smashed, heart smashed, abdomen smashed, her smile smashed, you must console me, come along.

So I returned and considered all the Oppressions that are done under the Sun

Franz, why do you sigh, Franzeken? Why must Eva be always gliding up to your side and asking you what you think, and she gets no reply, must always go away without an answer? Why are you so depressed, and why must you cringe, cringe, and cringe in a little nook, behind a little curtain, and take such tiny little steps? You know life, you didn't fall upon the earth yesterday, you have a nose for things and you can observe. But you see nothing, you hear nothing, you can only sense things, you dare not turn your eyes towards them, but look at them from the side, nor do you flee, you are too obstinate to flee, so you clench your teeth, you are no coward, only you don't know what may happen and whether you can take up the burden, whether your shoulders are strong enough to bear it.

How much did Job, the man from the land of Uz, suffer before he knew all and nothing could afflict him more. The Sabeans fell upon his servants, and slew them, the fire of God fell from heaven and burnt up the sheep and the servants, the Chaldeans fell upon and slew his camels and their drivers, his sons and daughters were sitting in their eldest brother's house, and there came a wind from the wilderness and smote the four corners of the house and the young men were slain.

That was much, but it was not enough. Job rent his mantle, bit his hands, and shaved his head and heaped ashes upon himself. But it was not yet enough. Job was stricken with sores, he had boils from the soles of his feet unto his crown, he sat down among the ashes and the pus flowed from him and he took him a potsherd to scrape himself withal.

His friends came and visited him, Eliphaz the Temanite, and Bildad the Shuhite, and Zophar the Naamathite, they came from afar to console him, they lifted up their voices and wept fearfully, they did not recognize Job; thus terribly was Job stricken. He had had seven sons and three daughters and seven thousand sheep and three thousand camels and five hundred yoke of oxen, and five hundred she-asses and a very great household.

Franz Biberkopf, you have not lost as much as did Job, the man of Uz, but it is slowly coming upon you, also. With little steps you draw yourself near to that which has befallen you, you say to yourself a thousand words of consolation, you flatter yourself, for you wish to risk it, you are resolved to draw nearer, you are resolved to affront the utmost, yea, woe is you, to affront the bitterest end. Not that, oh not that! You encourage yourself, you love yourself: come, nothing will happen, and we can't escape, anyway. But something in you wills it, refuses it. You sigh. How can I find shelter when disaster befalls, to what can I cling? Nearer it comes. And you, too, approach it like a snail; you are no coward, not only have you strong muscles, you are Franz Biberkopf, you are the cobra. See it coiling, inch by inch around the monster, that stands there, about to seize him.

You will lose no money, Franz, but you will be burnt up in your innermost soul! See how the whore rejoices! The whore of Babylon. And there came one of the seven angels which had the seven vials, and talked with me, saying unto me, Come hither; I will show unto thee the judgment of the great whore that sitteth upon many waters; and I saw a woman sit upon a scarlet colored beast, having a golden cup in her hand; and upon her forehead was a name written, MYSTERY. And I saw the woman drunken with the blood of the saints.

You sense her now, you feel her. Ah, will you now be strong, will you escape destruction?

In the pretty bright room of the Wilmersdorfer Strasse villa, Franz Biberkopf sits and waits.

The cobra coils itself, lies basking in the sun. A great bore all this, for he's vigorous and would like to do something, a fellow just lies around, they have not yet fixed up where to meet, fat Toni has supplied him with dark smoked glasses, I've got to get a brand-new outfit. I might get myself a student's scar on my face. There's somebody running across the courtyard. He's in a hurry all right. Nothing comes too late for me. If only people wouldn't hurry so much, they'd live twice as long, and get three times as much done. It's the same thing with the six-day bicycle race, they pedal and pedal, steadily all the time, they are patient, the milk won't boil over, let the public whistle, what do they know about it, anyhow?

There's a knock in the hallway. Well, why don't they ring? Damn it, I'll fly the coop, but there's only one exit. Let's listen.

With little steps you drag yourself up, you say to yourself a thousand words of consolation, you flatter yourself, lure yourself, you are ready for the utmost, but not for the very bitter, oh, not for the very bitterest end.

Let's listen. What's that? Don't I know her? I certainly know that voice. Screaming, crying, crying. Let's see. Terror, haunting terror, what are you thinking of now? There's so much one thinks about. Sure, I know her, it's Eva!

The door opens. Outside stands Eva, fat Toni has her arms around her. She's whimpering, sobbing, whatsa matter with the girl? A man thinks about so many things, all that's happened, Mieze screaming, Reinhold lying in the bed. "Howdy, Eva. Well, Eva, old girl, well, what is it, hold on, hold on, anything happened, it's not goin' to be as bad as all that." "Lemme go." How she grunts, probably got a good whacking somewhere, somebody must have beat her up, wait a minute. She must have told Herbert something, Herbert knows something about the child. "Did he beat you up, Herbert?" "Lemme go. Don't touch me." Her eyes looked so queer. Now she don't want to have anything to do with me any more. Didn't she want it herself? Whatsa matter, anyhow? What's wrong, more people coming, let's bolt the door. Toni stands there, talking excitedly to Eva. "Hush, Eva, don't worry. Now stop that, what's wrong, come in. Where's Herbert?" "I won't go in, I won't go in." "Well, come along, let's sit down. I've made some coffee. Go away Franz." "Why should I go away, I ain't done nothin'."

Then Eva's eyes grow bigger, terribly bigger, as if she wanted to eat up somebody, she starts screaming, grabs Franz by the vest: "He's got to come along, he's got to come in here, he must come in here with me. You got to come here with us." Whatsa matter with her, that woman's crazy, has anybody told her anything? Eva starts dithering on the sofa, beside fat Toni. The girl looks bloated and shaky, that's on account of her condition, but she got that from me, why, I ain't goin' to do nothin' to her. Eva puts her arms around fat Toni and whispers something in her ear; at first she cannot speak, but then she gets it out. Now something comes over Toni, too. She slaps her hands together, while Eva dithers and takes a crumpled piece of paper out of her pocket. They've all gone batty. Are they trying to stage something with me or what, what's that in the paper anyway, maybe about our job in the Stralauer Strasse? Franz stands up and shouts: those women are damned fools. "You monkeys. Don't start makin' scenes for my benefit, or I guess you think I'm your monkey." "For God's sake, for God's sake!" Fat Toni has sat down, Eva goes on blubbering, looking in front of her; she says nothing, just whimpers and shakes. Then Franz reaches across the table and tears the paper from fat Toni's hands.

There are two pictures on it, one next to the other, what horrible, horrible, ghastly fright, that's me—sure enough it's me. But why? On account of the Stralauer Strasse business? But why? Horror of horror, that's me and there's Reinhold. Headline: Murder. Murder of a Prostitute in Freienwalde, Emilie Parsunke of Bernau. Mieze. What's that? Me. Behind the stove a mouse is sitting, soon it will be flitting, flitting!

His hand grips the page convulsively. Slowly he sinks down on to the chair, he sits all shrunken within himself. What's that on the page? Behind the stove a mouse is sitting.

The two women gape at him, in tears; stare with goggly eyes towards him, what's the matter, murder? What's that, Mieze? I'm crazy, what's that, what does it all mean? His hand moves again towards the table, there it is in the paper, let's read it: my picture, me, and Reinhold, murder, Emilie Parsunke of Bernau, in Freienwalde, how did she get to Freienwalde? What paper is it, anyway, the *Morgenpost*. His hand moves up with the paper, down with the paper. Eva, what's Eva doing? Her look has changed, she comes over to him, her voice no longer strident: "Well, Franz?" A voice, somebody's speaking, I must say something, two women; a murder, what is a murder, in Freienwalde, so I murdered her in Freienwalde, but I never been to Freienwalde, where is that anyhow? "Now tell me Franz, say somethin'."

Franz looks at her, looks at her, his big eyes staring at her, he holds the paper on the flat of his hand, his head is shaking, he reads and babbles in jerks, stumbling, crackling. Murder in Freienwalde, Emilie Parsunke of Bernau, born June 12, 1908, it's Mieze, Eva. He scratches his cheek, looks at Eva with a vague, empty, hollow look, one can't see down into it. It's Mieze, Eva. It's Mieze, Eva. Yes. What—do you say, Eva? She's dead. That's why we didn't find her. "And you are in the papers, Franz." "Me?"

He takes the paper again and looks at it. It's my picture.

The upper part of his body is shivering. For God's sake, for God's sake, Eva! She grows more and more afraid. She moves a chair next to him. He is still rocking the upper part of his body. For God's sake, for God's sake! Swaying to and fro. Now he starts puffing and panting. From his face one would think he was amused. "For God's sake, what'll we do, Eva, what'll we do?" "Why did they put your picture there?" "Where?" "There?" "Well, I don't know. For God's sake, what does it mean?" "How come, ho, ho, that's really funny." Now he looks at her, helplessly trembling, and she is glad, that's a human look, tears are rolling from her eyes again, fat Toni starts whimpering, too, then his arm goes round behind her, and his hand rests on her shoulder, his face is on her neck. Franz whispers: "What's this, Eva, what's the matter with our Miezeken, what's happened? She's dead, something happened to her, now it's out. She didn't run away from me, somebody killed our Miezeken, my Miezeken, whatsa matter now? Is it true, tell me, it's not true!"

As he thinks of Miezeken something rises in him, fear arises, terror beckons him, there he is, there is that mower, Death's his name, hatchet and staff in hand he marches o'er the land blowing on a little flute, he wrenches his jaws apart, and takes a trumpet, to blare upon his trumpet, and beats the kettledrum and now it looms, a doom, gloom-black, battering ram, drooms, and softly drooooooms. . . .

Eva watches the slow gnashing and grinding of his jaws and clings to Franz. His head quivers, and now his voice is heard, at first a harsh rattle, then growing softer. But not an uttered word.

He lay beneath the auto, that was like it is now, there's a mill there, a quarry, it goes on pouring over me, but I'll hold fast, no matter how I hold on, it's no use, it wants to smash me to pieces, even if I am an iron girder, it wants to break me to pieces.

Franz murmurs through his teeth: "Something's coming." "What's coming?" What mill is this, revolving wheels, a windmill, a watermill? "Watch out, Franz, they are looking for you." So they say I killed her, me, he trembles again, his face is laughing again, I beat her once, maybe they think because I killed Ida. "Stay where you are, Franz, don't go downstairs, where do you wanta go? They're looking for you, they know you by that one arm." "They won't catch me, Eva, if I don't want 'em to; they won't catch me, you can depend on that. I must go out and look at the poster column, I've gotta see it. I've gotta read it in the saloon, in the papers, the stuff they write, how it happened." Then he stands in front of Eva, staring at her, can't get a word out, if he only don't start laughing. "Look at me, Eva, is there anything wrong with me, look at me." "No, no." She screams and clings to him. "Well, look at me, is there anything the matter with me? There must be somethin' wrong with me."

No, no, she screams, and wails, while he walks to the door, smiling, takes his hat from the bureau, and is gone.

Behold the Tears of Such as were oppressed and they had no Comforter

Franz has an artificial arm, but, as a rule, he rarely wears it; now, however, he goes out on the street with it, the false hand in the pocket of his overcoat, in the left a cigar. He had left the house with difficulty. Eva shrieked and threw herself at his feet before the hall-door, he promised her not to run away, and to watch out. "I'll be back for coffee," he said, and then went downstairs.

They did not catch Franz Biberkopf as long as he did not want to be caught. There were always two angels walking beside him, one on the left, the other on the right, who diverted people's eyes from him.

In the afternoon he comes upstairs for coffee at four. Herbert is there, too. Then for the first time in a long time they hear Franz talk at length. He has read the papers downstairs about his friend, Karl the tinner, he has read how he squealed on them. He does not know why he did that. So Karl the tinner went along to Freienwalde, where they had dragged Mieze. Reinhold did it by force. He had taken an auto, rode perhaps a little way with Mieze, and then Karl got in and between them they held her feet and dragged her to Freienwalde, probably at night. Maybe they had already killed her on the way. "And why did Reinhold do that?" "It was him who kicked me under the car, now you might as well know it, it was him, but it don't matter. I'm not angry at him for it, a fellow's gotta learn things, if he don't, he won't ever know nothin'. Then he runs around like a damn blockhead and knows nothin' about the world. I'm not angry at him, nope, nope. He wanted to knock me out, he thought he'd got me in his clutches, but it didn't happen that way, he found that out; that's why he took Mieze from me and did that to her, it wasn't her fault." Oh why, that's why. Roll of drums, battalion march, march. When the soldiers come marching along through the town, oh why, that's why, just because of tararara taraboomdeeay.

That's how I marched up, and that's how he answered me and it was a damned trick and all wrong for me to march with him.

It was all wrong for me to march, all wrong, all wrong.

But that doesn't matter, now it doesn't matter any more. Herbert opens his eyes wide. Eva can't say a word. Herbert: "Why didn'tcha tell Mieze somethin' about it?" "It's not my fault, there's nothing you can do about it, that guy mighta just as well shot me dead when I was in his room. I tell you, there's nothin' to be done about it."

Seven heads and ten horns, in her hand a cup full of abominations. We'll get 'em now, all right, there's nothin' can stop it now.

"Man alive, if you had just let one peep out, I tell you Mieze would still be living today, and another guy would be carrying his head under his arm." "It's not my fault. What a guy like that does, you'll never know. And you can't know what he's doin' now, you'll never find out." "I'll find out, all right." Eva pleads with him: "Don't go near that fellow, Herbert, I'm afraid, too." "We'll fix him up all right. First we'll find where he hangs out, and half an hour later the bulls'll get him." Franz nods. "Just you keep your fingers out of that pie, Herbert, he don't belong to you. Let's shake." Eva: "Shake, Herbert, what are you goin' to do, Franz?" "What do I care. You can throw me on the garbage-dump."

Then he moves quickly to the corner and stands with his back against the wall.

Now they hear a sobbing, sobbing, a whimpering, he is weeping for himself and for Mieze, they hear it, and Eva cries and weeps upon the table, the paper with "Murder" on it is still lying on the table, Mieze is murdered, nobody did anything, it just happened to her.

Wherefore I praised the Dead which were already Dead

Towards evening Franz Biberkopf is on his way again. Five sparrows, on the Bayrischer Platz, fly over him. They are five slain evil-doers, who have often met Franz Biberkopf before. They have considered what to do with him, what decision to take about him, how to make him anxious and uncertain, over which beam they shall make him stumble.

One of them screams: There he walks. Look, he has a false arm, he hasn't yet given up the game for lost, he does not want to be recognized.

The second says: That fine gentleman has certainly done a lot of shady things. He is a dangerous criminal, they should put him in the bull-pen, he ought to get life. Killing one woman and going around hooking things, burgling and then taking another woman, that's another of his crimes. What does he want now, I ask you?

The third: He's puffing himself up. He's playing the innocent. He's aping the honest man. Look at the louse. When a bull comes along, let's kick his hat off.

The first speaks again: Why should that fellow live any longer? I croaked in prison after nine years. I was much younger than this chap here, I was dead already then, and couldn't say boo. Take your hat off, you monkey, take off your damned glasses, you're not an editor yet, you jackass, why, you don't even know the multiplication table, and then you go putting on horn-rimmed glasses like a professor, look out, you'll see, they'll get you.

The fourth: Heh, don't scream so loud. What do you want to do to him? Look at the fellow, he has got a head, he walks on two legs. We little sparrows, we might let something drop on his hat.

The fifth: Go ahead and bawl him out. He's chewing his cud, he's got a screw loose. He goes walking about with two angels, his sweetheart is a mask at police headquarters, go ahead and do something to him. Go ahead and scream.

So they whir, scream, and twitter above his head. Franz raises his head, his thoughts are muddled, the birds squabble and mock at him.

Autumn weather. In the Tauentzien Palast they are playing *The Last Days of Francisco*; there are fifty dancing beauties at the Jäger Casino, for a bunch of lilacs you can kiss me. Then Franz decides: my life is at an end, it's all over, I've had enough.

The street-cars rattle along the streets, they are all going somewhere, but I don't know where to go. The Nord-End 51, Schillerstrasse, Pankow, Breitestrasse, Schönhauser Allee Depot, Stettin Depot, Potsdam Depot, Nollendorfplatz, Bayrischer Platz, Uhlandstrasse, Schmargendorf Depot, Grunewald, hop in. Howdy, here I am, they can take me anywhere they please. And Franz starts inspecting the city like a dog that has lost a trail. What kind of a city is this, anyway, this huge city, and what kind of a life, how many lives he has led in it. He gets out at Stettin Depot and then moves along Invalidenstrasse. Here's the Rosenthaler Tor. Fabisch's Ready-to-Wear Shop, here's where I stood, hawking tie-holders, last Christmas. He rides out to Tegel on the No. 41. The red walls appear, red walls on the left, the heavy iron gates, and now Franz grows silent. This is part of my life, and I must look at it, look at it.

The walls are red, and the roadway streams past them, car No. 41 rides past, General Pape Strasse, West Reinickendorf, Tegel, Borsig, they thunder by. Franz Biberkopf stands in front of the red walls, walks across the other side where there is a saloon. Then the red houses behind the walls begin to shake and tremble, and to puff out their cheeks. Convicts line all the windows, pushing their heads against the bars, their hair has been shaved close, almost to the skull. They look miserable, underweight, their faces are gray and scrubby, they roll their eyes and lament. There they stand, murderers, burglary, theft, forgery, rape; all the crimes of the code are there, and they wail with gray faces. There they sit, the gray men, and now they've twisted my Mieze's neck.

Franz Biberkopf roams around the giant prison; it goes on trembling and shaking and calling to him, across the fields, to the wood, back again to the tree-lined street.

Then he is in the street with the trees. I didn't kill Mieze. I didn't do it. I ain't got nothing to do here. That's all over. I ain't got nothing to do with Tegel any more, I don't know how all this came about.

Now it is six in the evening and Franz says, I want to go to Mieze. I must go to the cemetery, where they buried her.

The five criminals, the sparrows, are with him again. They sit up there on a telegraph post and scream down: Go to her, you scoundrel, have you the courage, ain't you ashamed to go to her? She called to you when she lay there in the hollow. Go and see her in the cemetery!

For the Repose of our Dead. In Berlin, in 1927, there died 48,742 persons, excluding infants born dead.

4570 deaths from tuberculosis, 6443 from cancer, 5656 from heart-disease, 4818 from vascular diseases, 5140 from apoplexy, 2419 from pneumonia, 961 from whooping cough, 562 children died of diphtheria, 123 of scarlet fever, 93 of the measles, 3640 deaths of children at the breast. There were 42,696 births.

The dead lie in the cemetery, in their garden plots, the guardian walks by with his stick, prodding scraps of paper.

It is half past six and still quite light; on her grave in front of a beech tree is seated a very young woman in a fur coat, without a hat, her head is bent and she is silent. She is wearing black kid gloves, she holds a sheet of paper in her hand, a small envelope. Franz reads: "I can live no longer. Give my love once more to my parents, my darling child. Life is a torture to me. Bieriger alone need have me on his conscience. But I hope he will go on enjoying life. I was a mere toy for him, and he exploited me. He is just a vulgar lout. I came to Berlin only on account of him, he alone made me miserable and I became a ruined woman."

Franz gives her back the envelope. "Oh my, oh my! Is my Mieze here?" Mustn't be sad, mustn't be sad. He weeps. "Oh my, oh my! where is my little Mieze?"

There is a grave like a big soft divan, and a learned professor is lying on it, he smiles at Franz. "Why are you grieved, my friend?" "I wanted to see Mieze. I just happened to pass by." "I'm dead, you see, one mustn't take life too seriously; nor death either. One can make everything easier. When I had had enough of it, and became ill, what did I do? Do you think I was willing to go on lying sick-a-bed till the end? What use would that have been? I had them put the morphine bottle near me and asked for some music, they were to play the piano, jazz, the latest hits. I had them read aloud something from Plato, the great *Symposium*, that's a beautiful dialogue, and, unobserved, I injected syringe after syringe underneath the sheets. I counted them, three times the fatal dose. I heard them banging away merrily, and my reader talking of old Socrates, yes, there are wise men and some less wise."

"Reading aloud, morphine, but where is Mieze?"

It is terrible, from a tree there hangs a man, and his wife stands beside him, wailing, when Franz comes by. "Come quickly, cut him down. He will not stay in his grave, he's always climbing the trees and dangling to one side." "Oh God, oh God, and why?" "My Ernst had been sick for such a long time, nobody could help him, and they didn't want to send him away, they always said he was pretending. So he went down to the cellar and took a nail and a hammer with him. I heard him hammering in the cellar and I wondered what he was doing; a good thing, I thought, for him to be working and not sitting around all the time, maybe he's building a rabbit-hutch. But he didn't come up that evening. I got afraid and puzzled as to where he could be, are those cellar keys up here, they weren't back in their place. Then the neighbors went down and fetched the police. He had hammered a stout nail into the ceiling, though he was quite a thin man, but he wanted to make sure, what are you looking for, young man? What are you whimpering about? Do you want to kill yourself?"

"No, they killed my girl, and I don't know if she's lying here."

"Well, you had better look for her back there, that's where the new ones are."

Now Franz is lying on the path beside an empty grave, he cannot shout, but bites into the earth. Mieze, what have we done anyway, why did they do that to you? You hadn't done anything, Miezeken. What can I do, why don't they throw me into the grave with you, how long is life going to treat me like this?

He gets up, but he can hardly walk, he rouses himself and goes out, staggering along between the rows of graves.

Franz Biberkopf, the gentleman with the stiff arm, gets into an automobile outside, which takes him to the Bayrischer Platz. He keeps Eva very, very busy. Eva is busy with him all day long and all night long. He does not live and he does not die. Herbert has practically vanished.

There follow a few days when Franz and Herbert are busy chasing Reinhold. Herbert is armed to the teeth and listens around everywhere, he's out to catch Reinhold. Franz does not want to at first, then he, too, feels the urge, it's the last medicine which will serve him in this world.

The Fortress is entirely Surrounded, the last Sallies are made, but they are only Feints

November is advancing. Summer has been over for a long time. The rain has continued into the autumn. Very far away are those weeks when a soft glow lay upon the streets and people walked about in light clothes and you would have said the women were in chemises. A light dress, a tight-fitting hat, that's what Franz's girl, Mieze, wore, she who once rode out to Freienwalde, and never came back again; that was in the summer. The court is in session to try Bergmann, the parasite, who preyed on the community, a public danger, devoid of scruples. The Graf Zeppelin, on a day of low visibility, flies over Berlin, the stars are bright when it leaves Friedrichshafen at 2.17 a.m. To avoid the bad weather, reported in Central Germany, the airship follows a course leading over Stuttgart, Darmstadt, Frankfort on the Main, Giessen, Kassel, Rathenow. At 8.35 it passes over Nauen, at 8.45 over Staaken. Shortly before nine o'clock the Zeppelin appears above the city, and in spite of the rainy weather, the roofs are crowded with sightseers who exultantly acclaim the airship as it moves to and fro in a loop to the east and north of the city. At 9.45 the first landing-rope is dropped in Staaken.

Franz and Herbert scour Berlin together. They are nearly always away from home. Franz haunts the shelters of the Salvation Army, men's almshouses, and watches out as he wanders through the August Shelter in Auguststrasse. He is sitting in Dresdener Strasse in the Salvation Army hall, where he once went with Reinhold. They sing Hymn No. 66 in the Hymn Book: Say, brother, why do you wait? Arise, and hurry to your goal! Your Saviour called you long ago, He'd like to give peace to your soul. Chorus: Why? Why don't you hurry to your goal, Why? Why don't you want peace in your soul? O brother, don't you feel in your heart the spirit's living might? Don't you want salvation from sin? Oh, hurry to Jesus in flight! Say, brother, why do you wait? Soon death will come and judgment-day too! Oh come, while the gate is still open, Jesus's blood is ready to pray for you!

Franz walks through Fröbelstrasse to the public flophouse, to the Palme, trying to find Reinhold. He lies down on a bunk, today in this one, tomorrow in another, hair-cut 10 pfennigs, shave 5, there they sit, get their papers in order, shoe and shirt peddlers, hey there, guess it's the first time you been here, no use undressing, or you'll be lookin' for your stuff tomorrow morning, your shoes, look here, you've got to put each one separate at the bottom of the bed, else they'll steal everything you got, even your teeth. Do you want to get tattooed? And rest. Night. Black rest, snoring like a sawmill, I haven't seen him. Keep quiet. Ding, dong, what's that, prison. Thought I was in Tegel. Wake up. A fight over there. Let's get out. Around six o'clock, the girls are over there, waiting for their sweethearts, they go into the dives with them and gamble away the money they begged.

Reinhold isn't there, it's damned hopless lookin' for him, he's probably out chasing a skirt again, Elfriede, Emilie, Caroline, Lilli; brown hair, fair hair.

Each night Eva watches Franz's drawn features, no caresses, not a single kind word, he eats and talks but little, just swills liquor and coffee, lies on the sofa with her and groans and groans. We can't find him. "Let him go!" "We can't find him. What'll we do, Eva?" "You've got to stop that, there's no sense in it, you'll go to pieces." "You don't know what we're going to do. That—you didn't go through that, Eva, you don't understand it, Herbert understands a little bit. What'll we do? I want to get him, yep, I'd go to church and get down on my knees if I could catch him."

But all that is unreal. Nothing is real. All this chasing after Reinhold is unreal, it's all a moaning and a terrible fear. Now the die is cast for him. He knows how it will fall. Everything will reveal its meaning, an unexpected, terrible meaning. This game of hide-and-seek won't last long now, my friend.

He spies around Reinhold's house, but his eyes avail him nothing, he looks around and feels nothing. Many people walk past the house and some go in. He has gone in himself, had a look, just because of tararara taraboomdeeay.

The house bursts into laughter, as it sees him standing there. It would like to be able to move in order to collect its neighbors, so that the cross-wise wing and the end wings could get a look at him. Here's a fellow with a wig and an artificial arm, a flaming fool, full of liquor, standing and jawing away about something.

"How do you do, lil' Biberkopf? This is November 22nd. Still rainy weather. Do you want to catch a cold? Wouldn't you rather go to your beloved saloon and get a cognac?"

"Give him up."

"Give in."

"Give Reinhold up."

"Go out to Wuhlgarten. Your nerves must be on edge."

"Give him up."

Then Franz Biberkopf works in the house one evening, he hides a gasoline can and a bottle.

"Come out, are you hiding there, you snake, you stinking dog? You haven't got the nerve to come out, have you?"

The house: "Why are you calling him when he's not here? Why don't you come in, you might have a look around."

"I can't look into all the holes."

"He isn't here. Do you think he'd be crazy enough to stay here?"

"Give him up to me. It'll go bad with you otherwise."

"You and your 'it'll go bad with you.' Go home, fellow, and get a good sleep, you must be pickled, it's because you don't eat nothin'."

Next morning he arrives there just behind the newswoman.

The street-lamps watch him run and start to rock: Fire! Fire! The flame's crawling higher!

Smoke, tongues of flame pour from the dormer-window, the firemen arrive at seven, but Franz is already with Herbert, his fist clenched: "I know nothing and you know nothing, needn't tell me anything. He'll be smoked outa there. Now he can go and look for something, yep, I set it on fire."

"Aw, he don't live there any more, you can bet on that."

"That was his dump all right, and he knows if it burns it was me. We've smoked him out, you'll see him marching up here yet." "I don't know, Franzeken."

But Reinhold doesn't appear. Berlin goes on rattling and rolling and roaring, there's nothing in the papers about their having caught him, he's escaped, gone abroad, they'll never get him.

And Franz stands before Eva, groaning and twisting his body. "I can't do a thing, and gotta stand it, he can smash me to pieces, he gave that girl the works and I'm standing still like a milk-sop. It ain't fair, it's unjust."

"Franz, it can't be changed." "I can't do nothin', I'm finished." "But why are you finished, Franzeken?" "I did what I could, it ain't fair, it's unjust."

The two angels walk beside him, Sarug and Terah are their names, and they talk together, Franz stands in the crowd, walks in the crowd. He is silent, but they hear him, the wild outcry within him. Bulls walk past on raiding parties, but don't recognize Franz. Two angels walk beside him.

Why do the two angels walk beside Franz, and what child's game is this, that angels should walk beside a man, two angels on Alexanderplatz in Berlin, in 1928, beside a former murderer, a burglar, and now a pimp? Yes, this tale of Franz Biberkopf, of his hard, true, and revealing existence, has now progressed thus far. Everything is growing clearer and clearer, the more Franz Biberkopf rears and rages. We are nearing the point where everything will become clear.

The angels talk beside him, their names are Sarug and Terah, and their conversation, while Franz is looking in Tietz's show-window, runs as follows:

"What do you think, Sarug, what would happen if we abandoned this fellow, if we let him go his own way and be caught?" Sarug: "Fundamentally it would make no difference, I think; they will catch him anyhow, that is inevitable. He looked towards that red building over there and he was right, he will be in there in a couple of weeks." Terah: "So you think we are superfluous?" Sarug: "A little, I think—as long as we are forbidden to take him away from this present life." Terah: "You are still a child, Sarug, you have seen this present life for a couple of thousand years only. If we take this man away from the Present, and set him elsewhere, in another existence, will he have accomplished what he could have done in the Here and Now? For every thousand beings and their lives, you must know, there are seven hundred, nay, nine hundred failures." "And what special reason is there, Terah, to protect this man, he is a commonplace man, I see no reason to protect him." "Commonplace, uncommon—what are these? Is the beggar 'commonplace' and the rich man so exceptional? The rich man may be a beggar and the beggar rich tomorrow. This man is on the brink of a vision. Many have reached that stage. But he is also on the point, I tell you, of becoming sentient. You see, Sarug, he who goes through much experience, and lives through much, is easily inclined towards mere knowledge, and then—towards escape, and death. He is no longer interested. He has passed along the road of experience and grown weary. His journey has outwearied body and soul. Do you understand?" "Yes."

"But after a man has experienced much and learned neither to hold fast, nor to go down, nor to die, but to stretch himself, to stretch himself, to feel, not evade things, but to stand straight, with a steadfast soul, that is something. You don't know, Sarug, how you came to be what you are, what you were, and how it comes about that you are walking with me here, protecting other beings." "That is true, Terah, I do not know that, my memory is all blotted out." "It will slowly come back to you. A man is never strong by himself, through himself, alone, unless there is something back of him. Strength must be acquired, you do not know how you acquired it, but you stand there and things which destroy others are no longer dangerous for you." "But he does not want me, this Biberkopf. You yourself say he wants to shake us off." "He'd like to die, Sarug. No man has ever made that great step forward, that terrible step, without desiring death. And you are right, that is how most men fail." "So you have hope for this man?" "Yes, because he is strong and unimpaired, and because twice already he has stood his ground. So let us stay beside him, Terah, I ask that favor of you." "Granted."

A young doctor, a giant of a man, is sitting before Franz. "Good morning, Herr Klemens. You'd better go on a trip, this often happens after a death in the family! You ought to get a change of air, the whole of Berlin will oppress you now, you need another climate. Don't you want to get a little diversion? You are his sister-in-law, aren't you, has he anybody to accompany him?" "I can start off alone, if necessary." "Necessary, I tell you, Herr Klemens, that's the only thing you can do. Just a little quiet diversion, something to take your mind off this, yes, but not too much of it, otherwise it might have the contrary effect. Always in moderation. There's still good weather everywhere just now. Where would you like to go?" Eva: "How about a tonic, Lecithin, wouldn't that be good for him, and then more sleep?" "I'll write it all down, wait a minute, Adalin." "I've given him Adalin already." (Don't want that poison!) "Then you had better take Phanodorn, one pill at night, with peppermint tea. Tea is good, it helps in taking the medicine; and then you might go to the Zoo with him." "Nope, I'm not interested in animals." "Well, then to the Botanical Gardens, a little diversion, but not too much." "Why not prescribe some nerve-tonic to strengthen him?" "We might give him a little opium to raise his spirits." "I drink already, Doctor." "No, opium is different. But I'll prescribe Lecithin, it's a new preparation, the instructions are written on the label. And then you must take baths, calming baths, of course, you have a bathroom, madame, haven't you?" "Certainly, Doctor." "Well, you see, that's the advantage of these new houses. That's why we all say 'certainly.' It wasn't like that in my place. I had to have everything installed, had to pay a wad of money, and then getting the rooms painted, you'd be astonished, if you saw it, that's what we haven't got here. All right, then, Lecithin and baths, one every other morning. And then a masseur should give his muscles a good kneading, to give his whole body some exercise." Eva: "That's right." "A good massage, you'll see, you're going to feel much freer, Herr Klemens. Don't worry, you'll feel all right again. And then, travel." "It's not easy with him, Doctor." "Doesn't matter, it'll come. Well, then, Herr Klemens, how about it?" "How about what?" "Don't let your spirits droop, take these things regularly, also this sleeping potion and the massage." "All right, Doctor; good-bye, and I thank you for the advice."

"Now you got what you wanted, Eva." "I'll fix up the baths, and the nerve-medicine." "Yes, go ahead." "And you'll stay upstairs till I get back." "All right, Eva, all righty."

Eva puts on her coat and goes downstairs. And a quarter of an hour later Franz goes, too.

The Battle begins. We ride to Hell with Trumpets and Drums

The battlefield calls, the battlefield!

We ride to hell with trumpets and drums. This world no longer interests us. It can go to hell with everything that's on it and below it and above it. With all its human beings, women and men, with all its infernal scoundrels, I'll never trust any of 'em again. If I were a little bird, I'd take a bag of slush, I'd toss it behind me with both feet and away I'd rush. If I were a horse, a dog, a cat, it would be best to drop dung on the earth, and then hustle off, as quickly as possible.

There's nothing happening in the world and I'm not itchin' to get soused again, I might do it, at that, boozing and boozing and boozing, and then the whole lousy show would start all over again. The good Lord created the earth, I wonder if a sky-pilot could tell me why. But still he made it much better than the sky-pilots know, he let us piss on the whole damned show, and he gave us two hands and a rope to use, to hell with the whole she-bang, that's what we can do, then this hellish racket's all over, happy days, my blessing to you, we ride to hell with trumpets and drums.

If I could catch Reinhold, my rage would be over, I would grab him by the neck and break his neck, and not let him live, I'd feel better then, and satisfied, too, that would be the right thing to do, and I'd have peace. But that dirty rat has given me so much trouble, he made a criminal out of me again, he broke my arm, and now he's laughing at me somewhere in Switzerland. Miserable as a mangy hound, that's the way I go running around, he can do whatever he wants with me, not a man will help me, not even the criminal police, they want to catch me, that's all, was it me who killed Mieze, didn't that crook do it, and he got me in trouble along with him. As the proverb says: The pitcher goes to the well until it breaks. I've stood enough, I've done enough, I can't do any more. Nobody can deny that I defended myself. But what's too much is too much. Because I can't kill Reinhold, I'll bump myself off. I'll just ride to hell with trumpets and drums.

Who is it standing in Alexanderstrasse, very slowly moving one leg after the other? It's Franz Biberkopf. What's he done? Well, you know all that, don't you? A pimp, a hardened criminal, a poor fool, he's been beaten, and how—he's in for it now. That cursed fist that beat him. That terrible fist that gripped him. The other fists hammered at him, but he escaped. A blow fell and the red wound gaped. But it healed one day. Franz didn't change and went on his way. Now the fist keeps up the fight, it is terrible in its might, it ravages him, body and soul, Franz advances with timid steps, he has learned his rôle: my life no longer belongs to me, I don't know what to set about. Franz Biberkopf is down and out.

It is November, late in the evening, about nine. The fellows are idling around in Münzstrasse, the noise of the street-cars and busses and newsvenders is terrific, the cops, carrying rubber maces, start out from their stations.

A group of people carrying red flags march along Landsberger Strasse: Awake, ye wretched of the earth!

"Mokka fix," Alexanderstrasse, excellent peerless cigars, well-brewed beer in fine mugs, card-playing is strictly prohibited, our guests are requested to watch their overcoats, as we are not responsible. Proprietor. Breakfast from 6 a.m. to 1 p.m., 75 pfennigs, one cup of coffee, two boiled eggs, bread and butter.

At the coffee-joint, in Prenzlauer Strasse, they cheer and acclaim Franz: "The noble Baron!" They take off his wig, he unbuckles his artificial arm, then orders a beer, and lays his overcoat across his knee.

Three men are sitting there with gray faces, and, no doubt about it, they're convicts, probably escaped. They're gabbing away like anything, talking a blue streak.

Well, so I'm thirsty, and I says to myself, why should I walk so far, there's a cellar, Polacks livin' in it, I'll show 'em my sausage and the cigarettes. They don't ask me where I got that stuff from, they buy it, and give me the booze. So I leaves everything there, and in the morning I waits till they're gone and then I slips down to the cellar, I got some hooks with me, everything's still there, my sausage and the cigarettes, and I blows. Fine business, what d'y say?

Police-dogs, a lot they kin do. Five of our men flew the coop through the wall. I can tell yez exactly how. The walls have metal on both sides, sheet-iron, a quarter of an inch at least. But those babies bore their way through the floor, yep, a cement floor, they dig a hole, workin' at night, of course, and from there under the walls. And them police-bunglers come along and say we shoulda heard it. Well, we were asleep. How'd we hear anything, and why us?

Laughter and merriment. Oh happy days, oh glorious days, at our table we sing a roundelay, hip-hip-hip-hurray!

And later, of course, who's this comes rolling up? Why, it's our friend, the police sergeant, First Sergeant Schwab, he wants to put on a lotta airs, and says he's heard all that day before yesterday, but he was out of town, away on duty, on the q.t. When something breaks loose, they've always been away on the q.t. Another mug, me, too, three cigarettes.

A young girl at the table is combing the hair of a tall blond man who sings: "O Sonnenburg, O Sunny Burg." When there comes a pause, he starts off, he has to sing something about the sun:

"O Sonnenburg, O Sonnenburg, how green are all your branches! This summer I was twenty-nine, but not in Berlin or Danzig did I serve my time, nor in Königsberg, either, where was it anyway? Don't you know, you sap, why, in Sonnenburg, in Sonnenburg.

"O Sonnenburg, O Sonnenburg, how green are all your branches! You're a model jail all right, where humanity rules from morn till night. There they don't beat you, don't razz you, don't mistreat you, they don't make life hell for you, there a fellow gets his fill, grub and smokes and beer to swill.

"Fine feathers in the beds, brandy, beer, and cigarettes. Say, boy, it's certainly grand, our guards are devoted to us, with heart and with hand, we want to make a present of military boots to the officers, you could give us cigarettes, with heart and with hand, ain't it grand. Just let us booze, with heart and with hand, we'll let you sell your military boots and uniforms left over from the war, it's grand, we won't have them altered, and you can sell 'em on the spot, we need the kale, for we are just poor prisoners in jail.

"There are a few proud comrades who want to give us away, but we'll break their bones for 'em, so they'd better think well before they start to bray, or we'll properly dust 'em up, and sorry will be the day when we'll bust 'em up.

"Only the warden is a boob, why—he never notices nothin'. The other day a fellow came and wanted to inspect the free penitentiary of Sonnenburg, it disagreed with him. Why it disagreed with him, why it disagreed with him. I'll tell you all about it now. We're in the saloon together. Two officers are sitting near and while we enjoy our booze and beer, who should turn up,—yes, who should turn up, yes, who turns up just then?

"It's, boom, boom, it's, boom, boom, it's the Inspector, what do you think o' that? Here's how, say we, long live our li'l Inspector, it's he, long may he stick to the ceiling, you see, take a cognac and sit next to me.

"What does the Inspector say? It's me, the Inspector, boom, boom, make way for the Inspector, I am the Inspector, boom, boom, there he is. I'll have you all locked up, convicts and officers, you'll catch something, when I get through with you, when you have to face the music, you'll feel blue, boom, boom, there he stands, boom, boom, there he is, boom, boom.

"O Sonnenburg, O Sonnenburg, how green are all your branches! We made hell out of his life, till he ran home to his wife, and took his revenge on her; boom, boom, united they stand, boom, boom, ain't he grand, boom, boom, the Inspector. Oh boy, now don't you look like a fool! ah don't be angry—just keep cool!"

Brown pants and a black cloth coat! One of them pulls a brown prison coat out of a package. Auction Sale: To the Highest Bidder! All goods at sacrifice prices, brown sales week, a coat to be had cheap, the price of a cognac. Who wants it? Merriment, joy, oh happy days, oh glorious days. Listen, mate, what's your sweetheart's name, let's drink another of the same. Then a pair of canvas shoes, familiar with local conditions of prison life, straw-soled, suitable for escapes, also a bed-cover. Gee, but you shoulda given that back to the old man.

The saloon-keeper's wife comes sneaking in and softly closes the door: not so much noise, there are some customers in the front room. One of the men looks towards the window. His neighbor laughs: the window's out of the question. When things get hot—look! He puts his hand under the table, opens a trap-door below; the cellar, and then you'd better slip quickly across the other courtyard, you don't have to climb, everything's smooth sailing. But keep your hat on, otherwise they'll notice something.

An old fellow grumbles: "Nice song you sang there. But there are lots of others. Not bad. Know this one?" He pulls a piece of paper out of his pocket, it's letter-paper, torn in shreds. Somebody had written on it in an unsteady hand: "The Dead Convict." "But not too sad!" "What d'y mean sad? It's as true as yours." "Hush-a-bye, don't you cry, when you wake, you'll have a little cake."

The dead convict. Poor, yet full of youth's enchantment, once he walked the righteous highway, sacred were to him things noble, mean things he left on the byway. But misfortune's evil spirit lurked at life's turn, him a-spying, held suspect of evil actions in the law's nets he was lying: (The chase, the pursuit, the damned pursuit, them dirty dogs chased me, how they chased me, they almost killed me. It goes on and on, a man don't know how to save himself, on and on, on and on, you don't know, you can't run fast enough, you run as fast as you can, but in the end they catch you anyway. Now they've got Franz, I guess I'll give up the game, I'm that far gone, well, here's how, happy days, old boy.)

All his crying, all his protests, all his rage was idle prating, evidence was dead against him, and the chains for him were waiting. Though the judges were mistaken (the chase, the pursuit, the damned chase), when his sentence they had spoken (how those damned hounds chased me), what availed his guiltless conscience, since his honor's shield was broken. Man, oh fellow-man, he whimpered, why oppress, why ruin me, did I do you injury? (It goes on, you can't see your way out. And on and on, you run, you can't run fast enough, you can just do the best you can.)

When from prison walls returning, he came back, with outlawed feeling, things were now the same no longer, changed, in dust they found him kneeling. To the river's bank he stumbled, but he found the bridge was sundered, sick at heart, and full of loathing, back into the night he wandered. All refused to still his hunger (the chase, the chase, the damned chase), bitterness oppressed him starkly, then he yielded to his fury—"Guilty this time," said Life darkly.

(Guilty, guilty, guilty, ah, that's it, you have to be, you had to be guilty, you ought to be guilty a thousand times more!) Such a deed is punished harshly, custom, morals have this meaning, to a cell within the prison back he wandered, sadly keening. (Franz, hallelujah, you can hear it, doomed to be a thousand times more guilty, a thousand times more guilty.) Yes, once more a jump to freedom, murder, robbery, and plunder, and without the smallest pity, tear that Beast, Mankind, asunder! He was gone, but soon in fetters he came back again. How fleeting, was his final drunken revel! And "Life" was the judges' greeting. (The chase, the chase, the damned chase, he was right; he did the right thing.)

Now he wailed no more for pity. Let them curse! It doesn't matter! Mute, he bore the yoke upon him, and he learned to fawn and flatter. Dully he went at his labors, always doing the same thing daily, long his spirit had been broken, like a dead man he walked palely. (The chase, the chase, the damned chase, they've kept on chasing me, I've always done the best I could, and now I'm down and out, but it's not my fault, what could I do? My name's Franze Biberkopf, and it still is, better watch out!)

And today his course is ended, with the springtime's golden gleaming, in the sod he's being lowered, it's the cell of convicts' dreaming. Now the prison-bell is ringing it's farewell with eerie sadness, to the man who lost his bearings and found death in prison madness. (Look out, gentlemen, you don't know Franz Biberkopf as yet, he won't sell himself for anything in the world, when that boy has to travel to his grave, he'll have as many friends as he has fingers, friends who'll have to present him to the Good Lord up above and say: First we'll come and then it'll be Franze's turn. You needn't be astonished, dear Lord, that he should come with a swell team like that, they chased him about so much, with the result that he now arrives in a handsome turn-out. He was so tiny on this earth, that now he's in heaven he's got to show what he is.)

Around the table they continue to sing and to gossip. Franz Biberkopf has been moping all the time, and now he feels bright and fresh again. He fixes himself up, ties his arm on, lost it in the war, it's always war with me. War never stops as long as you live, the main thing is to stand on your own feet.

Franz stands on the iron step of the coffee-joint, out in the street. And it is raining and dripping and pouring, it's dark, there's lots of activity in Prenzlauer Strasse. A mob is standing around in Alexanderstrasse, opposite. Cops among them. Franz turns around and goes slowly in that direction.

On Alexanderplatz is Police Headquarters

It is twenty past nine. In the lighted courtyard of headquarters a few persons stand talking. They tell each other jokes and shift from one foot to the other. A young police officer comes up and salutes. "It's now ten after nine, Herr Pilz, did you actually give that order? We need the car at nine." "One of our men has just gone upstairs to phone the Alexander Barracks; we ordered the car yesterday morning." A new man arrives: "Yes, they say the car started off at five before nine, it must've lost its way, so they're sending another." "That's it, lost its way, and we can just wait." "Well, I asked them where's the car? He says: who's talking? So I says, Secretary Pilz, so he says, this is Lieutenant So and So. Then I says to him: Well, I'm supposed to find out, it's the Chief's orders, we asked for the section car yesterday, it's for a raid at nine tonight, the order was given in writing, I'm to find out if the written order got there all right. You should have heard him, he became polite as the devil right away, that lieutenant did, well, of course, everything's on the way, there's been some trouble, and so on."

The cars arrive. Some ladies and gentlemen, detectives, inspectors, policewomen, get into one of them. That's the car in which later on Franz Biberkopf will come riding along, among fifty men and women, the angels will have abandoned him, his expression will be different from the one he had, when he left the coffee-joint, but the angels will dance, ladies and gentlemen, whether you believe or don't believe, it will certainly happen.

The car with its male and female occupants is on its way, it's not an armored car, albeit a vehicle of combat and law, a truck, people sit on benches, and it travels across Alexanderplatz between harmless trucks and taxis, and the people in the war car all look so comfortably at ease, it is an undeclared war, they ride in the performance of their duty, some of them quietly smoke their pipes, some of them their cigars, and the ladies observe: that gentleman in front must be a newspaper man, so everything will be in the papers tomorrow. Contentedly they ride up Landsberger Strasse to the right, they journey towards their goals by a roundabout way, lest the dives should know what's in the wind. But the people walking below get a good look at the car: they don't look very long, it's rather terrible, rather alarming, but it's quickly over, they're out to capture criminals, dreadful that such things should happen, let's go to the movies.

The car stops in Rückerstrasse, the passengers get out and go up the street on foot. The little street is empty, the raiding party wanders along the pavement, here's the Rücker Bar.

They occupy the doorway and stand guard in front of the entrance; a few take up their position across the way, the others enter the place. G'd evenin'. The waiter smiles. We know all about that! What'll you have, gentlemen? Thanks, got no time, get your accounts settled, it's a raid; everybody's to come along to headquarters. Laughter, protests, imagine it, don't get excited, damning and swearing, laughter; keep your shirt on, why, I got my papers with me, you're in luck, you'll be back in half an hour, that won't help me any, I gotta work, don't holler so much, Otto, free sightseeing at headquarters, night-illuminations. Hop right in. The car's as full as a sardine can. Somebody sings: Who's the guy rolled the cheese to the station, rolled along the cheese, the fresh louse, how dare he do such a thing, nobody had paid the custom-house fees for the cheese, for the cheese, so the cops got down on it and started to frown on it, 'cause they rolled along the cheese for which they hadn't paid the fees.

The car leaves. Handkerchiefs flutter: who's the guy rolled the cheese to the station, the cheese, the cheese, the cheese?

Well, that went pretty slick. We'll go on foot. A refined-looking gentleman crosses the street and salutes. Captain from the local station, the Commissioner? They enter a hallway, the others divide up, meeting-place Prenzlauer, corner Münz.

The Alexander Quelle is full up, it's Friday, everybody who's had his payday, has come to get a drink or two, music, radio, the bulls slide along the bar, the young commissioner talks with somebody, the band stops: Raid, Criminal Squad, everybody's to come along to headquarters. People are sitting around the tables, they laugh and don't let themselves be disturbed, they go on gabbling, the waiter continues serving. A girl standing in the aisle screams and weeps, between two others: but I left the other place and reported myself offa the register, only that woman in the new place hasn't sent my name in yet, well, then, you'll simply have to stay overnight, that's nothin', I won't go along, I won't let a cop touch me, don't get yourself all worked up, nobody ever got healthy with that. Lemme get out, what d'y mean out, you'll get out when it's your turn, the car's just left, why not get more cars then, now don't start telling us what we ought to do. Waiter, a bottle of champagne to wash my feet with. Heh, I gotta go to work, I gotta work at Lau's, he pays me by the hour, well, you've got to come along, that's all, I've gotta go to my building job, this is an attack on liberty, everybody's got to come along, you'll go along, Christ, don't get so excited, these people gotta make a raid once in a while, that's all, otherwise they wouldn't know what they were here for.

Out they go, in droves, traveling back and forth to headquarters, the bulls walk to and fro. There's noise of screams in the Ladies' Toilet, a virgin is lying on the floor, her friend stands over her, what's that man doing in the Ladies' Toilet? The girl has cramps, can't you see that? The bulls smile, have you got your papers, well, all right then, you can stay with her. She goes on screaming, watch out, when the coast's clear, she'll get up and they'll dance the tango together. I say the first guy that touches me gets a hook on the chin, a second would simply be violation of a corpse. The place is almost empty. At the door a man stands between two cops and roars: I've been in Manchester, in London, in New York, this never happens in a big city, things like this don't happen in Manchester or in London. They trot him off. Off with 'em, how do you feel, thanks, my regards to poor dead Towser.

At a quarter to eleven, when the raid is nearly over, and only a few tables remain occupied in the back where the staircase is and in the corner at the side, a man comes in, although, as a matter of fact, nobody is supposed to come in now. The coppers are energetic and won't let anybody pass; but here and there a girl peeps in through the window: Say, I've got a date, no, young lady, you'll have to come back at twelve, your sweetheart will be at headquarters till then. The old gentleman has been watching the rumpus that finally occurs, when the cops use their clubs, because more want to get out than can get into the car. Now the car's gone, things are less crowded. The man quietly walks through the door, past the two bulls both of whom are looking the other way, because some people are trying to get into the place and are argufying with the cops. Just at this moment, a squad of policemen marches out of the barracks and starts up the other side of the street with a lot of hallooing and hitching up of belts. The gray-haired man walks through the room and asks for a glass of beer at the bar; he gets it and goes upstairs where the woman is still yelling away in the Ladies' Toilet. As for the others, the few who are left, they laugh and prattle, just as if the whole business didn't concern them.

The man sits alone at a table, sipping his beer, he looks across the room. Then his foot knocks against something lying on the floor next to the wall; gee whiz, he reaches down, it's a revolver, somebody got rid of it, not bad, now I've got two. One on each finger, and if the Good Lord asks why, I'll say: I am traveling with a big turnout, all a fellow didn't get below, he can get above. They're pulling off a raid here, and they're right. Somebody had a heavy meal at headquarters and so he said: Let's pull off a raid, something's gotta be done that will be headlined in the papers. The higher-ups oughta know we're on the job all right, and then maybe one of those chaps wants to get an increase in salary, his wife needs a fur coat, and that's why they nab people and pick out a Friday, when the ghost walks.

He has kept his hat on, his right hand is in his pocket, his left hand also, except when he's reaching for his beer. A bull with a bristle brush on his hunter's hat, marches breezily through the room, everywhere there are empty tables, cigarette boxes on the floor, newspapers and chocolate wrappers. Everybody get ready now, the last car'll be here soon. He asks the old gentleman: "Did you pay up?" The old man grumbles and looks straight ahead: "I jus' come in." "Well, you didn't have to do that, but you gotta come along." "Jus' leave that to me." The bull, a sturdy, square-shouldered fellow, studies him from above, queer the way the man stares into space, he probably wants to start trouble. He does not say a word, but walks slowly downstairs through the room, and just then the sparkling eyes of the old man strike him, say, but he's got funny eyes, that one, there's something wrong with that chap. He walks to the door where the others are standing, and they whisper together, then they all walk out. A few minutes later the door opens. The bulls are coming back. Now for the rest of you, get out, everybody come along! The waiter laughs: "Next time you might take me along, too. I'd like to get a look at your shebang up there." "Oh, well, in another hour you'll be busy again, don't worry. There's already a few outside, just come back from the first car-load, they want to get in."

"Outside, sir, you gotta come along." He means me. When you've a sweetheart true, who has given her heart to you, you don't ask her when and how, if only she'll kiss you now.

The gentleman does not get excited: "Heh, there, got cotton in your ears? I tell you, you've gotta get up." You were sent me by the spring, my sweet, for until I came to know you, all my art was incomplete. Just let some more of 'em come along, one isn't nearly enough, there are five horses to my turn-out.

Three cops are already waiting on the stairs, the first comes up and then the bulls walk through the room. The tall young commissioner leads them, they're in a hurry. They've chased me enough, I did all I could, am I a human being or not?

Then he pulls his left hand out of his pocket, and, without rising from his seat, fires at the first cop who is about to rush furiously at him. Bang, we have settled all our accounts on earth, now we'll go riding to hell with trumpets, to hell with trumpets and drums.

The man staggers to one side. Franz gets up and wants to move towards the wall: the pack of them rush from the door into the room. That's nice, hop in, babies. He raises his arm, there's someone behind him, Franz thrusts him aside with his shoulder, and just then a blow crashes on his hand, another blow in his face, a blow on his hat, another on his arm. My arm, my arm, I've only got one arm and they're gonna smash my arm to bits, what'll I do, they'll kill me, first Mieze, then me. It's no use, it's no use, nothin's any use.

And he sinks down beside the railing.

Before he can shoot again, Franz Biberkopf has sunk down beside the railing. He has given up the game, he has cursed his life, surrendered his arms. There he lies.

The bulls and the coppers shove the tables and chairs aside and kneel beside him; they turn him over on his back, the man has an artificial arm, two revolvers, where are his papers, wait a minute, why, he's wearing a wig. Franz Biberkopf opens his eyes as they tear at his hair. Then they shake him, pull him up by the shoulders and set him straight, he can stand all right, he'll have to, they put his hat on. Outside they're all sitting in the car, Franz Biberkopf is being led through the door with a handcuff on his left wrist. There's a lot of noise in Münzstrasse, a mob, a shot was fired inside, look out, there he comes, that was him. They have already sent the wounded policeman away in an automobile.

This, then, is the car in which at half-past nine the commissioners, criminal police, and female officers, left headquarters, now they are starting back, Franz Biberkopf's in the car, his angels have left him, as I have already reported. In the lighted courtyard at headquarters the load is discharged. The prisoners walk up a little stairway in the back to a long, wide hallway, the women are put in separate rooms, and those who are discharged, their papers having been found in order, have to pass through the line of bulls, who examine everybody's chest, pants, right down to their shoes; the men laugh, there's a racket going on, a lot of cursing is heard in the corridor, the young commissioner and his officers walk back and forth, pacifying them, gotta be patient. The coppers are posted at the doors, no one can go to the toilet unaccompanied.

Inside officials in civilian clothes sit at their tables questioning the prisoners. They look at their papers, if they have any, then they write on a big sheet of paper: Place of Occurrence, District Court Area, Where arrested, Police Station, 4th Precinct. What's your name? Details of Arrest. When were you arrested last? Why not take me first, I gotta go to work. Chief of Police, Section 4, Arrested in the forenoon, afternoon, evening: Christian name, surname, calling or vocation, birthday, month, year, where born, no address, was unable to give an address, his statement *re* address proved false after inquiries made in the district. You'll have to wait till your station has answered, it doesn't go that fast, they've only got two hands, and, moreover, they've had people before who gave an address of some kind, it seemed O.K., there was somebody living there by the same name, only when you went there, it was somebody else, he simply had the other fellow's papers, hooked them from him, or he was his friend, or some other crooked game. Inquiries at the registry office for warrants of arrest, his gray card taken away, no gray card. Documents to be filed with the police report, exhibits concerning this or other misdemeanors, objects with which the suspect might injure himself or others, personal property, cane, umbrella, knife, revolver, brass knuckles.

They bring Franz Biberkopf in. It's all over with Franz Biberkopf. They have nabbed him. They lead him in, handcuffed. His head is hanging on his chest. They are going to question him downstairs, in the room of the commissioner on duty. But the man does not talk, he is rigid, he often touches his face, his right eye is swollen from the blow with the rubber mace. He quickly lets his arm drop, at which he gets a few more whacks.

Downstairs, across the dark courtyard, those who have been released wander toward the street, arm-in-arm with the girls they wend their way across the lighted courtyard. When you've a sweetheart true, who's given her heart to you, and so here we go, here we go, marching along, from one beer-saloon to the other, singing a song. I testify to the accuracy of the above statement, the signature has been taken, name and service number of the officer who seized the exhibit. To the District Court, Berlin Center, Section 151, Examining Judge 1 a.

At last Franz Biberkopf is introduced and held in custody. This man fired a shot during a raid in the Alexander Quelle, he has also committed other offenses punishable under the criminal code. They found him stretched out in the Alexander Quelle and half an hour later discovered that—in addition to eight other men wanted by the authorities, as well as the inevitable escaped reformatory inmates—the police had made an exceptionally good catch. As for the man who had fallen after the shooting, he had an artificial right arm and wore a gray wig. From this and from his photograph (which was in the records) they quickly established the fact that the disguised man was Franz Biberkopf who had been connected with the murder of the prostitute, Emilie Parsunke, in Freienwalde, and who had previously been convicted of manslaughter and procuration.

For some time he had neglected to make the prescribed police registrations; well, we have caught one of them, we'll soon get the other one too.

NINTH BOOK

Now Franz Biberkopf's earthly journey is ended. It is now time for him to be crushed outright. He falls into the hands of the dark power called death, and that, it seems to him, is a fitting place to stay. But he learns what this power thinks of him, in a way he did not expect, which surpasses everything he has met with up till now.

They settle accounts. He is enlightened concerning his ignorance, his pride, his every blunder. And then our old Franz Biberkopf breaks down, his whole life goes asunder.

The man's broken up. But a new Biberkopf will now be shown, superior to the man we've known, and of whom we may expect that he'll make a better job of things.

Reinhold's Black Wednesday, but this Chapter may be Skipped

As the police surmised: "Well, we've caught one of them, we'll soon get the other one too," so it turns out. Only not quite the way they anticipate. They think they'll catch him soon. But—they have him already, he's visited the same red headquarters, passed through other rooms and hands, and is now in Moabit.

With Reinhold things move quickly and he's made a definite end of it. The boy doesn't like a lot of watching and waiting. Don't we remember how he once acted towards Franz? Hardly had Reinhold known what the other was up to, when he knocked him down.

One evening Reinhold starts out for Motzstrasse, and he says to himself: those murder posters announcing that reward have been put up all over town, I gotta pull a job and get myself caught with false papers, snatching a handbag or something. Jail's the safest place when things begin to get hot. All this works according to schedule, except that he hands the fine lady a bit too vigorous a crack in the jaw. But what's the odds, thinks Reinhold, the main thing is, I must make myself scarce. So at headquarters they take his false papers from him, he's Moroskiewicz, a Polish pickpocket, off with him to Moabit. They don't notice at headquarters whom it is they have caught, the lad has never been in the coop before, and then who could remember by heart the description of every criminal? And very silently his trial proceeds, secretly, quietly and silently, just the way he had slipped through headquarters. But since he is a pickpocket, wanted by the Polish police, and this crook dares go out on the streets in a smart neighborhood and knock people down, snatching a lady's handbag, why, it's unheard of, we aren't in Russian Poland, after all, what did you think you were up to anyway, this should be an object lesson, so he gets four years in prison with five years' loss of citizenship, parole, and that sort of thing. His brass knuckles are confiscated. The defendant bears the cost of the trial, there's ten minutes' recess, the room is over-heated, please open the window in the meantime, have you anything else to say?

Reinhold, of course, has nothing to say, he reserves the right to a second trial, he's glad they talked to him that way, nothing can happen to him. So two days later everything is over, everything, everything. And we're out of the woods. All that damned bunk with Mieze and that jackass Biberkopf, but I didn't get into trouble, I did what I wanted, hallelujah, hallelujah, hallelujah.

Things have reached this point, when they catch Franz and take him to headquarters; the real murderer, Reinhold, is kept in Brandenburg, and nobody thinks about him, and he's drowned and forgotten, the world can go hang, they won't find him so easy here, don't you worry. No remorse tortures him, and if things had gone the way he expected them to go, he would still be sitting there today, or have escaped while being removed to another prison.

But such is life, the silliest proverbs prove to be true, and when a man thinks, now it's all right, it's not all right by a long shot. Man proposes, God disposes, and there's always that last straw to break the camel's back. How they catch Reinhold, and how he soon will have to travel a hard and cruel road—all this I shall now relate. But if any of my readers is not interested, let him simply skip the next few pages. All I have reported in this book, *Alexanderplatz, Berlin*, about Franz Biberkopf's fate is true, and you may read it twice or three times and learn it by heart; it contains a truth which can be grasped. But now Reinhold is through playing his rôle. Since, however, he represents that cold force which nothing in life can change, I will tell you about that force in its last bitter struggle. You will see him, hard and stone-like, right up to the last, unmoved, his life goes on—whereas Franz Biberkopf bends, and at last, like an element struck by certain rays, is transmuted into another element. Oh, it's easy to say we're all human beings. If there is a God—not only do we differ before him as regards our malevolence or kindness, we all have different natures and different lives, in kind, in origin, in future and destiny we are all different. Listen now to what finally happened to Reinhold.

*

It happens that Reinhold has to work in Brandenburg Prison with a man in the mat-weaving department who is also a Pole, but a real one, and he's real pickpocket, too, a very clever one who knows Moroskiewicz. He hears the name Moroskiewicz, why, I know him, where is he; then he sees Reinhold and says to himself, gee whiz, he's certainly changed, it's unbelievable. So then he acts as if he hadn't spotted anything and didn't know him, but one day he sidles up to Reinhold in the toilet where they are smoking away and gives him half a cigarette and talks to him; and it turns out that he doesn't know any Polish at all. Reinhold isn't pleased about this Polish conversation and gets himself transferred from the weaving department, and, because he sometimes shams weakness, the foreman takes him on as helper in the cell division where the others can't get near him. But Dluga, the Pole, keeps at it. Reinhold shouts from cell to cell: Finished work outside! When they are standing with the foreman near Dluga's cell and the foreman is just about to count the mats, Dluga whispers to Reinhold that he knows a fellow named Moroskiewicz from Warsaw, he's a pickpocket, are you any relation of his? Reinhold gets frightened, slips the Pole a small package of tobacco, and moves away. Finished work outside! The Pole is pleased about the tobacco, there's something in this for him, he starts to blackmail Reinhold, for that feller's always got money from somewhere.

This business threatens to become terribly dangerous for Reinhold, but this time he is still in luck. He parries the blow. He spreads the news that his countryman Dluga wants to squeal, he knows something about him. And right in the middle of recess, there develops a big row. Reinhold joins the others in giving the Pole a terrible clouting. For this he's given a week's isolation cell, with bedding and warm meals only every third day. Then he gets out and finds everything calm and tame as usual.

But then our Reinhold gets into trouble all by himself. Throughout his life the janes had brought him either evil days or good days. Now love is about to break his neck. That business with Dluga has caused him a lot of excitement, and he is raging because he has to sit around here all the time and let a goof like that get his goat. A fellow has no fun here, none at all, and it's lonesome, the whole thing is getting more and more on his nerves each week. He goes on like that for a time, he'd like to kill that fellow Dluga; then he gets to know a young chap, a burglar, who is here in Brandenburg for the first time, and is to be discharged in March. They first come together through tobacco-smuggling and calling Dluga all kinds of names, then they become true and loyal friends in a way Reinhold had never known before, and even if it's not a dame, but just a youngster, it's very nice, and Reinhold is now very happy in the Brandenburg Prison. So this damned affair with Dluga has brought me something after all. Only it's too bad the boy's got to leave so soon.

"I've gotta wear this black cap and this brown coat for a long time to come, and while I'm cooped up here, where will you be, my little Konrad?" Konrad is the lad's name, or rather that's what he says, he hails from Mecklenburg, and has the talent to become a big criminal. One of the two men with whom he had pulled a few jobs in Pomerania is here with ten years to do. One black Wednesday, the evening before Konrad's discharge, the two are together again in the dormitory, and Reinhold almost kills himself worrying because he's gonna be all alone again now and has nobody—but there'll be somebody all right—don't you worry, Reinhold, you'll soon get an outside job at Werder or somewhere else—but Reinhold can't pull himself together, he just can't, can't, no, sir, he just can't understand why things went so wrong with him, that damned bitch Mieze and that blockhead Franz Biberkopf, what are they to me, those boobs, those boneheads, I might be outside now playing the big boy, here there's nothin' but a lot of poor nuts who'll never get any farther. Then Reinhold almost has a fit and whimpers and wails and begs Konrad, you gotta take me along with you, you gotta take me along. Konrad consoles him as best he can, but it won't do, it's no use advising anybody to make a breakaway.

Through one of the polishers they get a small bottle of distilled alcohol from the carpenter-shop. Konrad gives Reinhold the bottle, they both take a nip. It's impossible to escape, two did it yesterday, or rather tried to do it, but one of them only got as far as Neuendorfer Strasse and tried to hop on a truck, when a patrol got him, the fellow had bled a lot from those damned pieces of glass they put on top of the wall, they had to take him to the hospital, who knows if his hands will ever get well again. As for the other, well, he was cleverer, all he did was to take a look at the glass, and off he went back into the courtyard.

"Nope, there's nothin' to this makin' a break, Reinhold." The latter is quite contrite and soft, he's got to stay here four years, and all on account of that fool business in Motzstrasse, and on account of that sow Mieze and that jackass, Franz. He sips some of the carpenter's alcohol and feels better, they've laid their things out, the knife on top of the bundles, closing-time, the lock's turned twice, the bolt's drawn, the beds are made. They whisper together, sitting on Konrad's bed, it's Reinhold's melancholy hour: "I'll tell you where to go in Berlin. When you get out, you go see my girl, who knows whose girl she is now, I'll give you her address and then lemme know, get me? And also find out what's happened about that case I was tellin' you about, y'know, this fellow Dluga smelled somethin'. I knew a feller in Berlin once, a real dumbbell, his name was Biberkopf, Franz Biberkopf—"

And so he whispers and tells stories and clings to Konrad who listens with his ears wide open, he just keeps on saying yes, and soon he will know everything. He has to help Reinhold get to bed, because Reinhold is weeping with rage and desolation and anger at his fate and feels he's caught in a trap. It doesn't help him when Konrad says, what's four years anyway? Reinhold can't, he simply can't, he just can't stand the gaff, he can't go on like this, it's a regular prison fit he has.

That's Black Wednesday. On Friday Konrad is with Reinhold's girl in Berlin. He gets a cordial reception, tells her a lot of stories, and gets money from her, too. That's Friday. On Monday it's all up with Reinhold. Konrad meets a friend in Seestrasse with whom he had once been in a reformatory, and who is now out of a job. Konrad starts boasting as to how things are going with him, pays for him in the beer-saloon, and they go with some girls to the movies. Konrad tells terrible stories about Brandenburg; after they get rid of the gals, they sit half the night in his friend's room, and that's the night before Tuesday, when Konard tells who Reinhold is. Moroskiewicz is just an assumed name, and he's a fine feller, you won't find the likes of him outside so easy, they're looking for him on a serious charge. Who knows how much reward there is on his head. He's hardly said that when he knows he's done a stupid thing, but the friend promises on his word of honor not to say anything, of course, we'll keep mum about it, and Konrad gives him 10 marks on top of that.

Then Tuesday comes around, and this friend is standing on the ground floor at Police Headquarters, scanning the posters to see if it's true, who's wanted by the police, if Reinhold, that's his name, is really on the list, and if a reward has been promised, and if Konrad has not been humbugging him perhaps.

He's fairly knocked out of his senses and can't believe his eyes when he reads the name, that's it, by God, murder of a prostitute, Parsunke, in Freienwalde, his name's actually there, wonder if it's really him, by God, why, it's a thousand reward, a thousand marks, wow! That fetches him, the thousand marks. So off he goes and comes back with his girl-friend that same afternoon; she says she'd met Konrad and he asked for him, yes, he smells a rat, what'll we do, what'll we do? Gee, why hesitate about it, is that man a murderer or isn't he? What's that to you? I wouldn't bother about Konrad, you'll never meet him again, and then how would he know it's you, all that money, imagine it, a thousand marks, you go and get the dole and yet you hesitate about a thousand marks. "Wonder if it's really him." "Well, come on, let's go in."

Inside, he makes a clear statement to the officer on duty of all he knows about Moroskiewicz, Reinhold, Brandenburg, etc., but he won't say how he found out about it. Since he has no papers, he and his girl-friend have to stay there for the time being. Then—everything's fine.

As Konrad rides out to Brandenburg on Saturday to visit Reinhold, carrying all kinds of things to give him, from Reinhold's girl and from Pums, he sees a paper lying on the floor of the car, it's an old paper dating from Thursday evening and on the first page it says: "Capture of the Freienwalde Murderer. In Prison Under Alias." The train rattles under Konrad, the tracks stretch on and on, and the train rattles. What's the date of this paper, what is it? *Lokalanzeiger*, Thursday evening.

So they got him. He's been taken to Berlin. I did that.

Women and love have brought luck, good and bad, to Reinhold all his life, and that's how in the end they brought him disaster as well. He was taken to Berlin, acting like a madman. A little more, and they would have rushed him to the same asylum in which his former friend Biberkopf is confined. After calming down in Moabit, he waits to see how his trial will shape up, what will develop from that quarter, to wit, Franz Biberkopf, his accomplice or instigator, but so far nobody knows anything at all about what's to become of him.

Buch Insane Asylum, Detention Ward

In the lock-up of the panoptical building at headquarters it is at first suspected that Franz Biberkopf is flying a kite, as it were, that he is shamming madness, because he knows his bean is at stake. But then the doctor has a good look at the prisoner and orders his removal to Moabit Hospital. They can't get a word out of him, it looks as if the man were really crazy, he lies there quite rigid or just blinks his eyes a bit. Having refused to eat for a few days, he is taken to the Buch Insane Asylum, where they place him in the detention ward. At any rate, that's the thing to do, the fellow has to be kept under observation, that's certain.

They first put Franz in the observation ward, because he was always lying around without a stitch on and didn't cover himself up; he even kept tearing off his shirt which was the only sign of life Franz Biberkopf gave for a few weeks. He kept his eyes shut tight all the time, lay perfectly stiff refusing all food so that they had to feed him forcibly; he lived for weeks on milk and eggs and a bit of cognac. The strong man grew so wasted that one guard alone could easily carry him to the bathtub. Franz greatly enjoyed his bath and while he was in it, even uttered sometimes a few words, opened his mouth, sighed or groaned, although nobody was able to make anything out of these sounds.

The Buch Asylum lies somewhat away from the village; the detention ward is detached from the dwellings of those who are only sick and have not committed a crime. The detention ward lies in an open lot out on the level plain; wind and snow, cold and rain, day and night, beset the house with might and main. There are no streets to hold up the elements, only a few trees and bushes, and a few telegraph wires, otherwise there is only rain and snow, wind and cold, day and night.

Boom, zoom, the wind stretches his chest, draws in his breath, then he exhales as if he were a barrel, each breath heavy as a mountain, the mountain approaches, and crash—it rolls against the house. Rumbling of basses. Boom, zoom, the trees sway, they can't keep time, they're swaying right, they're swaying left, and now he knocks them down. Falling weights, hammering air, a rattle and a roar, and a crash, boom, zoom. I'm yourn, come on, we'll soon be there, boom, night, night.

Franz hears the calls. Boom, zoom, they do not stop, can't they be quiet for a while? The guard sits at his table, reading, I can see him, he won't let this howling outside disturb him. I've been lying here a long time. The chase, the damned chase, they have chased me helter-skelter, my arms and legs are broken, my neck's smashed and broken. Boom, zoom, let it whimper, I've been lying here a long time, I won't get up, Franz Biberkopf won't get up again. And even if the Doomsday bugles should blow, Franz Biberkopf won't get up again. Let them shout all they want, let them bring up their old feeding-tube, now they're even pushing it down my nose because I won't open my mouth, but don't worry, I'll starve to death all right, what can they do with their medicine, they can do anything they like. Tripe, a lotta damned tripe, but all that's behind me. Now the guard is drinking his glass of beer, all that's behind me, too.

*

Boom, crash, zoom, crash, boom, a battering ram, zoom, a knock at the door. Rushing and whirling and crushing and skirling, the Powers of Storm get together and hold their conference, it is night and they set about awakening Franz, not that they want to break his limbs, but the walls are so thick, he cannot hear what they call; but if he were nearer them, outside, he would feel them and hear Mieze crying. Then his heart would open up, his conscience would be awakened, and he would arise and everything would be all right. Now, however, they don't know what to do. When a man takes a hatchet and slashes the solid wood, even the oldest tree begins to scream. But this rigid lying around, this self-effacement, this self-abasement before disaster, that's the worst thing in the world. We must not give up, either we'll break into the detention ward with our battering ram and smash the windows, or we'll raise the tiles on the roof; when he feels us, when he hears our screaming, Mieze's screaming, which we are bringing along with us, he will live again and know better what's up. We must put fear into him, we must frighten him, until he has no peace left in his bed, and then, how are we going to raise the coverlet, blast him to the floor, whirl the guard's book and beer from the table. Boom, zoom, how am I going to overturn his lamp, I'll kick the bulb down, maybe there'll be a short-circuit in the house, maybe there'll be a fire, boom, zoom, a fire in the madhouse, a fire in the detention ward.

Franz blocks his ears and stiffens up. Around the detention ward fair weather and rain follow each other day and night.

A girl from the village stands by the wall talking to a guard: "Can you see I've been crying?" "No, only one of your cheeks is a bit swollen." "My whole head, the back of my skull, everything, I tell you." She starts crying and takes her handkerchief from out of her bag. Her face has a sour expression. "What's more, I didn't do anything at all. I was told to go to the baker's and fetch something. I happened to know the young lady there, so I asked her what she was doing, and she says I'm going to the bakers' ball today. A person can't sit at home all the time, in this bad weather. She had an extra ticket and wanted to take me along. Don't cost me anything. That was nice of her, wasn't it?" "Why, yes." "But then you should hear my parents, my mother, I shouldn't go. But why not, isn't it a respectable ball? And then a girl would like a bit of fun, too, sometimes. What do I get out of life? No, I can't go, the weather's too bad, and father's sick. But I said, I'll go anyway. Then I got such a beating, is that nice?" She is crying again and stares into space. "The whole back of my head hurts.

And my mother says, now are you going to do us this favor and stay at home. That's going a little bit far, don't you think so? Why shouldn't I go out, I'm twenty years old now, Mother says you can go on Saturday and Sunday, well, then, why not on Thursday, because she's got the tickets anyway." "I can give you a handkerchief that long, if you want to." "Oh, I've used up six so far, crying so hard; and then I got a cold on top of it, crying all day long like this, and what'll I tell the young lady, why, I can't go to the store with that swollen cheek I just want to go away, get a change of air; you know about your friend Sepp, I've written him, it's all over between us, he hasn't answered, it's all over now." "Leave that fellow alone, you can see him in town every Wednesday with another girl on the string." "I like him a lot. That's why I want to run away."

An old man with a whisky-nose sits down on Franz's bed. "Heh, fellow, open them eyes of yours, you might listen to me a minute. I'm in the same boat as you are. Home Sweet Home, you know what that means for me: under the sod. When I'm not at home, I wanta be under the sod. The microcephalics want to make a troglodyte outa me, a cave-dweller. That's the cave they want me to live in. Y'know what a troglodyte is, don't you, that's us, awake, you wretched of the earth, doomed to starve, poor fallen victims of the fight in your holy love of mankind, you gave up your all for the people, life, liberty, and happiness. That's us, old boy. In his luxurious mansions the despot feasts, drowning his unrest in wine; but a hand has already been writing the menacing signs upon his sumptuous board. I'm an autodidact, I am, everything I learned I learned by myself, from the jail, the detention ward, and now they lock me up here, they're putting the people under tutelage, I'm too dangerous for society. You bet I am. I'm a freethinker, yes, sir, look at me, I'm the most peaceful man in the world, except when they get me excited. A time will come when the people will awake, strong and mighty and free, so rest in peace, my brothers, immense is the sacrifice you have made.

"Listen, brother, open them lamps of yours, I wanta know if you're listening to me—that's all right, you needn't do more than that. I won't give you away—what 'dja do, didja take one of them tyrants for a ride, death to you all, executioners and despots, sing ho. You're lying around here, y'know, and me, I can't sleep all night long, there's always that noise outside, boom, boom, don't you hear it too? One of these nights they'll be knocking down the whole shebang. They're right. Last night I figured out, I was doing it all night, how many revolutions the earth makes around the sun in a second, I calculate and I calculate, I think it's 28, and then I get a notion my old woman's sleeping beside me and I wake her up and she says: Don't get excited, darlin', but it was only a dream.

"They locked me up 'cause I drink, but when I drink I get in a rage, I tell ye, but only at myself, and then I gotta knock everything into smithereens, everything that comes my way, simply because I'm not able to control my will. So one day I goes to the office about my pension and they're all sitting around in the room, those lazy boobs, sucking their penholders and thinking they're our Lords and Masters. I comes in, I opens that door with a bang and starts talkin', and then they say what do you want here, who are you, anyway? Down goes my fist on their table: I don't wanta talk to you, whom have I the honor of addressing, my name's Schögel, please give me the telephone book, I want to call up the governor. So I smashed up the whole place, and two of them birds had to bite the dust, I tell ye."

Boom, crash, zoom, crash, boom, a battering ram, zoom, a hammering at the door. Bashing and crashing, crackling and smashing. Who is this lying fool, Franz Biberkopf, this crying mule, this sighing ghoul, he'd like to wait here till it snows, then, he thinks, we're gone and won't come back again. Wonder what he's thinking about, a feller like that can't be thinking a great deal, he's got water on the brain, he wants to lie around here and act like a mule. But never mind, we'll make things hot for him, we have bones made of iron, crash door, look out, smash door, hole in the door, crack in the door, look out, no door, just an empty hole, a gaping hole, boom, zoom, watch out, boom, zoom.

There is a clatter. A clatter invades the storm, a clattering sound is audible through all its mumbling and rumbling, a woman upon a scarlet beast turns around. She has seven heads and ten horns. She cackles, holding a glass in her hand, she sneers, she lies in wait for Franz, she lifts her glass to the Powers of Storm: cluck, cluck, pipe down, gentlemen, the feller is not much good, you won't be able to do much with that man, why, he's only got one arm, there's no flesh or fat on him, he'll soon be a stiff, they're beginning to put hot-water bottles in his bed, and I have his blood, he has only a wee bit left, he can't go bragging around with that any more. Shush, I tell you, gentlemen, pipe down.

This happens right before Franz's eyes. The whore moves her seven heads, cackles and nods. The beast plants its feet beneath her, lolling its head.

Grape-Sugar and Camphor Syringes, but in the end Somebody Else takes a Hand in it

Franz Biberkopf fights with the doctors. He can't tear the tube away from them, he can't pull it out of his nose, they pour oil on the rubber, and the tube slides down his throat and down his gullet, then milk and eggs flow down into his stomach. But after the feeding Franz starts to retch and to vomit. That's troublesome and painful, but it works, even if they tie a fellow's hands so that he can't stick his fingers in his throat. A man can vomit everything he wants, and we'll see who has the strongest will, they or I, and if anybody is going to coerce me in this damned world. I'm not here for doctors to experiment on me, and, anyway, they don't know what's wrong with me.

So Franz persists and grows weaker and weaker. They try all kinds of methods with him, they try to persuade him, they feel his pulse, they raise and lower him, they give him caffeine and camphor injections, they squirt grape-sugar and common salt into his veins, the prospects of his intestinal canal are discussed at his bedside, maybe we ought to make him inhale an extra amount of oxygen, he can't get rid of the mask. He asks himself why are those gentlemen, those big doctors worryin' about me all the time? A hundred men die in Berlin every day, and when a man's sick, the doctor only comes if he gets a lotta money. Now they all come rushing up, but they don't do it, because they want to help. They don't care a rap about me today, no more than they did yesterday, but maybe I'm an interesting case for 'em, and that's why they get so mad about me, because they can't do anything with me. And they don't want anybody to get away with it, not on your life, it's against the rules of the house here for somebody to die, it's against the discipline of the institution. If I croak, they may get a calling down, and then they wanta put me up for trial on account of Mieze and so on and I've gotta be on my feet first, why, they're hangman's assistants, that's all, not even hangmen, just assistants to the hangman, his beaters, and then they walk around in a doctor's blouse and they ain't ashamed, either.

There's a lot of sneering and whispering going on among the prisoners in the detention ward, after the doctor has made his round again, and Franz is lying just as before; they've gone to a lot of trouble with him, always new injections, next time they'll make him stand on his head, now they're starting to talk about blood-transfusion for him, but where are they goin' to get the blood from, there ain't nobody here as dumb as all that, lettin' em tap his blood, why not leave the poor feller alone, a man's will is his Paradise, and what a man wants, well, that's what he wants. The whole house is only interested to know what kind of injection our Franz is goin' to get today, and they laugh behind the doctor's back, for what's the use, they won't get anywhere with that feller, he's hard-boiled all right, he's hard as nails, he'll show 'em a thing or two, he knows what he wants.

The doctors put on their white blouses in the consultation-room, the Head Doctor, an assistant, two volunteers, and an interne, they all say it's a case of stupor. The younger gentlemen have opinions of their own about this case: they are inclined to consider Franz Biberkopf's trouble as psychogenic, that is, his rigidity derives from the soul, it is a pathological condition of inhibitions and constraint which would be cleared up by an analysis (perhaps it emanates from earlier psychic levels) if—the big If, a most regrettable If, it's too bad, a most irritating If—if only Franz Biberkopf would talk and sit down with them at the conference table to liquidate the conflict with them. The younger gentlemen envisage a Locarno with Franz Biberkopf. These younger gentlemen, the two volunteers and the interne, go, one by one, to the little ward, after the morning inspection and again in the afternoon, and visit Franz; each of them tries to start a conversation with him as best he can. They experiment, for instance, with the device of pretending nothing's wrong, and talk to him as if he were listening to everything, and that's all right, and as if they could coax him out of his isolation and break down his blockade.

But it doesn't work so well. One of the volunteers, therefore, insists on fetching an electrolytic machine from the ward across the way, and on galvanizing Franz Biberkopf, that is, the upper part of his body; and after that he directs the galvanic current particularly to the region of the jaws, throat, and palate. That's the region, he says, which needs special stimulation and excitation.

The older doctors are alive and full of worldly knowledge; they like to take a little constitutional by walking to the detention ward from time to time. They let a lot of things pass. The Head Doctor sits at his table in the consultation-room examining the documents which the head attendant hands him from the left side; the young generation, consisting of the interne and one of the assistants, is standing near the barred window chatting back and forth. The list of soporifics has been checked, the new attendant has been presented and has left the room with the head attendant, the gentlemen are alone and glance through the minutes of the last congress in Baden-Baden. The Head Doctor says: "They'll soon believe that paralysis is a psychic condition and that spirochetes are nothing but lice that happen to be in the brain. The soul, the soul—it's simply sentimental modern gush. Medicine soaring on the wings of Song."

The two gentlemen are silent, smiling inwardly. The older generation talks a lot, after a certain age a calcium deposit begins to form in the brain and nothing new is learnt. The Head Doctor puffs away, goes on signing papers, and continues:

"You see, electricity is all right, anyhow it's better than all that bunk. But suppose you use a weak current, that wouldn't help at all. And if you use a strong one, well, then you'll get the surprise of your life. We found out about it in the war, with that high-tension treatment. We can't allow that, it's modern torture." The two young gentlemen take heart and ask what's to be done in the Biberkopf case. "We need, first of all, a diagnosis, and, if possible, the right one. In addition to that indisputable soul—you see, we still know our daddy Goethe and Chamisso, even if it's some time since we read them—there are such things as bleeding at the nose, corns, and broken legs. They must be treated as a decent broken leg or corn demand from a doctor. You may do whatever you please about the broken leg, but it won't be cured merely by talking, and piano-playing won't cure it either. What it wants is to be put in a plaster cast with the bones properly set, and that'll fix it up. In the same way, a corn wants swabbing, or just a better pair of shoes. The latter cost more, but they're more practical." The wisdom of pension privileges, intellectual content: zero. "Well, what's to be done about this Biberkopf case, what's the Chief's opinion?" "Make the right diagnosis. Which, according to my naturally somewhat old-fashioned diagnostics, is called in this case: Catatonic stupor. Unless, of course, there is a serious organic condition back of it, such as tumor of the brain or something in the middle-brain, you remember what we learned during the epidemic of the so-called Spanish influenza, at least what we older men learned. We may perhaps find something sensational in the operating-room, it wouldn't be the first time." "Catatonic stupor?" He ought to buy himself a pair of new shoes, that one. "Yes, this rigidity of his, his fits of perspiration, that periodic twitching of the eyes, he observes us intently, but won't talk or eat, all that looks like catatonic trouble. A malingerer, or a psychogenic case, flops out of his rôle in the end, but starve, he'll never go that far." "And what's to be done for a man with such a diagnosis, Doctor, that alone won't help him a great deal." Now we've got him up a tree. The Chief laughs heartily and gets up. He steps to the window and slaps the assistant's shoulder: "Well, in the first place, he'll get out of both your clutches, my dear fellow. At least he can take a quiet snooze. That's an advantage for him. Don't you think that in the end he gets a bit bored with all the prayers you and your colleague recite over him? As a matter of fact, do you know what I am going to base my iron diagnosis on? You see, I've got it. Why, man alive, he would have made a grab for it long ago, if his trouble had been your so-called soul. When a confirmed jail-bird such as he is sees for himself that here are two young gentlemen who, of course, know only a lot of rubbish about him—excuse me, we're talking between us—and they want to do some prayer-healing with him, well, take it from me, a chap like that has been looking for you all his life. That's what fills his bill. And then what does he do, may have been doing all along? You see, supposing this fellow has sense and a bit of cunning—" Now the blind chicken thinks it's found a grain at last. How it cackles and cackles! "But he's inhibited, Chief, in our view it is a repression, conditioned by a psychic crisis, a loss of contact with reality, due to disappointments, failures, then infantile and instinctive demands on reality and a fruitless attempt to re-establish contact." "Psychic crisis be damned! In that case he would have other psychic moments. He'd give up those repressions and inhibitions. He's handing them to you as a Christmas present. In a week he'll be up and about with your assistance, good Lord, you really are a master-healer, bravo for the new therapy, you can send a telegram of congratulations to Freud in Vienna, a week later the lad is walking in the corridor thanks to your assistance, a miracle, a miracle, hallelujah; in another week he'll know all about the courtyard, and in another week, he'll be, hallelujah, hooray, skedaddling and away, thanks to your benevolent assistance." "I don't understand, we ought to try it sometime, I don't agree with you, Chief." (I know everything, you know nothing, cluck, cluck, we know everything.) "But that's the way I see it. You'll find out. It's a question of experience. All right, now don't go torturing the fellow, you can believe me, it's no use." (I'll have to go across to House 9, these smart-alecks, nearer my God to thee, what time is it anyway?)

Franz Biberkopf is now unconscious and drifting in space. He is very pale, jaundiced, water swelling at his joints, starvation sickness, he smells of hunger, of sweetish acetone; people entering the room notice at once that something queer is happening there.

Franz's soul has reached a deep stratum, and consciousness is present only at intervals. The gray mice who live up in the store-room understand him, so do the little squirrels and the field-rabbits leaping outside. The mice sit in their holes, between the detention ward and the big central Buch building. Something flutters from out of Franz's soul, it roams and searches, sputtering and questioning, it is blind and returns to its tenement which lies still breathing on the bed behind the wall.

The mice invite Franz to join them at their meals and not to be sad. What is it makes him sad, they ask. Then it develops that it is not easy for him to talk. They urge him on, why not make a complete end of it all? Man is a hideous beast: the enemy of enemies, the most loathsome creature on earth, far worse even than the cats.

He says: It is not good to be living in a human body. I'd rather cower under the earth or run across the fields and eat whatever I can find, and the wind blows and rain falls and the cold days come and go, that's better than living in a human body.

The mice scamper about, and now Franz is a field-mouse, and digs along with them.

In the detention ward he lies in bed, the doctors come and keep his body nourished, but meanwhile he grows paler and paler. Now they themselves admit it: he cannot be sustained any longer. All that was animal in him is wandering in the fields.

Now there slips away from him something that gropes and searches and makes itself free, something that he has felt within himself before, although rarely and dimly. It swims away across the mouse-holes, delving into the grass, groping in the earth, where the plants hide their roots and seeds. Something is talking with them, they are able to understand it, there is a blowing back and forth, a patter, as if the seeds were falling on the ground. Franz's soul is giving its seed-germs back to the earth. But it is a bad season, cold and frost-bound, who knows how many will be fruitful, although there is much space in the fields, and Franz has many seeds in him, each day he blows out of the house and scatters more seed-germs.

Death sings his slow, slow Song

The Powers of Storm are silent now, another song has started, they all know the song and him who sings it. When he lifts up his voice, they are always silent, even those who on earth happen to be the most impetuous.

Death has begun his slow, slow song, and he sings it like a stammerer, repeating each word; when he has finished singing a verse, he repeats the first before he starts anew. His song is like the hiss of a saw. Quite slowly the saw ascends and then plunges down into the flesh, shrilling louder, clearer and higher, till it comes to the end of a note, and rests. Then it withdraws, slowly, slowly, hissing, higher and clearer grows the note, it shrills, and then it plunges into the flesh once more.

Slowly Death is singing.

"It is time for me to appear beside you, for the seeds are already flying out of the window and you shake your winding-sheet as if you would never lie down again. I am not a mere mower, nor a mere sower, I have to be here because it is my duty to preserve. Oh, yes, oh, yes, oh, yes."

Oh, yes, this is the word Death speaks at the end of each stanza. And when he makes a strong movement, he also sings, oh, yes, because that pleases him. But those who hear it close their eyes, they cannot bear it.

Slowly, slowly, Death is singing and evil Babylon listens to him, the Powers of Storm listen to him.

"Here I stand and here I must record: He who lies here and offers up his life and his body is Franz Biberkopf. Wherever he may happen to be, he knows where he is going and what he wants."

That certainly is a beautiful song. Franz hears it and wonders what it means: Death is singing? If it were printed in a book, or read aloud, it would be rather like poetry, Schubert composed such songs, Death and the Maiden, but what about it?

I only want to tell the honest truth, the honest truth, which is: Franz Biberkopf hears Death, this Death, hears him slowly singing, singing like a stutterer, repeating himself over and over again like a saw cutting through wood.

"Franz Biberkopf, I have to record that you are lying here and that you want to come to me. Yes, you were right, Franz, in coming to me. How can a man prosper if he does not seek Death? Death, true and real. You preserved yourself all your life. To preserve, to preserve—that is man's terrible desire, and thus it stays in one spot, and it can't go on that way.

"I spoke with you for the first time when Lüders deceived you, you started drinking and—preserved yourself! Your arm broke, your life was in danger, Franz, confess, at no moment did you think of Death, I sent you everything, but you did not recognize me, and when you divined me, you ran away from me, growing more desperate and more frightened. It never entered your head to blame yourself and everything you had undertaken. You clung to force with might and main, and the spasm continues to reign, and it's no use, you realized it yourself, no use whatever, the moment comes, and vain is all endeavor. Death does not sing a gentle song for you, nor does he place a strangling necklace around your throat. I am life and truest strength, and now at last, at last, you will preserve yourself no longer."

"What? what! what do you want from me, what do you want to do with me?"

"I am life and truest strength, my strength is stronger than the biggest guns of war, and you don't want to live quietly anywhere before me. You want to experience yourself, to test yourself; without me life can mean nothing to you. Come, Franz, draw nearer, that you may really see me, look, in how deep an abyss you lie, but I will show you a ladder, and you will find a new outlook. You will climb up towards me now, I'll hold the ladder for you, although you have only one arm, catch hold, Franz, your foothold is firm, catch hold, climb up, come."

"I can't see a ladder in the dark, where is it, and I can't climb up with that one arm of mine."

"You don't climb with your arm, you climb with your legs."

"I can't grasp anything, there's no sense in what you ask me to do."

"It's because you don't want to come nearer me. All right then, I'll make a light for you and you'll find your way."

Then Death takes his right arm from behind his back, and now it becomes clear why he had concealed it behind his back.

"If you lack the courage to come to me in the dark, I shall make light for you, crawl nearer."

And a luminous hatchet flashes through the air, it flashes and is extinguished.

"Crawl nearer, nearer."

He swings the hatchet, and as he swings it up from behind his head, forward and farther forward in an arc, following the circle which his arm describes, the hatchet seems to whirl from his hand. But already his hand is rising again from behind his head and it swings another hatchet. It flashes, falls, guillotines in a half circle through the air before him, it strikes, it strikes, and another one whizzes up already, then another one whizzes up, and another.

Swing up, fall down, hack in, swing up, crash down, hack in, swing, fall, hack, swing fall hack, swing hack, swing hack.

And in the flash of the light, while the hatchet swings and flashes and hacks away, Franz creeps and gropes for the ladder; he screams and screams. Franz screams. But he does not crawl back. Franz screams. Death is here.

Franz screams.

Franz screams, creeps forward, screams.

He screams all night long. He got in motion, did Franz.

He screams into the day.

He screams into the forenoon.

Swing fall hack.

Screams into noon.

Screams into the afternoon.

Swing fall hack.

Swing, hack, hack, swing, swing hack, hack, hack.

Swing, hack.

Screams into the evening, into the evening. Night comes.

Screams on into the night, Franz screams into the night.

His body continues to thrust itself forward. One piece after the other is struck from his body on the block. His body automatically thrusts itself forward, it must press forward, he cannot help it. The blade whirls in the air, flashes and falls. Inch by inch he is hacked into pieces. And beyond, beyond those inches his body is not dead, it thrusts itself forward, slowly forward, but nothing falls, everything goes on living.

People from the outside walk past his bed, stand at his bed and raise his eyelids to see if the reflexes are still active. They feel his pulse, which is no more than a thread, and they hear nothing of all his outcry. They only see that Franz has opened his mouth, they think he is thirsty, and they cautiously pour a few drops into it, let's hope he won't vomit again, a good thing his teeth aren't clenched any more. How on earth does a man manage to keep alive that long?

"I am suffering. I am suffering."

"It is well that you are suffering. There is nothing better than suffering for you."

"Oh, do not let me suffer. Make an end of it."

"It is useless to do that. The end is near."

"Make an end of it. It lies in your hands to do so."

"I have only a hatchet in my hand. Everything else lies in your hand."

"What have I in my hand? Make an end of it."

Now the voice changes entirely and grows to a roar.

Rage immeasurable, rage uncontrolled, insensate rage, wholly immeasurable, ravening rage.

"So it has come to this, that I stand here and talk with you. That I stand here like a knacker or an executioner and choke you like a venomous, snapping beast. I called you again and again, and you take me for a mere talking-machine, a phonograph to turn on, whenever you please, then I have to call you, and when you have enough, you simply stop the record. That's what you take me for, or that's whatcha take me for. Go ahead and take me for it, but I tell you you are wrong."

"What did I do, heh? Haven't I taken enough trouble about it? I don't know nobody else who had things happen to 'im like I did, such wretched, miserable things."

"You were never there, you dirty louse, you. I ain't never seen Franz Biberkopf in my life. When I sent you Lüders, you didn't open your eyes, you went down like a house o' cards, and then you got boozed up and you went swiggin' away, swiggin' nothing but liquor and again liquor."

"I wanted to be a decent man, and that guy put one over on me."

"You didn't open your eyes, you poor fool! You curse and swear about crooks and their doin's, but you never look at people, and you don't ask about the how and why. What a fine judge o' men you are, where are your eyes? You've been blind, and pretty cocky at that, turning your nose up at the world, Herr Franz Biberkopf of Swankville, asking the world to be exactly like you'd like to be. It's different, m'boy, and now you notice it. It don't worry about you. When Reinhold grabbed you and kicked you under the car, your arm was run over, but did our Franz Biberkopf collapse then? Lying under the wheels he swore: I'm goin' to be strong! He didn't say, not he: let's think a minute, pull yourself together, old fellow. No, sir, he said: I want to be strong. And you didn't want to notice that I was talking to you. But now you're listening to me."

"What d'y mean 'notice'?"

"And finally Mieze—Franz, shame, shame on you. Say it. Shame, come on, yell: Shame!"

"I can't. I don't know why I should."

"Yell shame! She came to you, a lovely girl, protected you and was happy with you, and you, what did you care about a human being, a flower-like human being; why, you go and brag about her to Reinhold. The greatest feelin' we ever had. But you, all you wanted was to be strong. It gave you pleasure to fence with Reinhold, and to show your superiority, and then you went and got him excited about her. Now think it over, isn't it your fault she's dead? And you didn't shed a tear over her, the girl who died for you, just for you.

"A lotta palaver from you about 'I' and 'I,' and 'the wrong I'm suffering,' and what a noble man I am, how fine I am, and nobody wants to let me show what kind of a guy I am. Say shame. Yell shame!"

"How do I know?"

"You've lost the war, young man. It's all over with you, my son. You can chase yourself. Let 'em put you away with the moths. I've struck you off my list, and you can howl and whine as long as you like. You're a rotten specimen all right. Got a heart and a head and eyes and ears and he thinks it's a good thing to be decent, what he calls decent, but he sees nothing, hears nothing, and goes on living like a fool, unaware of anything people might do for him."

"Well, what, what do you want a feller to do?"

Death is roaring now: "Nothin', I'm tellin' you, don't talk rubbish to me. You got no bean, no ears. Why, you're not even born yet, you never saw the light of day. An abortion with hallucinations. Our Pope Biberkopf, he had to be born with cocky ideas, just to show us the way things are. The world needs fellows that are different from you, brighter ones who are a bit less cocky and can see how things actually are—not just made of sugar, but of sugar and dirt, and the whole caboodle mixed up. Out with your heart, you fool, and have done with you! I'll throw it into the dirt where it belongs. You can keep your big mouth for yourself."

"Wait a minute. Lemme think. Just a bit. Just for a little while."

"Out with your heart, you fool!"

"Just for a little while."

"Or I'll get it myself, damn you."

"Just for a little while."

Now Franz hears Death's slow Song

Lightning, lightning, lightning, the lightning lightning stops. Hacking falling hacking, the hacking falling hacking stops. It is the second night that Franz has screamed. The falling hacking stops. He no longer screams. The lightning stops. His eyes blink. He lies rigid. This is a room, a hall, people are moving about. You mustn't pinch your mouth like that. They pour warm stuff down his throat. No lightning. No hacking. Walls. A little while, just a little while, and then what? He shuts his eyes.

When Franz has shut his eyes, he starts doing something. You can't see what he's doing; you just think he's lying there, perhaps he'll soon be a goner, the man doesn't move a muscle. He calls and moves and roams about. He is calling together all that is his. He walks through the windows, across the fields, he shakes the grass and creeps into the mouse-holes. Get out, get out, what's in here, is there anything of me here? He fumbles in the grass: Outside, you bums, what's all this yapping about, it don't mean anything. I need you, I can't give any of you a furlough, there's lots of things to be done here, let's be gay, I need every one of you.

They pour broth down his throat, he swallows it and does not vomit. He doesn't want to vomit, he doesn't like to vomit.

Franz has Death's word in his mouth and nobody is going to tear it away from him, he turns it around in his mouth, it is a stone made of stone, and no nourishment comes out of it. At this stage many people have died. There was no Farther in life for them. They did not know that they had to suffer only one more pain to advance beyond that, only a little step was needed to get farther, but they could not take this step. They did not know it, it did not come quickly, or not quickly enough, there was a faintness, a spasm that lasted for minutes, for seconds, and already they had passed over there where their names were no longer Karl, Wilhelm, Minna, or Franziska—satiated, darkly satiated, red-flaming in rage and the palsy of despair, they had slept their way across. They did not know they had but to flame up whitely and then they would have become soft and all things would have been new.

So let it come—the night, however black and nothing-like it be! So let them come, the black night, those frost-covered acres, the hard frozen roads. So let them come: the lonely, tile-roofed houses whence gleams a reddish light; so let them come: the shivering wanderers, the drivers on the farm wagons traveling to town with vegetables and the little horses in front. The great, flat, silent plains crossed by suburban trains and expresses which throw white light into the darkness on either side of them. So let them come—the men in the station, the little girl's farewell to her parents, she's traveling with two older acquaintances, going across the big water, we've got our tickets, but good Lord, what a little girl, eh, but she'll get used to it over there, if she's a good little girl it'll be all right. So let them come and be absorbed: the cities which lie along the same line, Breslau, Liegnitz, Sommerfeld, Guben, Frankfort on the Oder, Berlin, the train passes through them from station to station, from the stations emerge the cities, the cities with their big and little streets. Berlin with Schweidnitzer Strasse, with the Grosse Ring of the Kaiser-Wilhelm Strasse, Kurfürstendamm, and everywhere are homes in which people are warming themselves, looking at each other with loving eyes, or sitting coldly next to each other; dirty dumps and dives where a man is playing the piano. Say, kiddo, that's old stuff, you'd think there was nothing new in 1928, how about "I kiss your hand, Madame," or "Ramona."

So let them come: the autos, the taxis, you know how many you have sat in, how they rattled, you were alone, or else somebody sat next to you, or maybe two. License Number 20147.

A loaf is put in the oven.

It is an open-air oven near a farm-house, back of it lies a field, it looks like a little heap of tiles. The women have sawed a lot of wood and gathered dry twigs, which they have heaped beside the oven, and now they are stuffing it in. One of them walks across the courtyard carrying big molds containing the dough. A young man quickly opens the door of the oven, it glows inside, it glows and glows, a tremendous heat, they shove the tins in with poles, the bread will rise there and the water will evaporate; the dough will turn brown.

Franz is sitting half up. He has swallowed and now he is waiting; almost everything that was running around outside is back with him again. He trembles, what was it Death had said? He ought to know what Death had said. The door opens. Now it will come. The curtain's up. I know him. It's Lüders. I have been expecting him.

So they come in, awaited with trembling. What can be the matter with Lüders? Franz has made a sign and they thought he had difficulty in breathing, because he was lying flat, but he just wants to lie a bit higher and straighter. For they are coming now. He is lying high. Go ahead.

One by one they come. Lüders, he's a miserable cuss, such a funny little man. Let's see what's the matter with him. He walks upstairs peddling shoe-laces. Yes, that's what we did. A fellow goes to the dogs in his rags, still the same old outfit left over from the war, Makko shoe-laces, I just wanted to ask you, Ma'am, can't you let me have a cup o' coffee, what about your husband, probably died in the war; claps his hat on. All right now, hand over the change! That's Lüders, he was with me. The woman's face is flaming red, but one cheek's snow-white, she fumbles in her pocketbook, she squeals and topples over. He digs around among kitchen things. A lotta chicken-feed, let's hustle off, or she'll start screamin'. Through the hallway, slam that door, downstairs. Yes, he did it. Hooks something. Hooks a lot. They give me the letter, it's from her, what's happening to me now, suddenly my legs are hacked off, my legs hacked off, but why, I can't get up. Do you want a cognac, Biberkopf, probably a death in the family, yes, oh why, just why, why are my legs hacked off, I don't know. Gotta ask him, gotta talk to him. Listen, Lüders, good mornin', Lüders, how are you, not well, me neither, come here a minute, sit down on that chair, now don't go away, did I do anything to you, don't go away.

Let them come. Let them come, the black night, the autos, the hard frozen roads, the little girl's farewell from her parents, she's traveling with a man and a woman, she'll get used to it over there, got to stay nice and good, and it'll be all right. Let them come!

Reinhold, here's Reinhold. Ugh! the bastard! So here you are, what d'you want here, d'you wanta play the big gazook with me, no rain will ever wash you clean, you crook, you murderer, you big scoundrel, take that pipe out of your mug when you talk to me. It's a good thing you came, I missed you, come on, you dirty louse, haven't they caught you yet, you with your blue overcoat on? Look out, they'll nab you in that outfit. "Who are you, Franz?" Me, you crook? Not a murderer, you know who you murdered? "And who showed me the girl, and who didn't look out for the girl, and I gotta lie under the bed-cover, you fathead you, who was it?" But you needn't have killed her for that. "What of it, didn't you nearly beat her black and blue yourself? And then how about a certain other woman we've heard about, she lived in Landsberger Allee; she didn't get to the cemetery all by herself, did she? Well, what about it? Now you got nothin' to say, what has Herr Franz Biberkopf, our big-mouth by profession, to say now?" You kicked me under the car, you let'em run over my arm. "Hah, hah, well, you can get one made of cardboard. If you're jackass enough to take up with me!" A jackass? "Well, don't you realize you're a jackass? Now you're in Buch playing the wild man from Borneo, but I'm doin' well: who's a jackass now?"

There he goes, and hell-fire flashes from his eyes, horns grow out of his head, and he yells: Why don't you fight with me, come on, show what you are, Franzeken, Franzeken Biberkopf, dear little Biberkopf, ha, ha! Franz presses his eyelids together. I shouldn't have started anything with him, I shouldn't have fought him. Why did I fall for that so hard?

"Come on, Franzeken, let's see who you are! Have you got any strength?"

I shouldn't have fought. He's teasin' me, he's still teasin' me, makin' me mad, my God, he's a dog. I shouldn'a done it. I can't do anything against him, I shouldn'a done it.

"You gotta have strength, Franz."

I should'na had any strength, not against him. Now I see it, it was all wrong. A fine mess I made of things! Away, away with him!

He doesn't go.

Away, away with—!

Franz screams and twists his hands: I must see somebody else, nobody else is coming, why does he stay on?

"I know it, you don't want none o'me. I don't taste nice. But somebody else is comin' right away."

Then let him come. Let them come, the great, flat, silent plains, the lonely tiled houses whence gleams a reddish light, cities which lie along the same line, Frankfort on the Oder, Guben, Sommerfeld, Liegnitz, Breslau, from the stations the cities emerge, cities with their big and their little streets. Then let them come: the cabs driving along, the rushing, gliding automobiles.

Reinhold leaves. Then he stands there once more flashing a look at Franz. "Well, who is the strong man? Who won, Franzeken?"

Franz trembles: Not me, and I know it.

Then let them come.

Somebody else is coming right away.

Franz draws himself up still higher, he has clenched his fists.

A loaf to be put in the oven, a giant oven. The heat is terrific and the oven crackles.

Ida! Now he's gone. Thank God, Ida, you've come. He was the biggest crook the world has ever seen, Ida, it's a good thing you've come. He made me mad and got me excited, what do you think of that? I've had a lotta trouble and now I'm here, you know where that is, Buch, the Insane Asylum, under observation or maybe I'm already crazy. Come on, Ida, don't turn your back on me. What's she doin'? She's standin' in the kitchen. Yes, the girl's standin' in the kitchen pottering about, probably wiping the plates. But why does she keep on crumplin' up like that, her side is crumplin' up as if she had sciatica, as if somebody was kickin' her in the ribs. Don't kick her, you fool, that's inhuman, stop that, oh my, oh my, who's that beatin' her, she can't stand up any more, stand up straight, girlie, turn around, look at me, who's beatin' you so terribly?

"You, Franz, it was you who struck me dead."

Nope, nope, it wasn't me, look it up in the Court Records, it was only mayhem, it wasn't my fault. Don't say that, Ida.

"Yes, you killed me, look out, Franz."

He screams, no, no, he clenches his hands and puts his arm before his eyes, but he can see it nevertheless.

Then let it come. Let them come: the travelers, the strangers with potato-sacks slung on their backs, a boy is coming with a pushcart behind them, his ears are freezing, it's 18 degrees below freezing. Breslau and its Schweidnitzer Strasse, Kaiser-Wilhelm Strasse, Kurfürstenstrasse.

Franz groans: Then I might as well be dead, it's unbearable, it would be best if somebody came along and killed me, I didn't do all this, I didn't know anything about it, he whimpers, stammers, he can't talk. The guard guesses that he wants something. He asks him. The guard gives Franz a sip of warm red wine; the other two patients in the room insist on his warming up the red wine.

Ida keeps crumpling up, don't crumple up, Ida, wasn't I in Tegel for it, I got mine, didn't I? Now she stops crumpling up and she sits down; she hangs her head, grows smaller and darker. There she lies—in the coffin, and does not—move.

Groaning, Franz is groaning. His eyes. The guard sits beside him and holds his hand. Take that away, somebody move the coffin away, I can't get up, no, I can't!

He moves his hand. But the coffin does not move. He can't reach it, and Franz weeps despairingly, staring dully and despairingly at it. Through his tears and his despair the coffin vanishes. Franz, however, continues weeping.

But, ladies and gentlemen, you who are reading all this, I ask you, why is Franz Biberkopf weeping? He weeps because he suffers, and about his suffering and himself as well. Because he had done all this, because he was like this, that's why Franz Biberkopf is weeping. Now Franz Biberkopf is weeping about himself.

It is high noon, and the meals are being served in the house. The kitchen-wagon is moving about downstairs, then back to the main building, the kitchen attendants and two patients less seriously ill push it from the annex.

And now at noon, Mieze comes to Franz. Her face is very quiet, calm and gentle. She is in her street-dress with a tight-fitting hat that hides her ears and covers her forehead. She looks very quietly and tenderly at Franz, the way she did when he used to meet her in the street or in the saloon. He asks her to come nearer and she comes nearer. He asks her to give him her hands. She puts both her hands into one of his. She is wearing a pair of kid gloves. Take those gloves off. She takes them off and gives him her hands. Come here, Mieze, don't be such a stranger, and give me a kiss. Calmly she comes up close to him, looks tenderly at him, so tenderly, and kisses him. Stay here, he says, I need you, you must help me. "I can't, Franzeken. I'm a dead one, dontcha know that?" Please stay. "I'd like to, but I can't." She kisses him again. "Y'know all about Freienwalde, don'tcha, Franz? And you aren't angry with me, are ye?"

She's gone. Franz writhes and tears his eyes open. But he can't see her now. What have I done? Why haven't I got her any more? Why did I show her to Reinhold, if only I hadn't started going around with that fellow! What have I done! And now . . .

A stammering sound comes from his terribly tortured face. She must, she must come back again. The guard who understands only the word "again" pours some more wine into his parched and gaping mouth. Franz has to drink, what else can he do?

The dough lies in the heat, it rises, the yeast thrusts it up, bubbles form, the bread rises, it browns.

The voice of Death, the voice of Death, the voice of Death:

What is the use of all your strength, what is the use of all this being respectable. Oh, yes, oh, yes, look upon it. Know and repent.

All that Franz possesses now surrenders. He keeps nothing back.

Now we must depict what Pain is

Now we must depict what pain and suffering are. How pain burns and ravages. For it is pain that now surges up. Many have described pain in their poems. And every day the cemeteries witness pain.

Now we must describe what pain does to Franz Biberkopf. Franz does not resist, he surrenders and gives himself up as pain's victim. He lies down in the blazing flame in order that he may be slain, destroyed, and burnt to ashes. Now let us acclaim what suffering makes of Franz Biberkopf. Let us set forth the annihilation achieved by pain. A breaking asunder, a lopping off, an overthrow, a dissolution. That is what pain achieves.

To everything its season. A time to strangle and a time to heal, to cast down and to build, to weep and to laugh, to wail and to dance, to seek and to lose, to rend and to sew. Now is the time to strangle, to wail, to seek and to rend.

Franz wrestles, awaiting Death, merciful Death.

Now, he thinks, Death, the Merciful, the All-Ending One, is coming near. He trembles, as towards evening he lifts himself up again to receive him.

They who cast him down at noon come now for the second time. Franz says: So be it, it is I. Away with you goes Franz Biberkopf, take me away with you.

With a deep shudder, he greets the specter of that wretch Lüders. Evil Reinhold sloshes up to him. With a deep shudder he encounters Ida's voice, Mieze's face, it is she, everything is fulfilled. Franz weeps and weeps. I'm guilty, I'm not a human being, I'm just a beast, a monster.

Thus died, in that evening hour, Franz Biberkopf, erstwhile transport-worker, burglar, pimp, murderer. Another man lay in the bed, and that other one has the same papers as Franz, he looks like Franz, but in another world, he bears a new name.

This then has been the fall of Franz Biberkopf which I have tried to describe, beginning with Franz's discharge from Tegel Prison up to his end in the Buch Insane Asylum during the winter of 1928–1929.

Now I will append a report about the first hours and days of a new man, having the same identity papers as he.

Exit the Evil Harlot, Triumph of the Great Celebrant, the Drummer and Wielder of the Hatchet

Dirty snow covers the fields of the bleak landscape before the red walls of the institution. There is a beating of drums and again a beating of drums. The whore of Babylon has lost. Death is the victor and he drums her away.

The harlot hisses and fusses, drools and screams: "What about him, what can you get out of this fellow, Franz Biberkopf? Preserve him in alcohol, if you want, this funny man of yours!"

Death beats a tattoo on his drum: "I cannot see what you have in your cup, you hyena. This man Franz Biberkopf is here. I have beaten him to a pulp. But since he is strong and good, he may now start a new life. So get out of my way, our argument is ended."

But she becomes mulish and keeps on drooling. Now Death makes a move, gets in motion, his huge gray cloak flutters; scenes and landscapes become visible, they are swimming around him, winding themselves about his feet and upwards towards his breast. And screams and shots and clamor and triumph and rejoicing resound about him. Triumph and rejoicing. The beast whereon the woman rides shies and kicks.

The river, the Beresina, marching legions.

The legions march along the Beresina, icy cold, an icy wind. They have crossed from France and the great Napoleon leads them. Roaring wind, flurries of snow, bullets whine. They fight on the ice, they charge and fall. And always that cry: Long live the Emperor! Long live the Emperor! The sacrifice, the sacrifice—and that is Death!

Rolling of railroads, thunder of guns, bursting hand-grenades, curtain-fire, Chemin des Dames, Langemarck, Dear Fatherland be comfort thine, be comfort thine! Shattered dug-outs, fallen soldiers. Death folds his cloak singing: Oh yes, oh yes, oh yes.

Marching, marching. We march to war, with iron tread, a hundred minstrels march ahead. Red of morning, red of night, shines on us death's early light. One hundred minstrels beat the drum, drumm, brumm, drumm, if we can't walk straight, we'll walk crooked, by gum, drumm, brumm, drumm.

Death folds his cloak and sings: Oh yes, oh yes, oh yes.

An oven burns, an oven burns, before an oven stands a mother with seven sons and the groaning of a people is behind them. They shall deny the God of their people. Quietly radiant there they stand. Will you deny and submit? The first says No and suffers tortures, the second says No and suffers tortures, the third says No and suffers tortures, the fourth says No and suffers tortures, the fifth says No and suffers tortures, the sixth says No and suffers tortures, the seventh says No and suffers tortures. The mother stands there cheering her sons. Finally, she, too, says No and suffers tortures. Death folds his cloak and sings: Oh yes, oh yes, oh yes.

The woman with the seven heads tugs at the beast, but the beast cannot rise.

Marching, marching, we ride to war, a hundred minstrels march before, with fife and drum, drumm, brumm, for one the road goes straight, for the other it goes to the side, one stands fast, another's killed, one rushes past, the other's voice is stilled, drumm, brumm, drumm.

Cries and rejoicings. On they march, by sixes, by twos, and by threes, the French Revolution marches on, the Russian Revolution marches on, the Peasants' Wars march on, the Anabaptists, all march behind Death, and they rejoice behind him, onward to freedom, to freedom they go, the old world must fall, awake, O morning breeze, drumm, brumm, drumm, brumm, by sixes, by twos, by threes, brothers towards the sun and freedom, brothers towards the light, from the darkness of past ages gleams our future bright, get in step, to the left, to the right, to the left, to the right, drumm, brumm, drumm.

Death folds his cloak and laughs and beams and sings: Oh yes, oh yes, oh yes.

Now Babylon, the Great, can at last pull her beast up onto its legs, it starts trotting, races across the fields, sinks down in the snow. She turns around, howls at the gleaming figure of Death. At her outcry, the beast falls on its knees and the woman sways over the neck of the beast. Death draws his cloak around him. He sings and beams: Oh yes, oh yes, oh yes. The field murmurs: Oh yes, oh yes, oh yes.

The first Steps are the Hardest

In Buch the detectives and doctors question at great length the death-pale invalid who once was Franz Biberkopf, as soon as he has begun to talk and look around; the detectives, in order to find out what he's been up to, the doctors for their diagnosis. The detectives inform him that a man named Reinhold who played a part in his life, his former life, is in the nets of the police. They talk about Brandenburg, and ask him if he knows a certain

Moroskiewicz, and where he is to be found. He has them repeat this several times and keeps very quiet. Now they have left him in peace for a whole day. There is a mower, Death yclept. When he 'gins his scythe to whet, sharper it grows and sharper yet. Look out, little blue flower!

Next day he made his statement to the Chief of Detectives: he had had nothing to do with that old Freienwalde case. If this man Reinhold says the contrary, then—he is mistaken. This pale man, this wreck of a man, is then asked to produce an alibi. It takes days before this is possible. Everything in the man struggles against walking back along that road. It seems a closed thoroughfare. Groaning, he utters a few dates. Groaning, he begs them to let him be. He looks anxiously ahead of him, like a dog. The old Biberkopf is gone, the new Biberkopf is still sleeping. He does not utter a single incriminating word against Reinhold. We all lie under the same ax. We all lie under the same ax.

His statements are confirmed, they agree with the statement made by Mieze's gentleman-friend and the latter's nephew. The doctors get a clearer view of the case. The diagnosis of catatonia moves into the background. It was a psychic trauma, involving a sort of twilight coma, his family history is not untarnished, he's been on good terms with old John Barleycorn, that's obvious. When all's said and done, this fight about his diagnosis is the bunk, the fellow certainly was not a malingerer, he had a bat in his belfry, and it was some bat, and that's all there's to it. All right now, that's that. As for the shooting affray in the Alexander Quelle, he is punishable under Paragraph 51. Wonder if we'll get him back here again.

This wobbly fellow, whom we'll call Biberkopf after the dead man, is unaware, as he moves about this house in the capacity of kitchen help, and no questions asked, that a lot of things are still going on behind his back. The detectives are still nibbling at him, what happened to his arm, where did he lose it, where did he receive medical treatment? They make inquiries at the Magdeburg Hospital, but that's old stuff, still, the bulls are interested in old stuff, even what happened as far back as twenty years ago. As it is, they don't get anything out of him, aren't we near the happy end, Herbert's a pimp, too, the boys've all got fine girls, they saddle them with everything and pretend they get their money from them. None of the bulls, of course, believes that, it's quite possible they get money from the girls here and there, but in the meantime they work independently as well. About this subject, however, the boys keep mum.

This thunderstorm also passes over our man, albeit this time he might be let off. This time, sonnie, you got a return ticket.

*

Then comes the day when he is discharged. The police leave him no doubt about it, they'll keep an eye on him outside as well. They fetch all of old Franz's belongings from the store-room, and he gets everything back; he puts his things on again, there's still some blood on his coat, that's where a cop hit him over the head with the club, I don't want that false arm, you can keep the wig too, if you want, might need it, when you're giving theatricals, we always give theatricals in this place, but we don't wear any wigs, well, here's your discharge paper, good-bye, Chief, look us up one of these days, when the weather's nice out here in Buch, we'll do that all right, you bet, and thanks a lot, I'll open the gate for you.

Well, well, that's behind us, too.

Dear Fatherland, be Comfort thine, I'll watch, and use these Eyes o' Mine

For the second time Biberkopf now leaves a house in which he had been held prisoner, we are at the end of our long road and have just one more little step to take with Franz.

The first house he left was Tegel Prison. Frightened, he had stood beside the red wall, and, as he went away and No. 41 came along and took him to Berlin, the houses did not stand still and the roofs were about to fall upon Franz; he had to walk a long time and sit down until everything was quiet around him, and he grew strong enough to remain there and start all over again.

Now he has no strength. He can no longer see the detention ward. But, lo and behold, as he gets out at Stettin Station, at the suburban section, and the great Baltikum Hotel greets his eyes, nothing moves—nothing at all. The houses keep still, the roofs lie quiet, he can move securely below them, he need not creep into any dark courtyards. Yes, this man—let's call him Franz Karl Biberkopf, to make a difference between him and the former one, Franz got that second name, at his christening, after his grandfather, his mother's father—this man now walks slowly up Invalidenstrasse past Ackerstrasse, towards Brunnenstrasse, past the yellow Market Hall, and looks quietly at the stores and houses, what a lot of people there are dashing around, I haven't seen it for a long time and now here I am back again. Biberkopf had been away a long time. Now Biberkopf is back again: your Biberkopf is back again.

Then let them come, let them come, the wide plains, the red-tiled houses, in which light is gleaming. Then let them come: the shivering travelers with bags slung on their backs. It is a re-encounter, more than a re-encounter.

He sits in a café on Brunnenstrasse and picks up a paper. Wonder if my name's in here, or Mieze's, or Herbert's, or Reinhold's. Nothing. Nothing. Where shall I go? Where'll I go? Eva, I must see Eva.

She is not living with Herbert any more. The landlady opens the door: Herbert's got nabbed, the bulls went through all his things, he did not come back, his stuff is still up there on the floor, how about selling it, I'll find out. Franz Karl meets Eva in the West End, in her gentleman-friend's apartment. She takes him in. She is glad to welcome Franz Karl Biberkopf.

"Yes, Herbert got nabbed, they sent him up for two years, I do what I can for him, they asked a lot of questions about you, first in Tegel, and what are you doin', Franz?" "I'm all right, I'm out of Buch, they gave me my hunting-permit." "I saw it in the paper the other day." "Funny, how they always have to write up things. But I'm weak, Eva. You know what the food is like in a place like that."

Eva notices the expression in his eyes, a dark, silent, searching expression, she's never seen that in Franz before. She doesn't talk about herself; as a matter of fact, something's happened to her, too, something that concerns him, but he is very lame, she gets him a room, she helps him, he mustn't do anything. He himself says it as he sits in the room and she is about to go: "Nope, I can't do nothin' now."

And then what does he do? He starts little by little to go about the streets, he walks around Berlin.

Berlin: 52° 31' North Latitude, 13° 25' East Longitude, 20 main-line stations, 121 suburban lines, 27 belt lines, 14 city lines, 7 shunting stations, street-car, elevated railroad, autobus service. There's only one Kaiser Town, there's only one Vienna. A Woman's Desire in three words, three words comprise all a woman's desire. Imagine it, a New York firm advertises a new cosmetic which gives a yellowish retina that fresh bluish tint only possessed by youth. The most beautiful pupil, from deep blue to velvet-brown, can be got from our tubes. Why spend so much on having your furs cleaned?

He walks around the town. There are many things to make a man well, if only his heart keeps well.

First the Alex. It's still there. There is nothing to be seen there. It was terribly cold all winter, so they did not work and left everything lying around, just as it was, the big steam-shovel is now standing on the Georgenkirchplatz, they are dredging sand and dirt from Hahn's Department Store, they've put in a whole lot of rails there, maybe they are going to build a railway station. A lot of other things are happening on the Alex, but the main thing is: it's still there. The people keep crossing the square, the slush is something awful, the Berlin municipality is so noble and humane that it lets all the snow dissolve quietly, *peu à peu*, of its own accord, into mud, nobody's supposed to touch it. When automobiles go by, you'd better jump into the nearest house, or else you'll get a load of garbage, free of charge, all over your top-hat, and you'll risk a suit for appropriating public property. Our old "Mokka Fix" is closed. At the corner there is a new joint called "Mexico," a world sensation: the chef stands beside his grill in the window, Indian Blockhouse. They are putting a fence around the Alexander Barracks, wonder what's doing there, they are tearing down some stores. And the street-cars are chock-full of people, all of them have something to do, the tickets still cost 20 pfennigs, a fifth of a mark in cash: or if you prefer, you can pay 30 pfennigs, or buy yourself a Ford. The elevated also goes by, no firsts or seconds, third-class only, everybody's sitting on comfortable plush-seats, unless they happen to be standing up, which is also possible. Getting off while the train is in motion is prohibited and liable to fines up to 150 marks, but who would dare do that, we'd simply risk an electric shock. Everybody admires the shoe that's brightly polished with "Egu." Passengers are requested to get on and off quickly, during the rush-hour kindly move towards the center-aisle.

All these are nice things that can help a man get on his feet, even if he is a bit weak, provided his heart is in good condition. Don't stand near the door. Well, Franz Karl Biberkopf is healthy all right, wish everybody was as solid as he is! It wouldn't be worth while telling such a long story about a man if he were not solid on his legs, now would it? And one day, when an itinerant bookseller was standing in the street, during a terribly rainy spell, cussing about his poor receipts, Cäsar Flaischlen stepped up to the book-cart. He quietly listened to the man's cussing, and then, tapping him on his wet shoulder, said: "Stop that cussing, keep sunshine in your heart!" Thus he consoled him and disappeared. This was the starting-point for the famous sun-poem. It was just such a sun, but different, of course, that Biberkopf had in his heart: and he also poured a little flask of booze and a lot of malt-extract into his soups. Thus slowly he gets in shape again. May I, therefore, take the liberty of offering you a share in my excellent barrel of Trabener Würzgarten, 1925, at the special price of 90 marks for 50 bottles, packing included, F. O. B., or 1.60 marks per bottle, not counting the bottles and boxing which I take back at the agreed price? Dijodyl for arteriosclerosis. Biberkopf has not got arteriosclerosis, he only feels weak, he certainly had a tremendous fast in Buch, nearly starved to death, a man needs time to fill himself out again. That's why he doesn't need to see the magneto-pathologist, where Eva wants to send him, because he helped her once.

A week later, when Eva goes with him to Mieze's grave, she finds cause for surprise right away and she notices how much better he is. No tears are shed, he just puts a handful of tulips on the grave, strokes the cross, and immediately after takes Eva's arm and off they go.

He sits with her in the pastry shop across the way, eating a honey-cake in honor of Mieze, you see she never could get enough of it, it really tastes good, but nothing to write home about, at that. So now we have been to see our little Mieze, a man shouldn't go to cemeteries too much, might catch a cold, maybe next year again, on her birthday. You see, Eva, I don't have to run out here to see Mieze, you can take my word for it, she's always there for me, cemetery or no cemetery, and then Reinhold, well, I won't forget him so easy, either. And even if my arm should grow again, I wouldn't forget him. There are so many things in this world, a fellow would have to be a big boob, and not a human being, to forget 'em. And so Biberkopf talks with Eva, while eating honey-cake.

Eva once wanted to be his mistress, but now she's quite given up the idea. This business with Mieze, and then the Insane Asylum, that was too much for her, however much she still likes him. The baby she had expected by him didn't come either, she had a miscarriage. It would have been so lovely, but it was not to be, but it's the best thing in the long run, especially since Herbert isn't there, and her gentleman-friend prefers, by a long shot, that she shouldn't have a kid, as in the end, the good man had found out that the baby might very likely be by somebody else, you can't blame him for that.

They sit quietly together, thinking backwards and forwards, eating honey-cake and devil-cake with whipped cream.

Forward March and get in Step and Right and Left and Right and Left

We see our man once more at the trial of Reinhold and Matter the tinner, alias Oskar Fischer, charged with murder and complicity, respectively, in the affair of Emilie Parsunke, of Bernau, on the date of September 1, 1928, in Freienwalde near Berlin. Biberkopf is not a defendant. This one-armed man excites general interest, quite a sensation, in fact, the murder of his sweetheart, love-life in the underworld, he was mentally unbalanced after her death and suspected of being an accomplice, a tragic destiny.

During the trial, the one-armed man who, as the experts state, has now recovered and can be questioned, gives the following testimony: Deceased (he calls her Mieze), did not have an affair with Reinhold. Reinhold and he were good pals, but Reinhold had a terrible, abnormal craving for women, that's how it came about. Whether Reinhold has predispositions to sadism, he doesn't know. He suspects that Mieze resisted Reinhold in Freienwalde, so he did it in a fit of rage. Do you know anything about his youth? No, I didn't know him then. Has he not told you anything? Did he drink? Yes, I'll tell you how it was: In the old days he did not drink, but finally he did start drinking, how much I can't say, but formerly he could only stand a sip of beer, always drank mineral water and coffee.

That's all they can get out of Biberkopf about Reinhold. Nothing about his arm, nothing about their quarrel, their fight, I shouldn't have done it, I shouldn't have taken up with him. Eva and some members of the Pums gang are sitting in the court-room. Reinhold and Biberkopf stare fixedly at each other. The one-armed man has no pity for the man in the prisoner's box between the two policemen, who is getting his neck in a sling, he has only a curious devotion for him. I once had a faithful comrade, never a better one could there be. I must look at him, keep on looking at him, nothing seems more important than to look at you. The world is made of sugar and dirt. I can look at you quietly, without batting an eye. I know who you are. I now find you here, m'boy, in the prisoner's box, outside I'll meet you a thousand times more, but my heart will not turn to stone on account of that.

Reinhold has planned, if anything should go wrong at the trial, to expose the whole Pums gang, he'll get them all into trouble if they make him mad, he is keeping that up his sleeve, especially in case Biberkopf starts shooting off his mouth before the judge, that dirty son of a bitch, it's on his account I'm in this hole. But then the Pums crowd are all sitting in the court-room, that's Eva over there, that's a coupla detectives, we know those bulls. Then he gets calmer, hesitates, thinks things over. A man is dependent on his friends, I'll get out some time, and I may need 'em inside, too, I won't make things so easy for the bulls, and then, strange to say, Biberkopf is acting white. They tell me he's been doin' time in Buch. Funny, how that boob has changed, queer look he's got, as if he couldn't turn his eyes around, they musta gone rusty on him out in Buch, and how slow he talks. He probably still has a screw loose somewhere. But Biberkopf knows that, although Reinhold does not testify, he owes him no gratitude for it.

Ten years' prison for Reinhold, murder while temporarily insane, alcoholism, impulsive disposition, unprotected youth. Reinhold accepts the sentence.

Somebody in the court-room screams, when the sentence is pronounced, and sobs aloud. It is Eva, the thought of Mieze has overpowered her. Biberkopf, hearing her, turns around in the witness box and then he, too, sinks heavily into himself, and holds his hand in front of his forehead. There is a mower, Death yclept; I'm yourn, she came to you so lovable, protected you, and you, oh Shame, cry Shame!

Immediately after the trial Biberkopf is offered a job as assistant door-man in a medium-sized factory. He accepts. I have nothing further to report about his life.

We have come to the end of our story. It has proven a long one, but it had to unfold itself, on and on, till it reached its climax, that culminating point which at last illuminates the whole thing.

We have walked along a dark road, at first there was no street-lamp burning, we only knew it was the right road, but gradually it grew bright and brighter, till at last we reached the light and under its rays were able to make out the name of the street. It was a process of revelation of a special kind. Franz Biberkopf did not walk along the streets the way we do. He rushed blindly through this dark street, knocking against trees, and, the more he ran, the more he knocked against trees. Now it was dark, and, as he knocked against the trees, he shut his eyes in terror. And the more he knocked against them, the greater became his terror, when he shut his eyes tightly. His head all bunged up, almost at his wits' end, at last he reached his goal. As he fell down, he opened his eyes. Then the street-lamp shone bright above him, and he was able to read the sign.

Now at last he is assistant door-man in a medium-sized factory. He is no longer alone on Alexanderplatz. There are people to the right, and people to the left of him, some walk in front of him, others behind him.

Much unhappiness comes from walking alone. When there are several, it's somewhat different. I must get the habit of listening to others, for what the others say concerns me, too. Then I learn who I am, and what I can undertake. Everywhere about me my battle is being fought, and I must beware, before I know I'm in the thick of it.

He is assistant door-man in a factory. What is fate anyway? One is stronger than I. If there are two of us, it grows harder to be stronger than I. If there are ten of us, it's harder still. And if there are a thousand of us and a million, then it's very hard, indeed.

But it is also nicer and better to be with others. Then I feel and I know everything twice as well. A ship cannot lie in safety without a big anchor, and a man cannot exist without many other men. The true and the false I will know better now. Once I got myself into trouble for a single word and had to pay bitterly for it, this shan't happen to Biberkopf again. The words come rolling up to us, we must be careful not to get run over; if we don't watch out for the autobus, it'll make apple-sauce out of us. I'll never again stake my word on anything in the world. Dear Fatherland, be comfort thine, I'll watch, and use these eyes o'mine.

Often they march past his window with flags and music and singing. Biberkopf watches coolly from his door, he'll not join the parade any more. Shut your trap, in step, old cuss, march along with the rest of us. But if I march along, I shall have to pay for it later on with my head, pay for the schemes of others. That's why I first figure out everything, and only if everything's quite O. K., and suits me, I'll take action. Reason is the gift of man, jackasses replace it with a clan.

Biberkopf is working as assistant door-man, takes numbers, checks cars, sees who comes in and goes out.

Keep awake, keep awake, for there is something happening in the world. The world is not made of sugar. If they drop gas-bombs, I'll have to choke to death; nobody knows why they are dropped, but that's neither here nor there, we had the time to prepare for it.

If war comes along and they conscript me, and I don't know why, and the war's started without me, well, then it's my fault, it serves me right. Keep awake 'mid the strife, we're not alone in life. Let it hail and storm, there's no way of guarding against it, but we can defend ourselves against many other things. So I will not go on shouting as once I did: Fate, Fate!

It's no use revering it merely as Fate, we must look at it, grasp it, down it, and not hesitate.

Keep awake, eyes front, attention, a thousand belong together, and he who won't watch out, is fit to flay and flout.

The drums roll behind him. Marching, marching. We tramp to war with iron tread, a hundred minstrels march ahead, red of night and red of day, deathward leads the way.

Biberkopf is a humble workman. We know what we know, the price we paid was not low.

The way leads to freedom, to freedom it goes. The old world must crumble. Awake, wind of dawn!

And get in step, and right and left and right and left, marching: marching on, we tramp to war, a hundred minstrels march before, with fife and drum, drrum, brrum, for one the road goes straight, for another it goes to the side, one stands fast, another's killed, one rushes past, another's voice is stilled, drrum, brrumm, drrumm!

THE END

Question what you thought before

Continuum Impacts - books that change the way we think

AESTHETIC THEORY - Theodor Adorno 0826476910
I AND THOU - Martin Buber 0826476937
ANTI-OEDIPUS - Gilles Deleuze & Félix Guattari 0826476953
A THOUSAND PLATEAUS - Gilles Deleuze & Félix Guattari 0826476945
DISSEMINATION - Jacques Derrida 0826476961
BERLIN ALEXANDERPLATZ - Alfred Döblin 0826477895
PEDAGOGY OF HOPE - Paolo Freire 0826477909
MARX'S CONCEPT OF MAN - Erich Fromm 0826477917
TRUTH AND METHOD - Hans-Georg Gadamer 082647697X
THE ESSENCE OF TRUTH - Martin Heidegger 0826477046
JAZZ WRITINGS - Philip Larkin 0826476996
LIBIDINAL ECONOMY - Jean-François Lyotard 0826477003
DECONSTRUCTION AND CRITICISM - Harold Bloom et al 0826476929
DIFFERENCE AND REPETITION - Gilles Deleuze 0826477151
THE LOGIC OF SENSE - Gilles Deleuze 082647716X
GOD IS NEW EACH MOMENT - Edward Schillebeeckx 0826477011
THE DOCTRINE OF RECONCILIATION - Karl Barth 0826477925
CRITICISM AND TRUTH - Roland Barthes 0826477070
ON NIETZSCHE - George Bataille 0826477089
THE CONFLICT OF INTERPRETATIONS - Paul Ricoeur 0826477097
POSITIONS - Jacques Derrida 0826477119
ECLIPSE OF REASON - Max Horkheimer 0826477933
AN ETHICS OF SEXUAL DIFFERENCE - Luce Irigaray 0826477127
LITERATURE, POLITICS AND CULTURE IN POSTWAR BRITAIN - Alan Sinfield 082647702X
CINEMA 1 - Gilles Deleuze 0826477054
CINEMA 2 - Gilles Deleuze 0826477062
AN INTRODUCTION TO PHILOSOPHY - Jacques Maritain 0826477178
MORAL MAN AND IMMORAL SOCIETY - Reinhld Niebuhr 0826477143
EDUCATION FOR CRITICAL CONSCIOUSNESS - Paolo Freire 082647795X
DISCOURSE ON FREE WILL - Desiderius Erasmus & Martin Luther 0826477941
VIOLENCE AND THE SACRED - René Girard 0826477186
NIETZSCHE AND THE VICIOUS CIRCLE - Pierre Klossowski 0826477194

www.continuumbooks.com